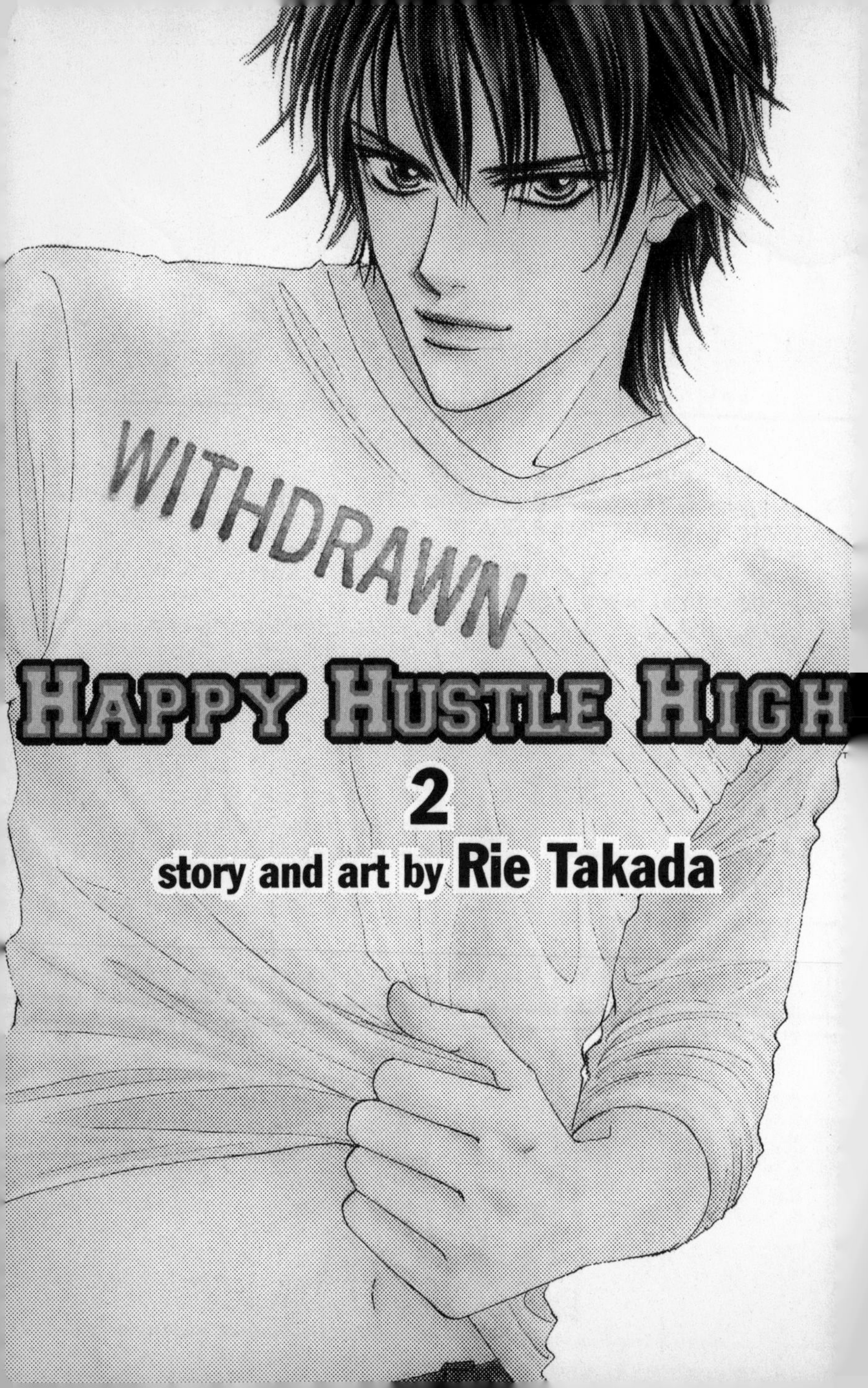

HAPPY HUSTLE HIGH

2

story and art by Rie Takada

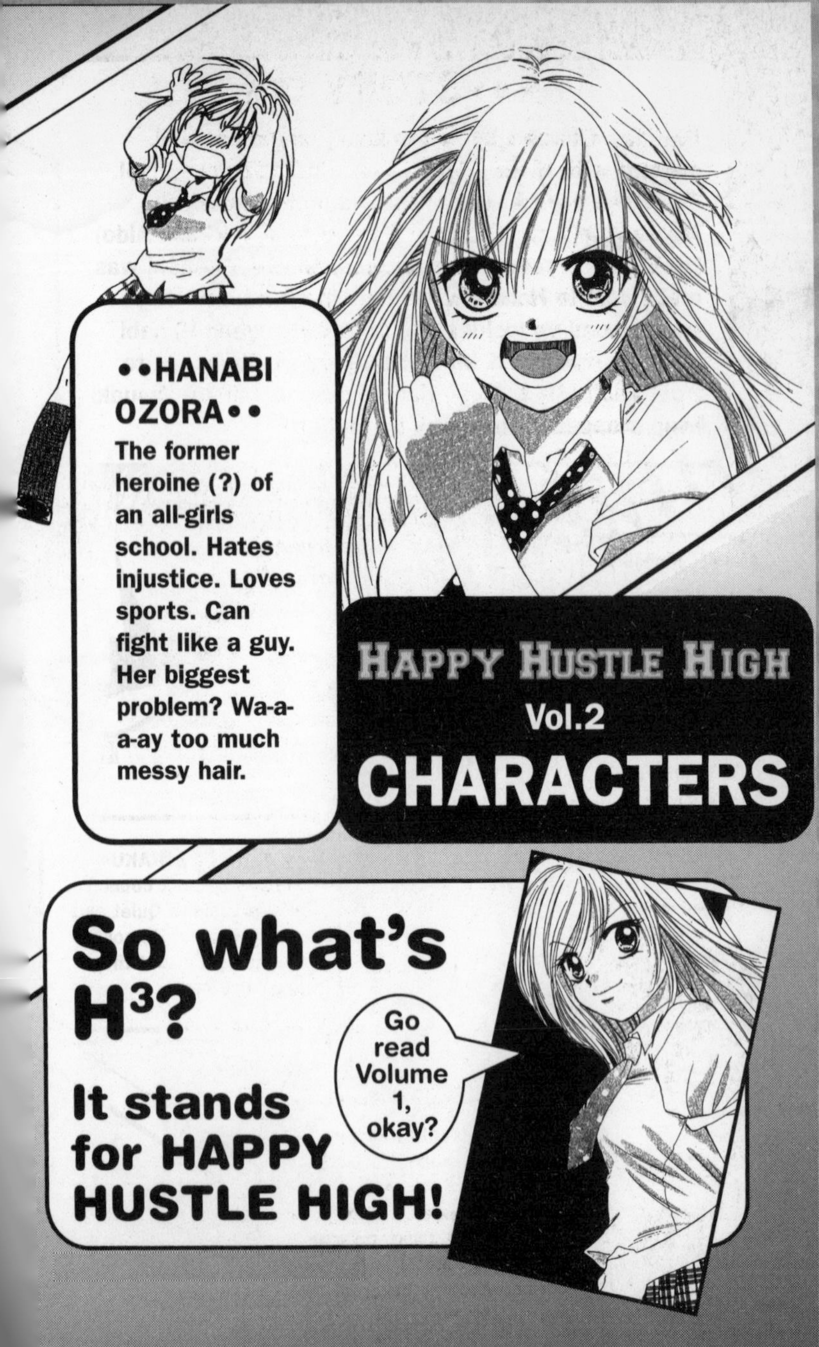
HAPPY HUSTLE HIGH
Vol.2
CHARACTERS
••HANABI OZORA••
The former heroine (?) of an all-girls school. Hates injustice. Loves sports. Can fight like a guy. Her biggest problem? Wa-a-a-ay too much messy hair.
So what's H^3?
It stands for HAPPY HUSTLE HIGH!
Go read Volume 1, okay?

•••STORY•••

One day, Otome High, an ordinary all-girls school, merged with Meibi High, a very elite all-boys school. The three pretty boys of the student council (Yoshitomo Kuon, Yasuaki Garaku, and Tokihisa Aido) became everybody's instant heartthrobs. Yasuaki was really cold to Hanabi when they first met, but they soon wound up locking lips (aka CPR) when Hanabi fell off a surfboard! After that, they slowly began to trust each other. When Hanabi missed school, Yasuaki even stopped by to check up on her.

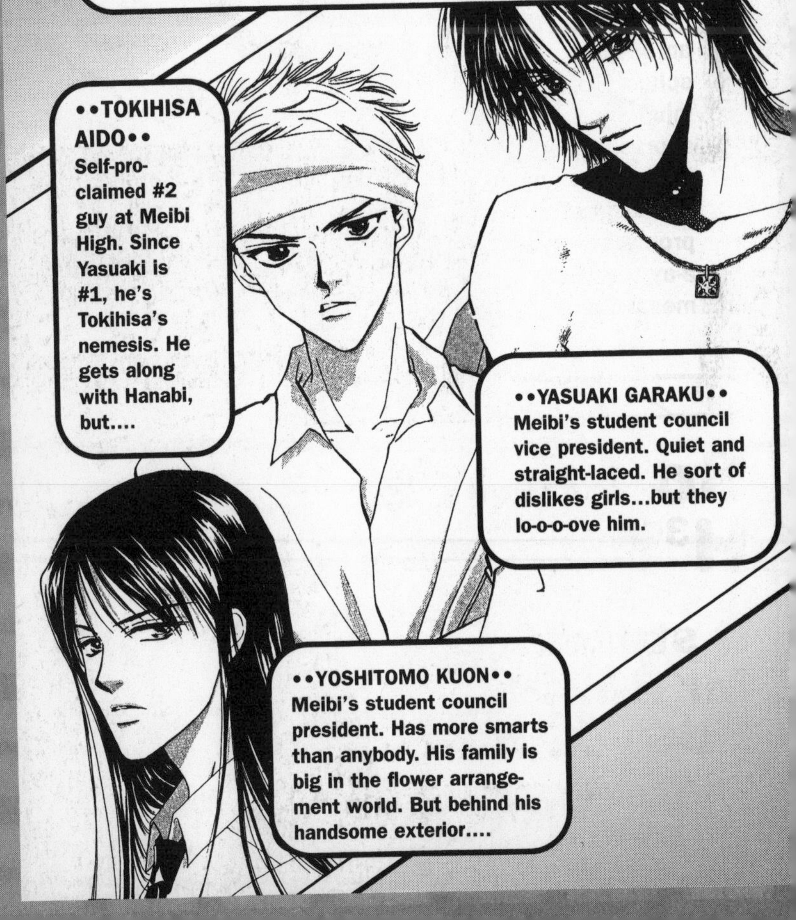
••TOKIHISA AIDO••
Self-proclaimed #2 guy at Meibi High. Since Yasuaki is #1, he's Tokihisa's nemesis. He gets along with Hanabi, but....
••YASUAKI GARAKU••
Meibi's student council vice president. Quiet and straight-laced. He sort of dislikes girls...but they lo-o-o-ove him.
••YOSHITOMO KUON••
Meibi's student council president. Has more smarts than anybody. His family is big in the flower arrangement world. But behind his handsome exterior....

HAPPY HUSTLE HIGH

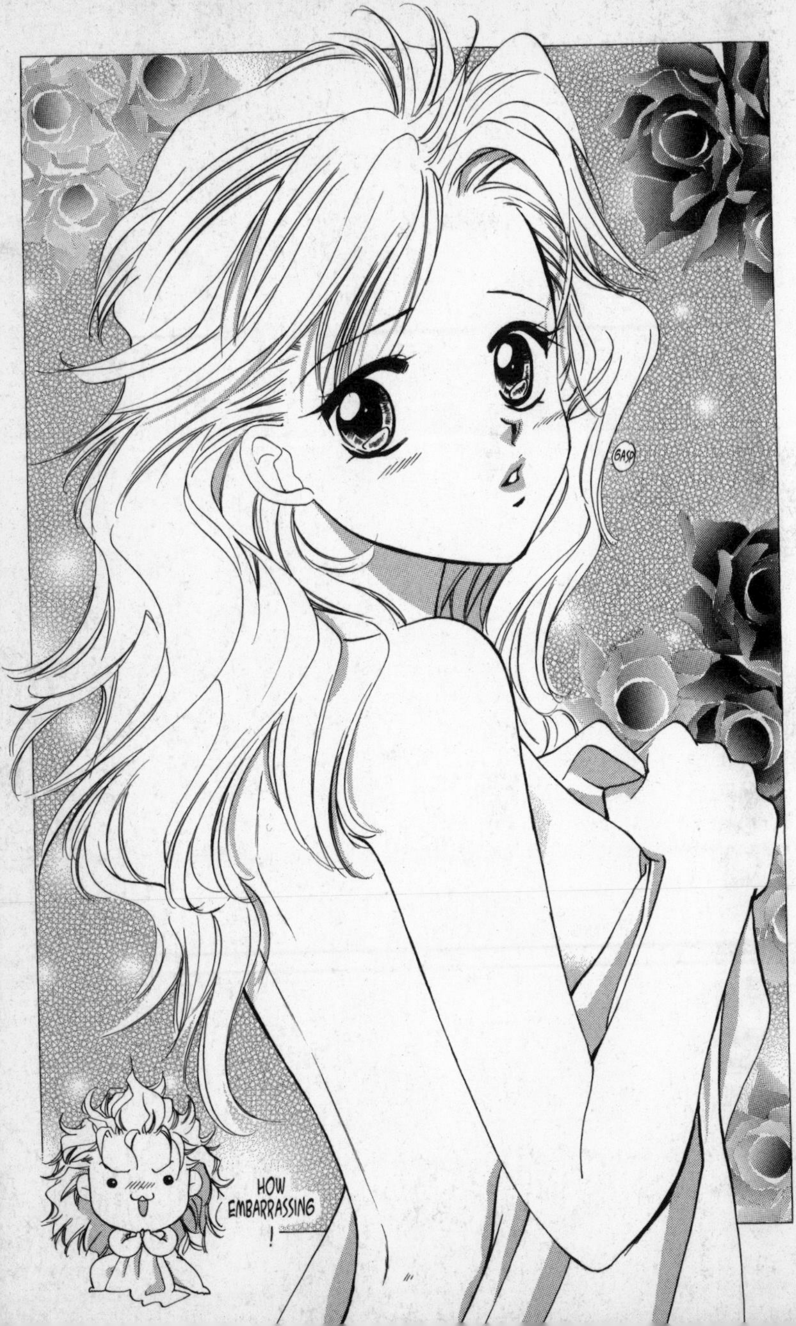
GASP
HOW EMBARRASSING!

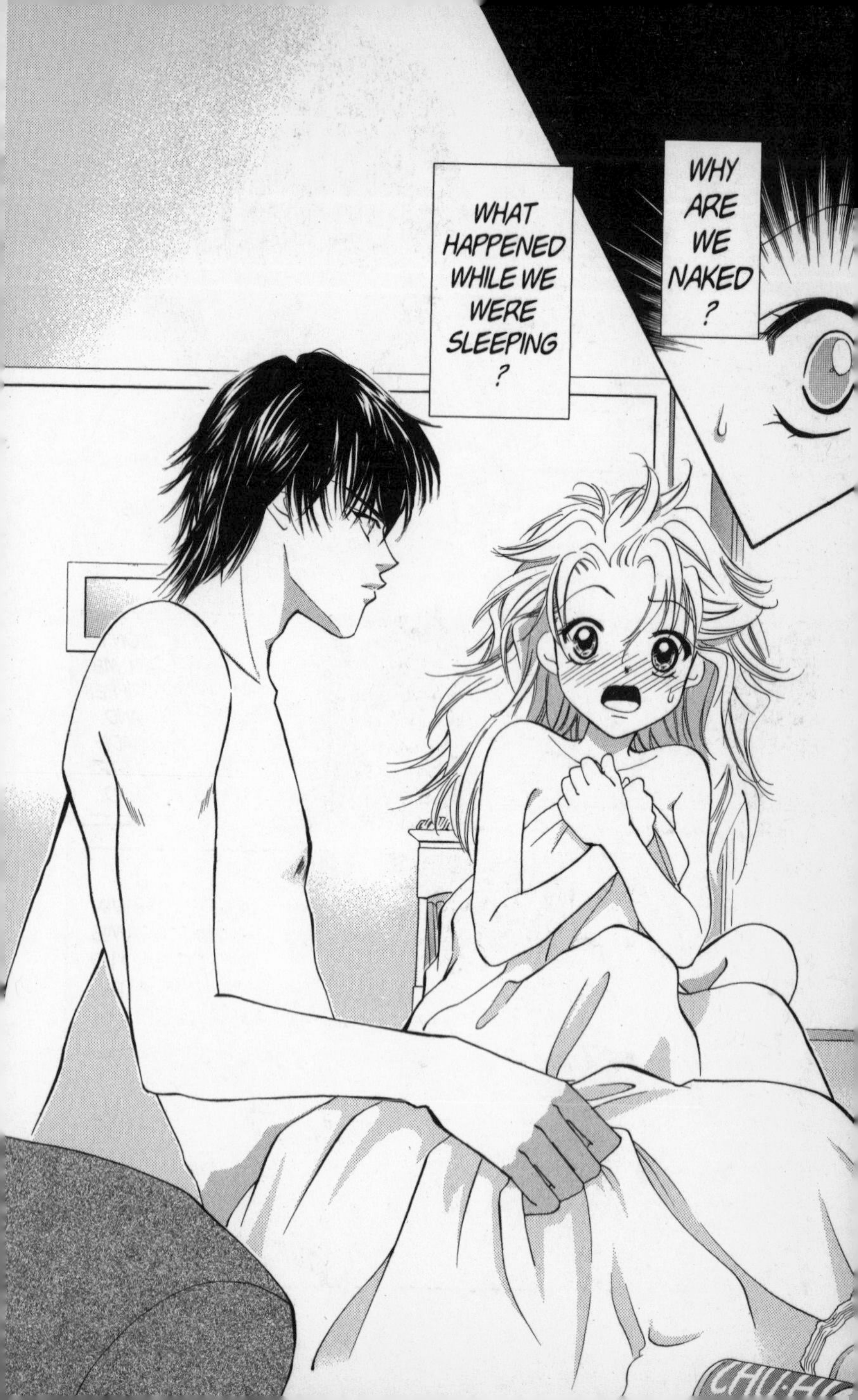
WHY ARE WE NAKED?
WHAT HAPPENED WHILE WE WERE SLEEPING?

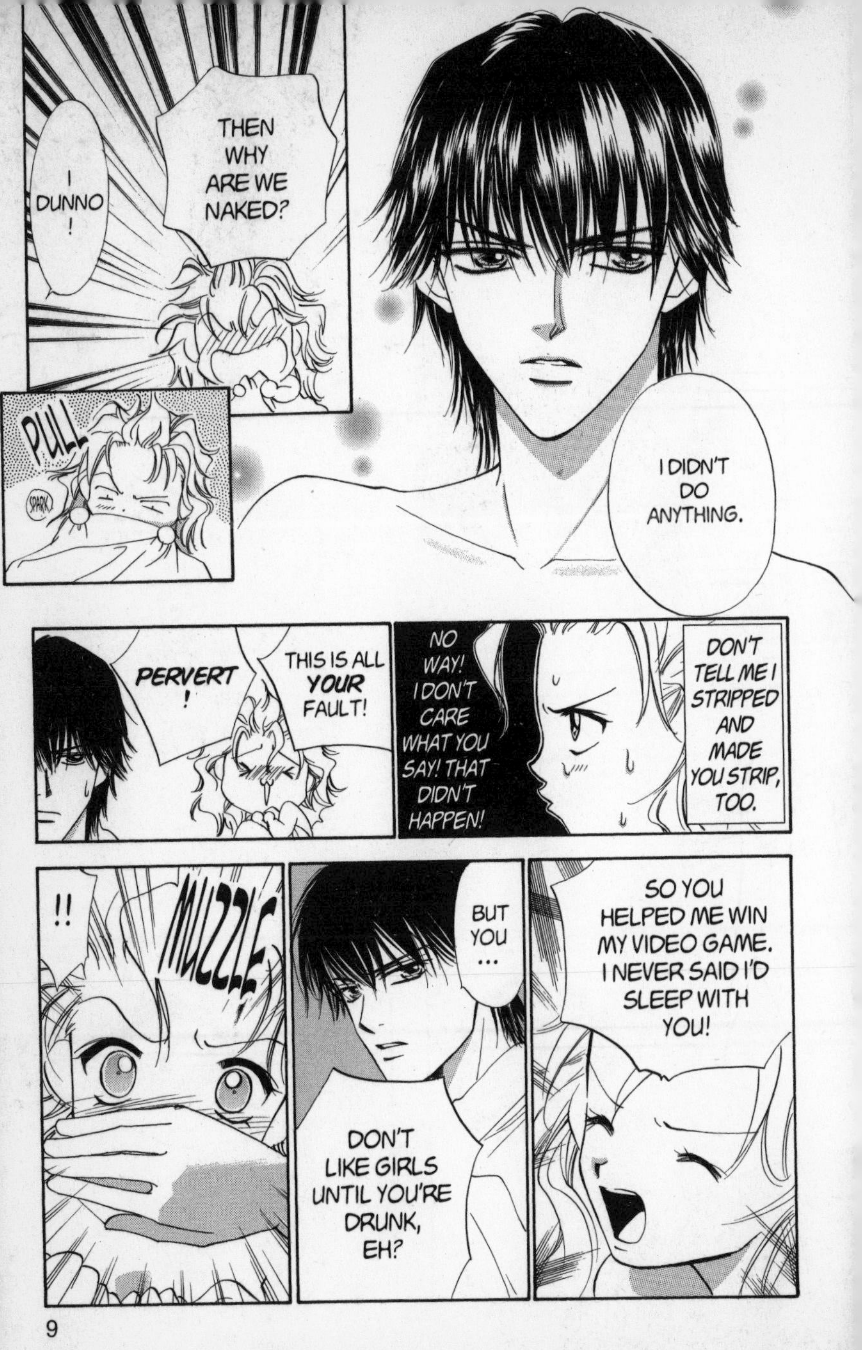
I DIDN'T DO ANYTHING.
THEN WHY ARE WE NAKED?
I DUNNO!
PULL
SPARK
DON'T TELL ME I STRIPPED AND MADE YOU STRIP, TOO.
NO WAY! I DON'T CARE WHAT YOU SAY! THAT DIDN'T HAPPEN!
THIS IS ALL YOUR FAULT!
PERVERT!
SO YOU HELPED ME WIN MY VIDEO GAME. I NEVER SAID I'D SLEEP WITH YOU!
BUT YOU...
DON'T LIKE GIRLS UNTIL YOU'RE DRUNK, EH?
MUZZLE
!!

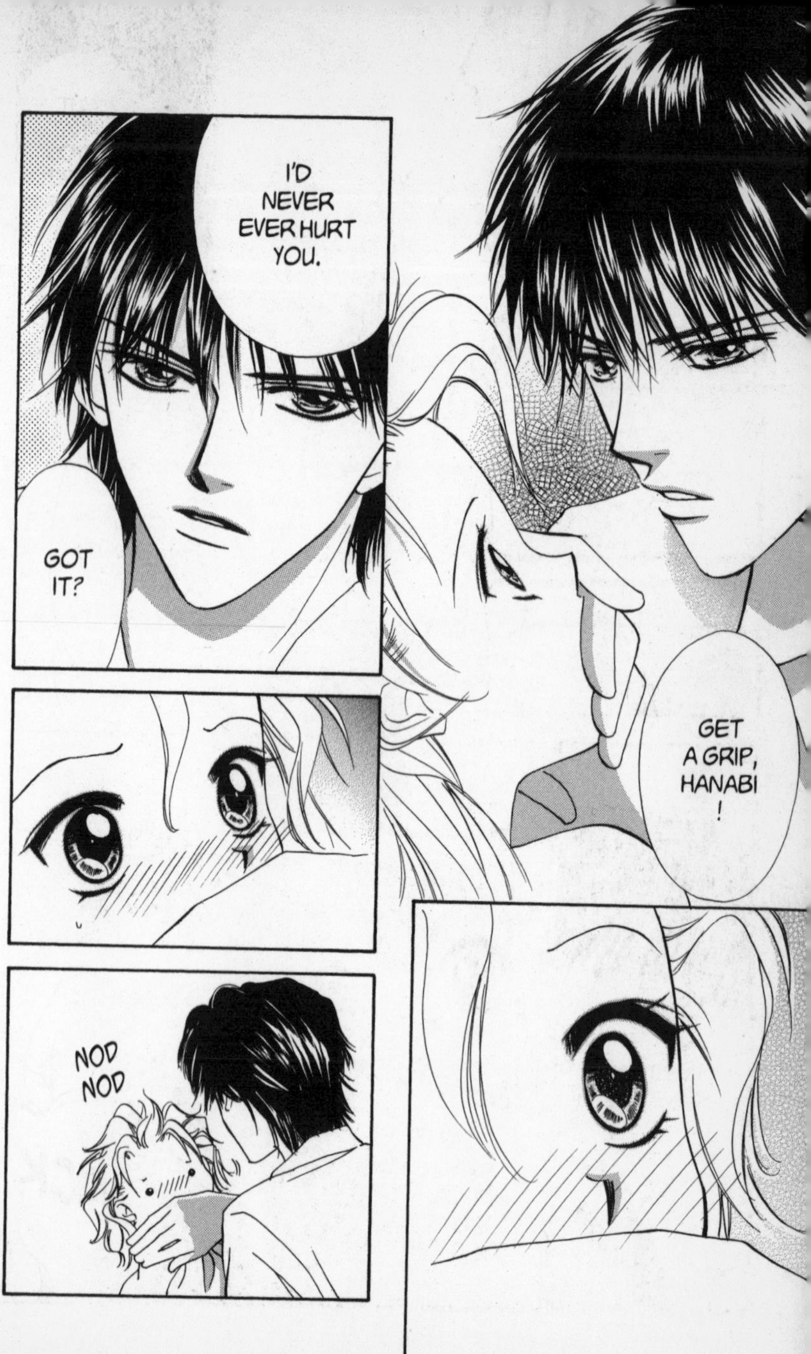
GET A GRIP, HANABI!
I'D NEVER EVER HURT YOU.
GOT IT?
NOD NOD

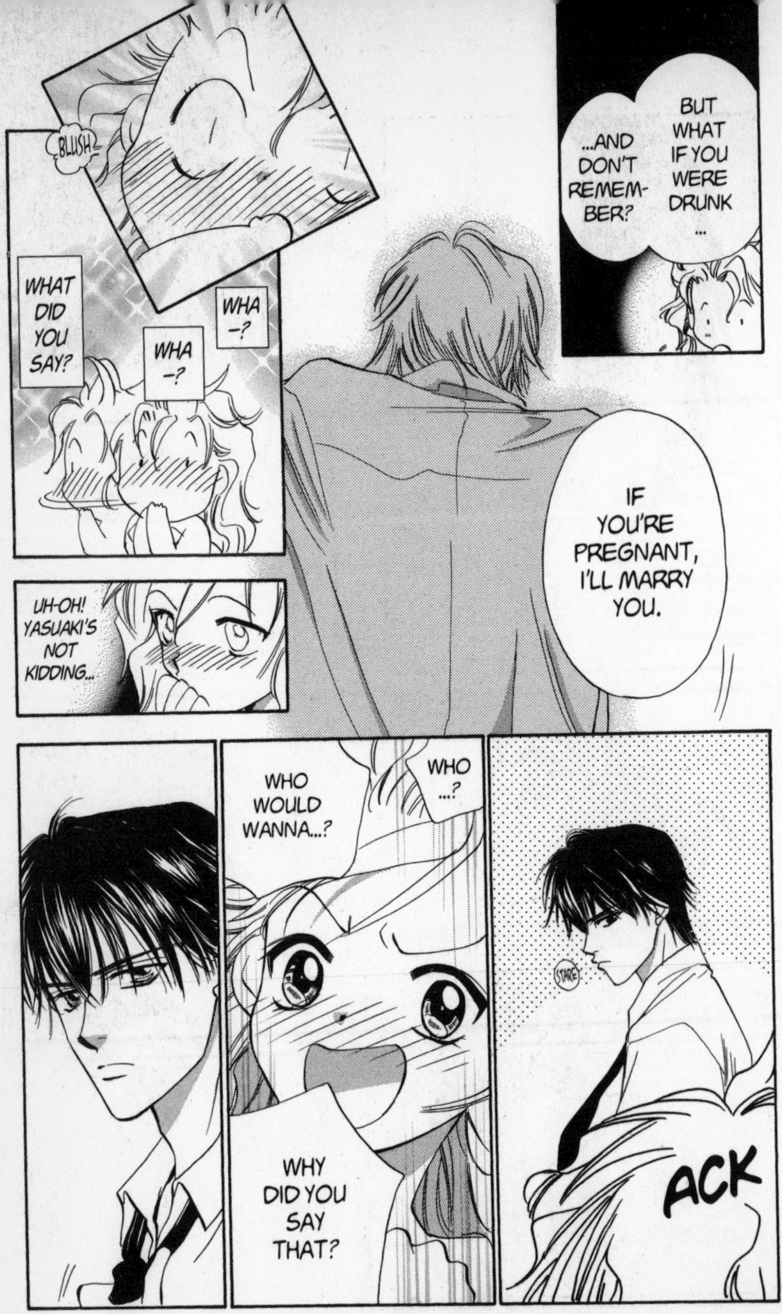
BUT WHAT IF YOU WERE DRUNK ...
...AND DON'T REMEM-BER?
IF YOU'RE PREGNANT, I'LL MARRY YOU.
BLUSH
WHA –?
WHA –?
WHAT DID YOU SAY?
UH-OH! YASUAKI'S NOT KIDDING...
STARE
ACK
WHO ...?
WHO WOULD WANNA...?
WHY DID YOU SAY THAT?

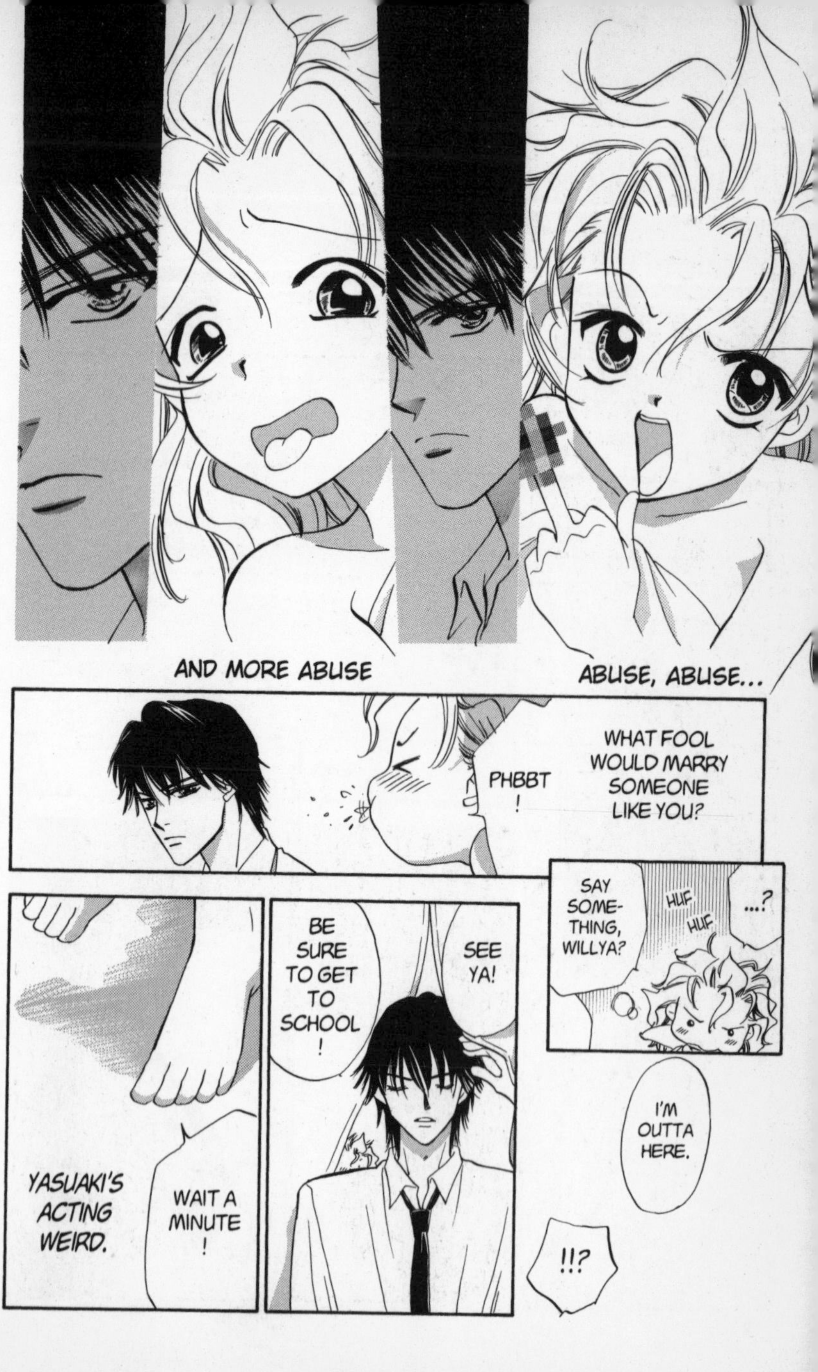
ABUSE, ABUSE...
AND MORE ABUSE
WHAT FOOL WOULD MARRY SOMEONE LIKE YOU?
PHBBT!
...?
HUF HUF
SAY SOME-THING, WILLYA?
I'M OUTTA HERE.
!!?
SEE YA!
BE SURE TO GET TO SCHOOL!
WAIT A MINUTE!
YASUAKI'S ACTING WEIRD.

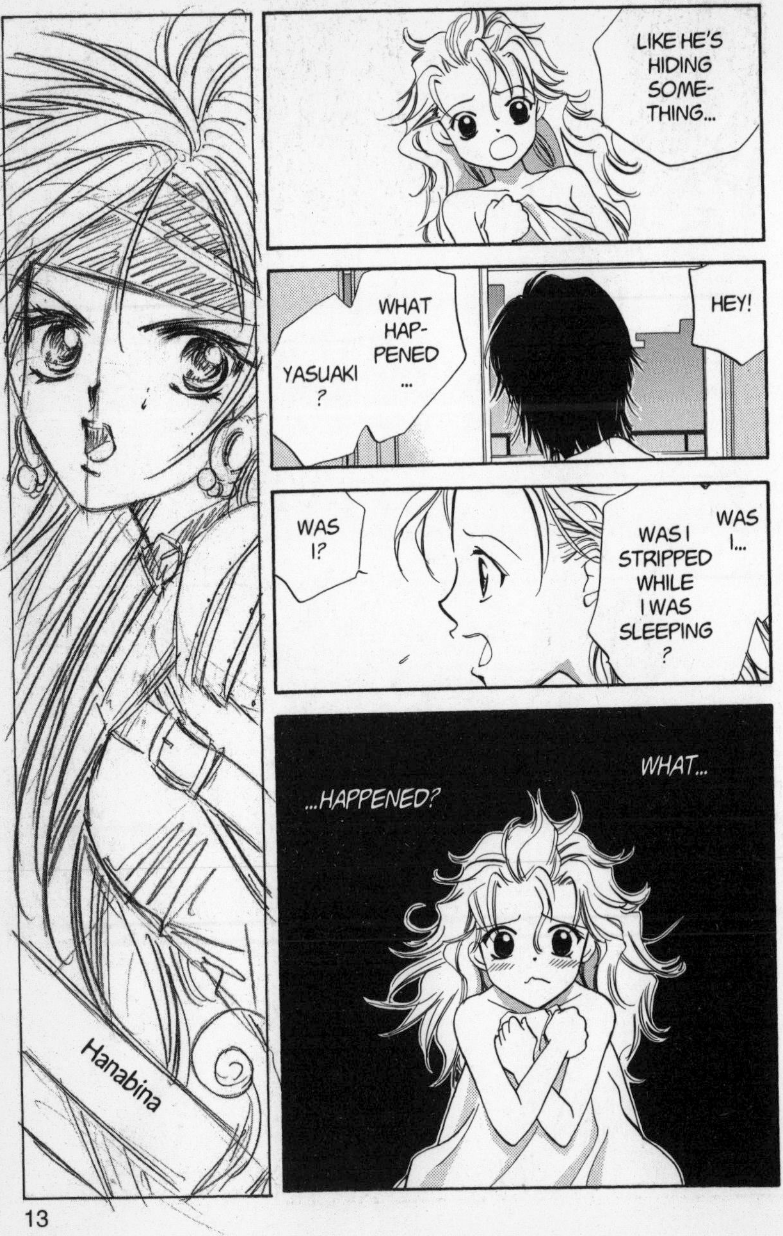
LIKE HE'S HIDING SOME-THING...
HEY!
WHAT HAP-PENED ...
YASUAKI ?
WAS I...
WAS I STRIPPED WHILE I WAS SLEEPING ?
WAS I?
WHAT...
...HAPPENED?
Hanabina

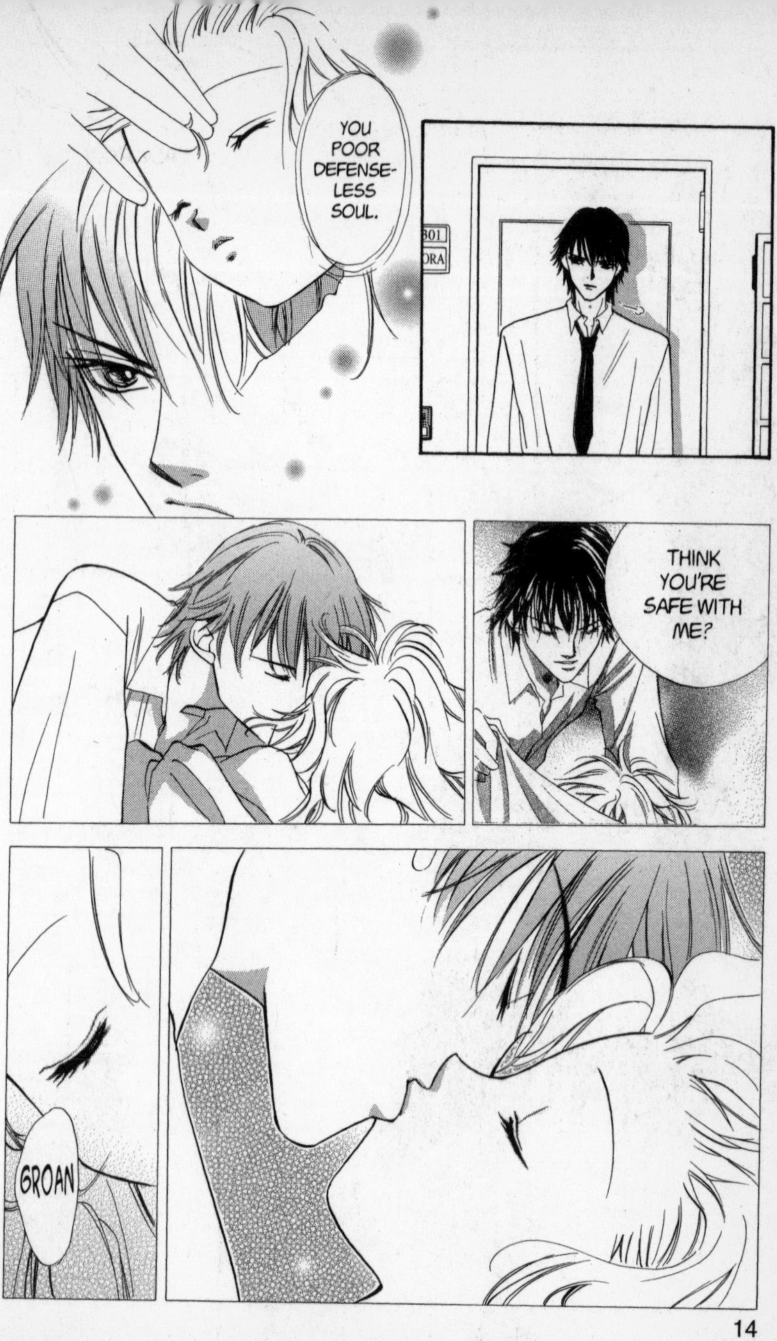
YOU POOR DEFENSE-LESS SOUL.
THINK YOU'RE SAFE WITH ME?
GROAN

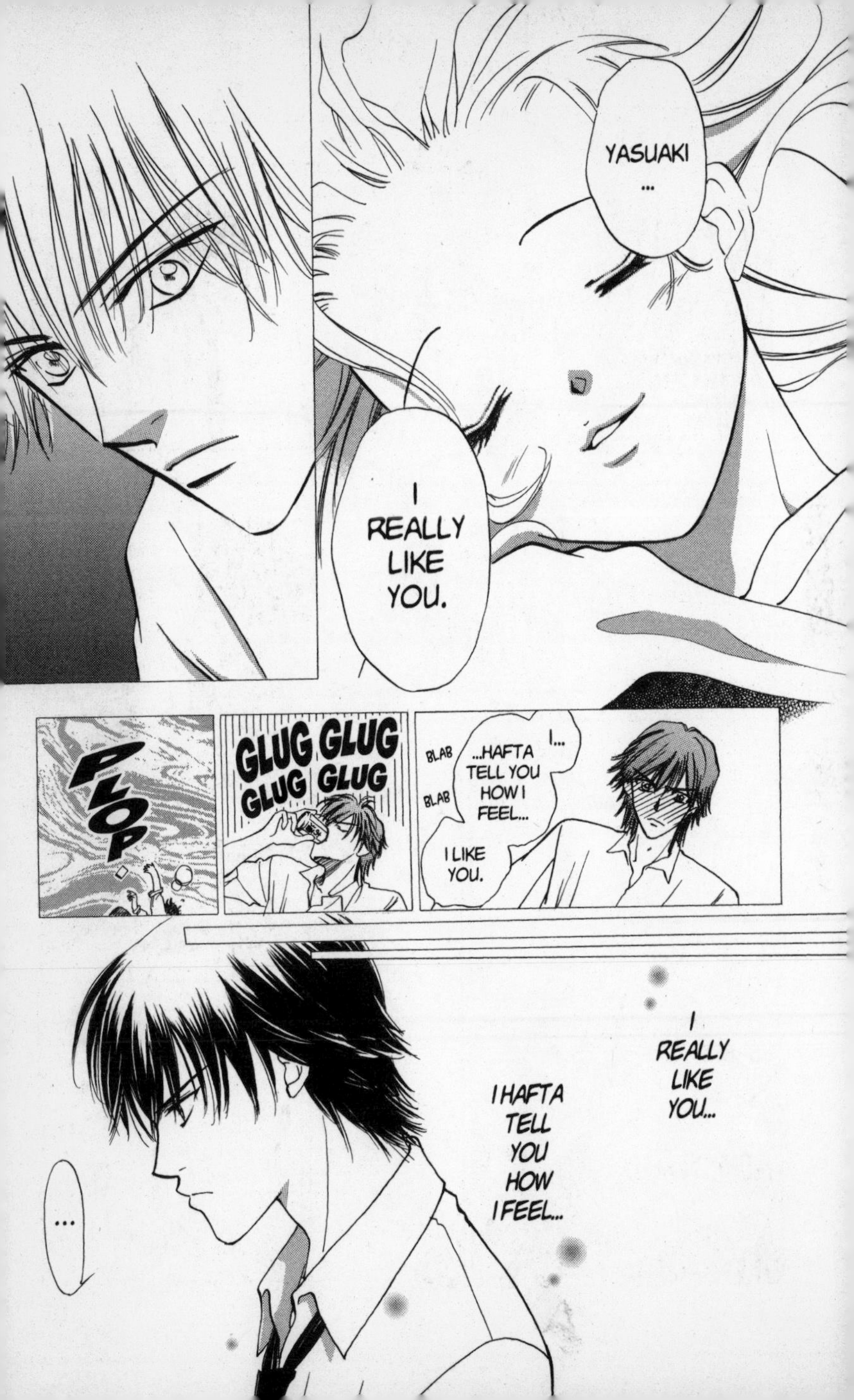
YASUAKI ...
I REALLY LIKE YOU.
I...
...HAFTA TELL YOU HOW I FEEL...
BLAB BLAB
I LIKE YOU.
GLUG GLUG GLUG GLUG
PLOP
I REALLY LIKE YOU...
I HAFTA TELL YOU HOW I FEEL...
...

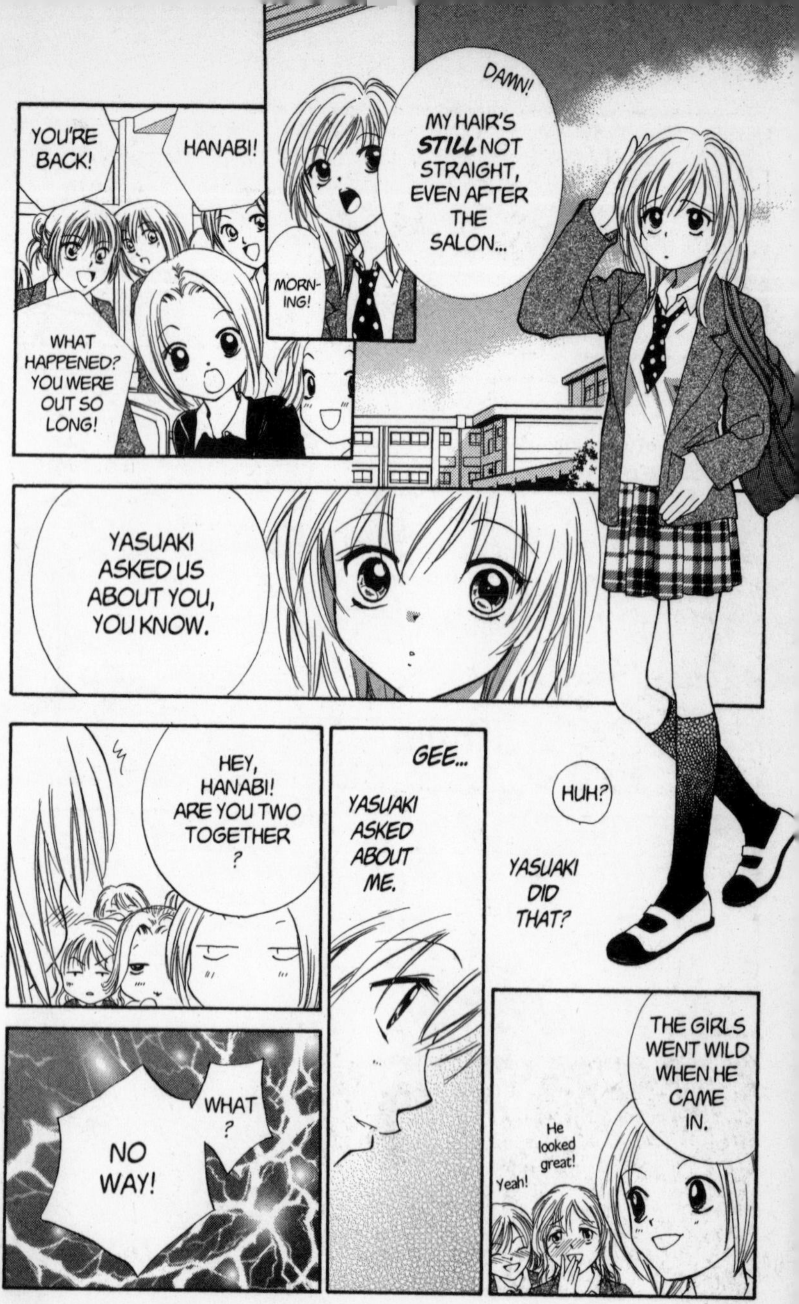
DAMN!
MY HAIR'S **STILL** NOT STRAIGHT, EVEN AFTER THE SALON...
MORNING!
HANABI!
YOU'RE BACK!
WHAT HAPPENED? YOU WERE OUT SO LONG!
YASUAKI ASKED US ABOUT YOU, YOU KNOW.
HUH?
YASUAKI DID THAT?
THE GIRLS WENT WILD WHEN HE CAME IN.
He looked great!
Yeah!
GEE...
YASUAKI ASKED ABOUT ME.
HEY, HANABI! ARE YOU TWO TOGETHER?
WHAT?
NO WAY!

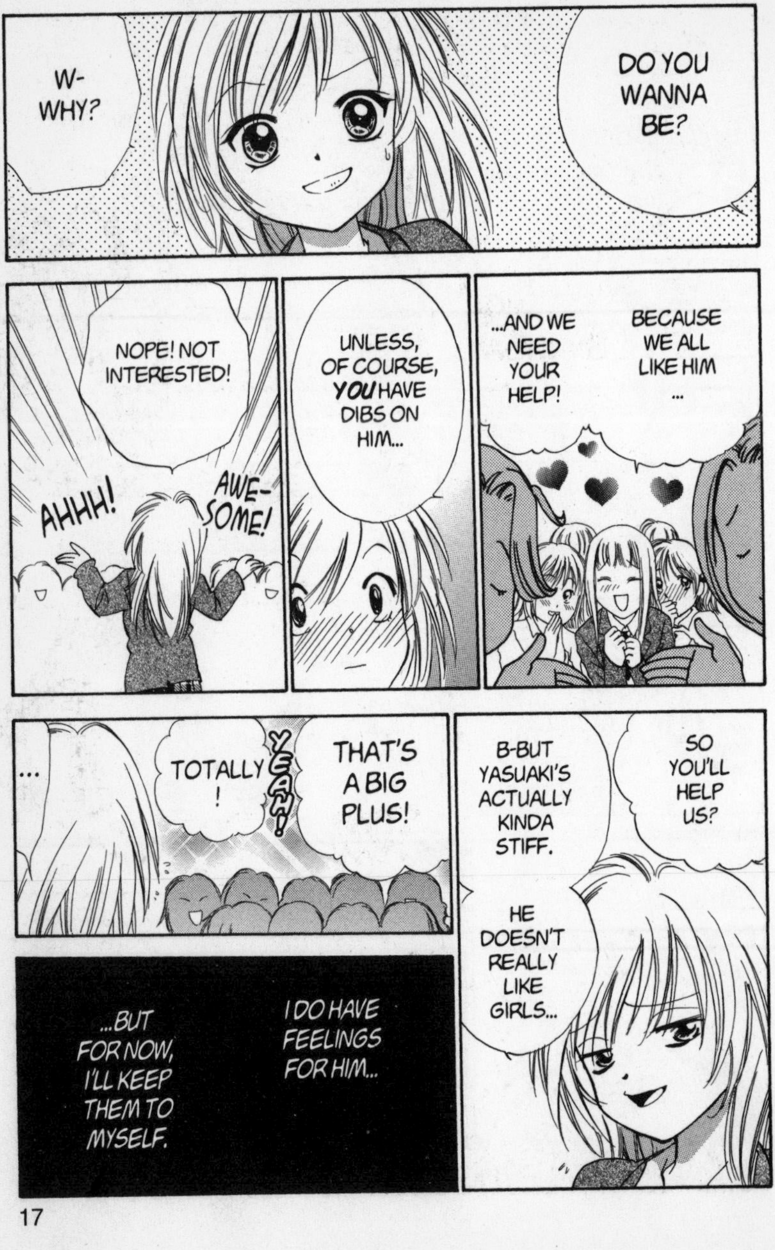
DO YOU WANNA BE?
W- WHY?
BECAUSE WE ALL LIKE HIM ...
...AND WE NEED YOUR HELP!
UNLESS, OF COURSE, YOU HAVE DIBS ON HIM...
NOPE! NOT INTERESTED!
AWE- SOME!
AHHH!
SO YOU'LL HELP US?
B-BUT YASUAKI'S ACTUALLY KINDA STIFF.
HE DOESN'T REALLY LIKE GIRLS...
THAT'S A BIG PLUS!
YEAH!
TOTALLY!
...
I DO HAVE FEELINGS FOR HIM...
...BUT FOR NOW, I'LL KEEP THEM TO MYSELF.

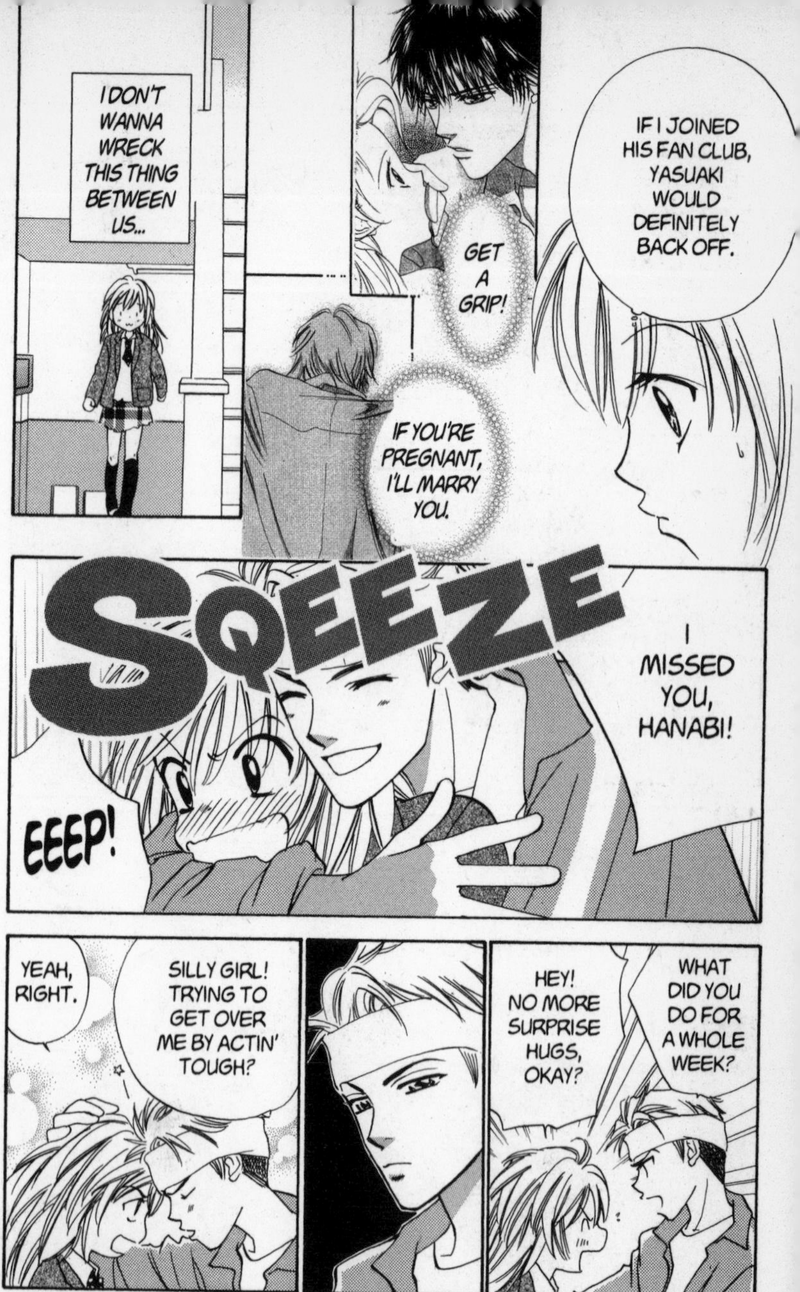
IF I JOINED HIS FAN CLUB, YASUAKI WOULD DEFINITELY BACK OFF.
GET A GRIP!
IF YOU'RE PREGNANT, I'LL MARRY YOU.
I DON'T WANNA WRECK THIS THING BETWEEN US...
SQEEZE
I MISSED YOU, HANABI!
EEEP!
WHAT DID YOU DO FOR A WHOLE WEEK?
HEY! NO MORE SURPRISE HUGS, OKAY?
SILLY GIRL! TRYING TO GET OVER ME BY ACTIN' TOUGH?
YEAH, RIGHT.

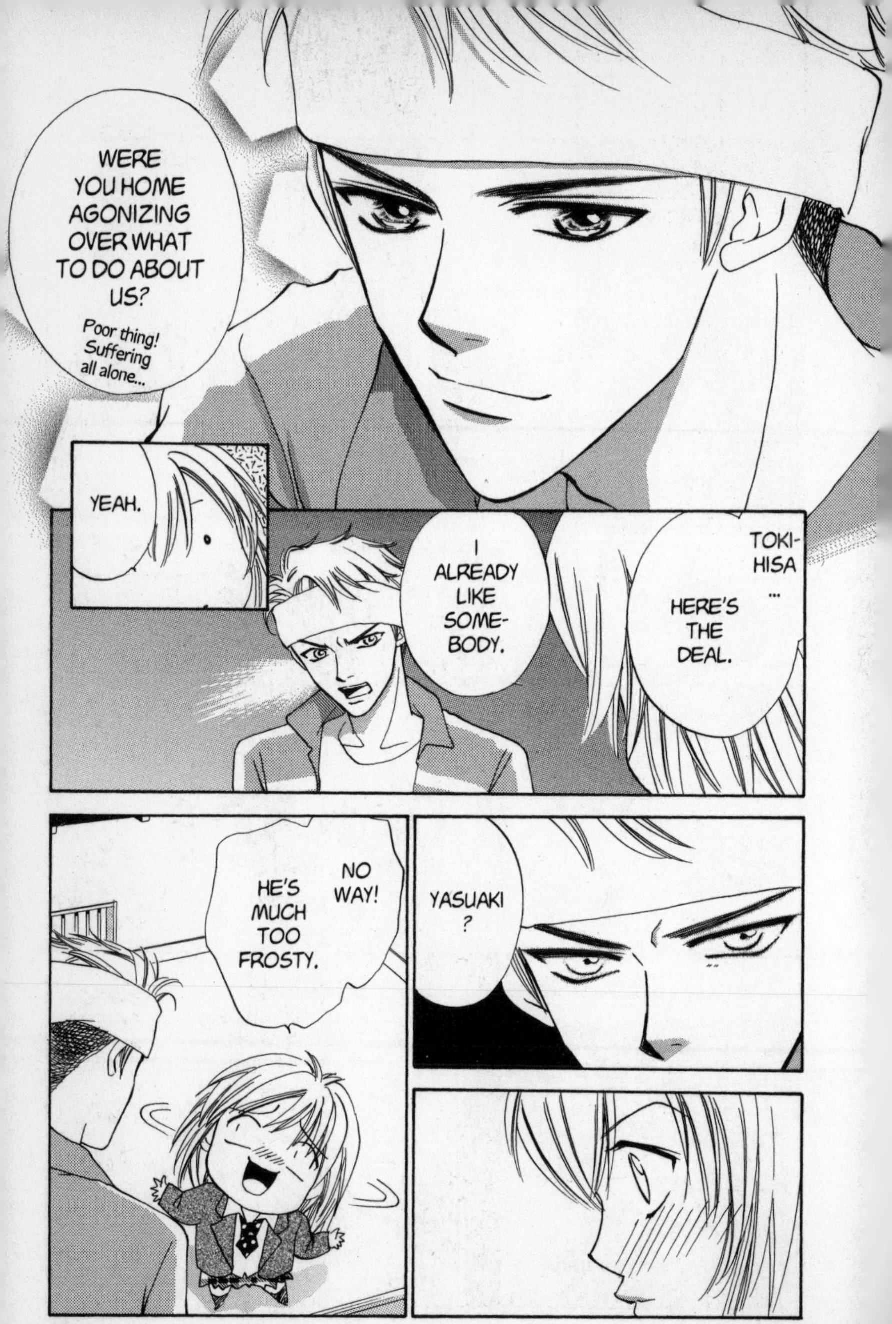
WERE YOU HOME AGONIZING OVER WHAT TO DO ABOUT US?
Poor thing! Suffering all alone...
YEAH.
TOKI-HISA...
HERE'S THE DEAL.
I ALREADY LIKE SOME-BODY.
YASUAKI?
NO WAY!
HE'S MUCH TOO FROSTY.

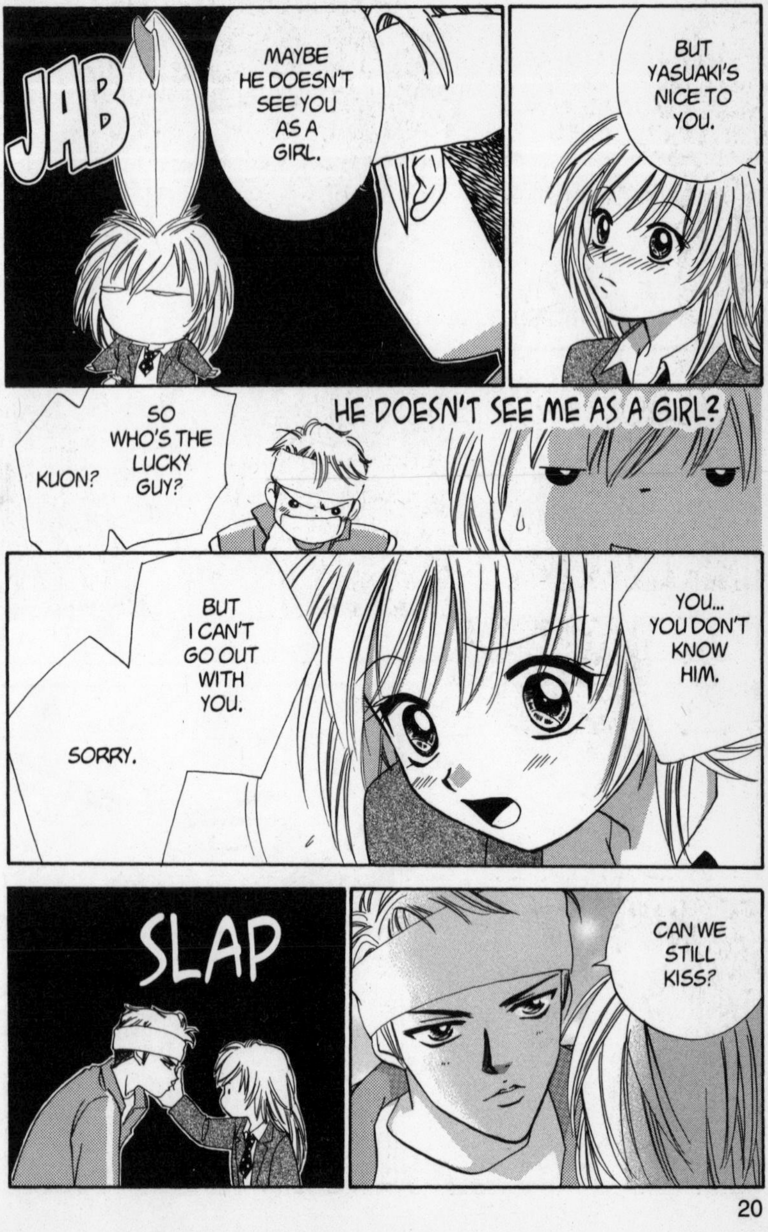

BUT YASUAKI'S NICE TO YOU.
MAYBE HE DOESN'T SEE YOU AS A GIRL.
JAB
HE DOESN'T SEE ME AS A GIRL?
SO WHO'S THE LUCKY GUY?
KUON?
YOU... YOU DON'T KNOW HIM.
BUT I CAN'T GO OUT WITH YOU.
SORRY.
CAN WE STILL KISS?
SLAP

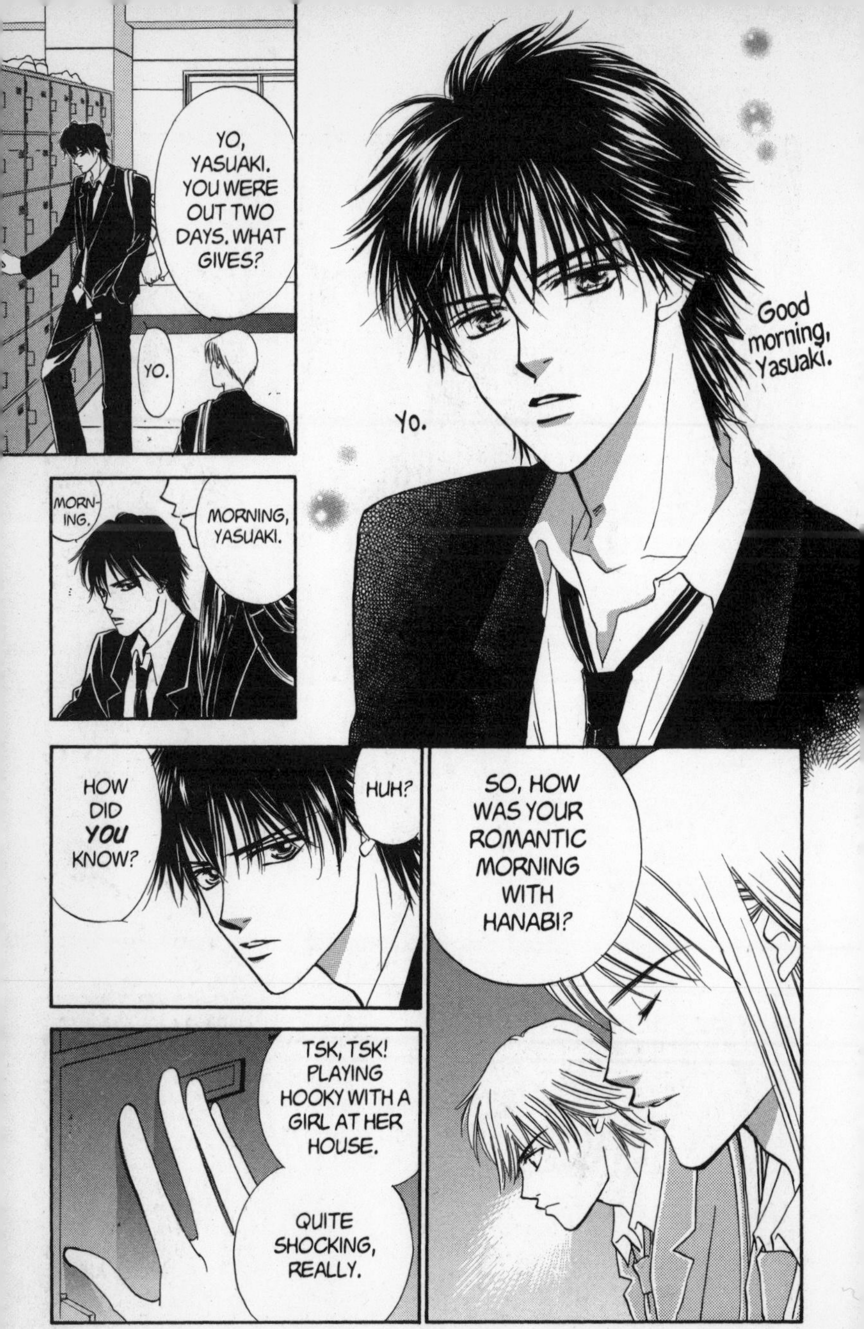

Good morning, Yasuaki.
Yo.
YO, YASUAKI. YOU WERE OUT TWO DAYS. WHAT GIVES?
YO.
MORNING, YASUAKI.
MORNING.
SO, HOW WAS YOUR ROMANTIC MORNING WITH HANABI?
HUH?
HOW DID ***YOU*** KNOW?
TSK, TSK! PLAYING HOOKY WITH A GIRL AT HER HOUSE.
QUITE SHOCKING, REALLY.

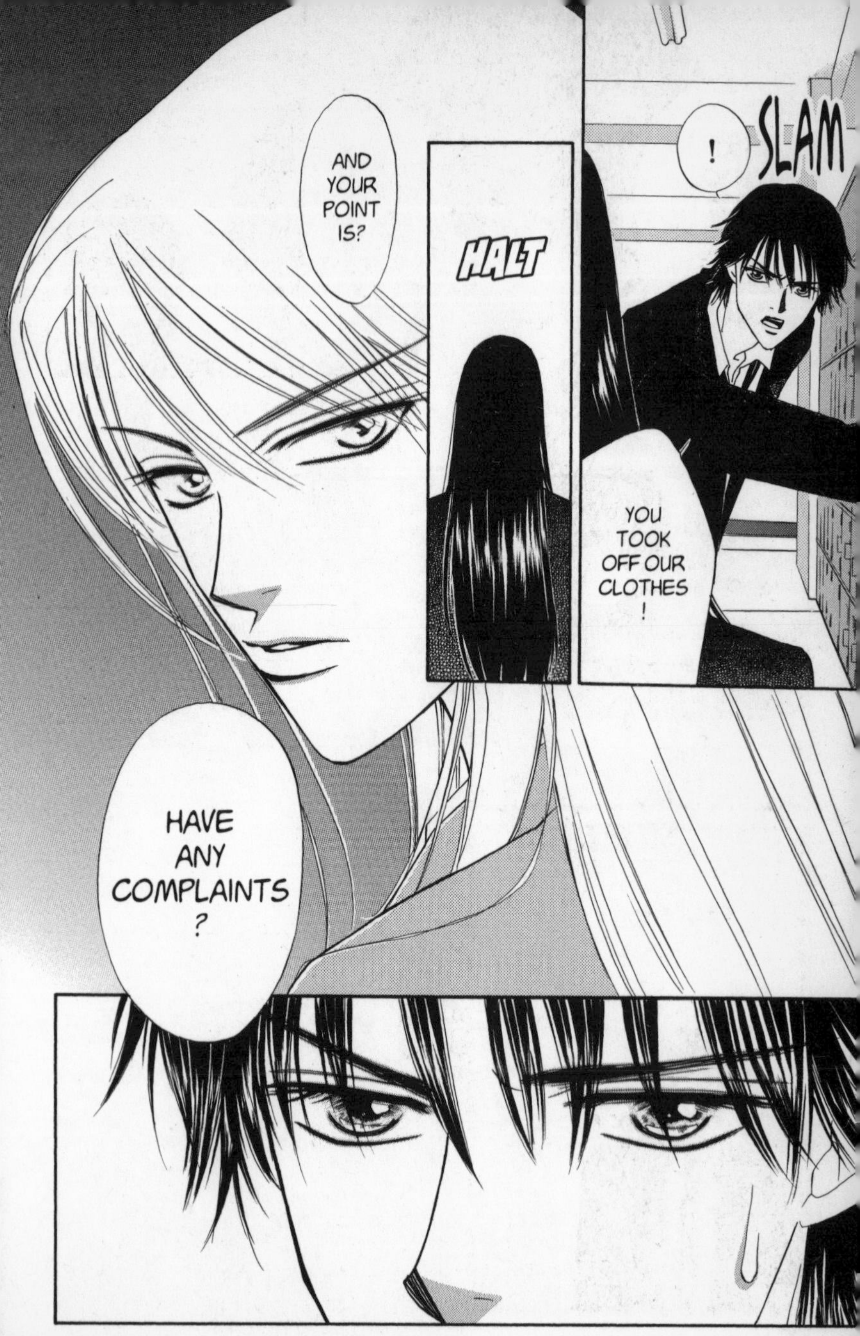
SLAM
!
YOU TOOK OFF OUR CLOTHES!
HALT
AND YOUR POINT IS?
HAVE ANY COMPLAINTS?

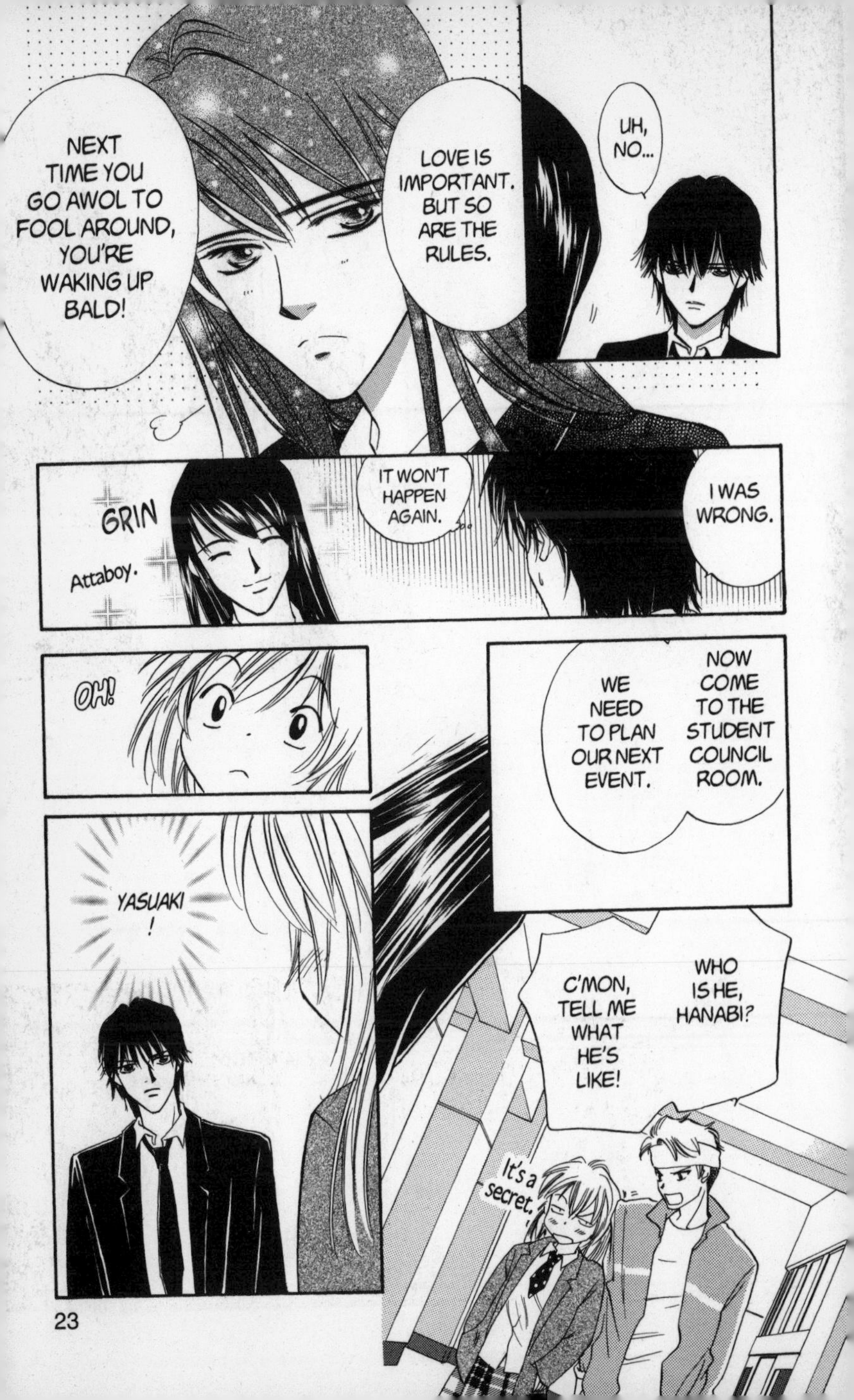

UH, NO...
LOVE IS IMPORTANT. BUT SO ARE THE RULES.
NEXT TIME YOU GO AWOL TO FOOL AROUND, YOU'RE WAKING UP BALD!
I WAS WRONG.
IT WON'T HAPPEN AGAIN.
GRIN
Attaboy.
NOW COME TO THE STUDENT COUNCIL ROOM.
WE NEED TO PLAN OUR NEXT EVENT.
WHO IS HE, HANABI?
C'MON, TELL ME WHAT HE'S LIKE!
It's a secret.
OH!
YASUAKI!

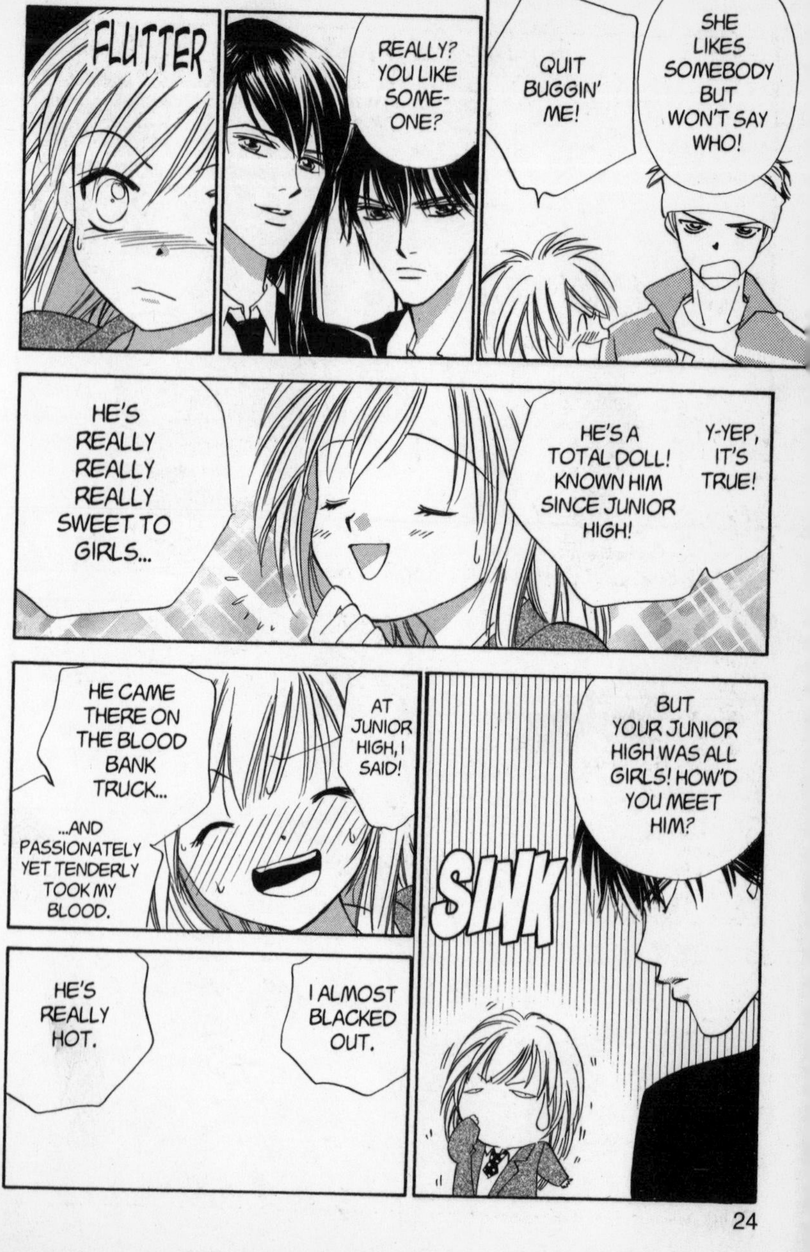
SHE LIKES SOMEBODY BUT WON'T SAY WHO!
QUIT BUGGIN' ME!
REALLY? YOU LIKE SOME-ONE?
FLUTTER
Y-YEP, IT'S TRUE!
HE'S A TOTAL DOLL! KNOWN HIM SINCE JUNIOR HIGH!
HE'S REALLY REALLY REALLY SWEET TO GIRLS...
BUT YOUR JUNIOR HIGH WAS ALL GIRLS! HOW'D YOU MEET HIM?
SINK
AT JUNIOR HIGH, I SAID!
HE CAME THERE ON THE BLOOD BANK TRUCK...
...AND PASSIONATELY YET TENDERLY TOOK MY BLOOD.
I ALMOST BLACKED OUT.
HE'S REALLY HOT.

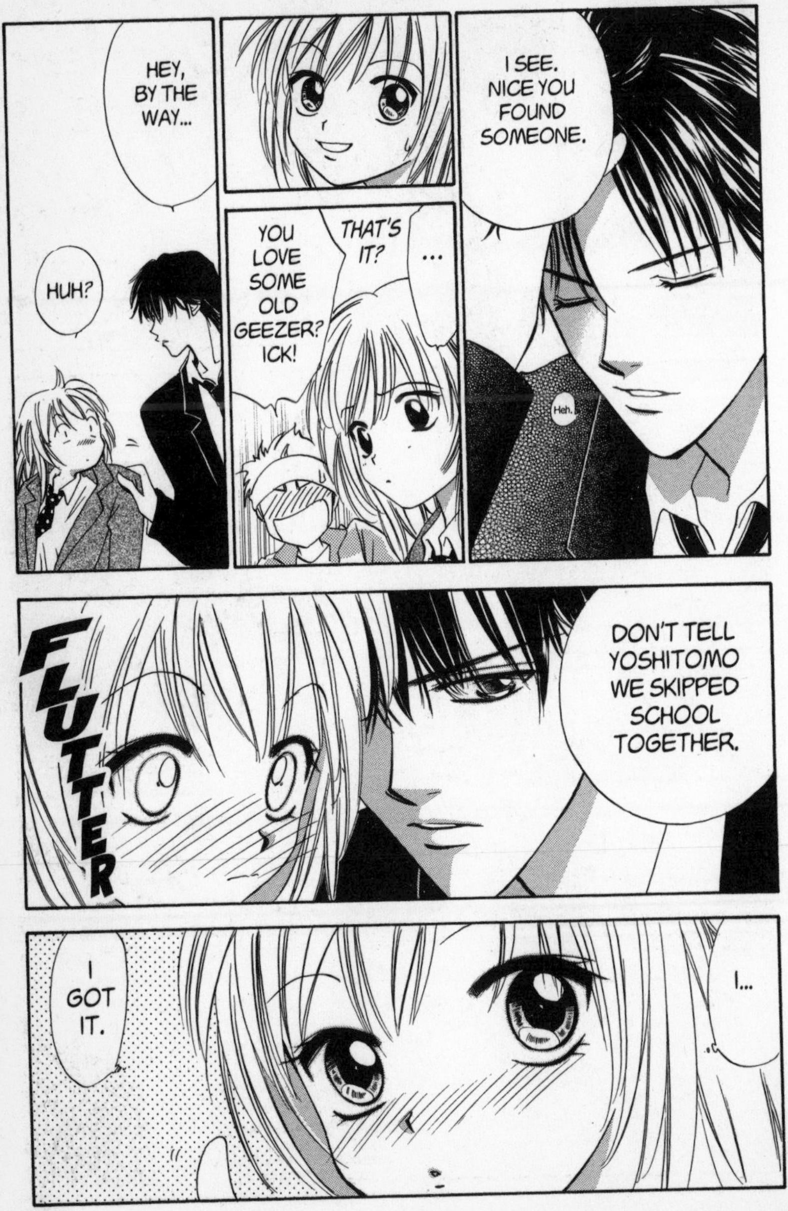
I SEE. NICE YOU FOUND SOMEONE.
Heh.
...
THAT'S IT?
YOU LOVE SOME OLD GEEZER? ICK!
HEY, BY THE WAY...
HUH?
DON'T TELL YOSHITOMO WE SKIPPED SCHOOL TOGETHER.
FLUTTER
I...
I GOT IT.

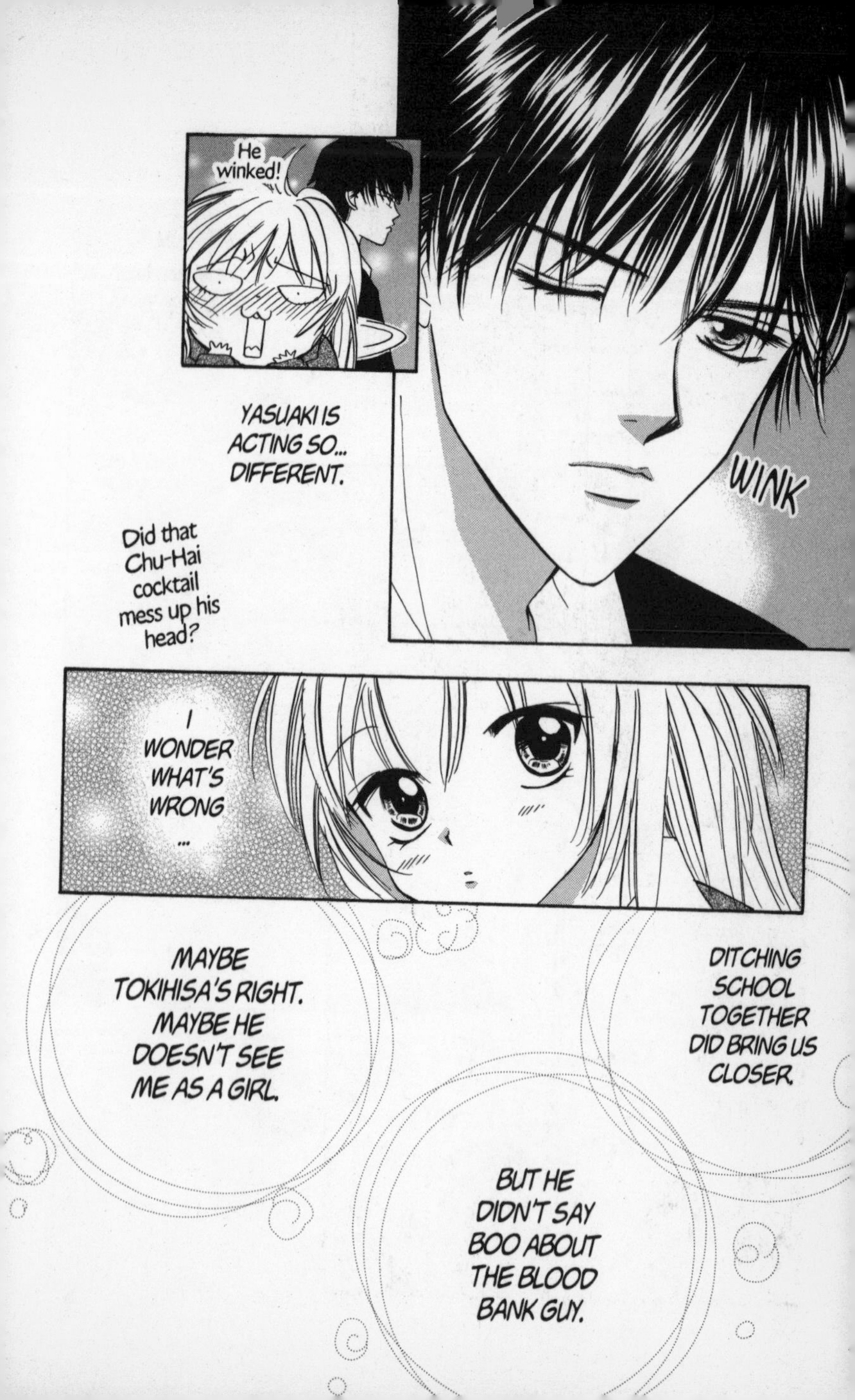
WINK
He winked!
YASUAKI IS ACTING SO... DIFFERENT.
Did that Chu-Hai cocktail mess up his head?
I WONDER WHAT'S WRONG ...
DITCHING SCHOOL TOGETHER DID BRING US CLOSER.
BUT HE DIDN'T SAY BOO ABOUT THE BLOOD BANK GUY.
MAYBE TOKIHISA'S RIGHT. MAYBE HE DOESN'T SEE ME AS A GIRL.

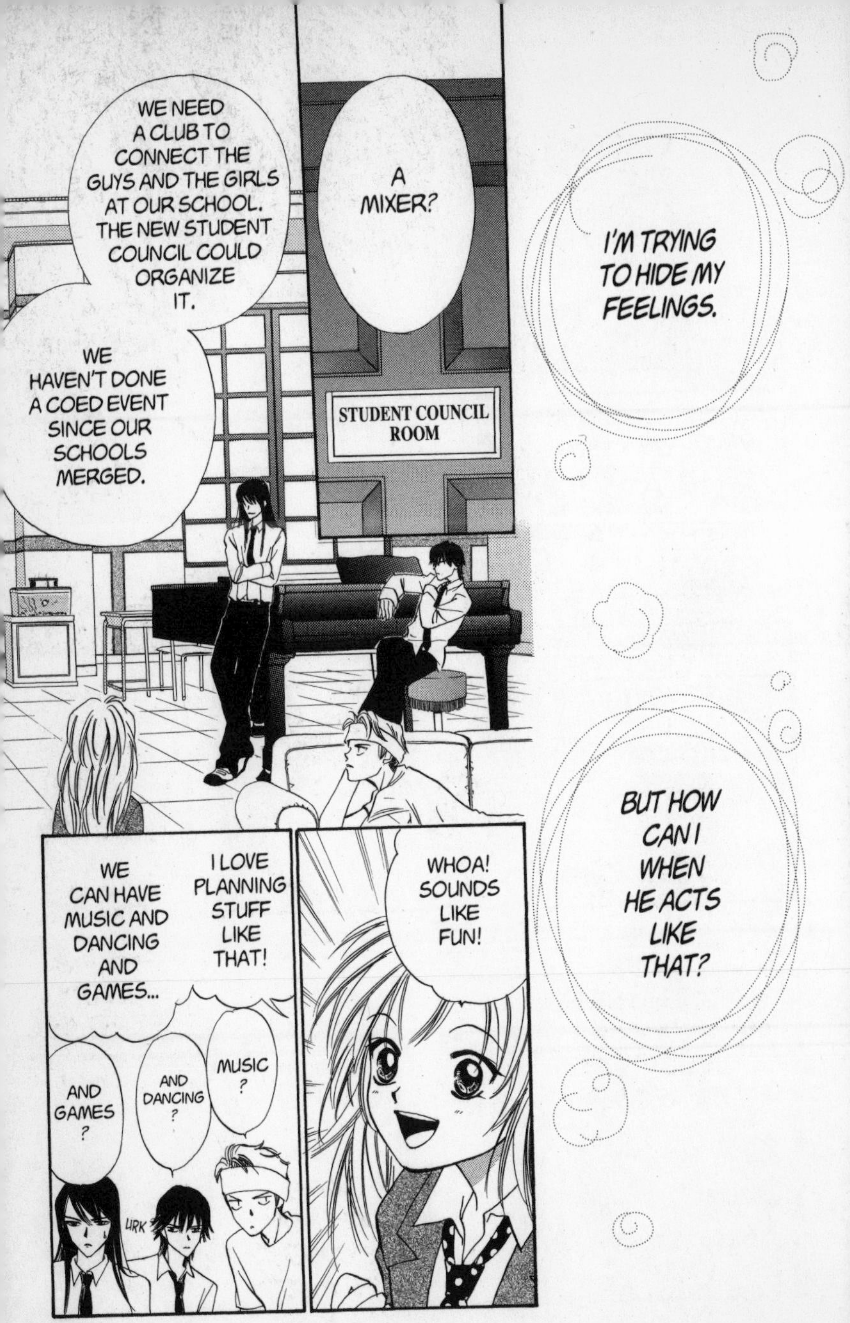
I'M TRYING TO HIDE MY FEELINGS.
BUT HOW CAN I WHEN HE ACTS LIKE THAT?
A MIXER?
STUDENT COUNCIL ROOM
WE NEED A CLUB TO CONNECT THE GUYS AND THE GIRLS AT OUR SCHOOL. THE NEW STUDENT COUNCIL COULD ORGANIZE IT.
WE HAVEN'T DONE A COED EVENT SINCE OUR SCHOOLS MERGED.
WHOA! SOUNDS LIKE FUN!
I LOVE PLANNING STUFF LIKE THAT!
WE CAN HAVE MUSIC AND DANCING AND GAMES...
MUSIC?
AND DANCING?
AND GAMES?
URK

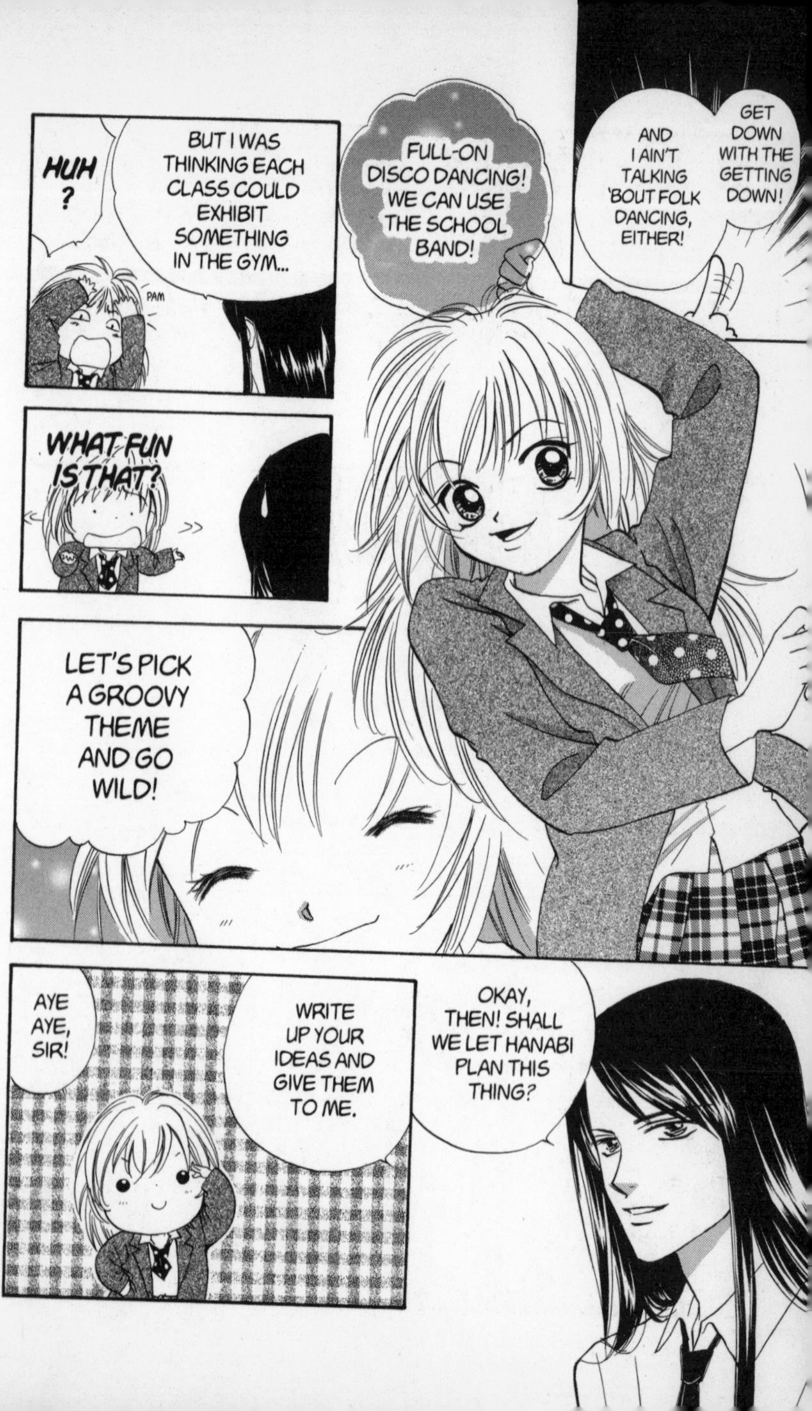
GET DOWN WITH THE GETTING DOWN!
AND I AIN'T TALKING 'BOUT FOLK DANCING, EITHER!
FULL-ON DISCO DANCING! WE CAN USE THE SCHOOL BAND!
BUT I WAS THINKING EACH CLASS COULD EXHIBIT SOMETHING IN THE GYM...
HUH?
PAM
WHAT FUN IS THAT?
LET'S PICK A GROOVY THEME AND GO WILD!
OKAY, THEN! SHALL WE LET HANABI PLAN THIS THING?
WRITE UP YOUR IDEAS AND GIVE THEM TO ME.
AYE AYE, SIR!

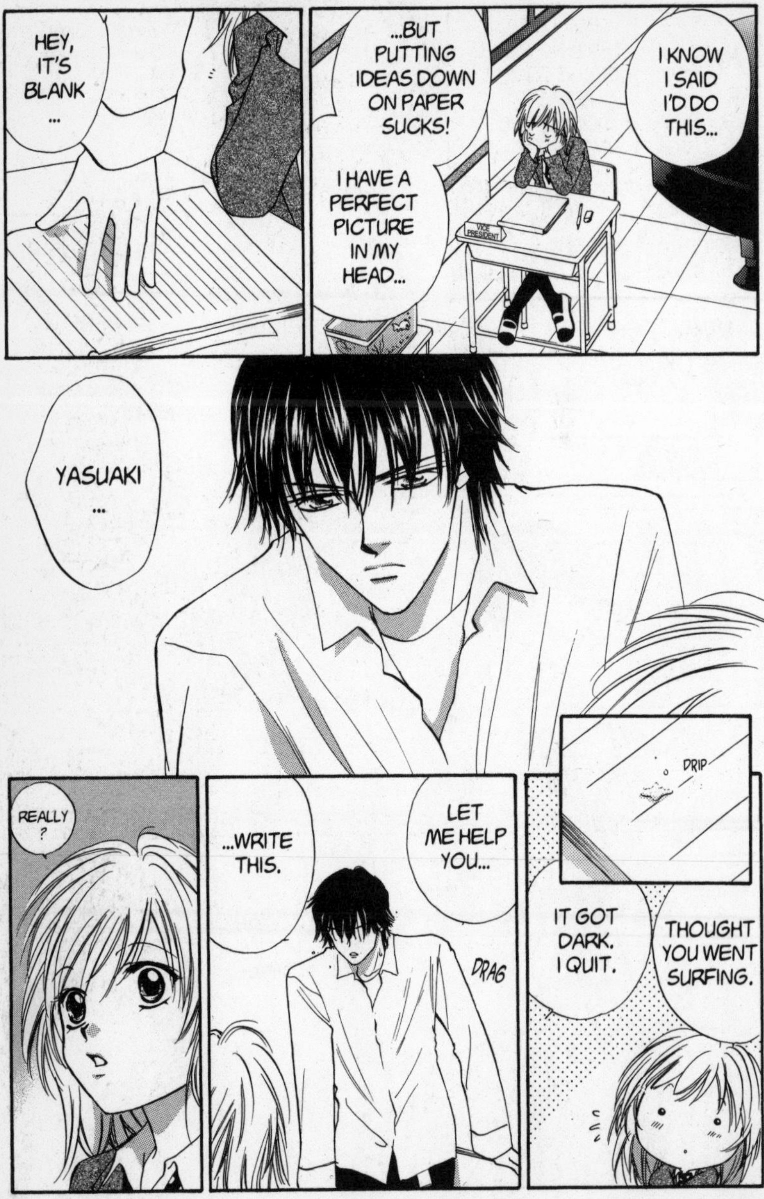
I KNOW I SAID I'D DO THIS...
...BUT PUTTING IDEAS DOWN ON PAPER SUCKS!
VICE PRESIDENT
I HAVE A PERFECT PICTURE IN MY HEAD...
HEY, IT'S BLANK...
YASUAKI...
DRIP
THOUGHT YOU WENT SURFING.
IT GOT DARK. I QUIT.
LET ME HELP YOU...
...WRITE THIS.
DRAG
REALLY?

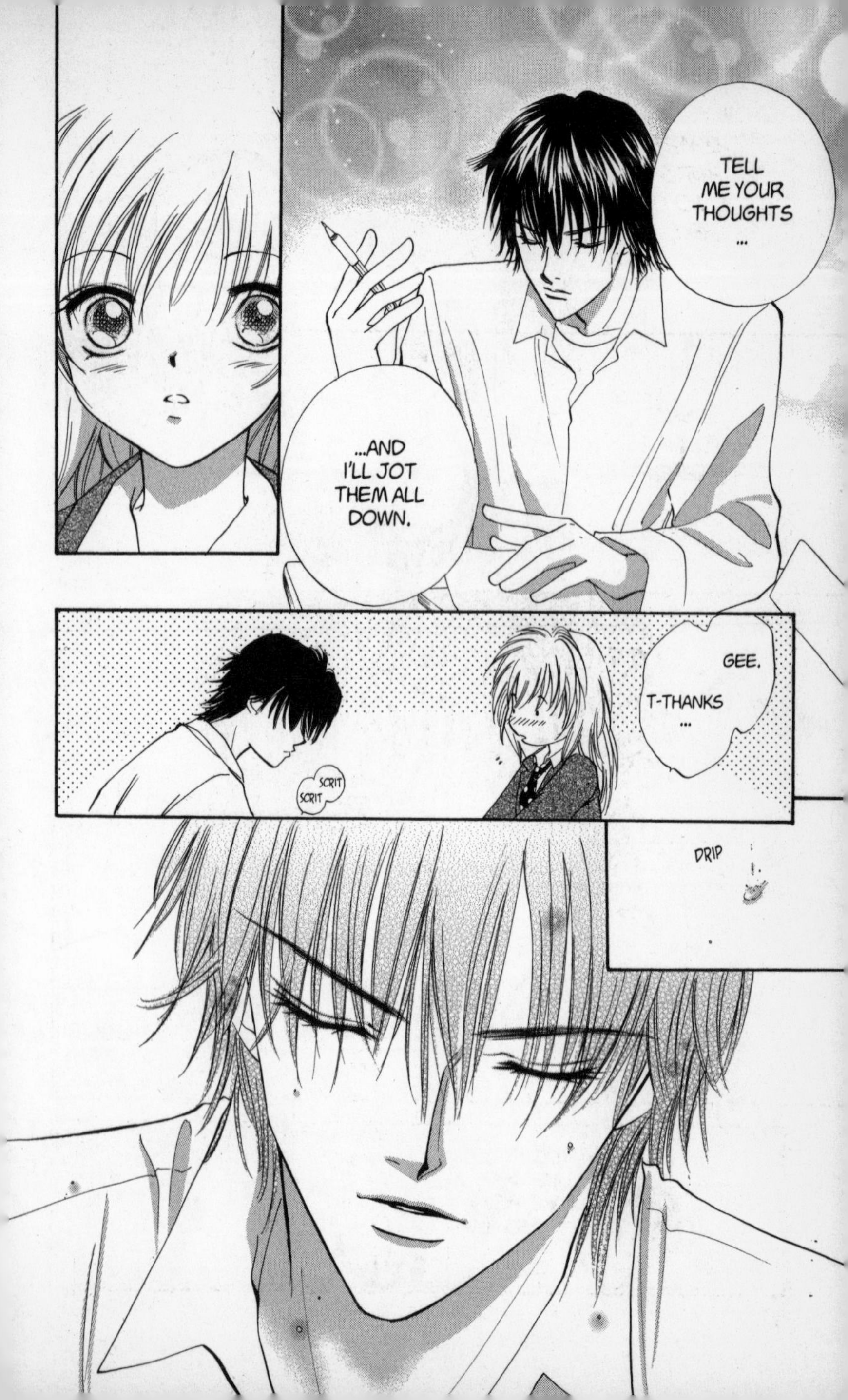
TELL ME YOUR THOUGHTS ...
...AND I'LL JOT THEM ALL DOWN.
GEE. T-THANKS ...
SCRIT SCRIT
DRIP

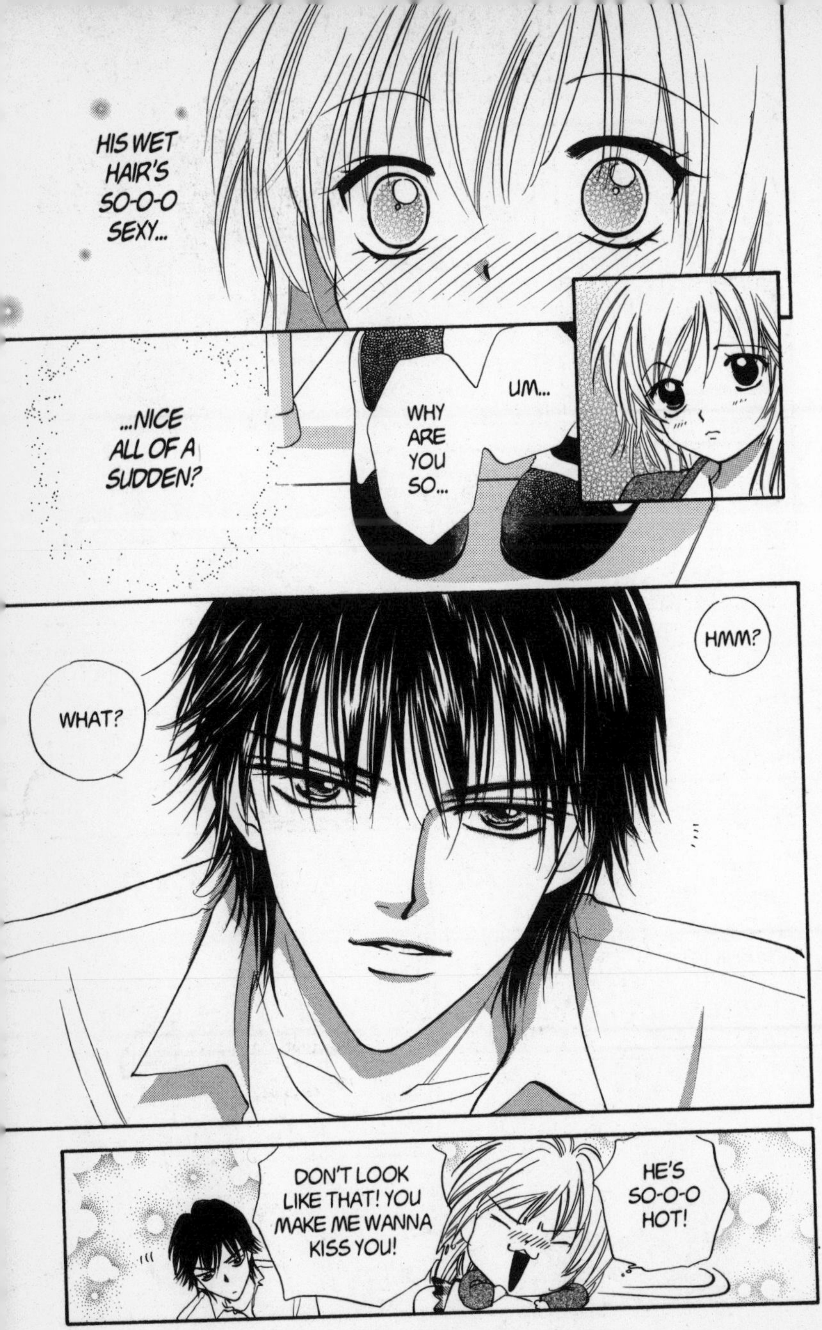
HIS WET HAIR'S SO-O-O SEXY...
UM...
WHY ARE YOU SO...
...NICE ALL OF A SUDDEN?
HMM?
WHAT?
HE'S SO-O-O HOT!
DON'T LOOK LIKE THAT! YOU MAKE ME WANNA KISS YOU!

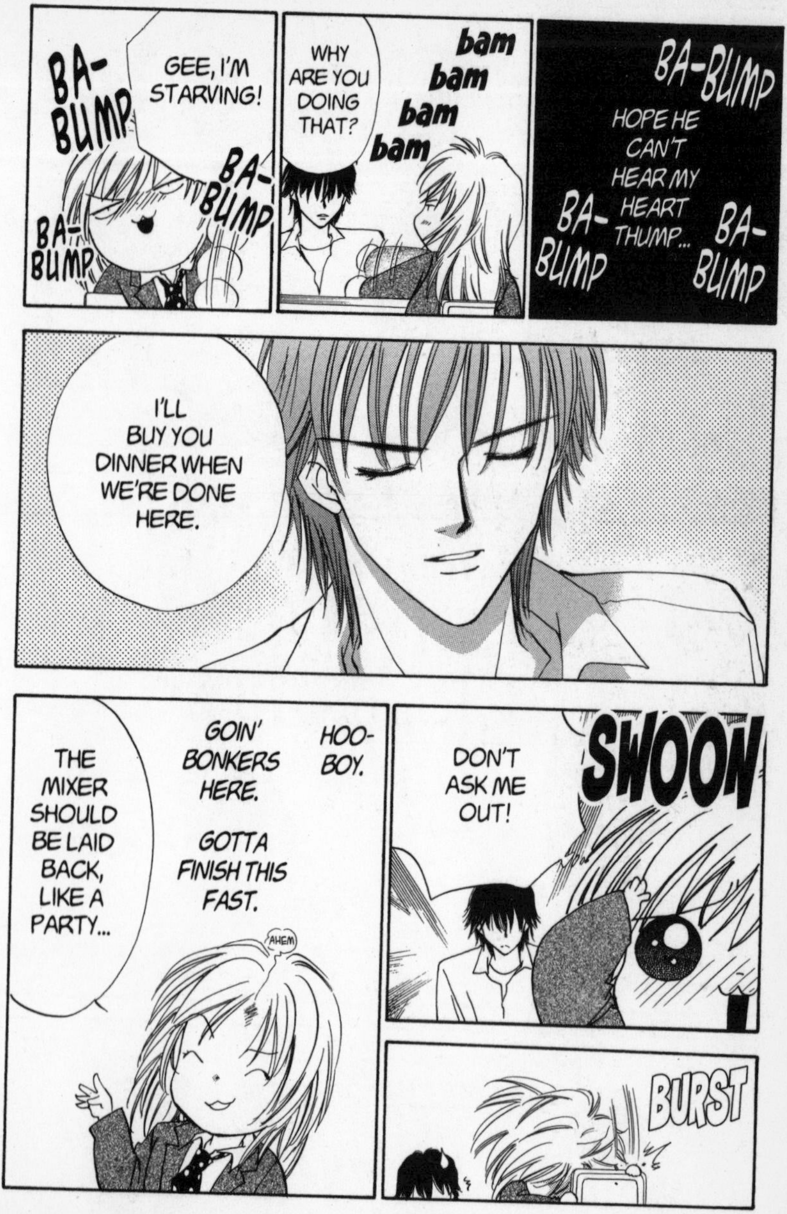
BA-BUMP
HOPE HE CAN'T HEAR MY HEART THUMP...
BA-BUMP
BA-BUMP
bam bam bam bam
WHY ARE YOU DOING THAT?
BA-BUMP
GEE, I'M STARVING!
BA-BUMP
BA-BUMP
I'LL BUY YOU DINNER WHEN WE'RE DONE HERE.
SWOON
DON'T ASK ME OUT!
BURST
HOO-BOY.
GOIN' BONKERS HERE.
GOTTA FINISH THIS FAST.
THE MIXER SHOULD BE LAID BACK, LIKE A PARTY...
AHEM

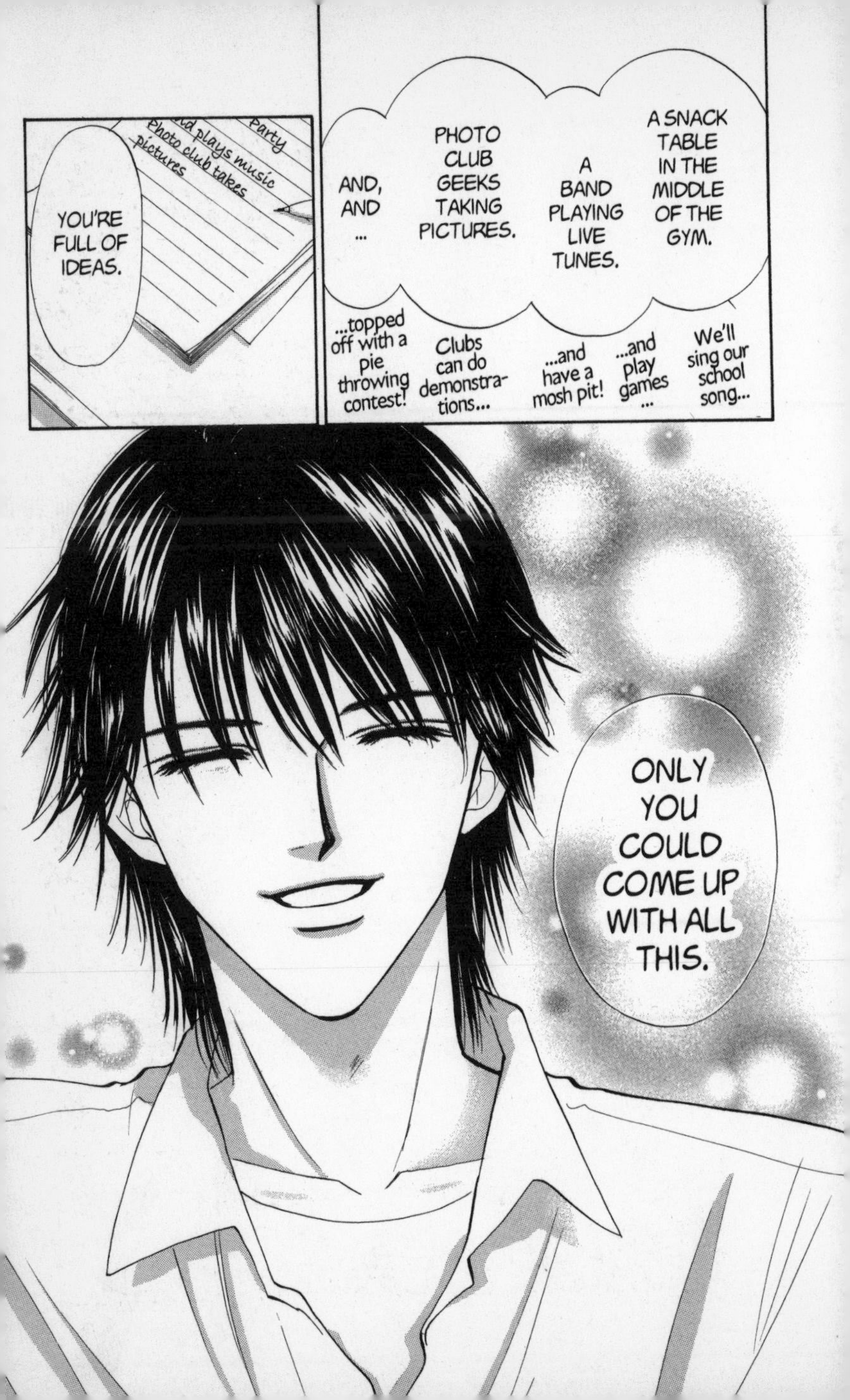
A SNACK TABLE IN THE MIDDLE OF THE GYM.
A BAND PLAYING LIVE TUNES.
PHOTO CLUB GEEKS TAKING PICTURES.
AND, AND ...
We'll sing our school song...
...and play games ...
...and have a mosh pit!
Clubs can do demonstrations...
...topped off with a pie throwing contest!
Party
plays music
Photo club takes pictures
YOU'RE FULL OF IDEAS.
ONLY YOU COULD COME UP WITH ALL THIS.

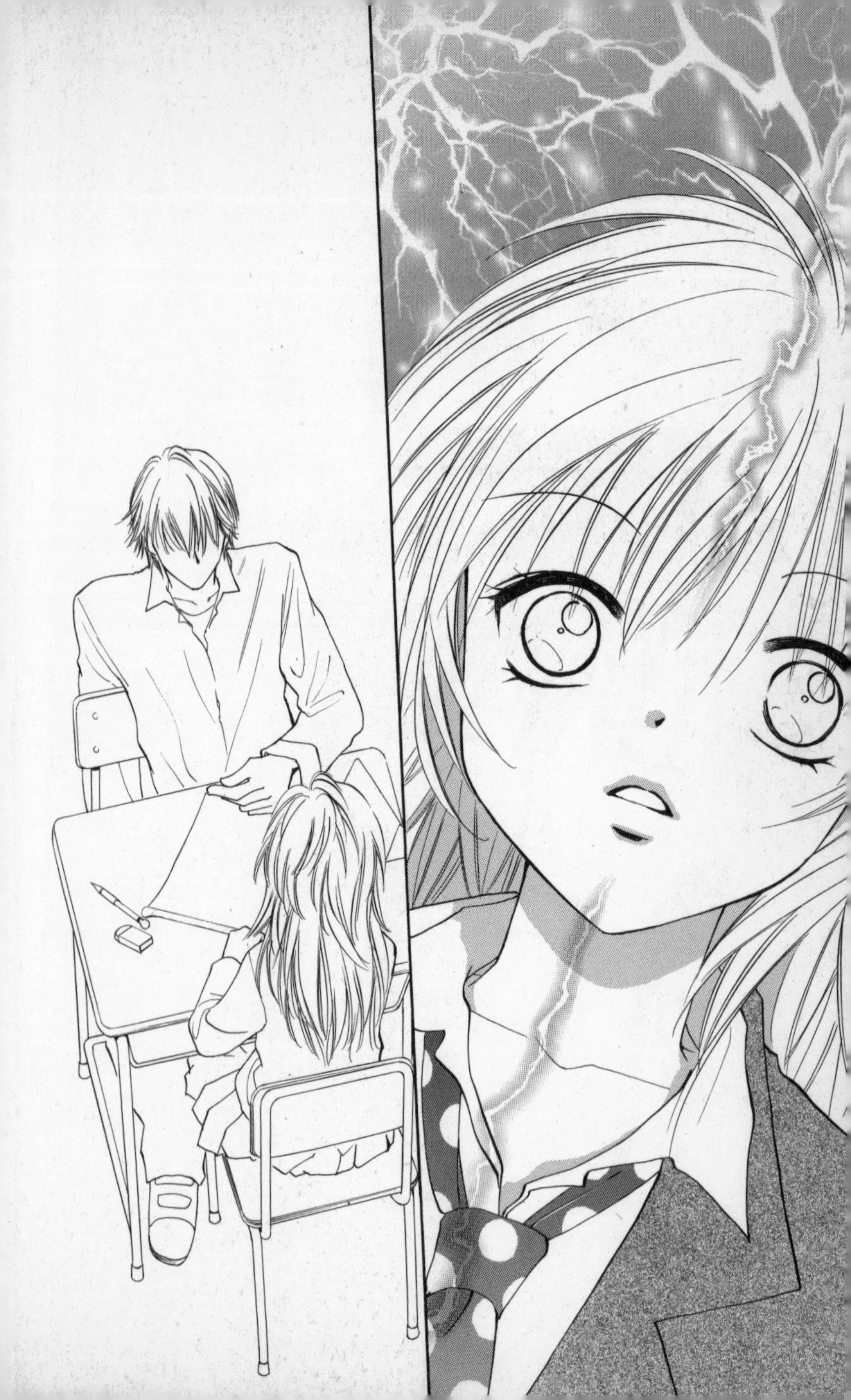

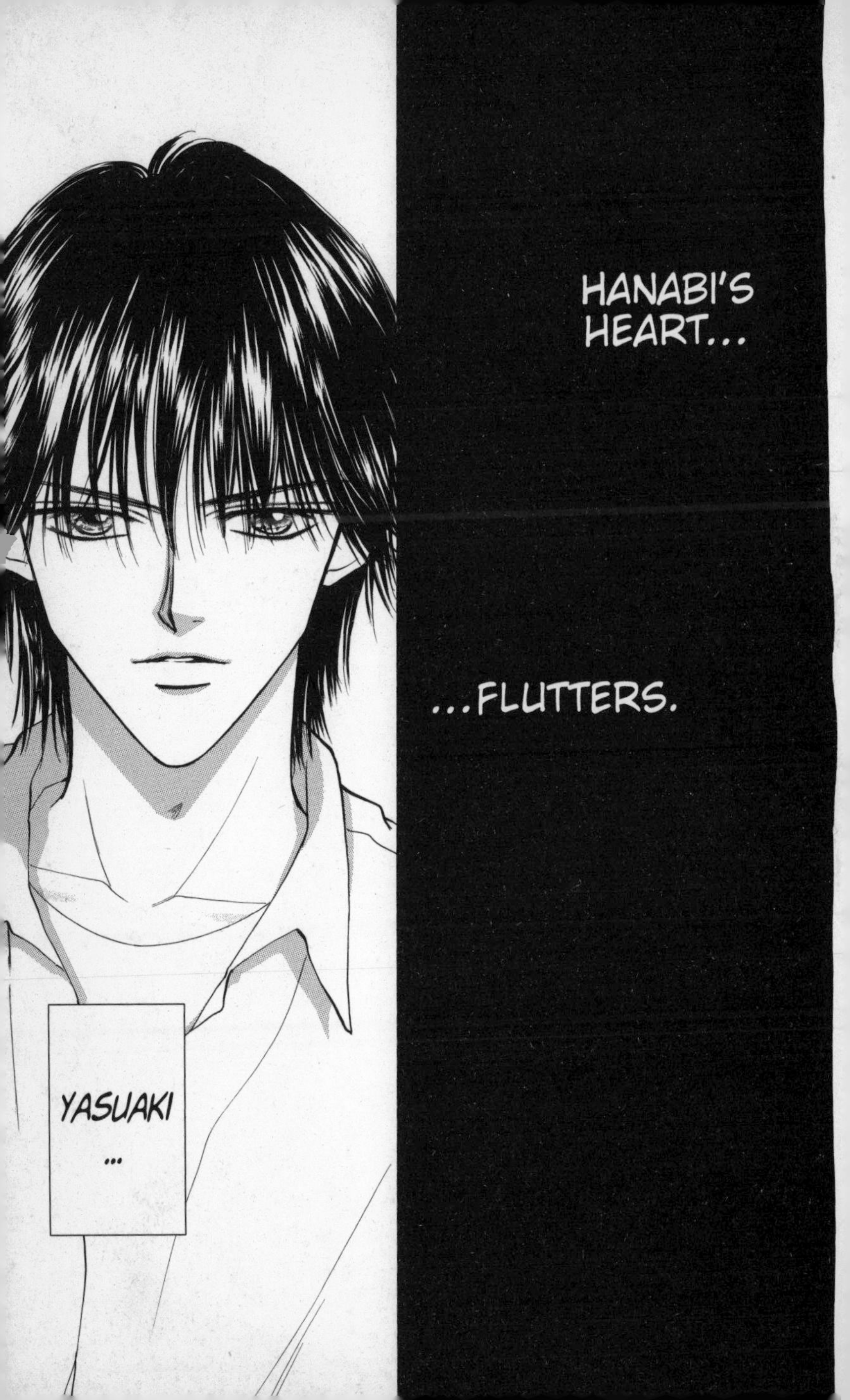
HANABI'S HEART...
...FLUTTERS.
YASUAKI ...

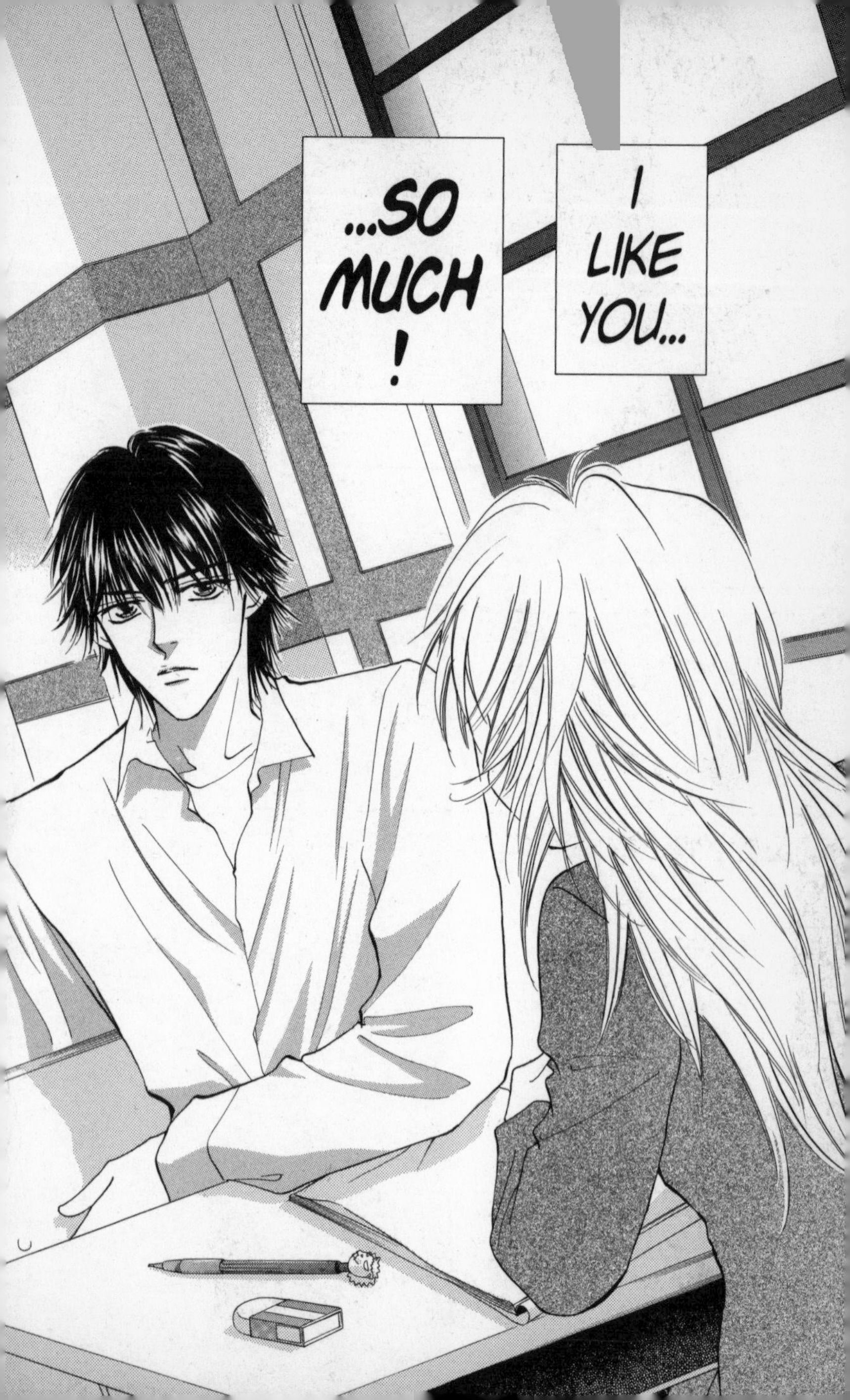
I LIKE YOU...
...SO MUCH!

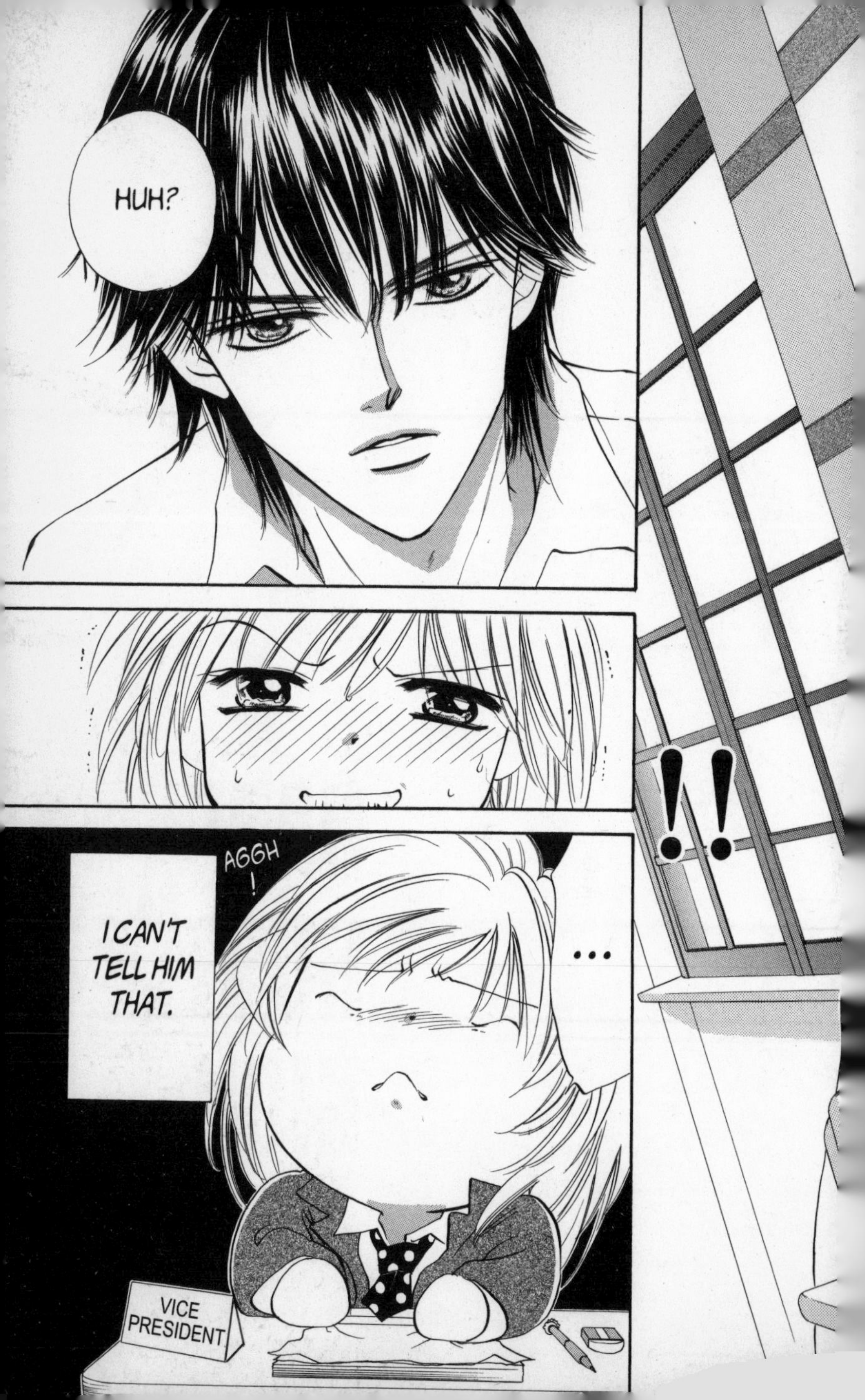
!!
HUH?
...
AGGH!
I CAN'T TELL HIM THAT.
VICE PRESIDENT

HAPP

HUST

HIGH

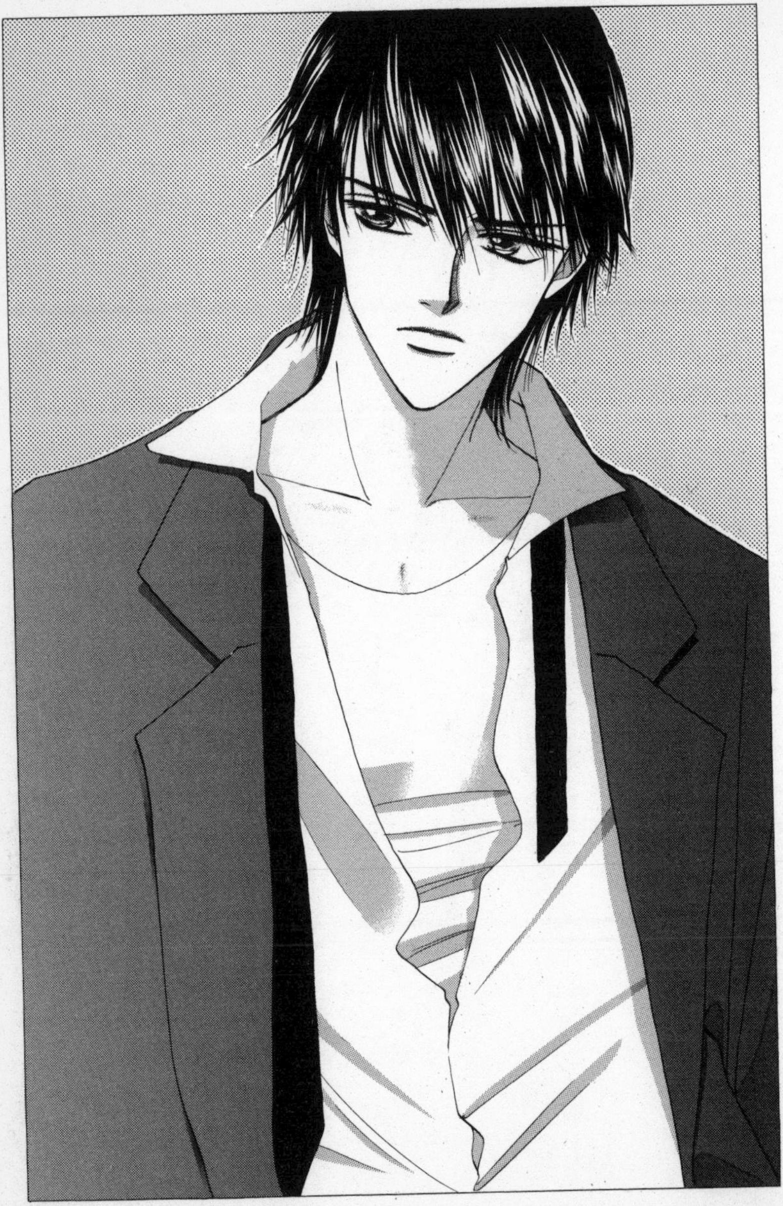

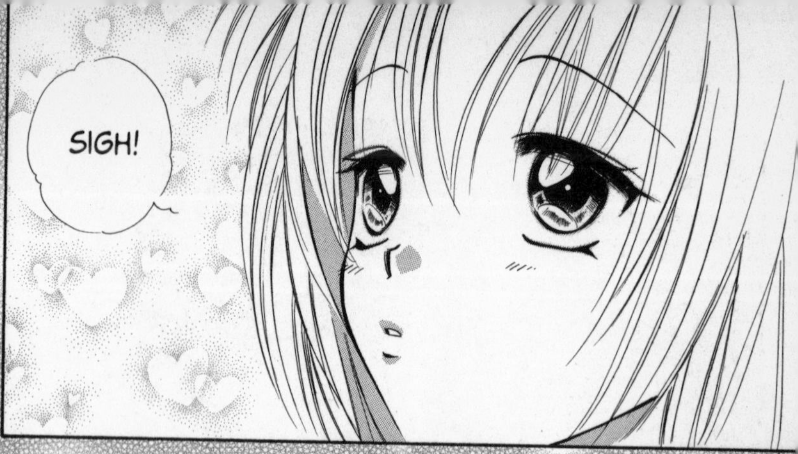
SIGH!

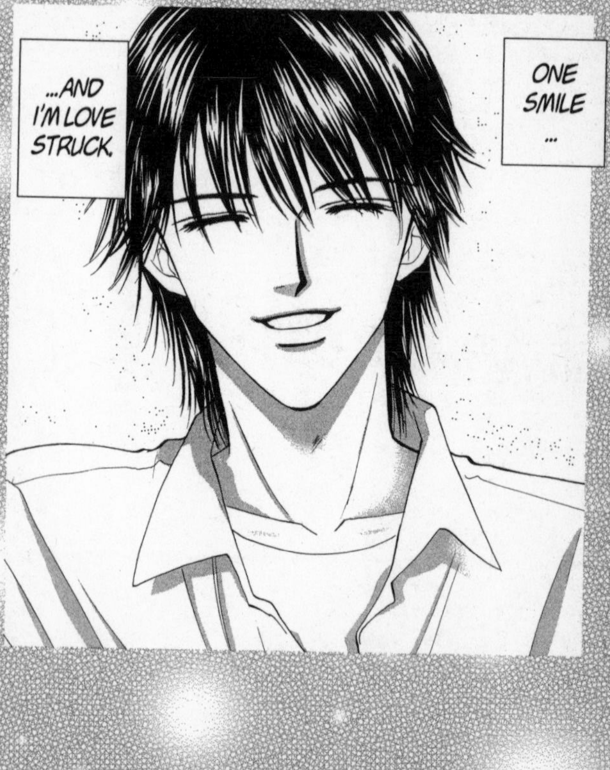
ONE SMILE ...
...AND I'M LOVE STRUCK.

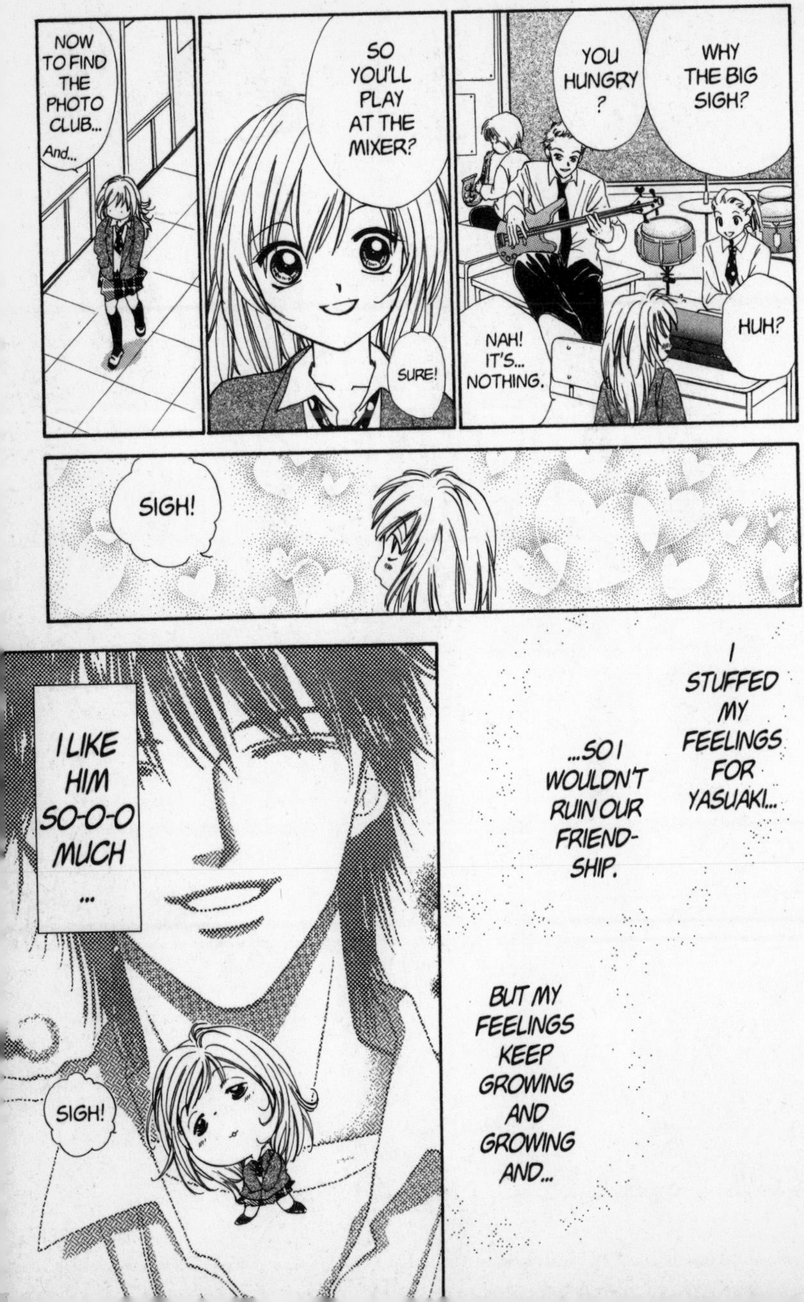
WHY THE BIG SIGH?
YOU HUNGRY?
HUH?
NAH! IT'S... NOTHING.
SO YOU'LL PLAY AT THE MIXER?
SURE!
NOW TO FIND THE PHOTO CLUB...
And...
SIGH!
I STUFFED MY FEELINGS FOR YASUAKI...
...SO I WOULDN'T RUIN OUR FRIENDSHIP.
BUT MY FEELINGS KEEP GROWING AND GROWING AND...
I LIKE HIM SO-O-O MUCH...
SIGH!

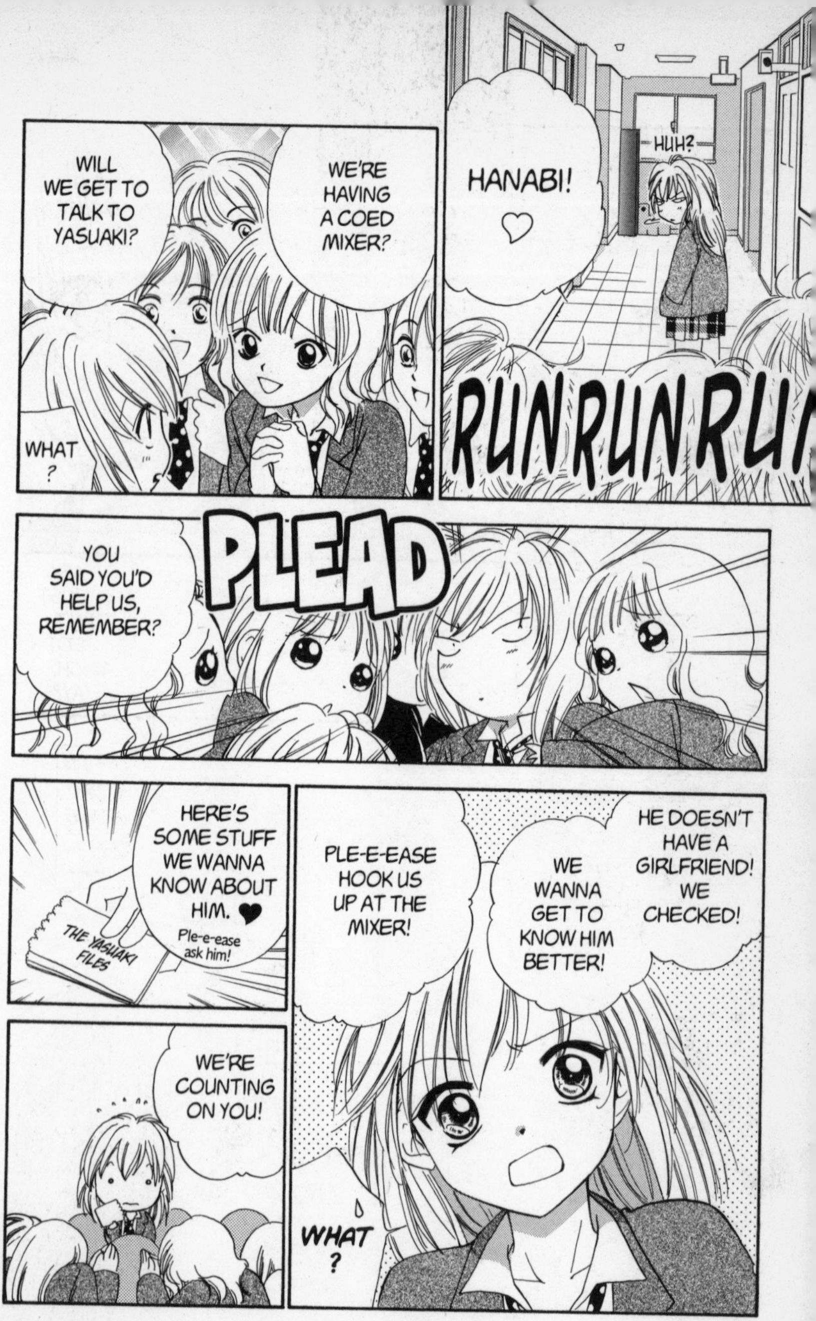
HANABI! ♡
HUH?
RUN RUN RU
WE'RE HAVING A COED MIXER?
WILL WE GET TO TALK TO YASUAKI?
WHAT ?
PLEAD
YOU SAID YOU'D HELP US, REMEMBER?
HE DOESN'T HAVE A GIRLFRIEND! WE CHECKED!
WE WANNA GET TO KNOW HIM BETTER!
PLE-E-EASE HOOK US UP AT THE MIXER!
WHAT ?
HERE'S SOME STUFF WE WANNA KNOW ABOUT HIM. ♥
Ple-e-ease ask him!
THE YASHAKI FILES
WE'RE COUNTING ON YOU!

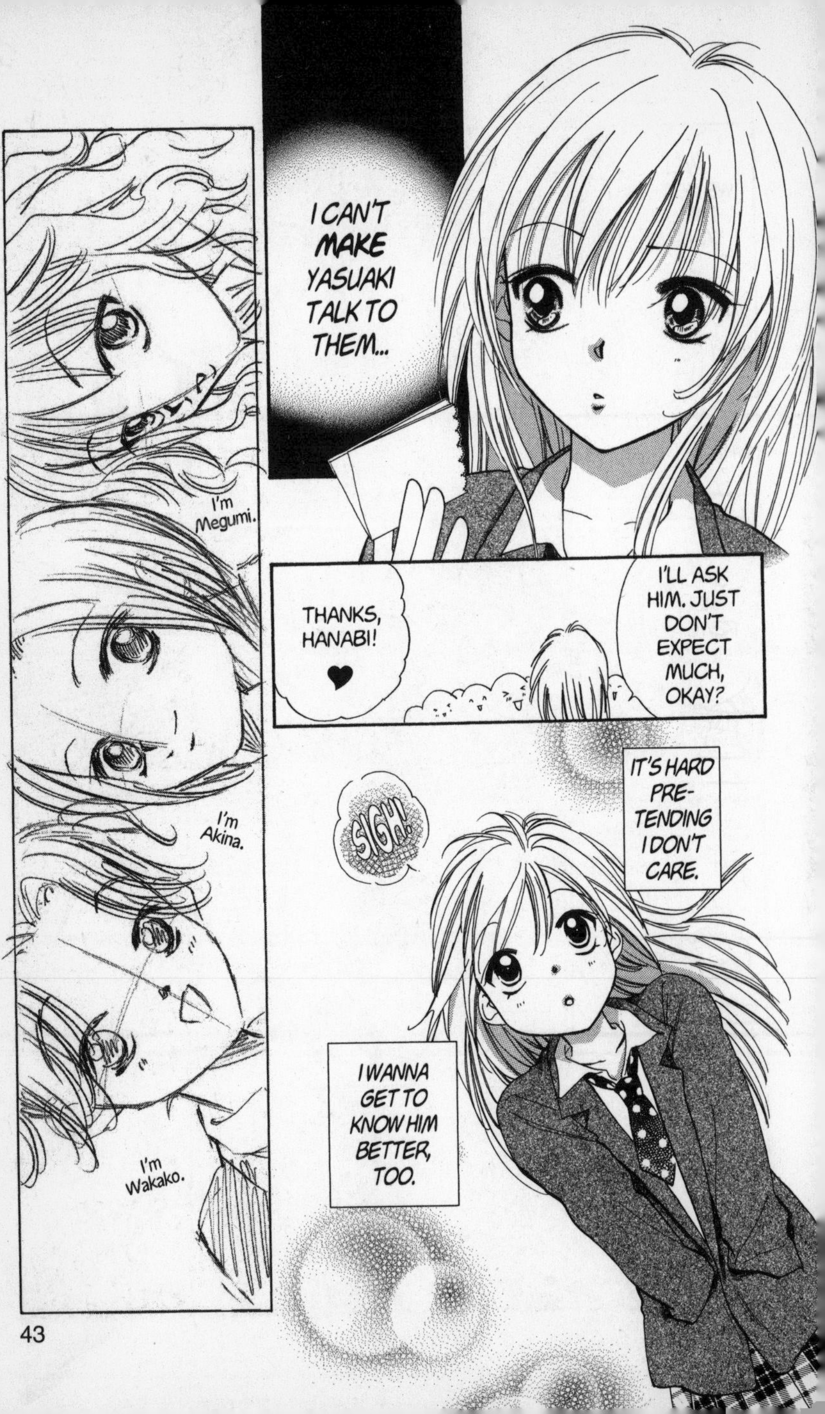
I CAN'T MAKE YASUAKI TALK TO THEM...
I'LL ASK HIM. JUST DON'T EXPECT MUCH, OKAY?
THANKS, HANABI! ♥
IT'S HARD PRETENDING I DON'T CARE.
SIGH!
I WANNA GET TO KNOW HIM BETTER, TOO.
I'm Megumi.
I'm Akina.
I'm Wakako.

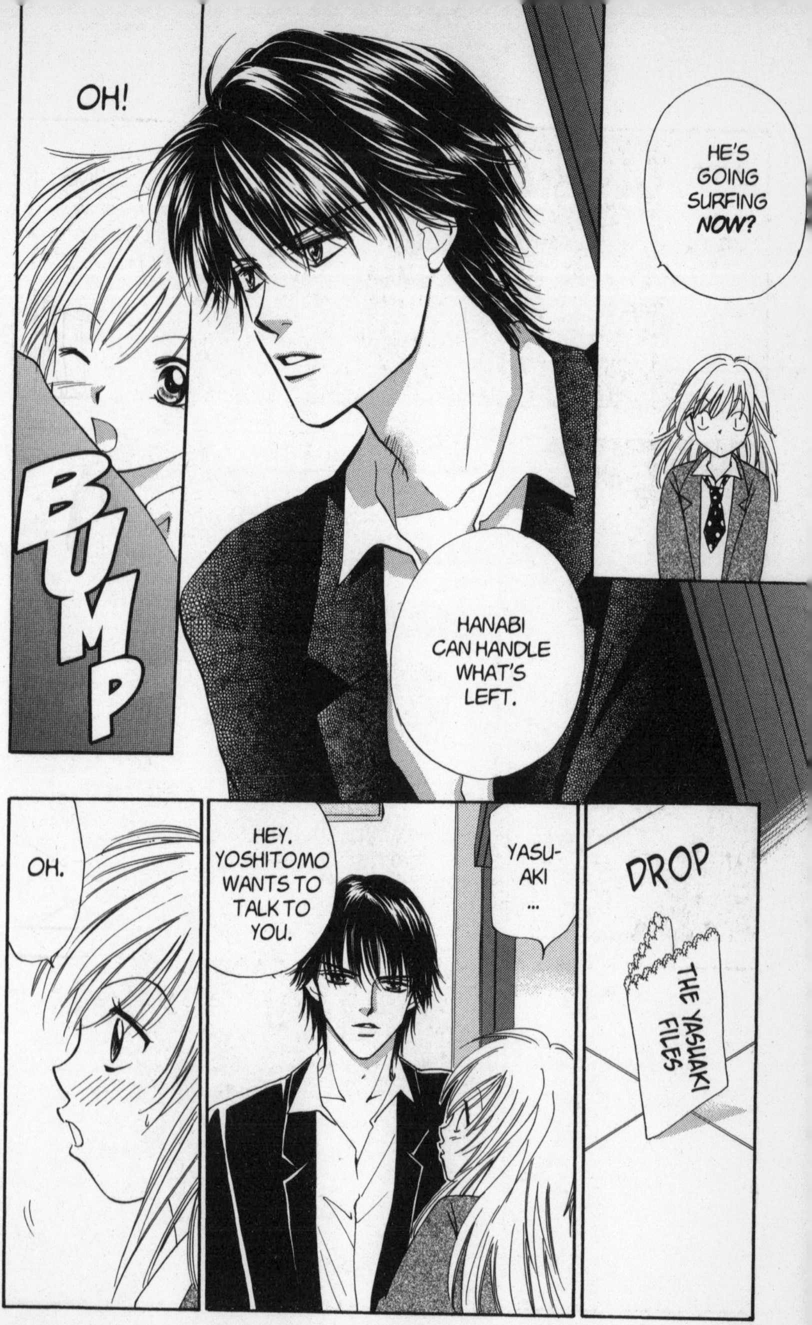
HE'S GOING SURFING NOW?
HANABI CAN HANDLE WHAT'S LEFT.
OH!
BUMP
DROP
THE YASUAKI FILES
YASU-AKI ...
HEY. YOSHITOMO WANTS TO TALK TO YOU.
OH.

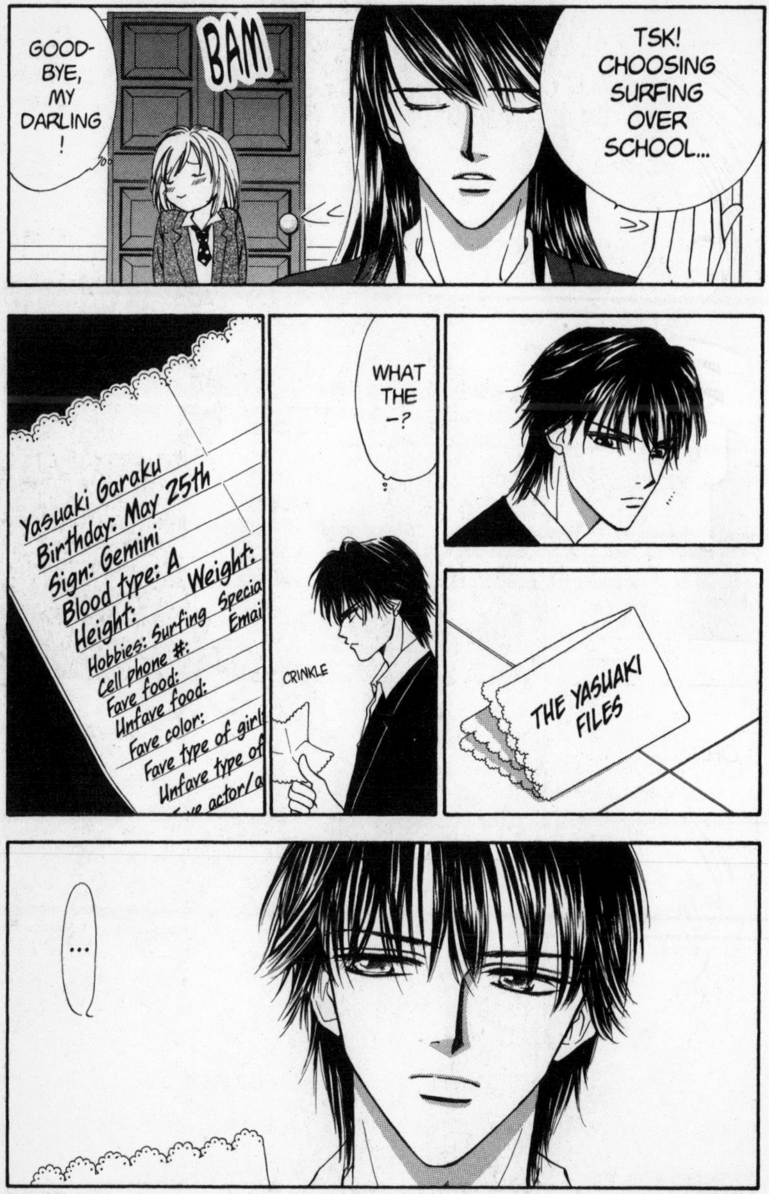
TSK! CHOOSING SURFING OVER SCHOOL...
BAM
GOOD-BYE, MY DARLING!
...
THE YASUAKI FILES
WHAT THE —?
CRINKLE
Yasuaki Garaku
Birthday: May 25th
Sign: Gemini
Blood type: A
Height: Weight:
Hobbies: Surfing Specia
Cell phone #: Emai
Fave food:
Unfave food:
Fave color:
Fave type of girl
Unfave type of
...

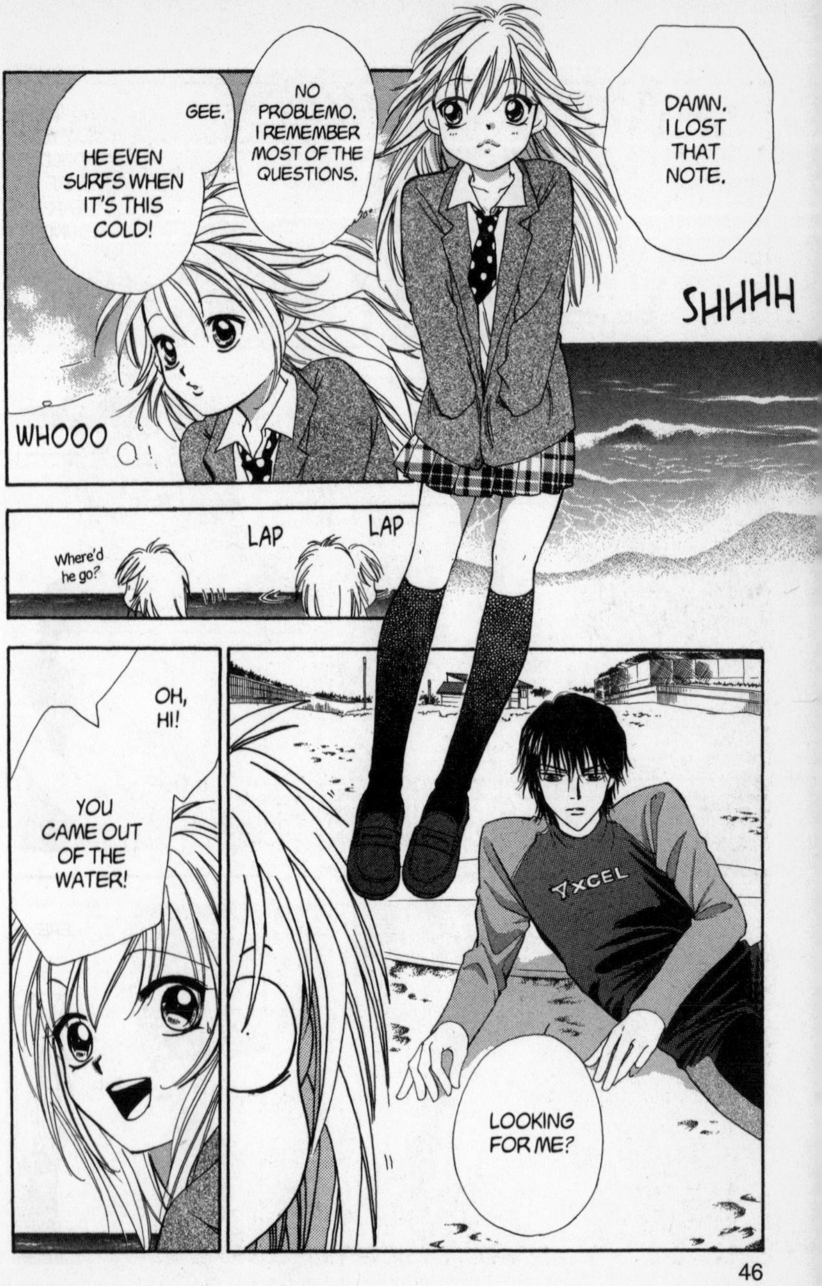
DAMN. I LOST THAT NOTE.
SHHHH
NO PROBLEMO. I REMEMBER MOST OF THE QUESTIONS.
GEE.
HE EVEN SURFS WHEN IT'S THIS COLD!
WHOOO
LAP
LAP
Where'd he go?
LOOKING FOR ME?
OH, HI!
YOU CAME OUT OF THE WATER!

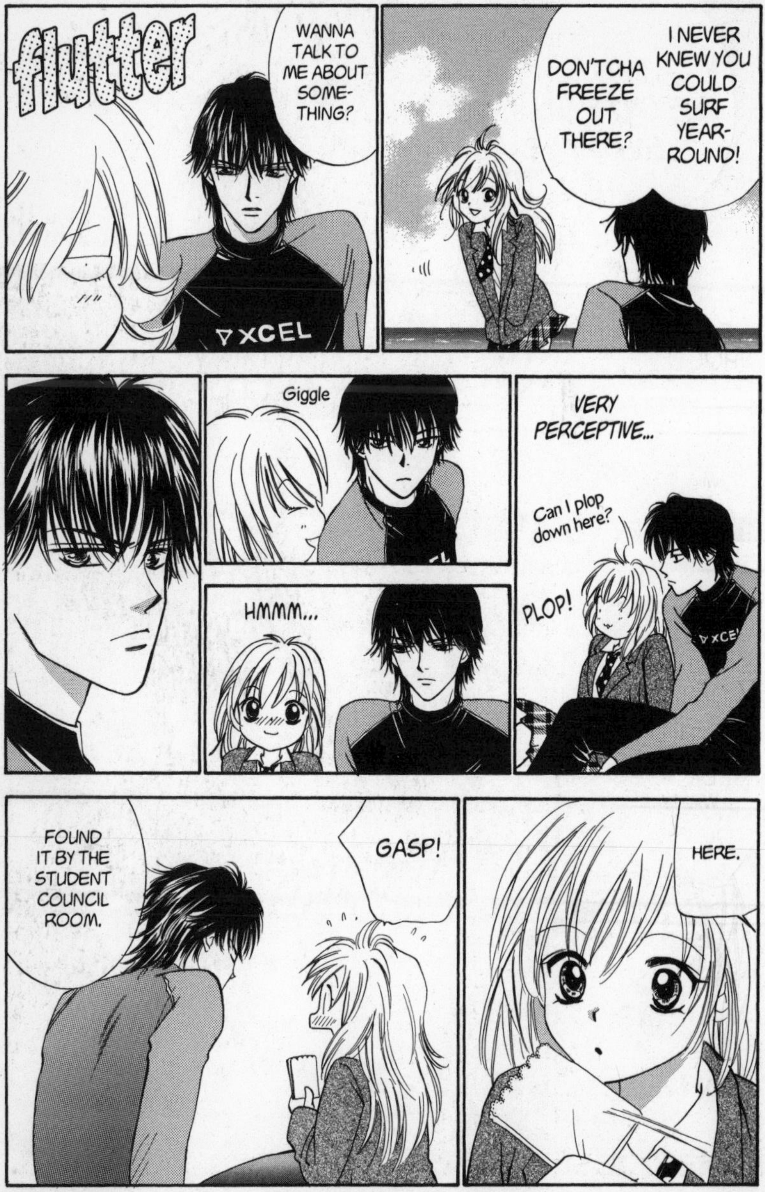
I NEVER KNEW YOU COULD SURF YEAR-ROUND!
DON'TCHA FREEZE OUT THERE?
flutter
WANNA TALK TO ME ABOUT SOME-THING?
VERY PERCEPTIVE...
Can I plop down here?
PLOP!
Giggle
HMMM...
HERE.
GASP!
FOUND IT BY THE STUDENT COUNCIL ROOM.

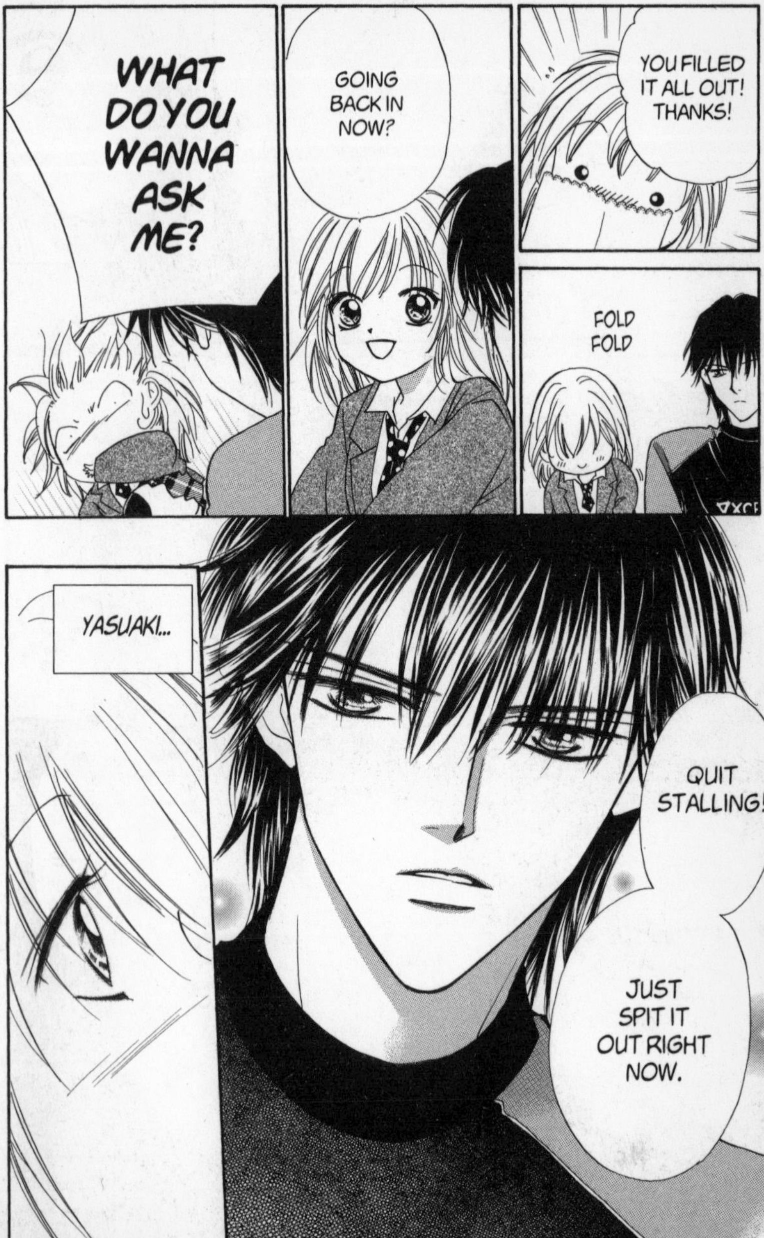
YOU FILLED IT ALL OUT! THANKS!
FOLD FOLD
GOING BACK IN NOW?
WHAT DO YOU WANNA ASK ME?
QUIT STALLING!
JUST SPIT IT OUT RIGHT NOW.
YASUAKI...

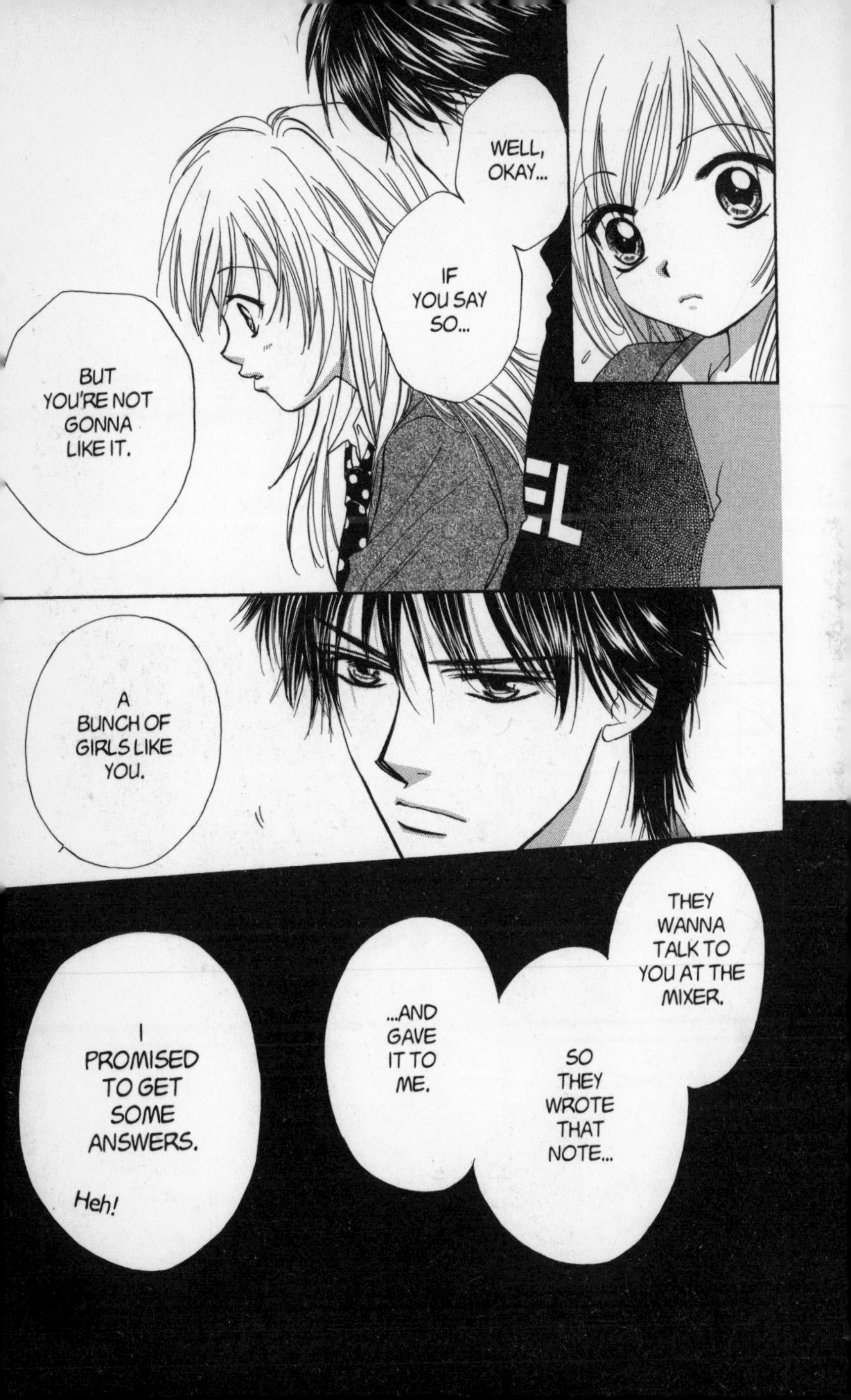
WELL, OKAY...
IF YOU SAY SO...
BUT YOU'RE NOT GONNA LIKE IT.
A BUNCH OF GIRLS LIKE YOU.
THEY WANNA TALK TO YOU AT THE MIXER.
SO THEY WROTE THAT NOTE...
...AND GAVE IT TO ME.
I PROMISED TO GET SOME ANSWERS.
Heh!

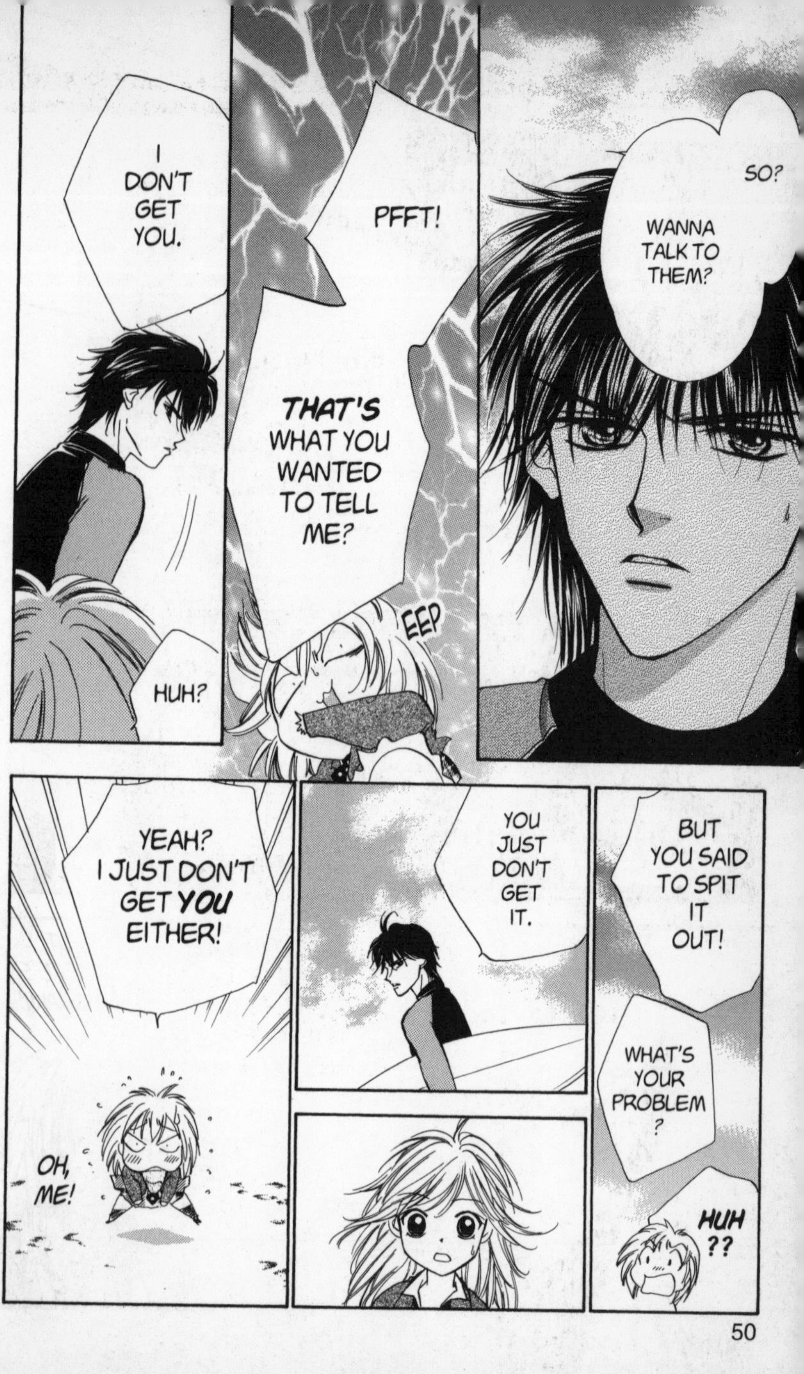

SO?
WANNA TALK TO THEM?
PFFT!
THAT'S WHAT YOU WANTED TO TELL ME?
EEP
I DON'T GET YOU.
HUH?
BUT YOU SAID TO SPIT IT OUT!
WHAT'S YOUR PROBLEM?
HUH??
YOU JUST DON'T GET IT.
YEAH? I JUST DON'T GET YOU EITHER!
OH, ME!

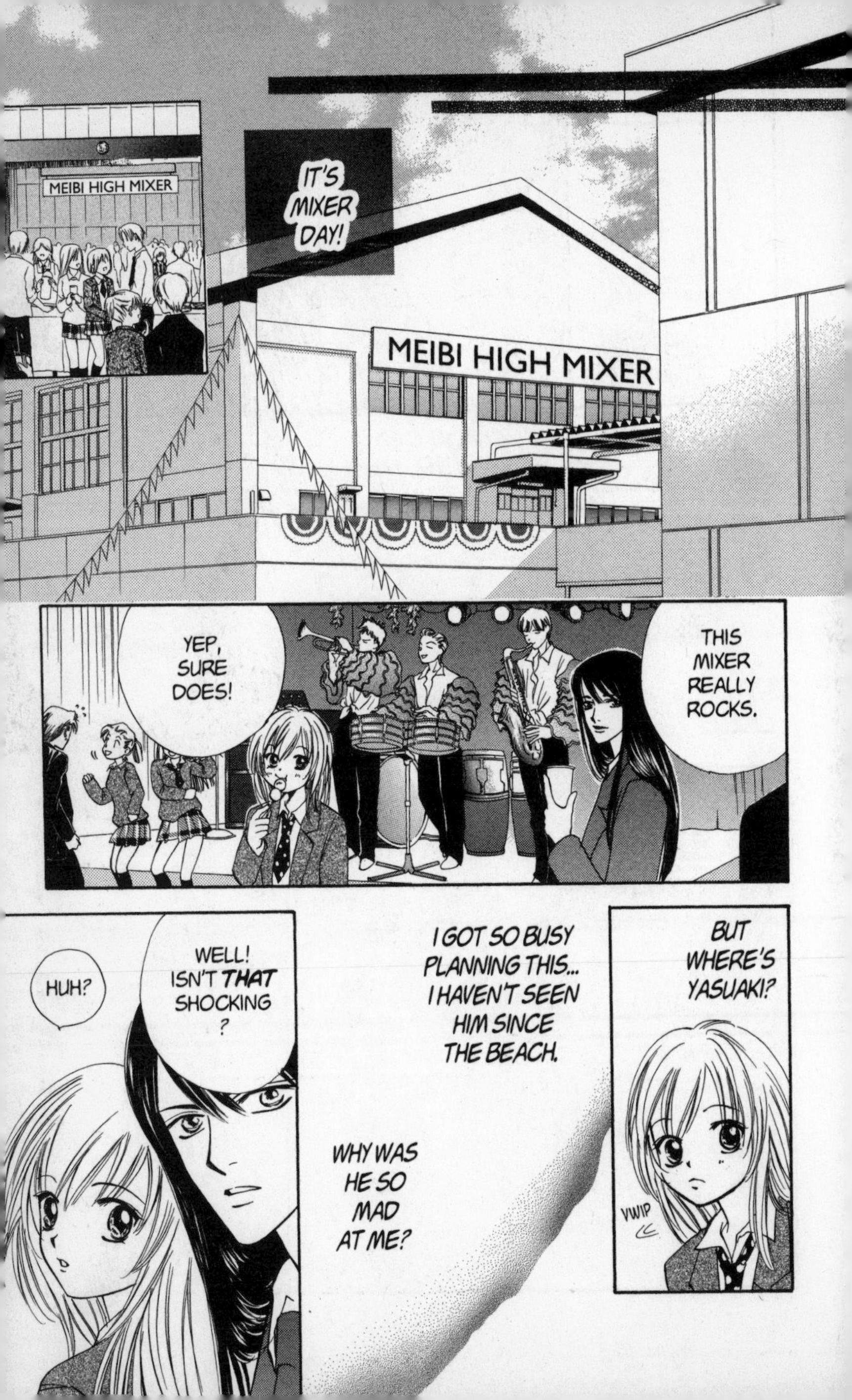
IT'S MIXER DAY!
MEIBI HIGH MIXER
MEIBI HIGH MIXER
THIS MIXER REALLY ROCKS.
YEP, SURE DOES!
BUT WHERE'S YASUAKI?
VWIP
I GOT SO BUSY PLANNING THIS... I HAVEN'T SEEN HIM SINCE THE BEACH.
WHY WAS HE SO MAD AT ME?
WELL! ISN'T **THAT** SHOCKING?
HUH?

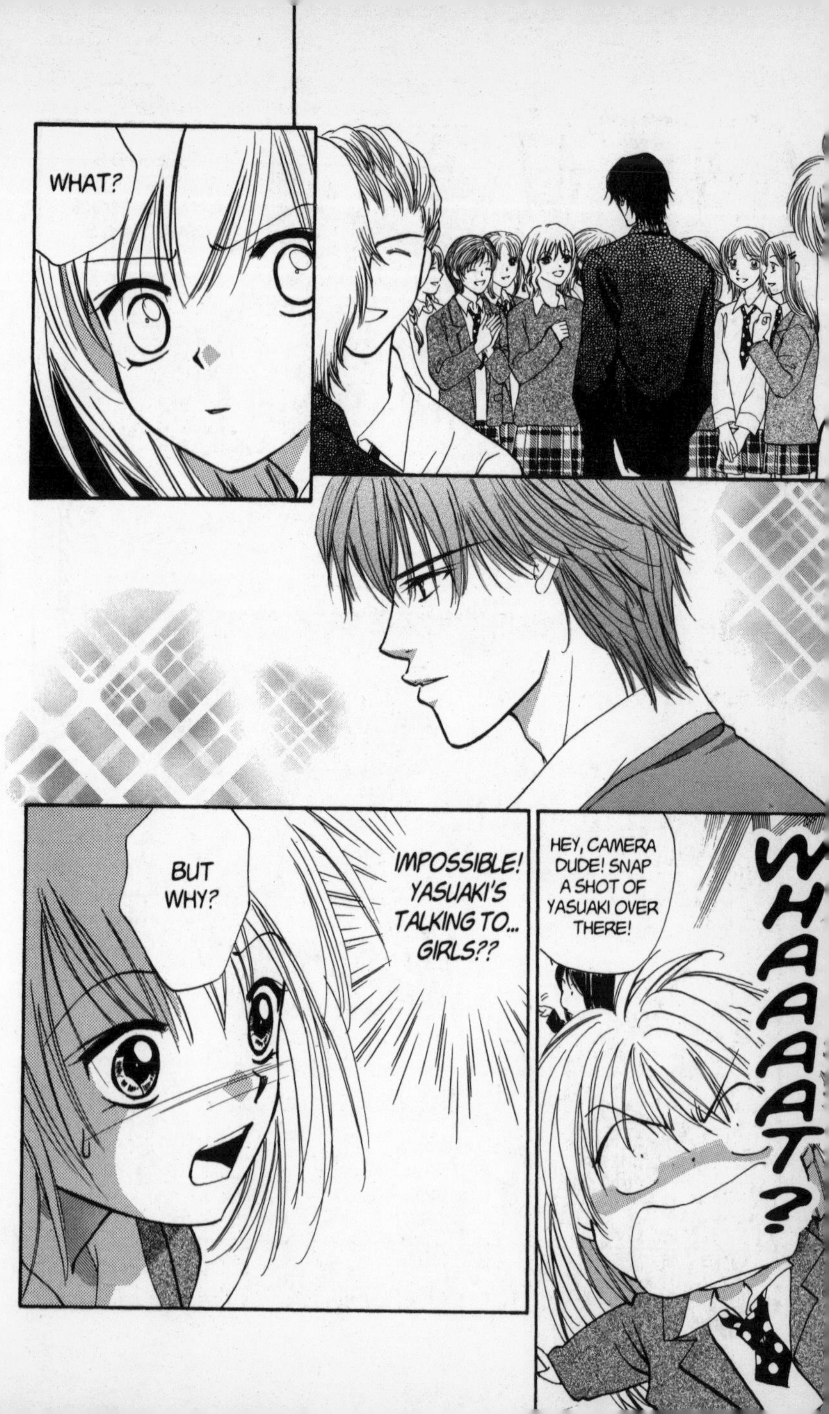
WHAT?
WHAAAAAT?
HEY, CAMERA DUDE! SNAP A SHOT OF YASUAKI OVER THERE!
IMPOSSIBLE! YASUAKI'S TALKING TO... GIRLS??
BUT WHY?

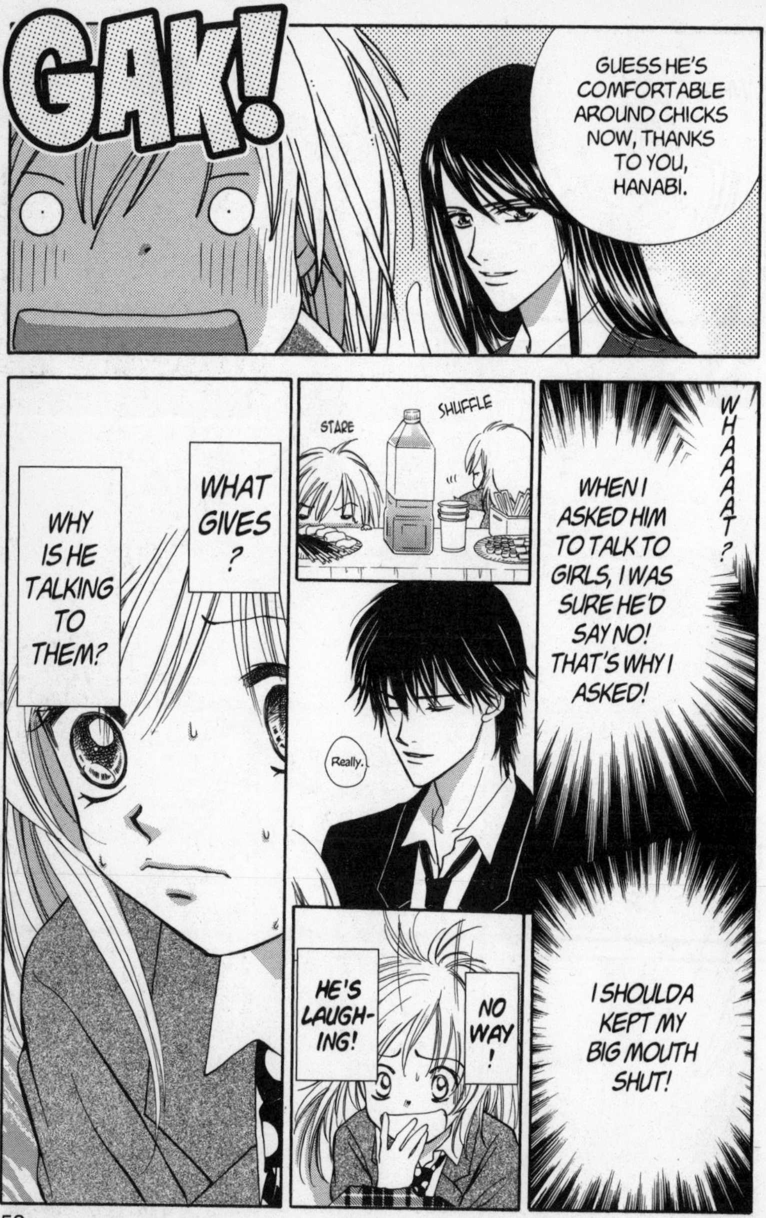
GUESS HE'S COMFORTABLE AROUND CHICKS NOW, THANKS TO YOU, HANABI.
GAK!
WHAAAAT?
WHEN I ASKED HIM TO TALK TO GIRLS, I WAS SURE HE'D SAY NO! THAT'S WHY I ASKED!
I SHOULDA KEPT MY BIG MOUTH SHUT!
SHUFFLE
STARE
Really.
NO WAY!
HE'S LAUGH-ING!
WHAT GIVES?
WHY IS HE TALKING TO THEM?

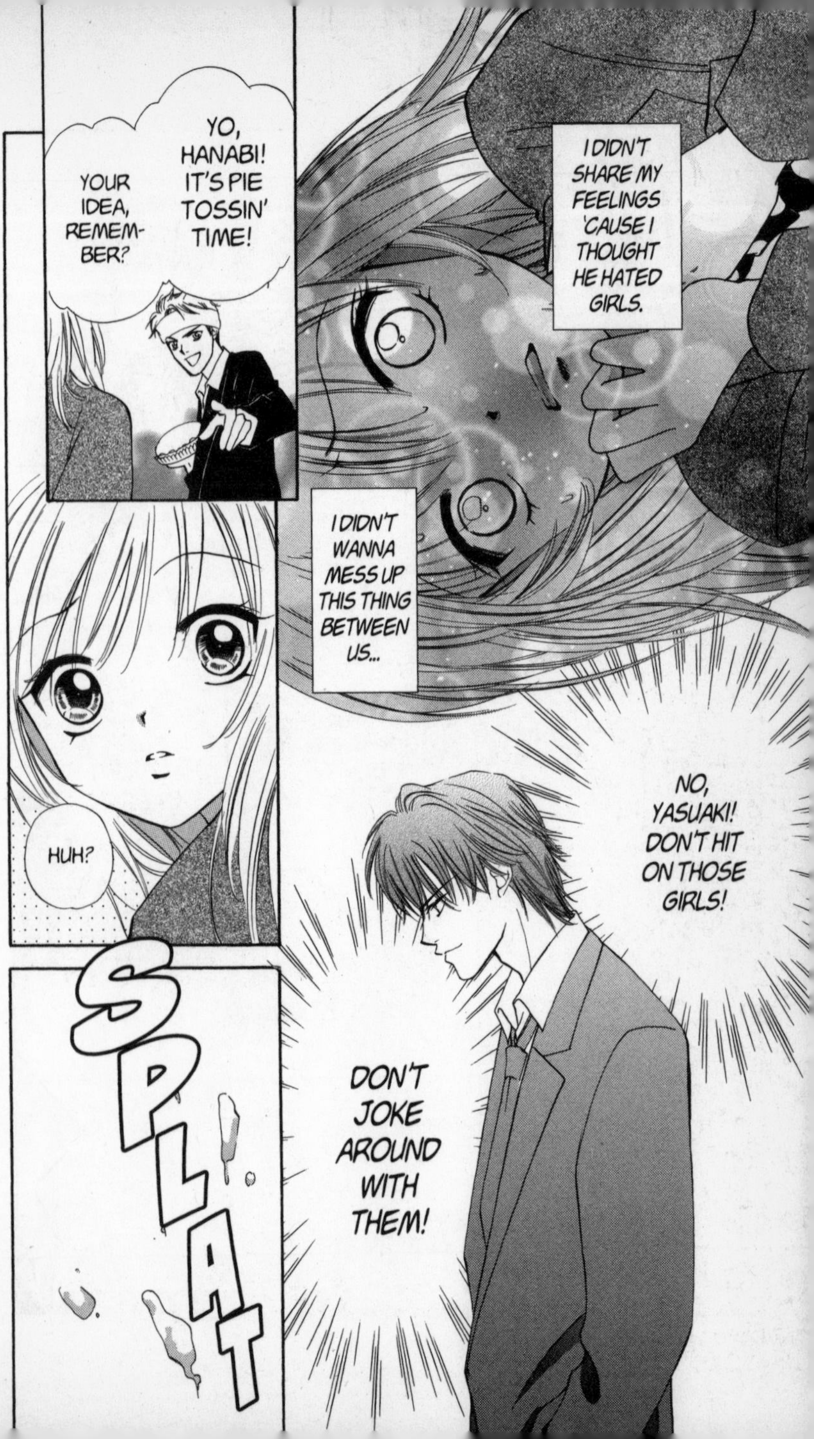

I DIDN'T SHARE MY FEELINGS 'CAUSE I THOUGHT HE HATED GIRLS.
I DIDN'T WANNA MESS UP THIS THING BETWEEN US...
YO, HANABI! IT'S PIE TOSSIN' TIME!
YOUR IDEA, REMEMBER?
HUH?
NO, YASUAKI! DON'T HIT ON THOSE GIRLS!
DON'T JOKE AROUND WITH THEM!
SPLAT

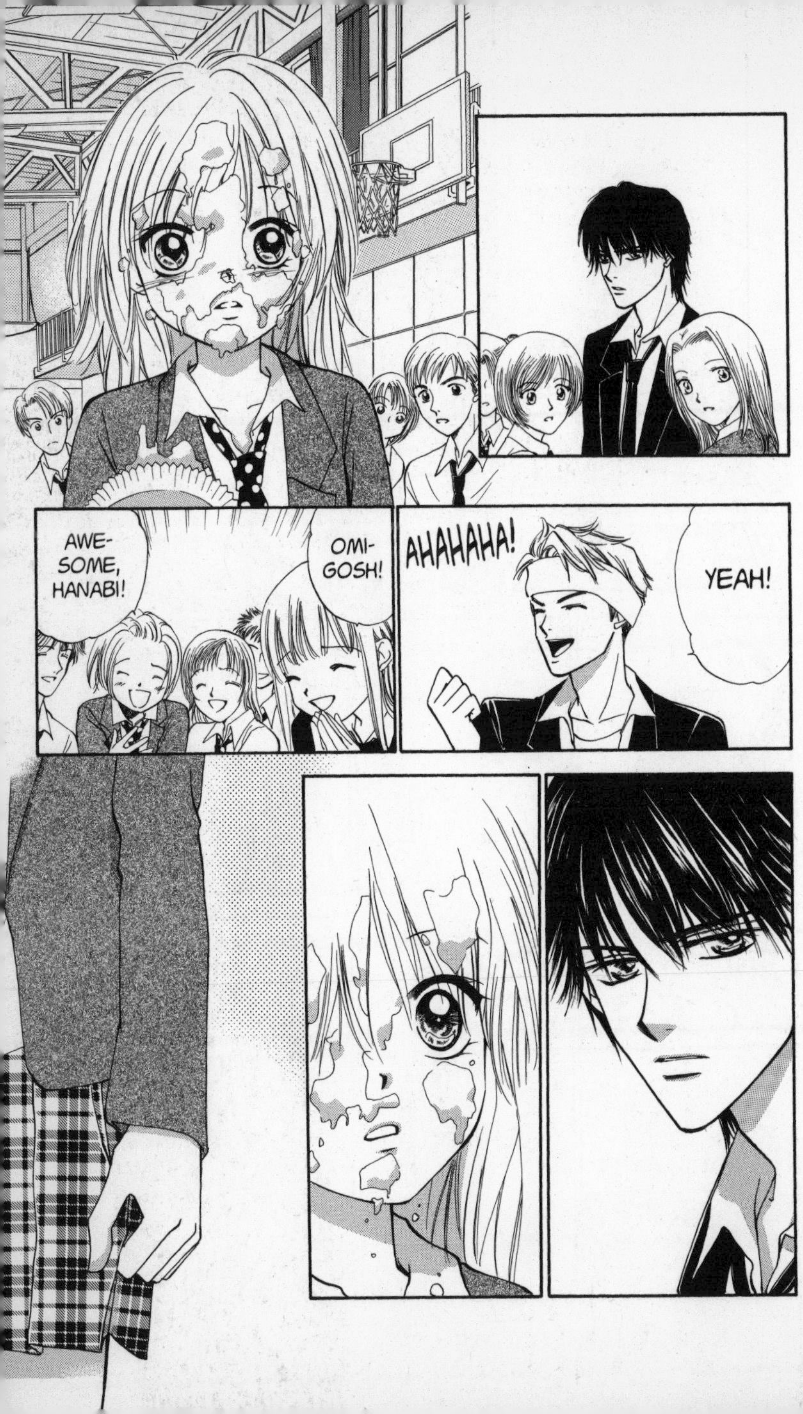
YEAH!
AHAHAHA!
OMI-GOSH!
AWE-SOME, HANABI!

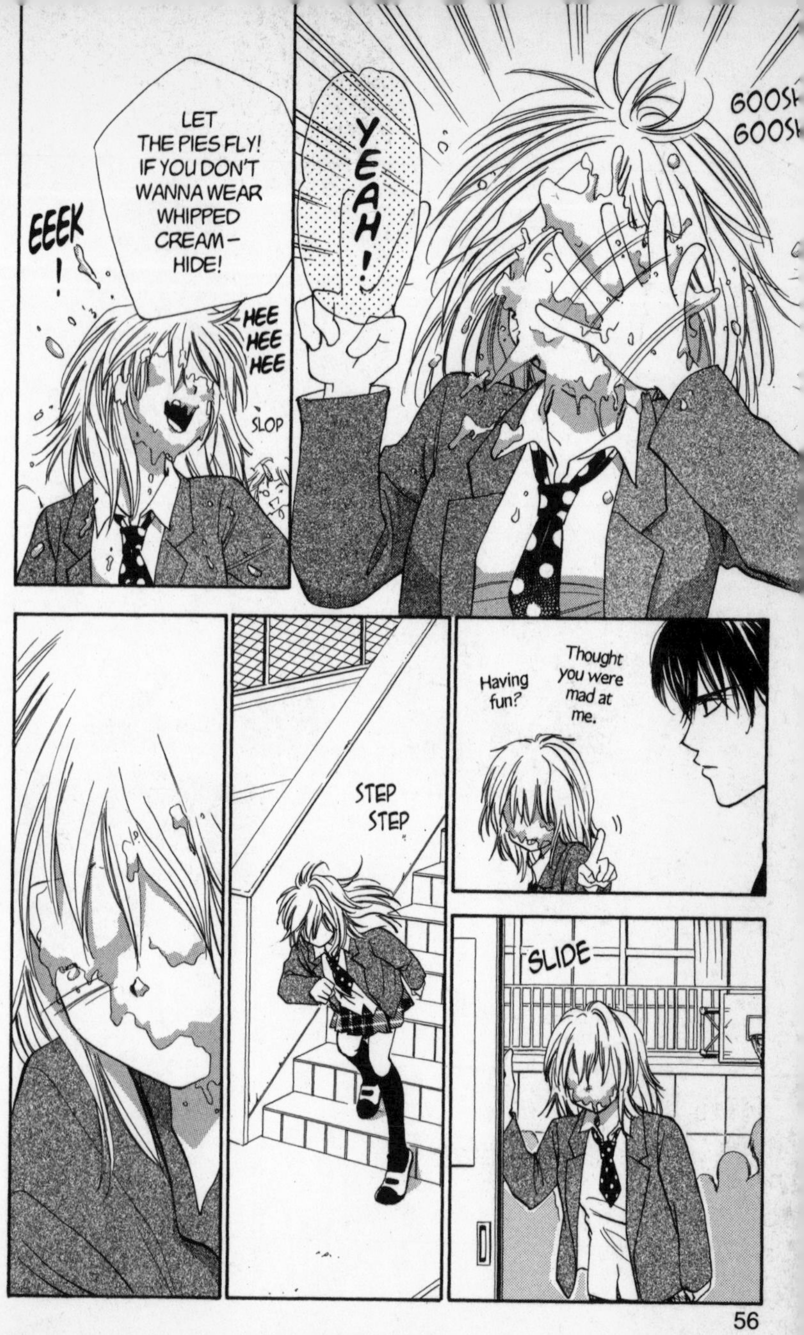
GOOS
GOOS
YEAH!
LET THE PIES FLY! IF YOU DON'T WANNA WEAR WHIPPED CREAM—HIDE!
EEEK!
HEE HEE HEE
SLOP
Thought you were mad at me.
Having fun?
SLIDE
STEP STEP

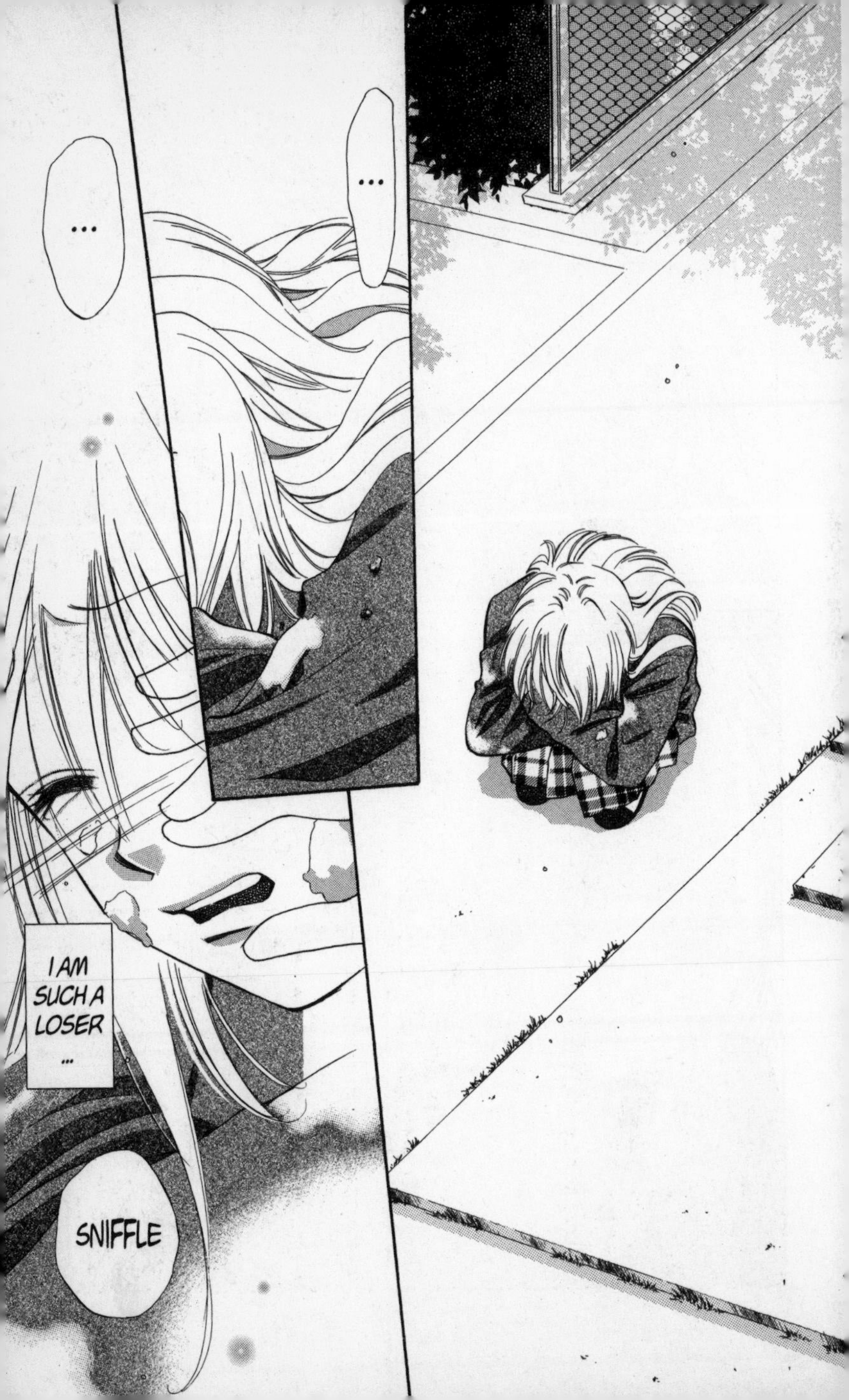
...
...
I AM SUCH A LOSER ...
SNIFFLE

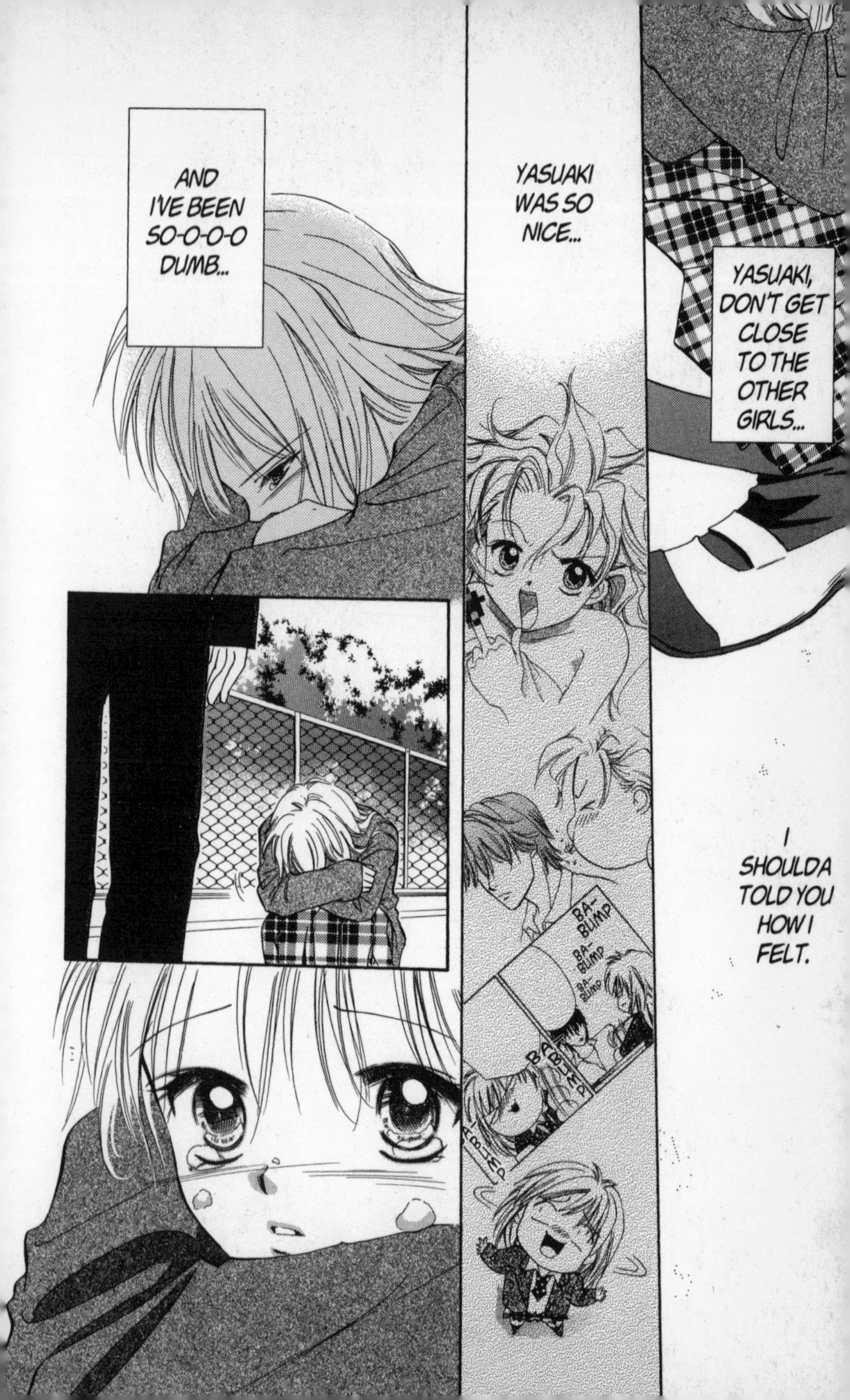
YASUAKI, DON'T GET CLOSE TO THE OTHER GIRLS...
I SHOULDA TOLD YOU HOW I FELT.
YASUAKI WAS SO NICE...
BA-BUMP
BA-BUMP
BA-BUMP
BA-BUMP
AND I'VE BEEN SO-O-O-O DUMB...

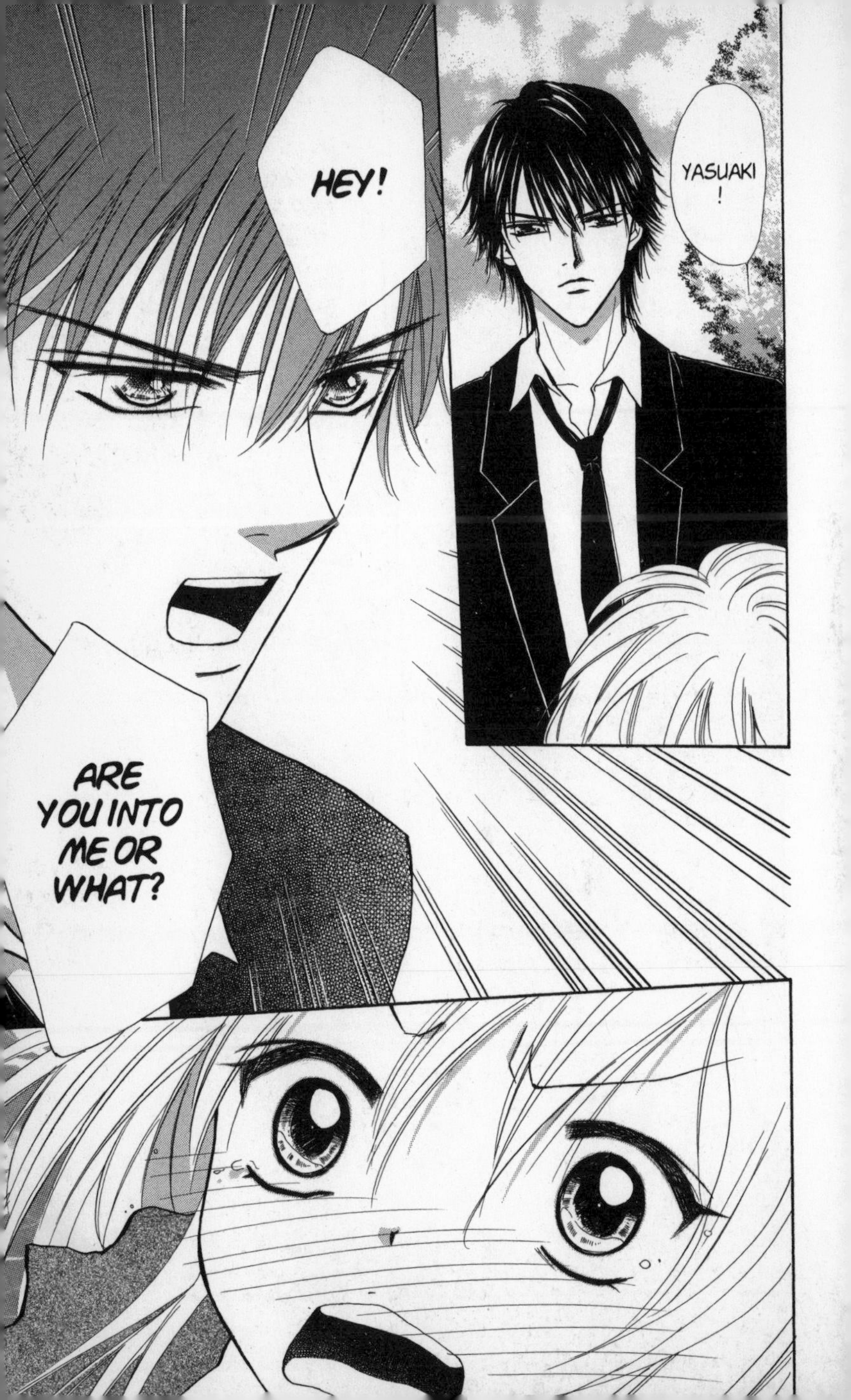
YASUAKI!
HEY!
ARE YOU INTO ME OR WHAT?

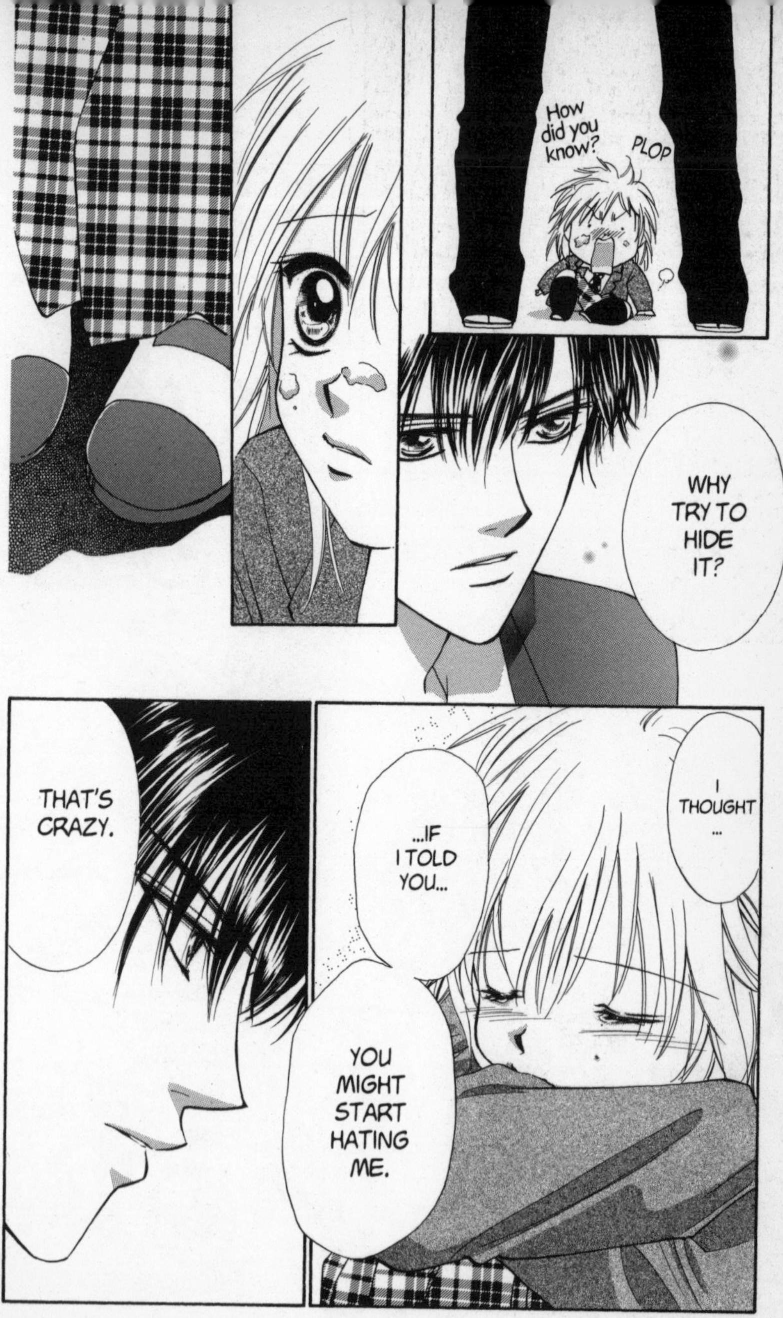
How did you know?
PLOP
WHY TRY TO HIDE IT?
I THOUGHT...
...IF I TOLD YOU...
YOU MIGHT START HATING ME.
THAT'S CRAZY.

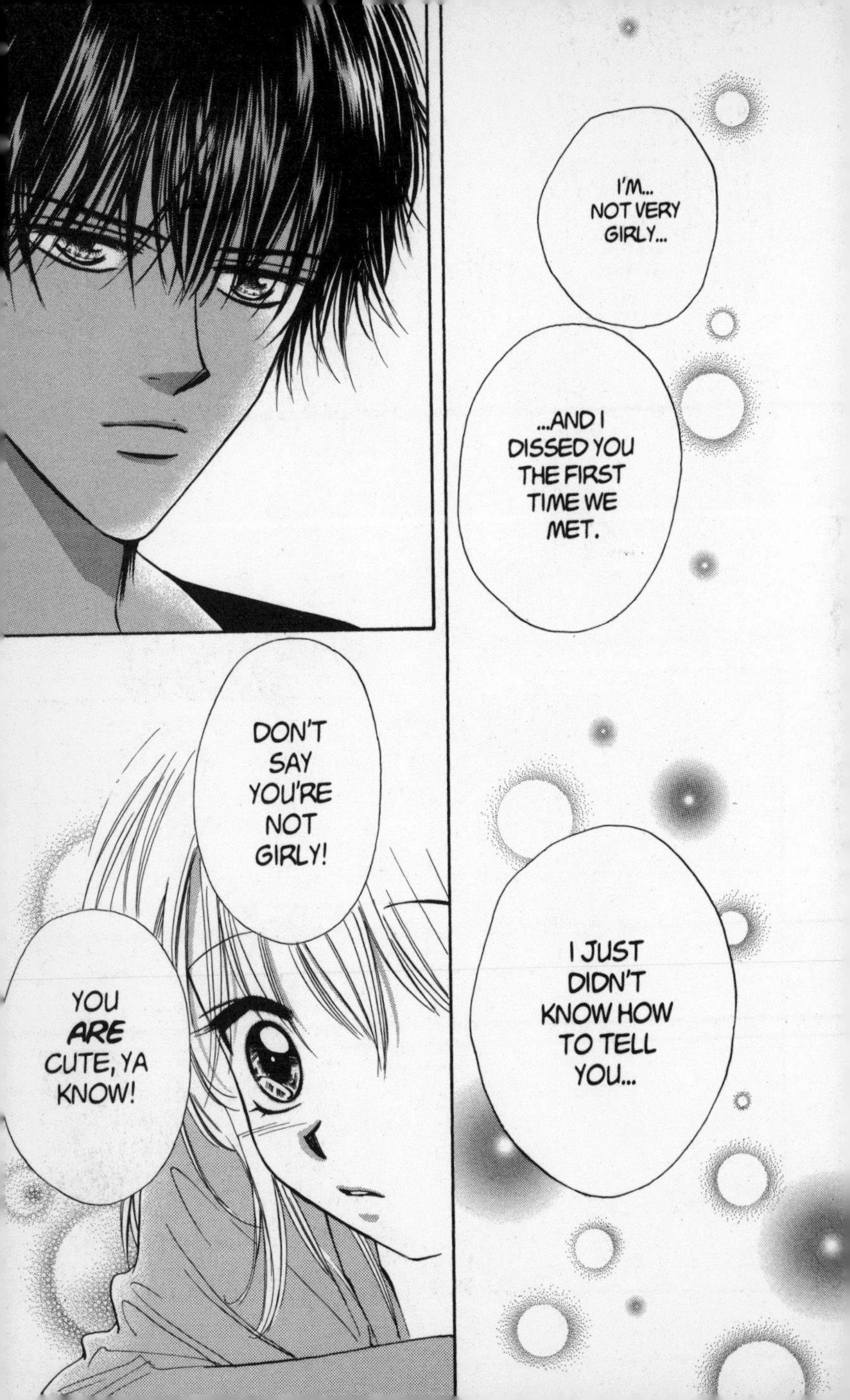
I'M... NOT VERY GIRLY...
...AND I DISSED YOU THE FIRST TIME WE MET.
I JUST DIDN'T KNOW HOW TO TELL YOU...
DON'T SAY YOU'RE NOT GIRLY!
YOU **ARE** CUTE, YA KNOW!

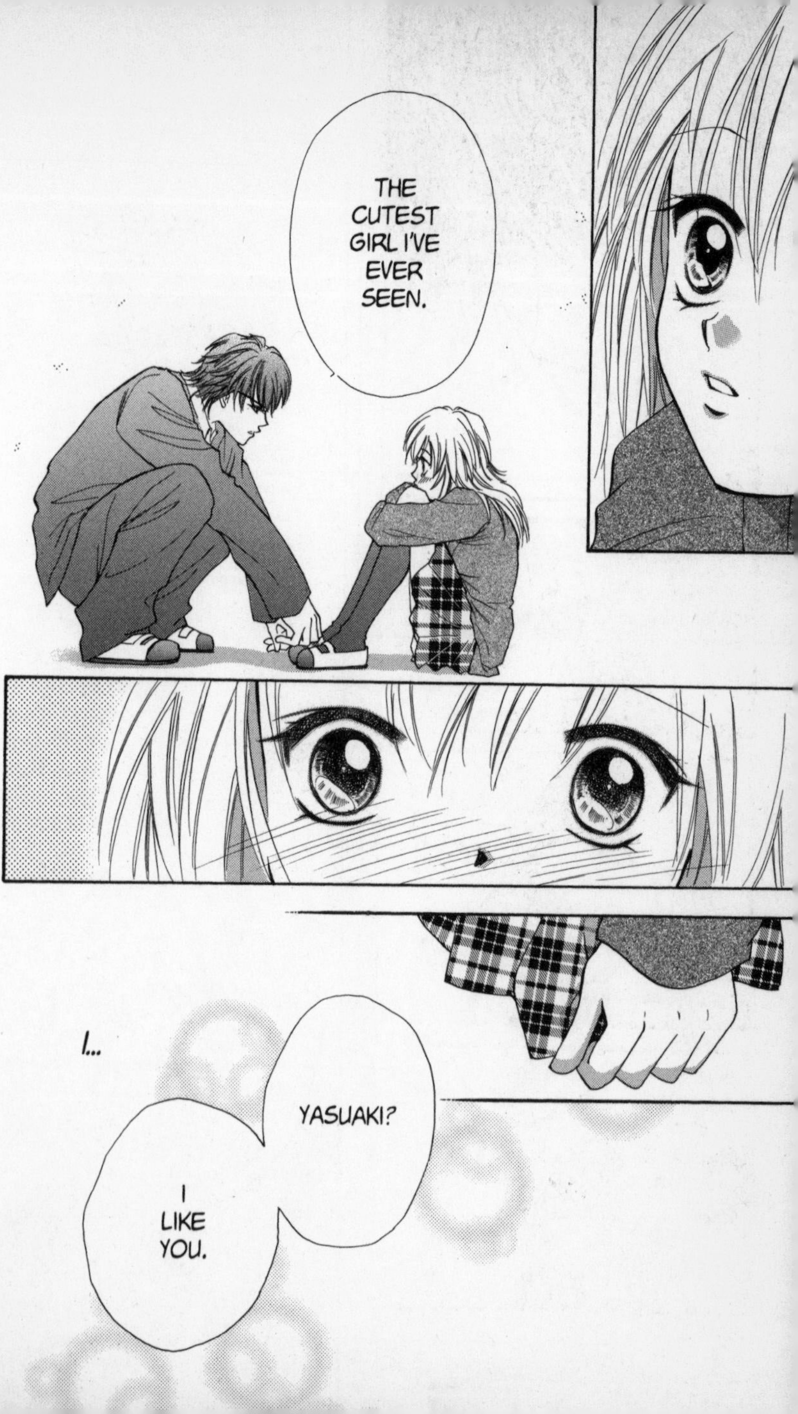
THE CUTEST GIRL I'VE EVER SEEN.
YASUAKI?
I...
I LIKE YOU.

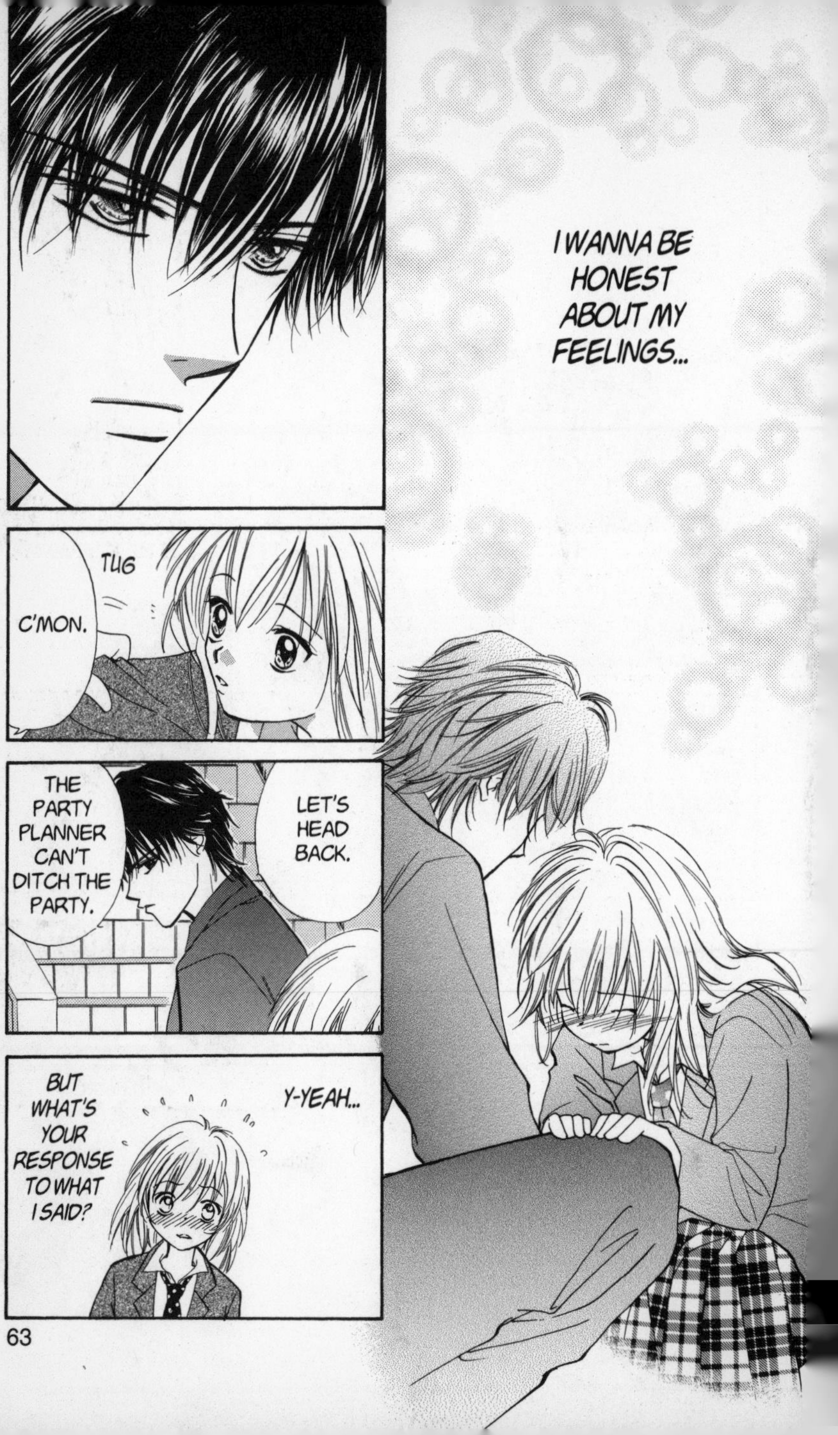
I WANNA BE HONEST ABOUT MY FEELINGS...
TUG
C'MON.
LET'S HEAD BACK.
THE PARTY PLANNER CAN'T DITCH THE PARTY.
Y-YEAH...
BUT WHAT'S YOUR RESPONSE TO WHAT I SAID?

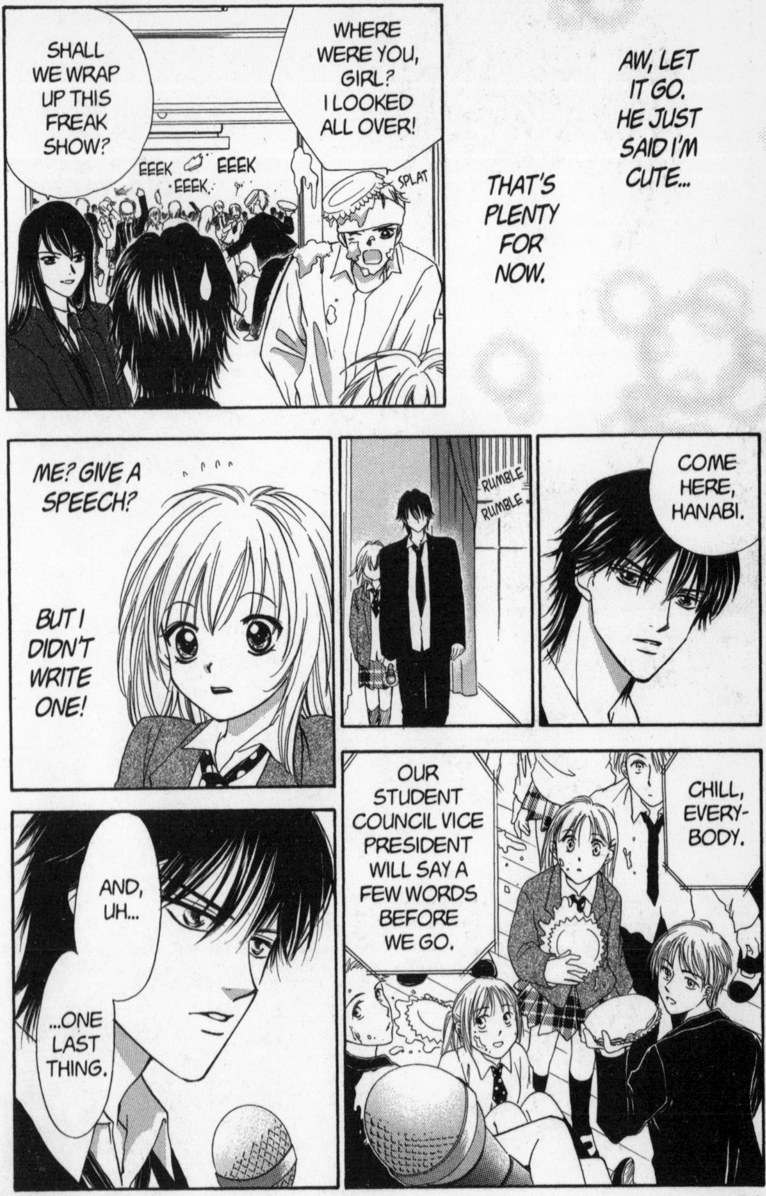
AW, LET IT GO. HE JUST SAID I'M CUTE...
THAT'S PLENTY FOR NOW.
WHERE WERE YOU, GIRL? I LOOKED ALL OVER!
SPLAT
EEEK EEEK EEEK
SHALL WE WRAP UP THIS FREAK SHOW?
COME HERE, HANABI.
RUMBLE RUMBLE
ME? GIVE A SPEECH?
BUT I DIDN'T WRITE ONE!
CHILL, EVERYBODY.
OUR STUDENT COUNCIL VICE PRESIDENT WILL SAY A FEW WORDS BEFORE WE GO.
AND, UH...
...ONE LAST THING.

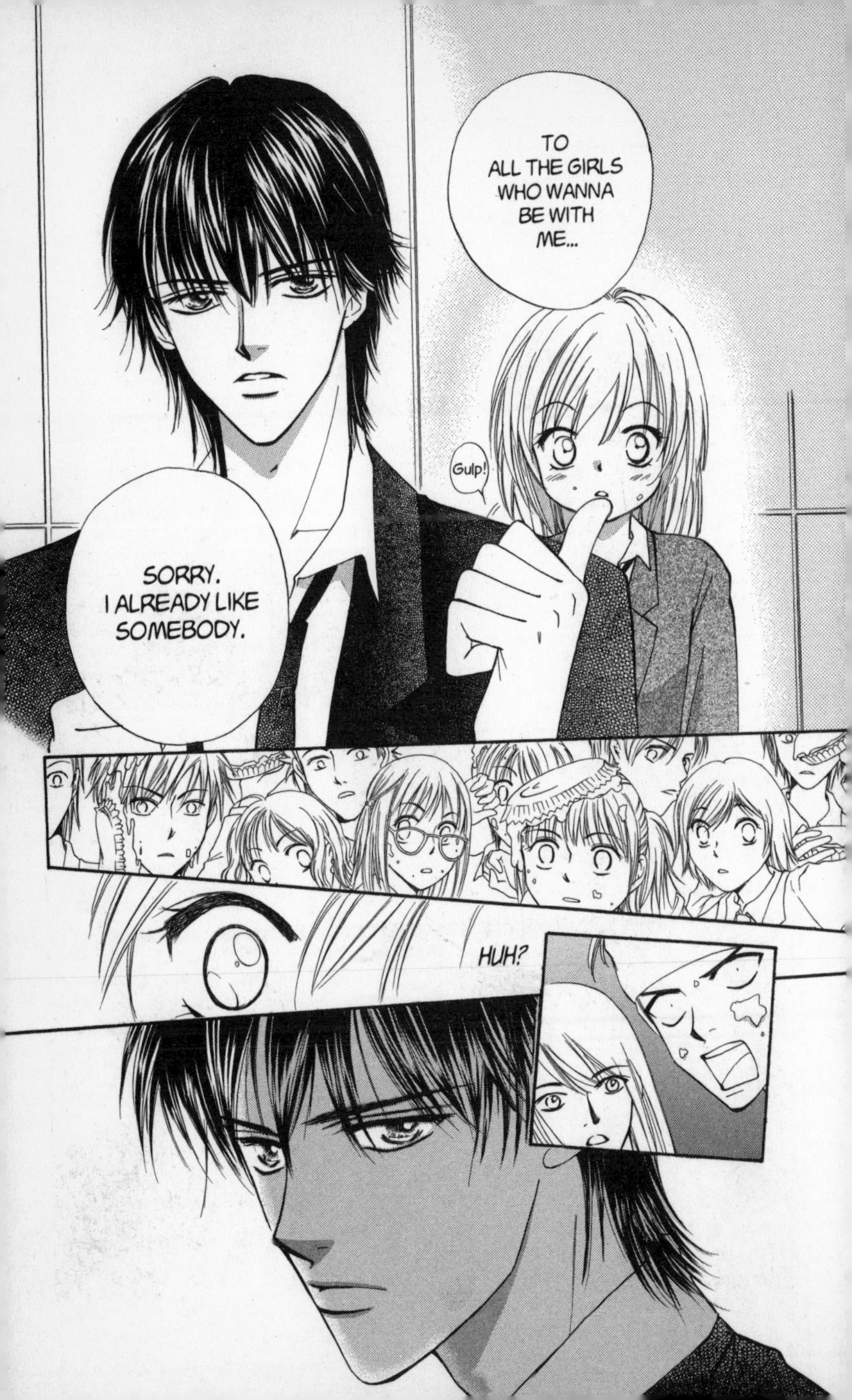
TO ALL THE GIRLS WHO WANNA BE WITH ME...
Gulp!
SORRY. I ALREADY LIKE SOMEBODY.
HUH?

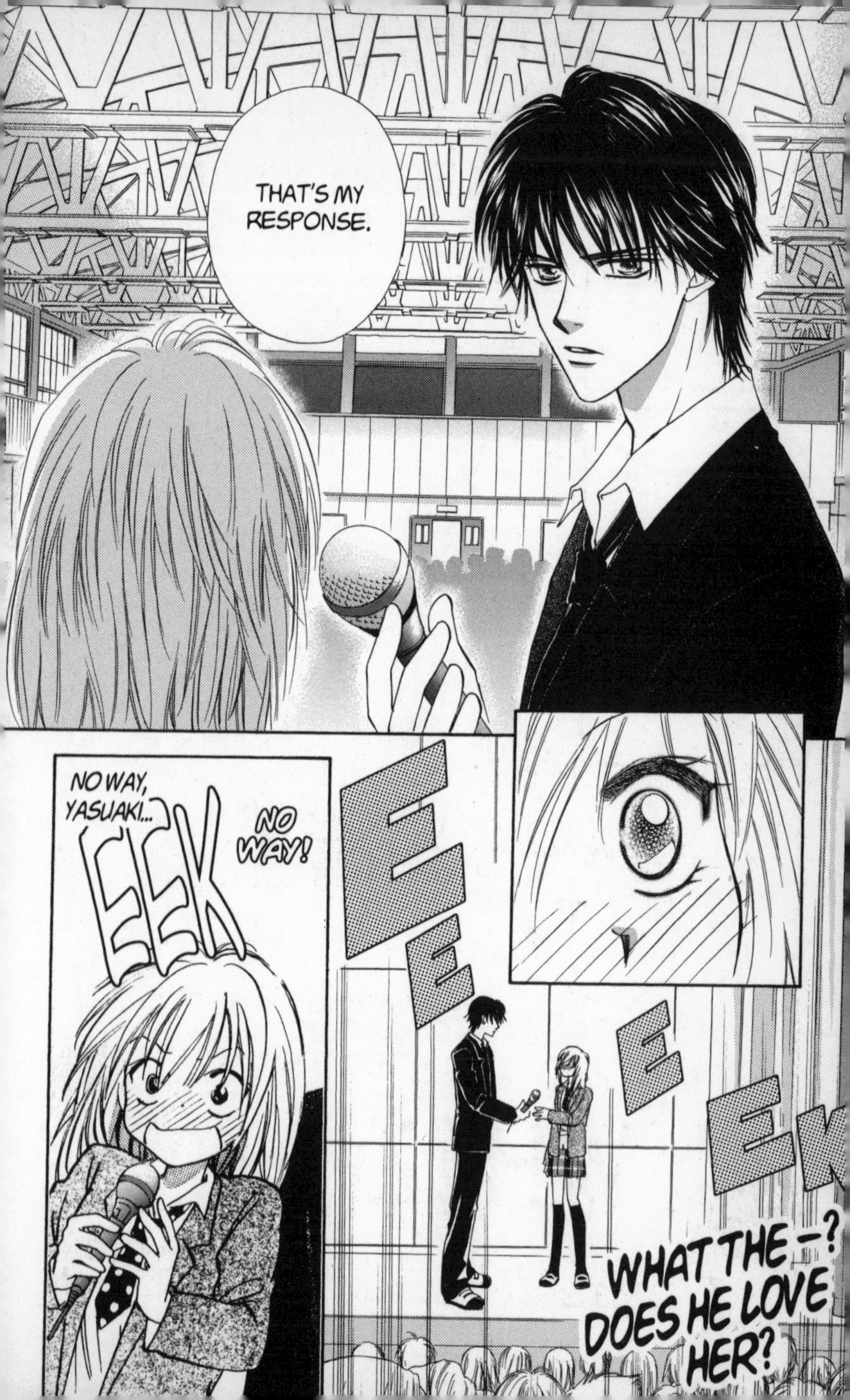
THAT'S MY RESPONSE.
EEEEK
WHAT THE—? DOES HE LOVE HER?
NO WAY, YASUAKI...
EEK
NO WAY!

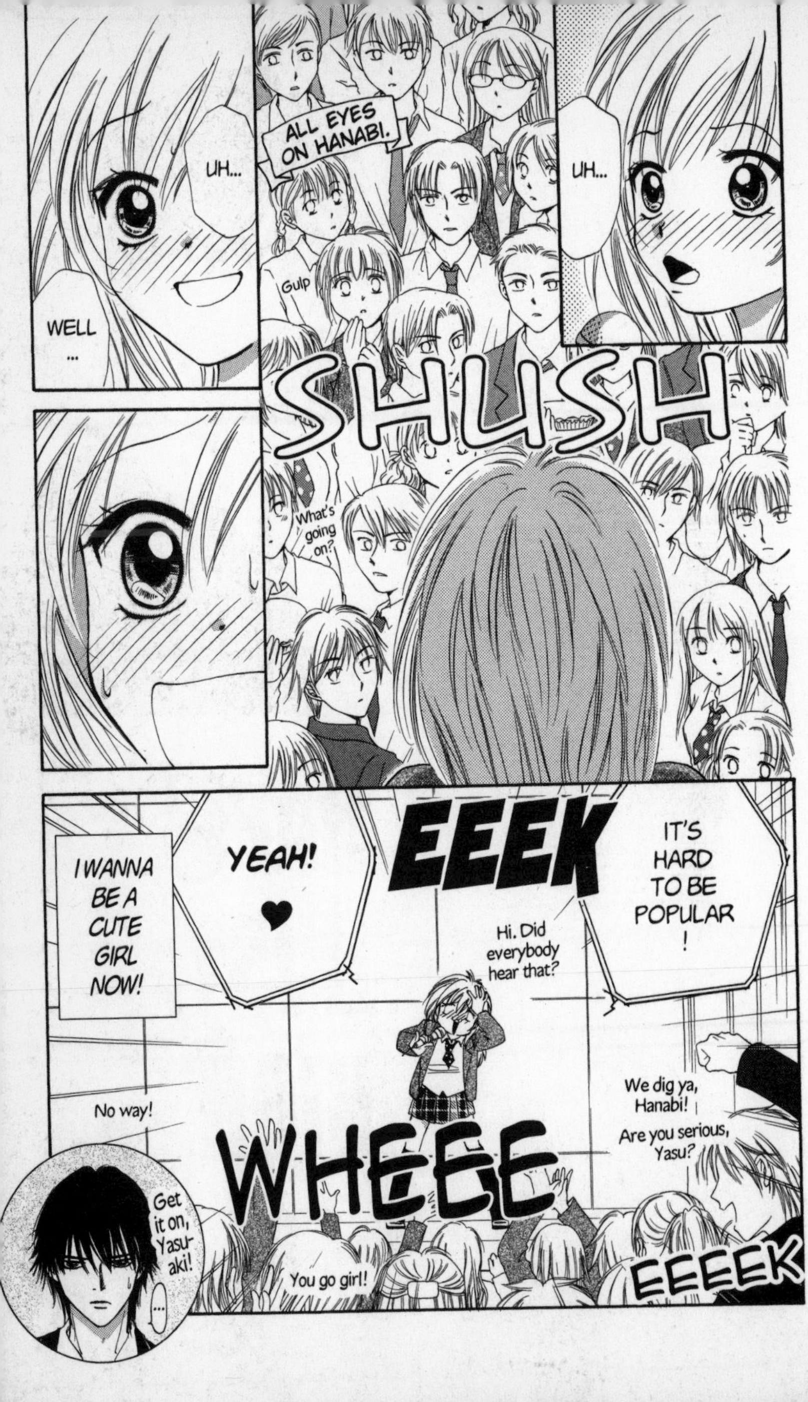
UH...
ALL EYES ON HANABI.
Gulp
SHUSH
What's going on?
UH...
WELL ...
IT'S HARD TO BE POPULAR!
EEEK
Hi. Did everybody hear that?
YEAH! ♥
I WANNA BE A CUTE GIRL NOW!
We dig ya, Hanabi!
Are you serious, Yasu?
EEEEK
No way!
WHEEE
You go girl!
Get it on, Yasu-aki!
...

HAPPY HUSTLE HIGH

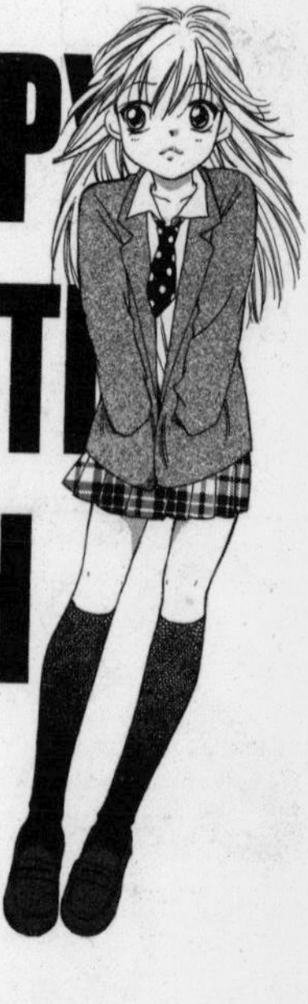

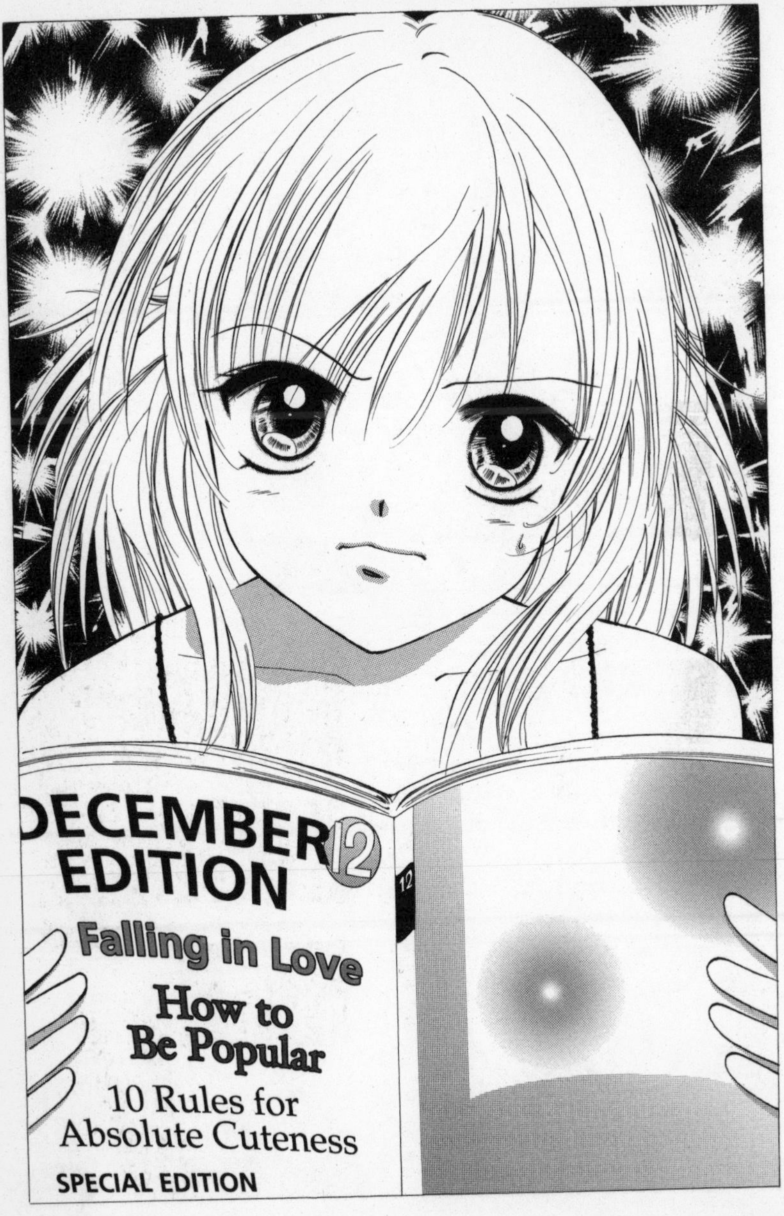
DECEMBER EDITION
12
Falling in Love
How to Be Popular
10 Rules for Absolute Cuteness
SPECIAL EDITION
12

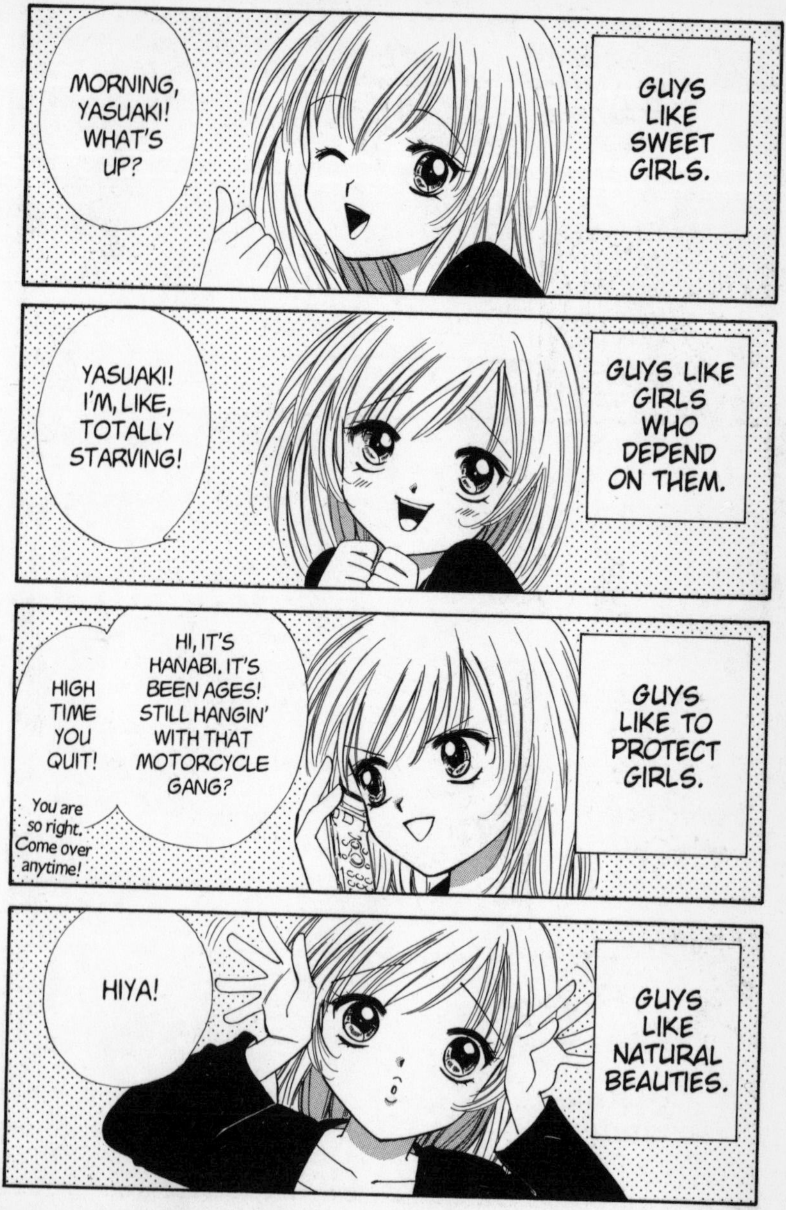

GUYS LIKE SWEET GIRLS.
MORNING, YASUAKI! WHAT'S UP?
GUYS LIKE GIRLS WHO DEPEND ON THEM.
YASUAKI! I'M, LIKE, TOTALLY STARVING!
GUYS LIKE TO PROTECT GIRLS.
HI, IT'S HANABI. IT'S BEEN AGES! STILL HANGIN' WITH THAT MOTORCYCLE GANG?
HIGH TIME YOU QUIT!
You are so right. Come over anytime!
GUYS LIKE NATURAL BEAUTIES.
HIYA!

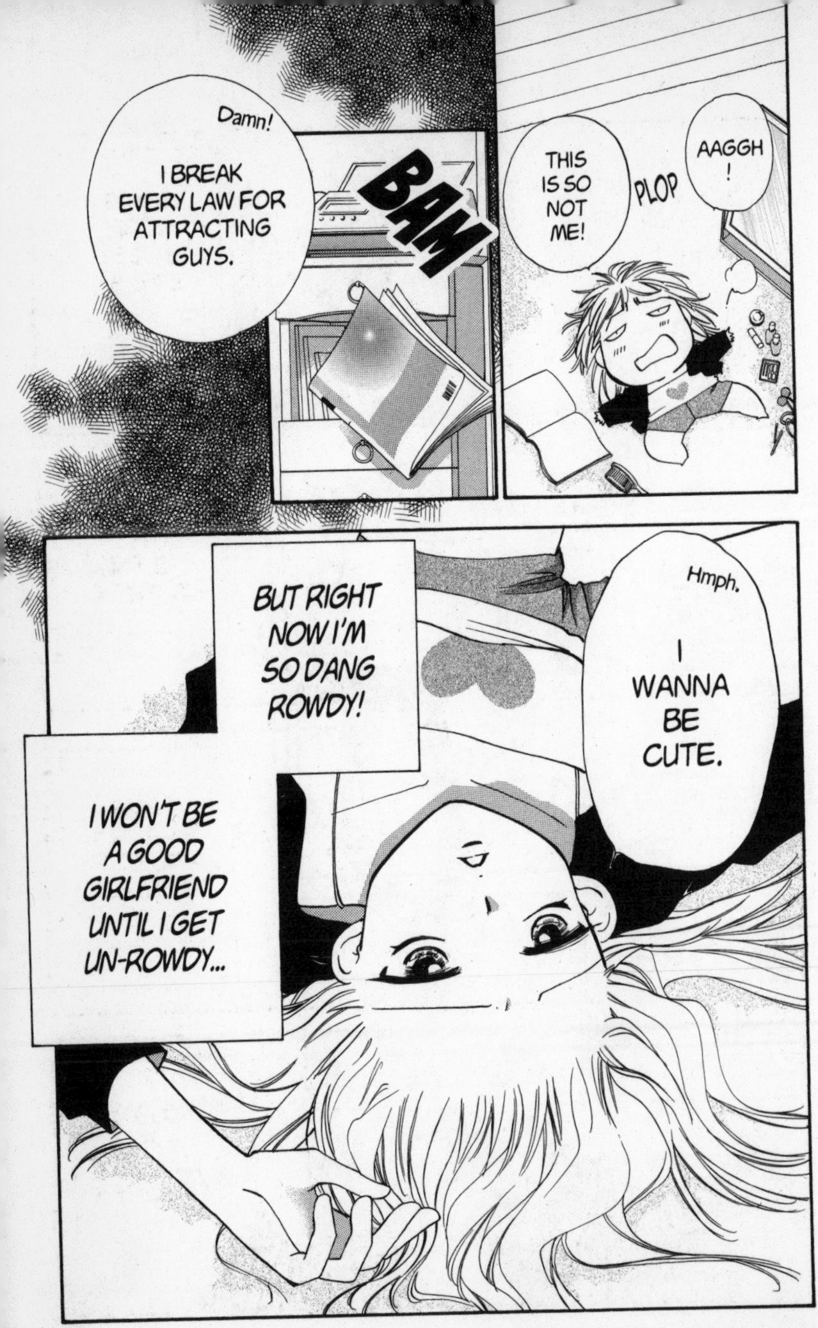
AAGGH!
PLOP
THIS IS SO NOT ME!
BAM
Damn!
I BREAK EVERY LAW FOR ATTRACTING GUYS.
Hmph.
I WANNA BE CUTE.
BUT RIGHT NOW I'M SO DANG ROWDY!
I WON'T BE A GOOD GIRLFRIEND UNTIL I GET UN-ROWDY...

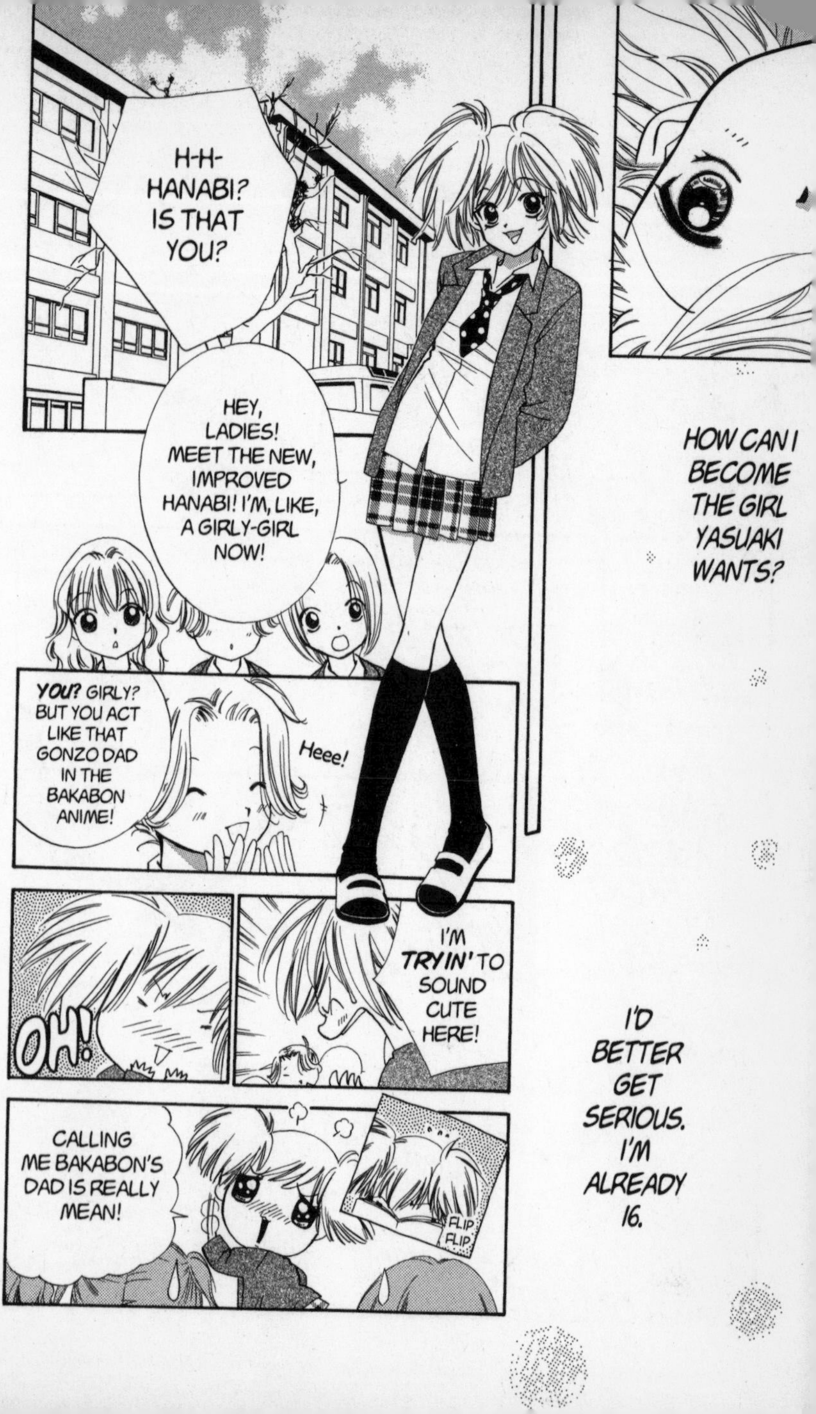

HOW CAN I BECOME THE GIRL YASUAKI WANTS?
I'D BETTER GET SERIOUS. I'M ALREADY 16.
H-H-HANABI? IS THAT YOU?
HEY, LADIES! MEET THE NEW, IMPROVED HANABI! I'M, LIKE, A GIRLY-GIRL NOW!
Heee!
YOU? GIRLY? BUT YOU ACT LIKE THAT GONZO DAD IN THE BAKABON ANIME!
I'M TRYIN' TO SOUND CUTE HERE!
OH!
FLIP FLIP
CALLING ME BAKABON'S DAD IS REALLY MEAN!

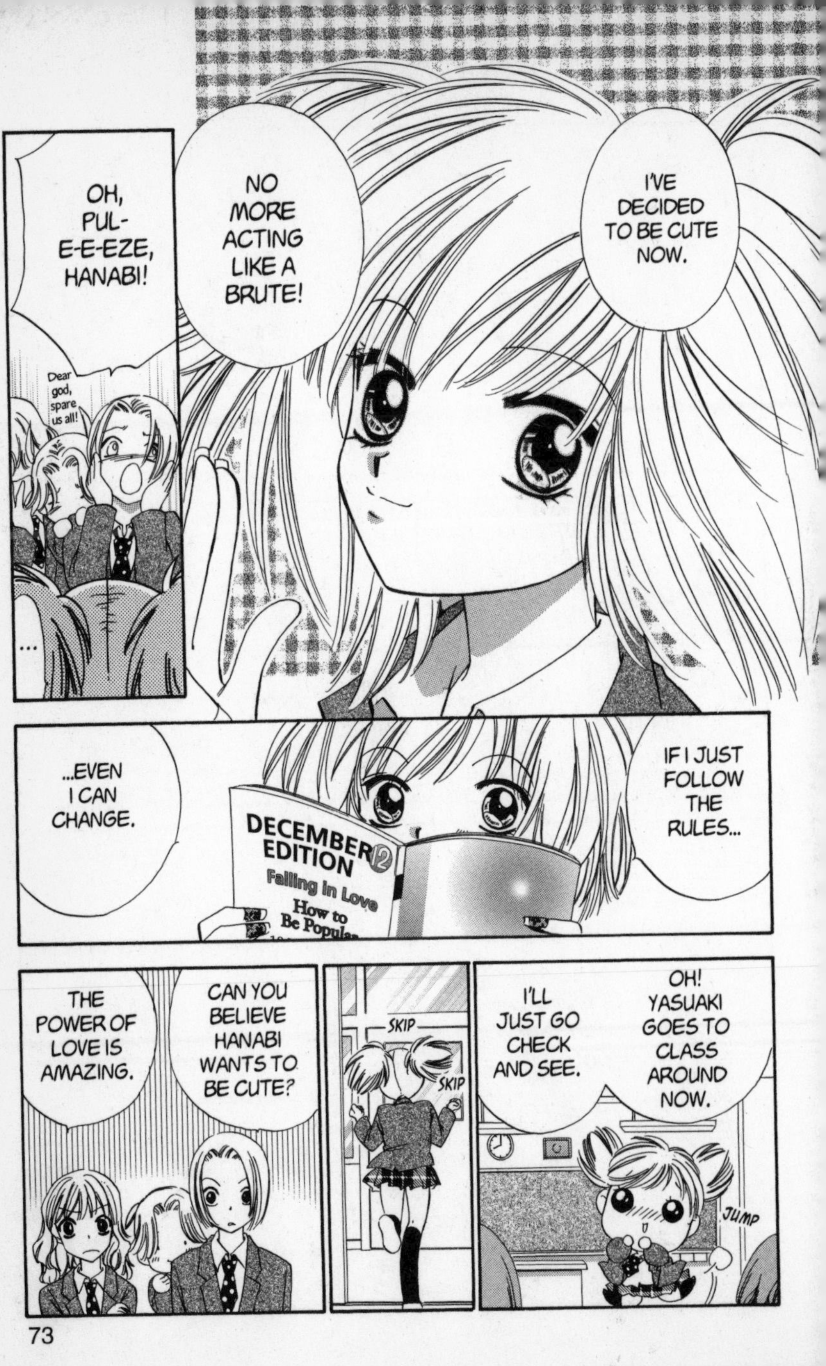
I'VE DECIDED TO BE CUTE NOW.
NO MORE ACTING LIKE A BRUTE!
OH, PUL-E-E-EZE, HANABI!
Dear god, spare us all!
...
IF I JUST FOLLOW THE RULES...
DECEMBER 12 EDITION
Falling in Love
How to Be Popula
...EVEN I CAN CHANGE.
OH! YASUAKI GOES TO CLASS AROUND NOW.
I'LL JUST GO CHECK AND SEE.
JUMP
SKIP
SKIP
CAN YOU BELIEVE HANABI WANTS TO BE CUTE?
THE POWER OF LOVE IS AMAZING.

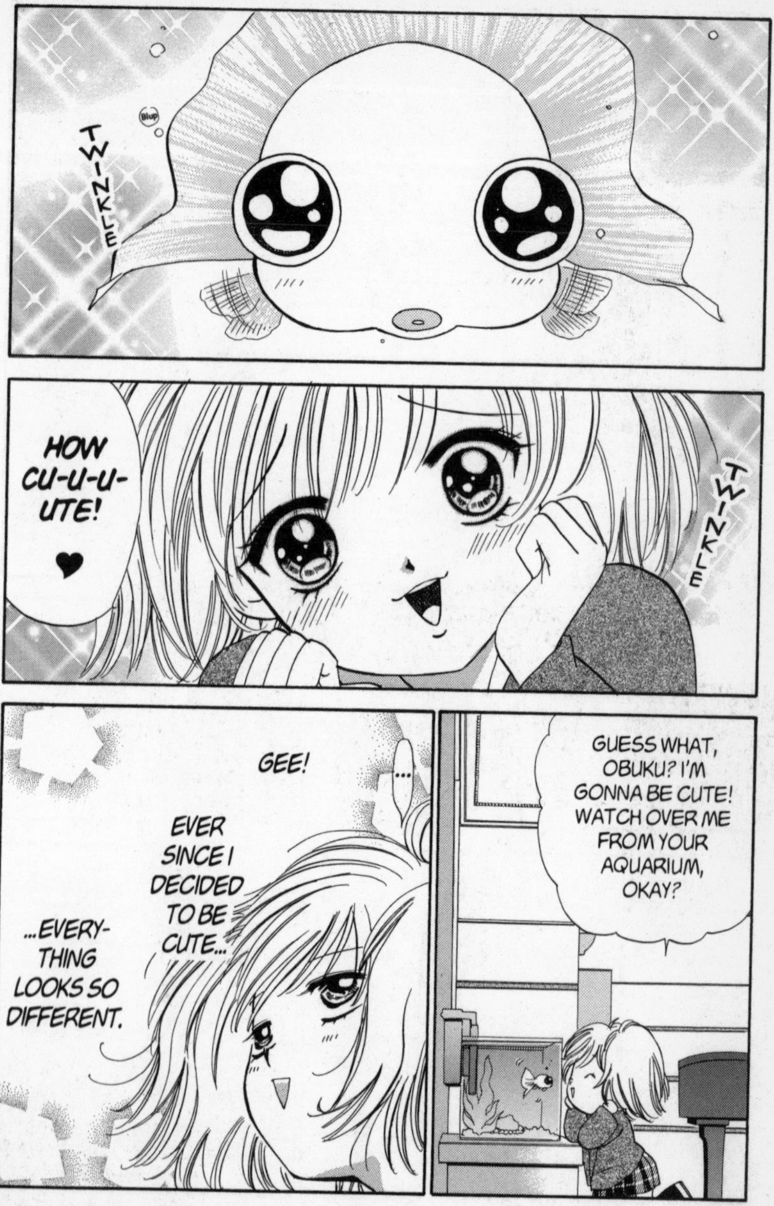
Blup
TWINKLE
TWINKLE
HOW CU-U-U-UTE! ♥
GUESS WHAT, OBUKU? I'M GONNA BE CUTE! WATCH OVER ME FROM YOUR AQUARIUM, OKAY?
...
GEE!
EVER SINCE I DECIDED TO BE CUTE...
...EVERYTHING LOOKS SO DIFFERENT.

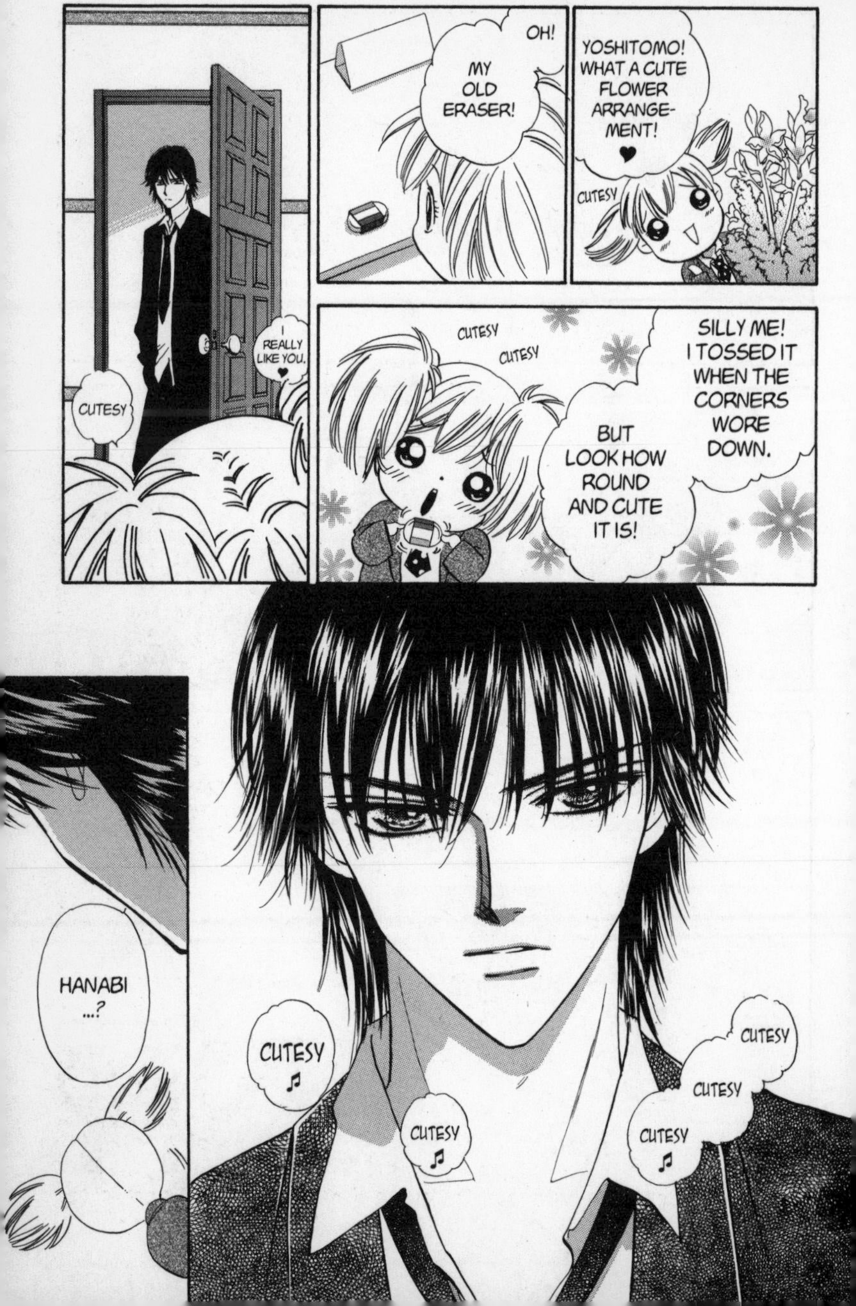
YOSHITOMO! WHAT A CUTE FLOWER ARRANGE-MENT! ♥
CUTESY
OH!
MY OLD ERASER!
CUTESY
CUTESY
SILLY ME! I TOSSED IT WHEN THE CORNERS WORE DOWN.
BUT LOOK HOW ROUND AND CUTE IT IS!
I REALLY LIKE YOU. ♥
CUTESY
CUTESY
CUTESY
CUTESY ♪
CUTESY ♪
CUTESY ♪
HANABI ...?

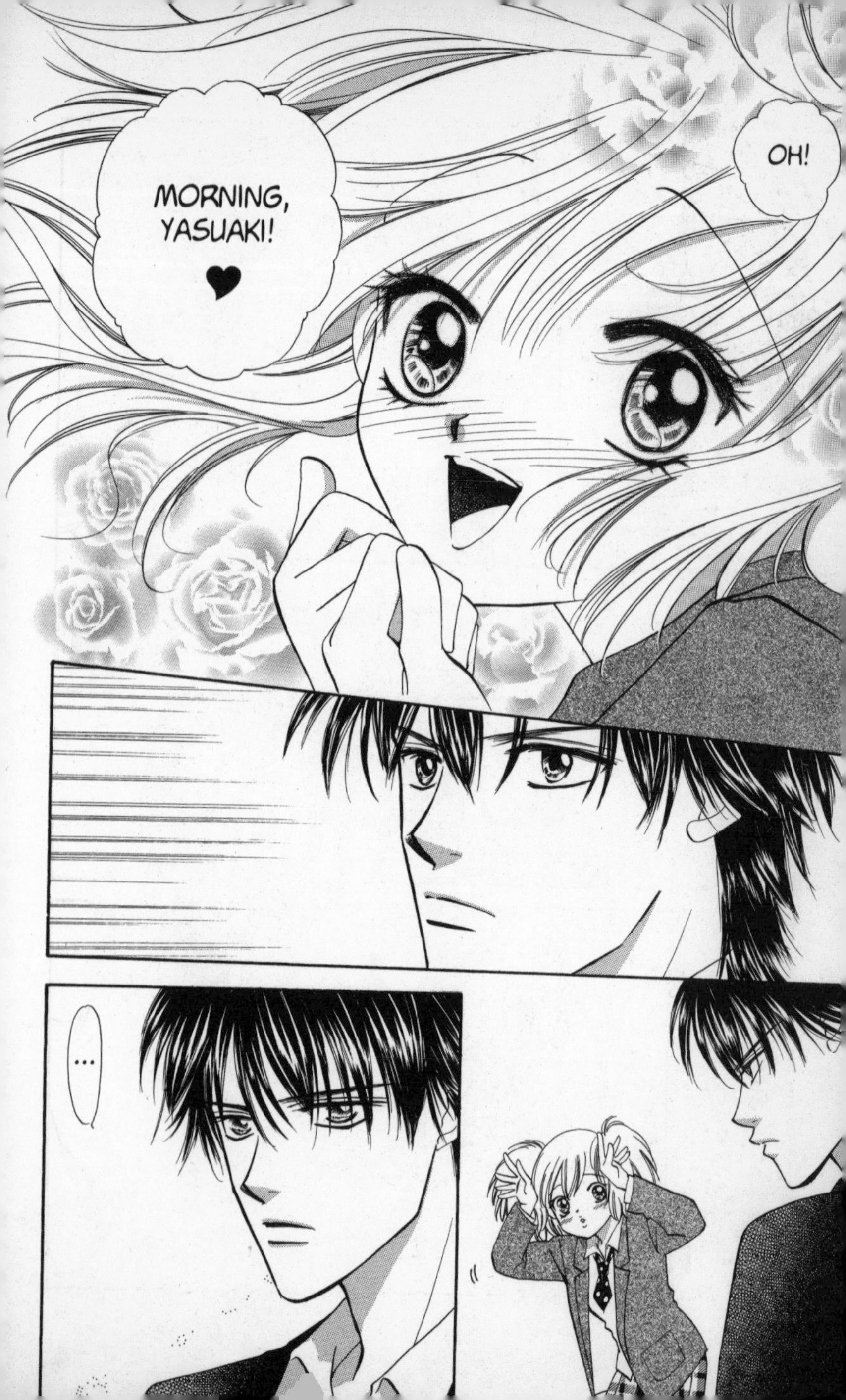
OH!
MORNING, YASUAKI! ♥
...

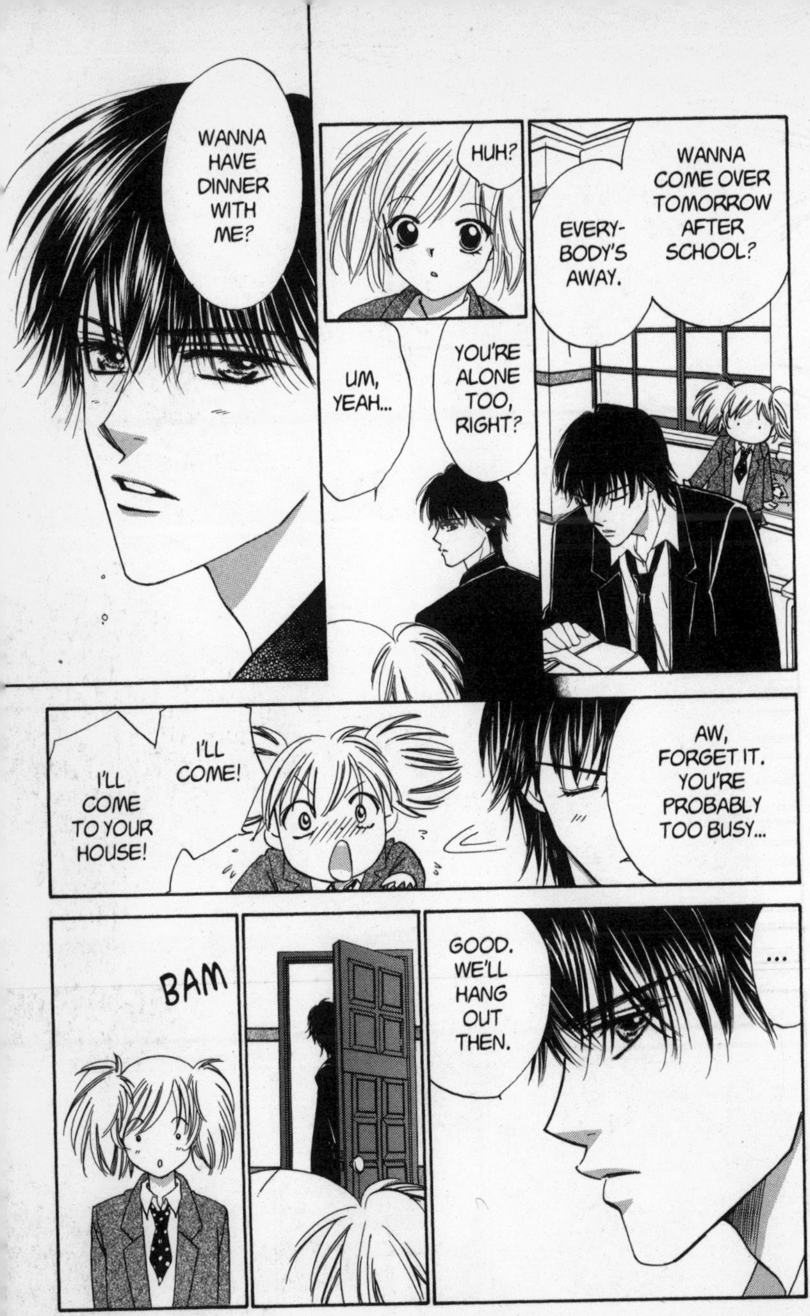

WANNA COME OVER TOMORROW AFTER SCHOOL?
EVERY-BODY'S AWAY.
HUH?
YOU'RE ALONE TOO, RIGHT?
UM, YEAH...
WANNA HAVE DINNER WITH ME?
AW, FORGET IT. YOU'RE PROBABLY TOO BUSY...
I'LL COME!
I'LL COME TO YOUR HOUSE!
...
GOOD. WE'LL HANG OUT THEN.
BAM

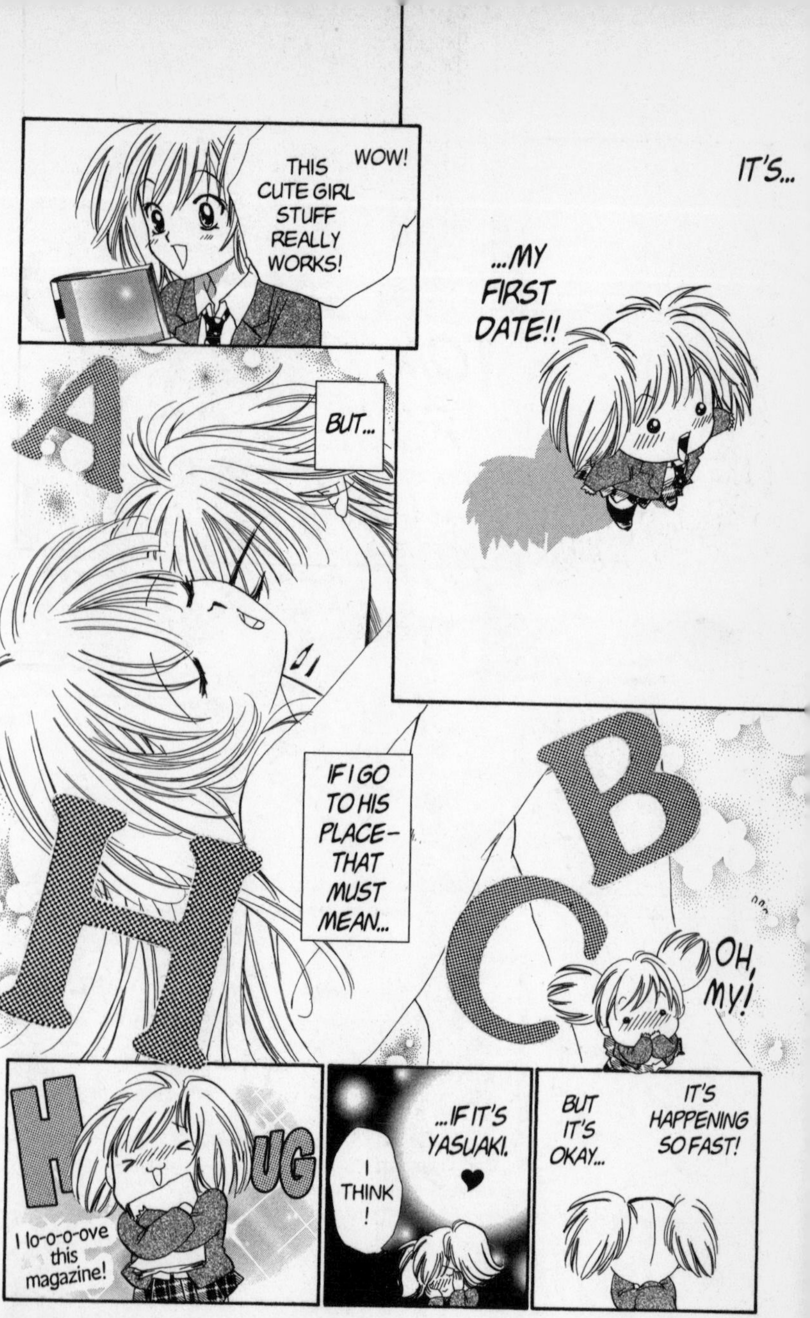
IT'S...
...MY FIRST DATE!!
WOW!
THIS CUTE GIRL STUFF REALLY WORKS!
A
BUT...
B
IF I GO TO HIS PLACE—THAT MUST MEAN...
C
H
OH, MY!
IT'S HAPPENING SO FAST!
BUT IT'S OKAY...
...IF IT'S YASUAKI. ♥
I THINK!
HUG
I lo-o-o-ove this magazine!

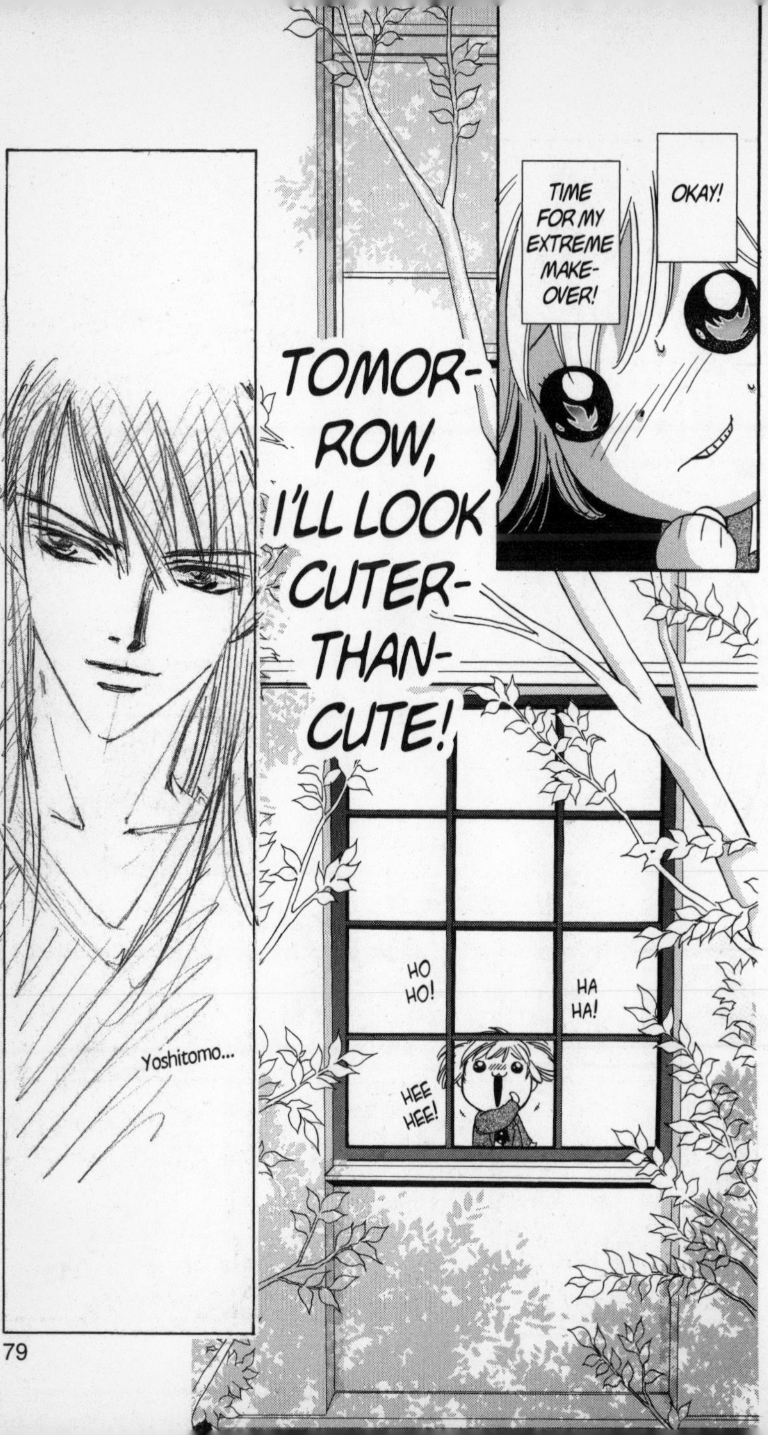
OKAY!
TIME FOR MY EXTREME MAKE-OVER!
TOMOR-ROW, I'LL LOOK CUTER-THAN-CUTE!
HA HA!
HO HO!
HEE HEE!
Yoshitomo...

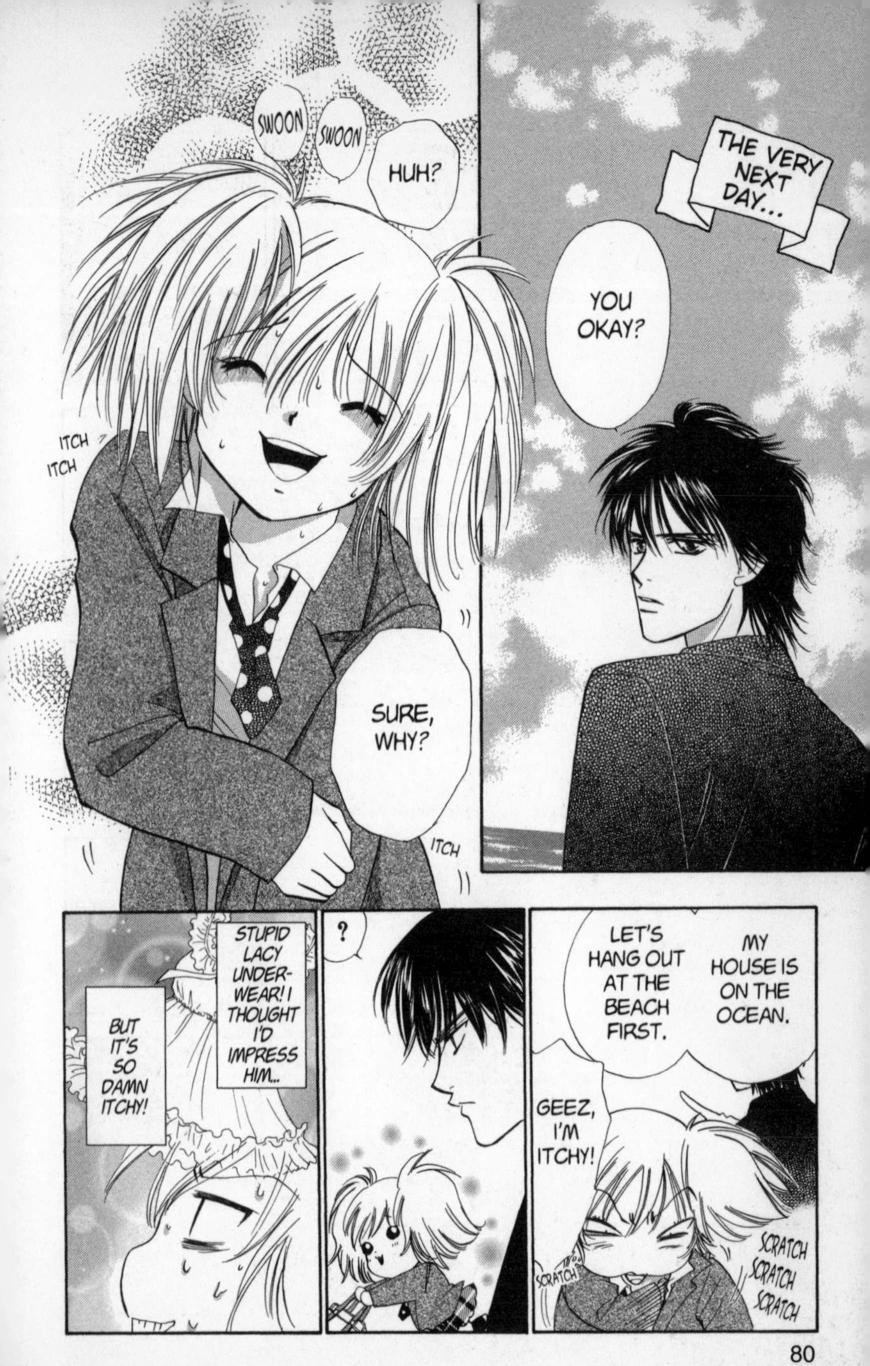
THE VERY NEXT DAY...
YOU OKAY?
SWOON
SWOON
HUH?
ITCH
ITCH
SURE, WHY?
ITCH
MY HOUSE IS ON THE OCEAN.
LET'S HANG OUT AT THE BEACH FIRST.
GEEZ, I'M ITCHY!
SCRATCH
SCRATCH
SCRATCH
SCRATCH
?
STUPID LACY UNDER-WEAR! I THOUGHT I'D IMPRESS HIM...
BUT IT'S SO DAMN ITCHY!

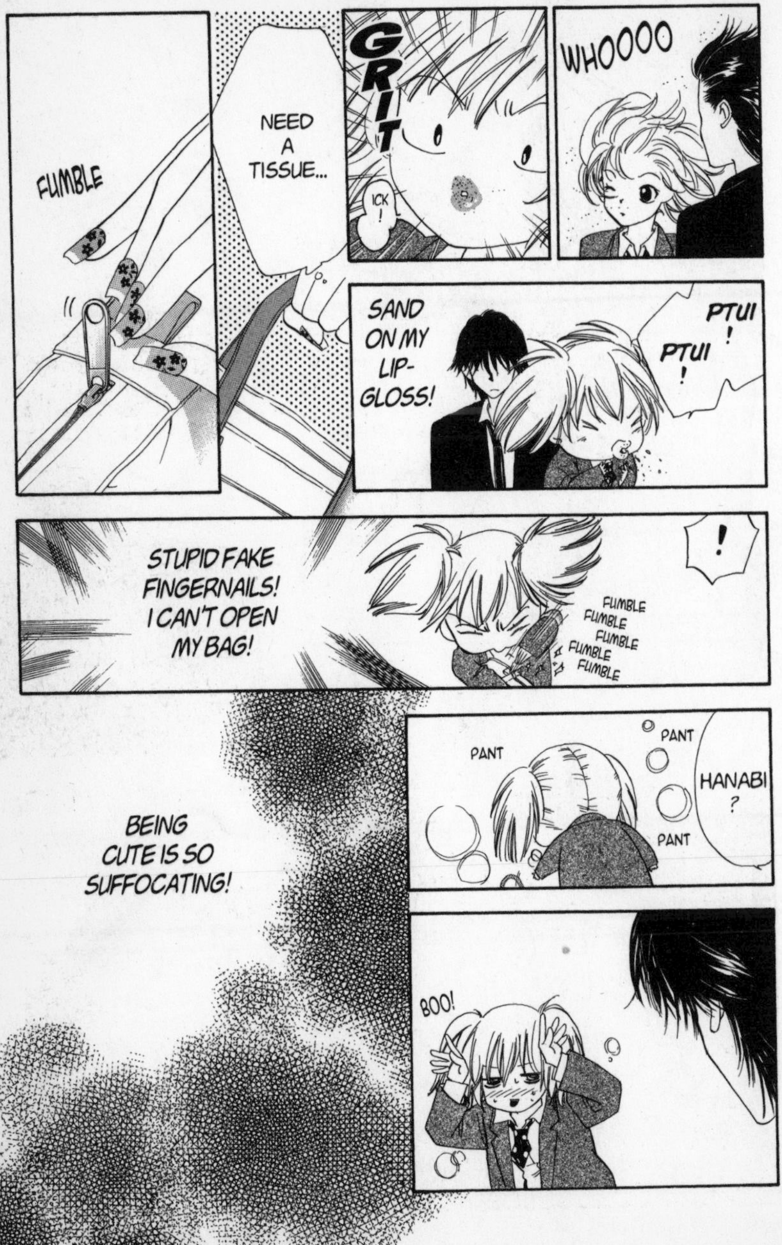
WHOOOO
GRIT
ICK!
PTUI!
PTUI!
SAND ON MY LIP-GLOSS!
NEED A TISSUE...
FUMBLE
!
FUMBLE FUMBLE FUMBLE FUMBLE FUMBLE
STUPID FAKE FINGERNAILS! I CAN'T OPEN MY BAG!
HANABI?
PANT
PANT
PANT
BOO!
BEING CUTE IS SO SUFFOCATING!

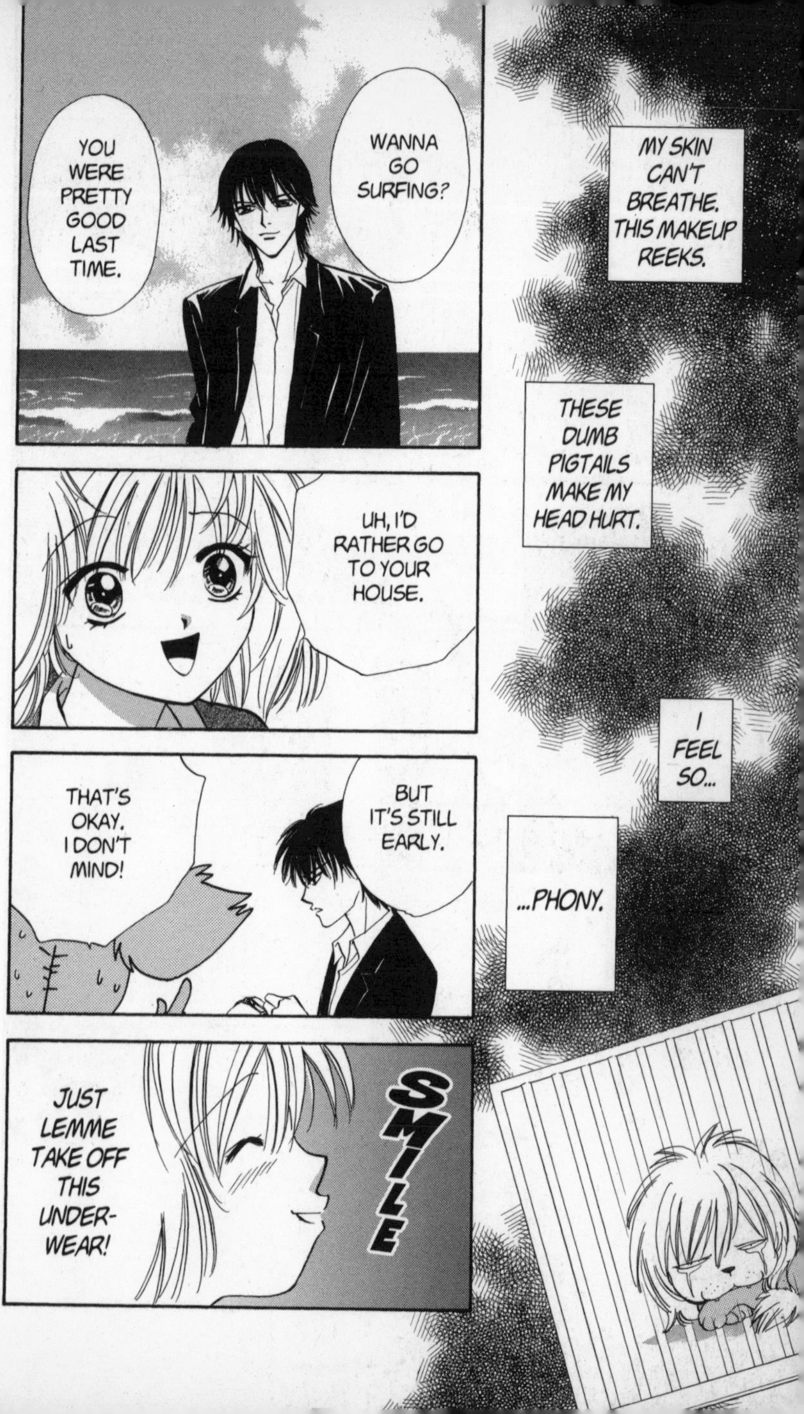
MY SKIN CAN'T BREATHE. THIS MAKEUP REEKS.
THESE DUMB PIGTAILS MAKE MY HEAD HURT.
I FEEL SO...
...PHONY.
WANNA GO SURFING?
YOU WERE PRETTY GOOD LAST TIME.
UH, I'D RATHER GO TO YOUR HOUSE.
BUT IT'S STILL EARLY.
THAT'S OKAY. I DON'T MIND!
SMILE
JUST LEMME TAKE OFF THIS UNDER-WEAR!

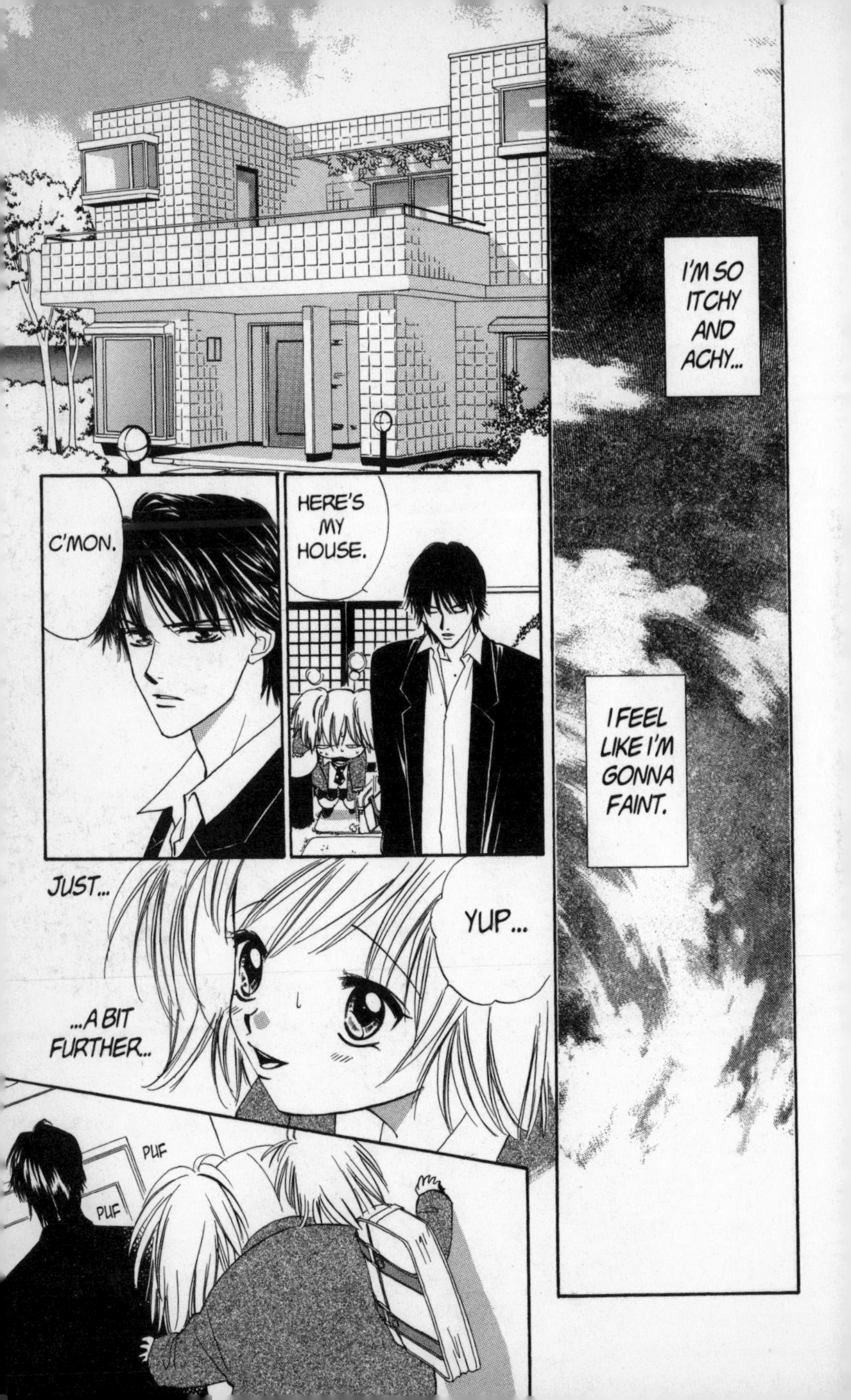
I'M SO ITCHY AND ACHY...
I FEEL LIKE I'M GONNA FAINT.
HERE'S MY HOUSE.
C'MON.
YUP...
JUST...
...A BIT FURTHER...
PUF
PUF

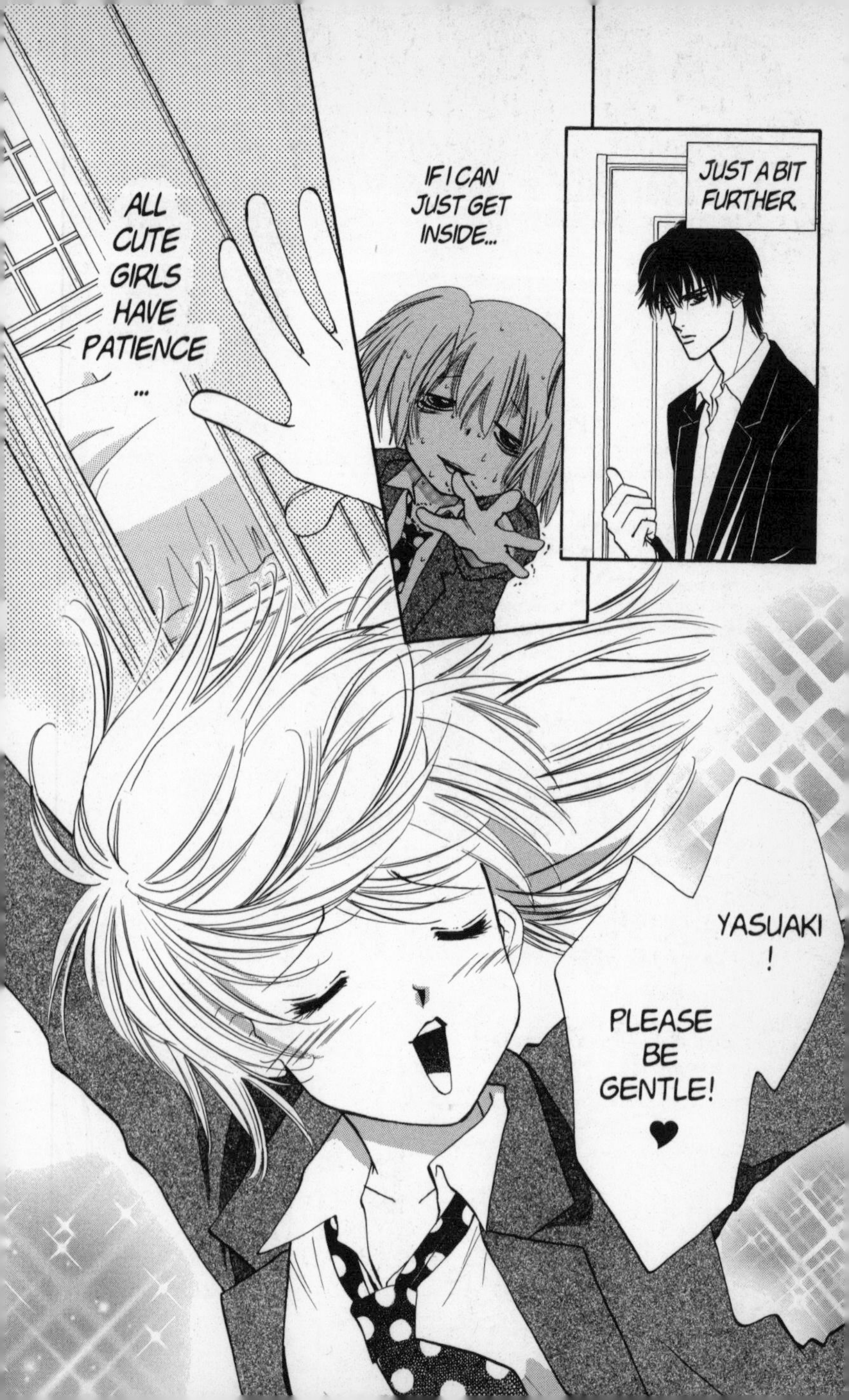
JUST A BIT FURTHER.
IF I CAN JUST GET INSIDE...
ALL CUTE GIRLS HAVE PATIENCE...
YASUAKI!
PLEASE BE GENTLE! ♥

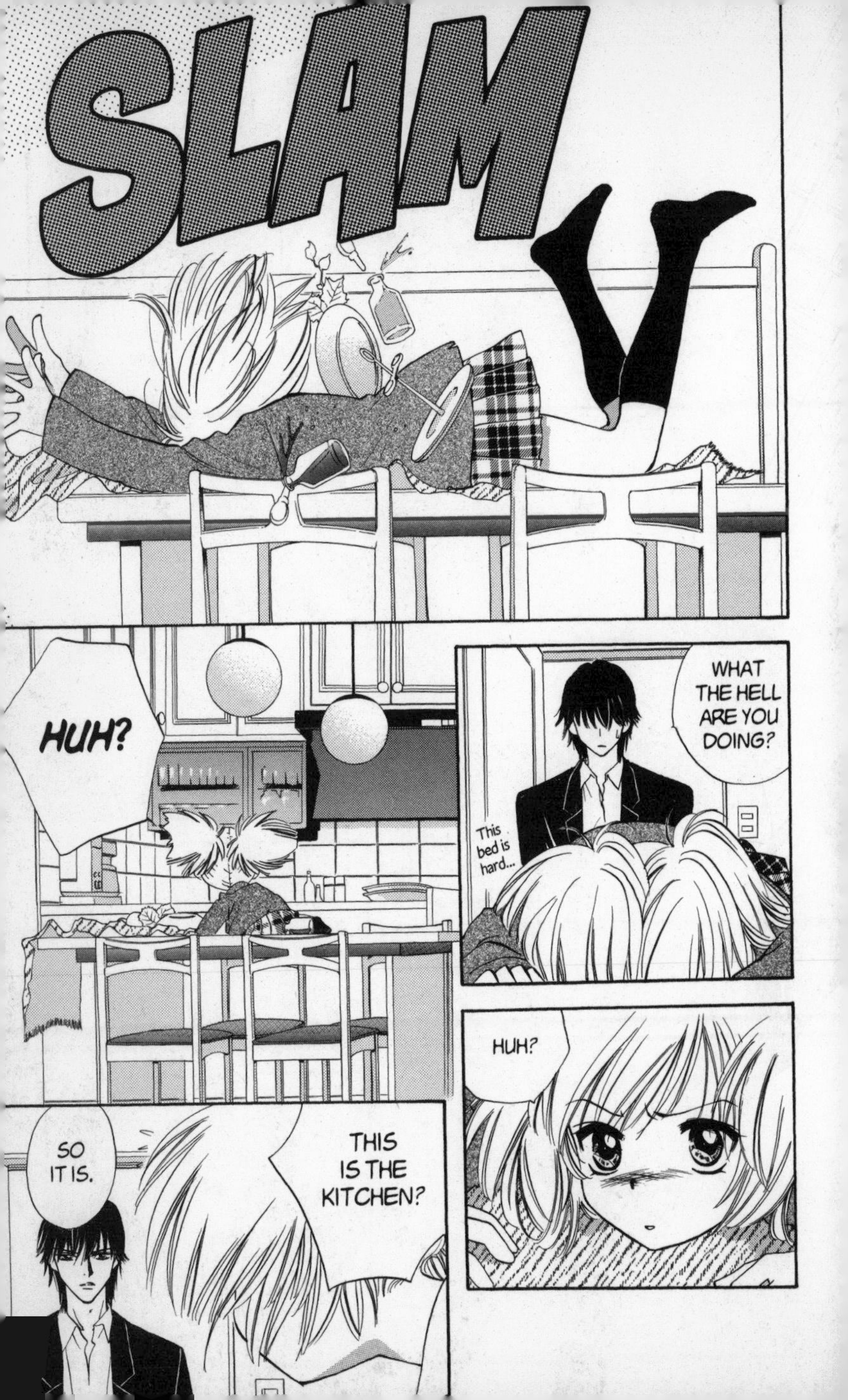
SLAM
WHAT THE HELL ARE YOU DOING?
This bed is hard...
HUH?
HUH?
THIS IS THE KITCHEN?
SO IT IS.

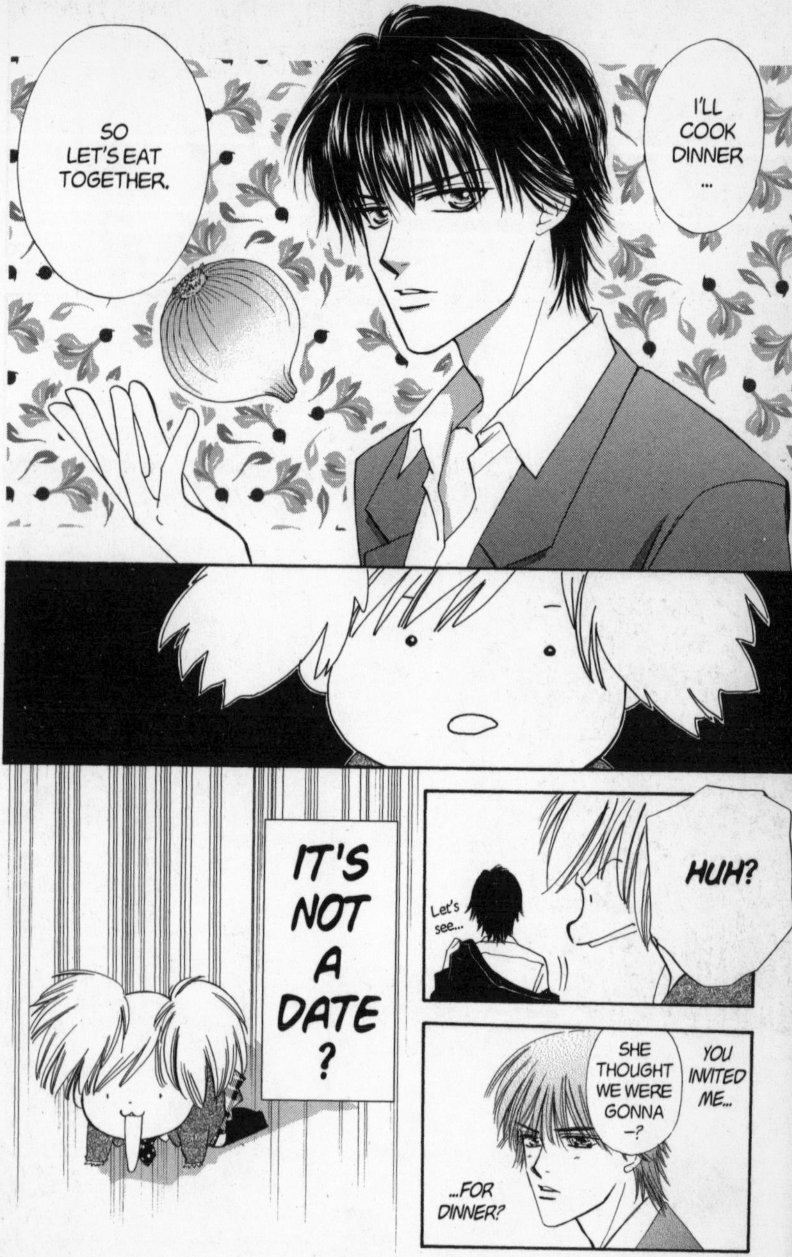
I'LL COOK DINNER ...
SO LET'S EAT TOGETHER.
HUH?
Let's see...
YOU INVITED ME...
SHE THOUGHT WE WERE GONNA —?
...FOR DINNER?
IT'S NOT A DATE ?

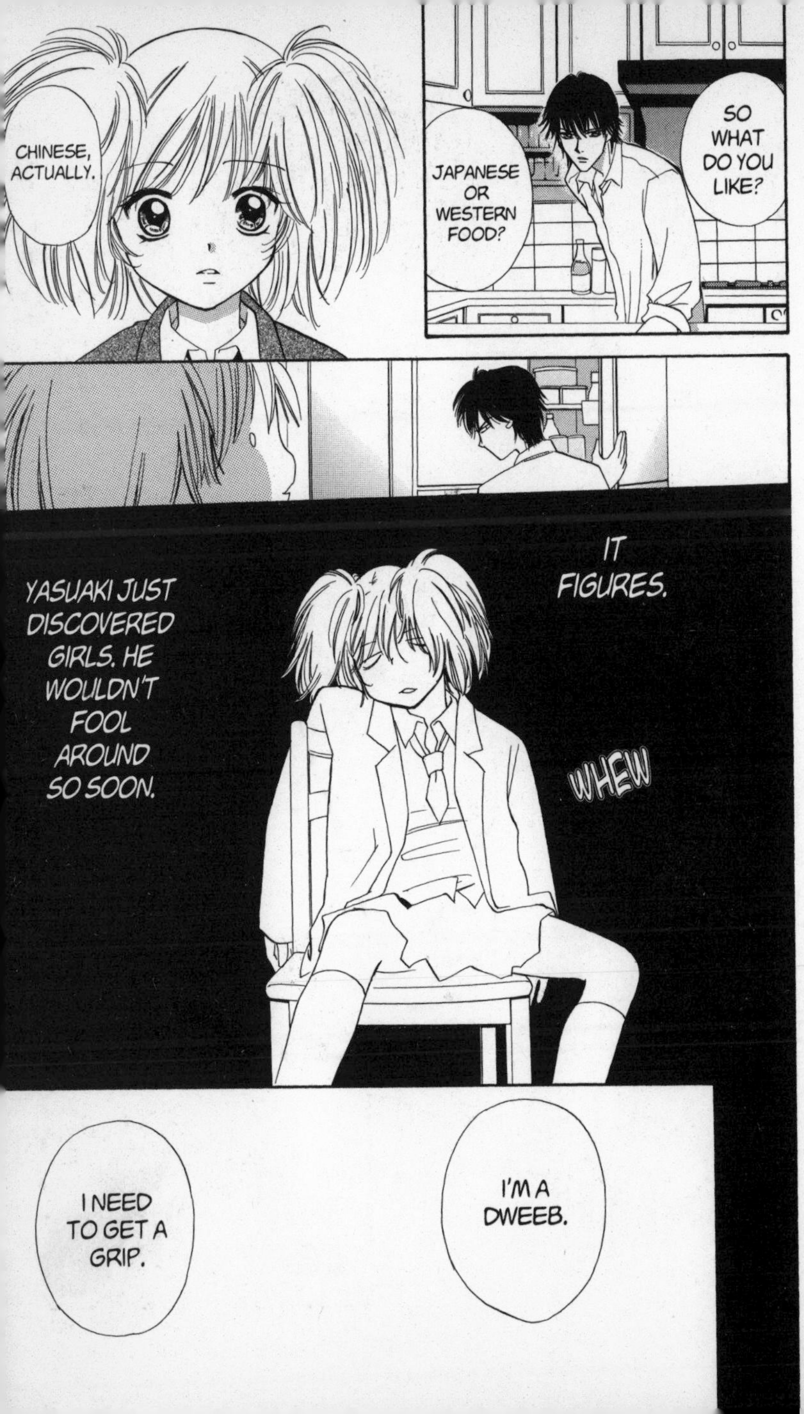
SO WHAT DO YOU LIKE?
JAPANESE OR WESTERN FOOD?
CHINESE, ACTUALLY.
IT FIGURES.
YASUAKI JUST DISCOVERED GIRLS. HE WOULDN'T FOOL AROUND SO SOON.
WHEW
I'M A DWEEB.
I NEED TO GET A GRIP.

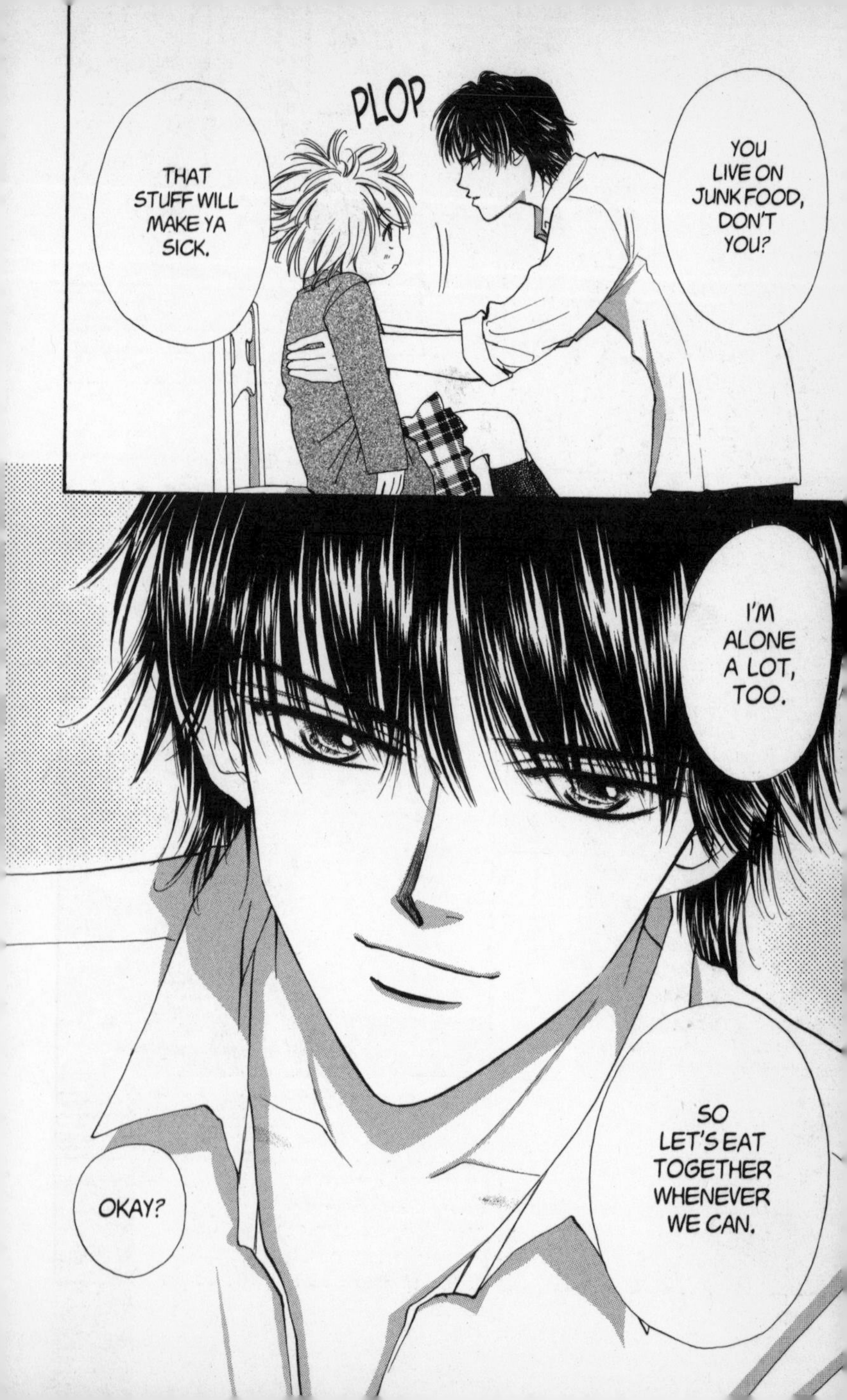
YOU LIVE ON JUNK FOOD, DON'T YOU?
PLOP
THAT STUFF WILL MAKE YA SICK.
I'M ALONE A LOT, TOO.
SO LET'S EAT TOGETHER WHENEVER WE CAN.
OKAY?

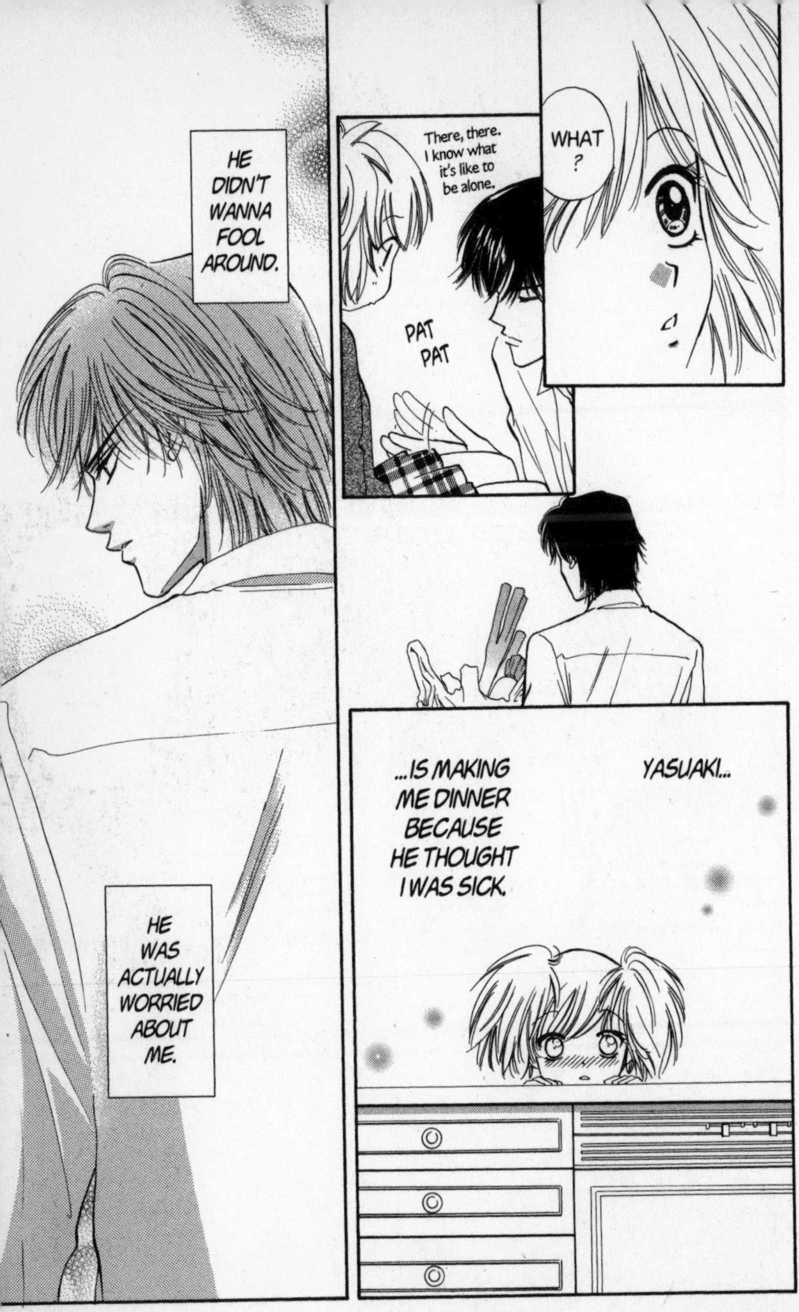
WHAT?
There, there. I know what it's like to be alone.
PAT PAT
YASUAKI...
...IS MAKING ME DINNER BECAUSE HE THOUGHT I WAS SICK.
HE DIDN'T WANNA FOOL AROUND.
HE WAS ACTUALLY WORRIED ABOUT ME.

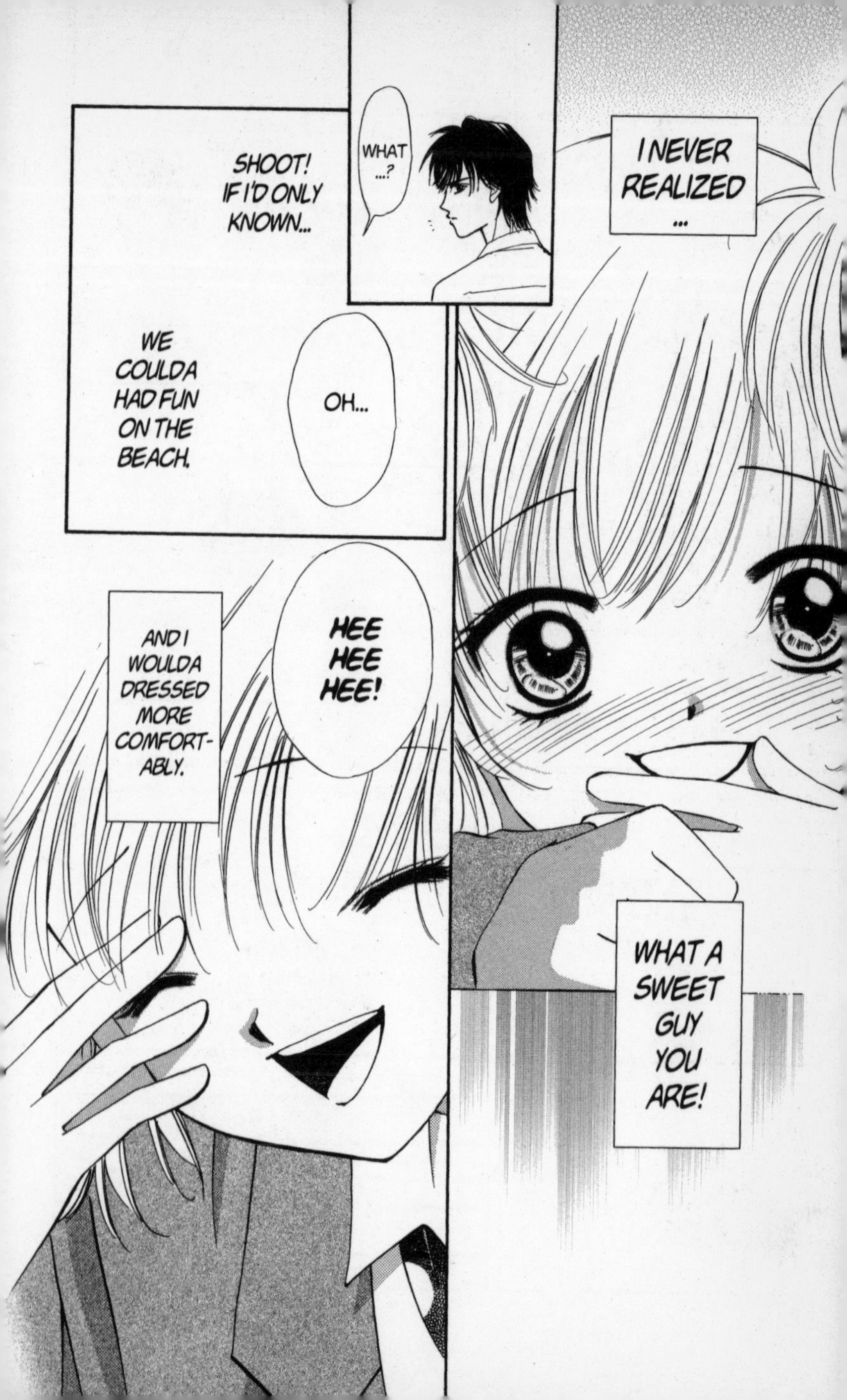
I NEVER REALIZED ...
WHAT A SWEET GUY YOU ARE!
WHAT ...?
SHOOT! IF I'D ONLY KNOWN...
WE COULDA HAD FUN ON THE BEACH.
OH...
HEE HEE HEE!
AND I WOULDA DRESSED MORE COMFORT-ABLY.

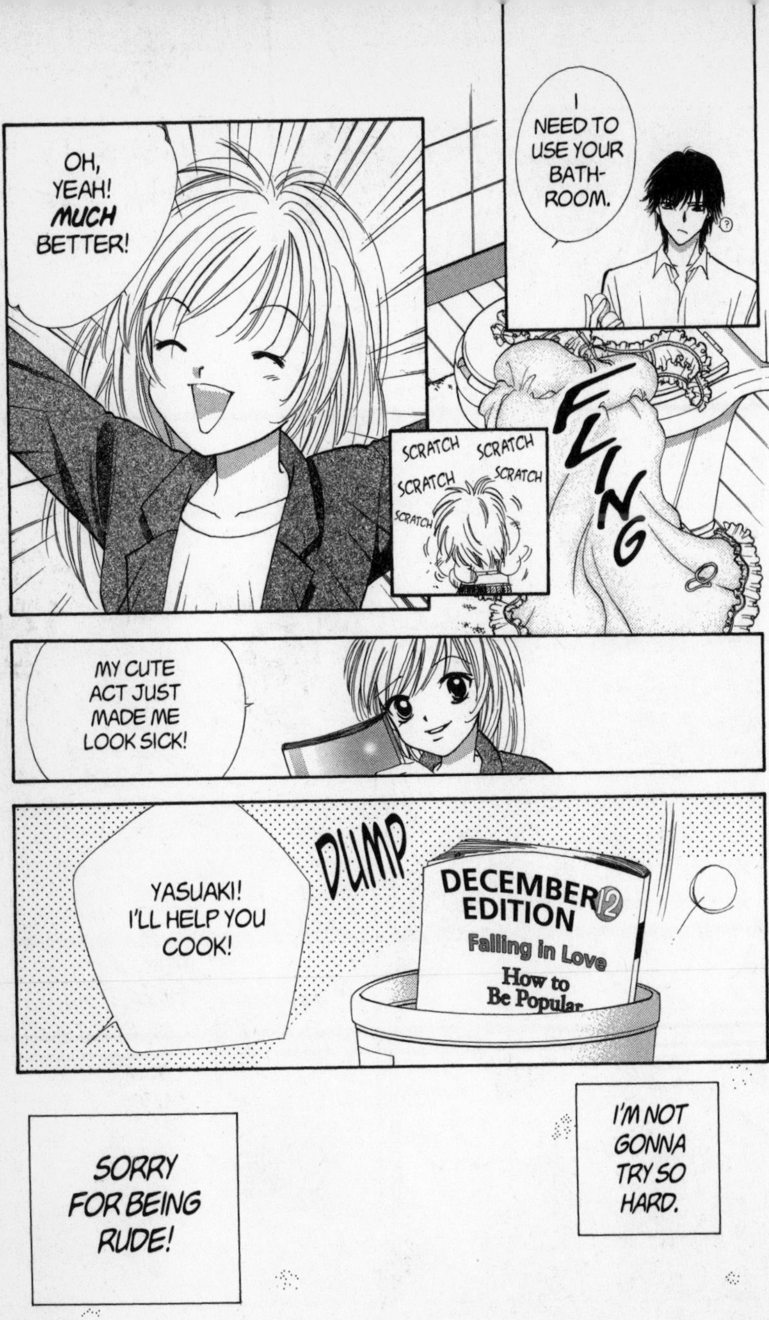
I NEED TO USE YOUR BATH-ROOM.
?
FLING
SCRATCH SCRATCH SCRATCH SCRATCH SCRATCH
OH, YEAH! MUCH BETTER!
MY CUTE ACT JUST MADE ME LOOK SICK!
DECEMBER EDITION 12
Falling in Love
How to Be Popular
DUMP
YASUAKI! I'LL HELP YOU COOK!
I'M NOT GONNA TRY SO HARD.
SORRY FOR BEING RUDE!

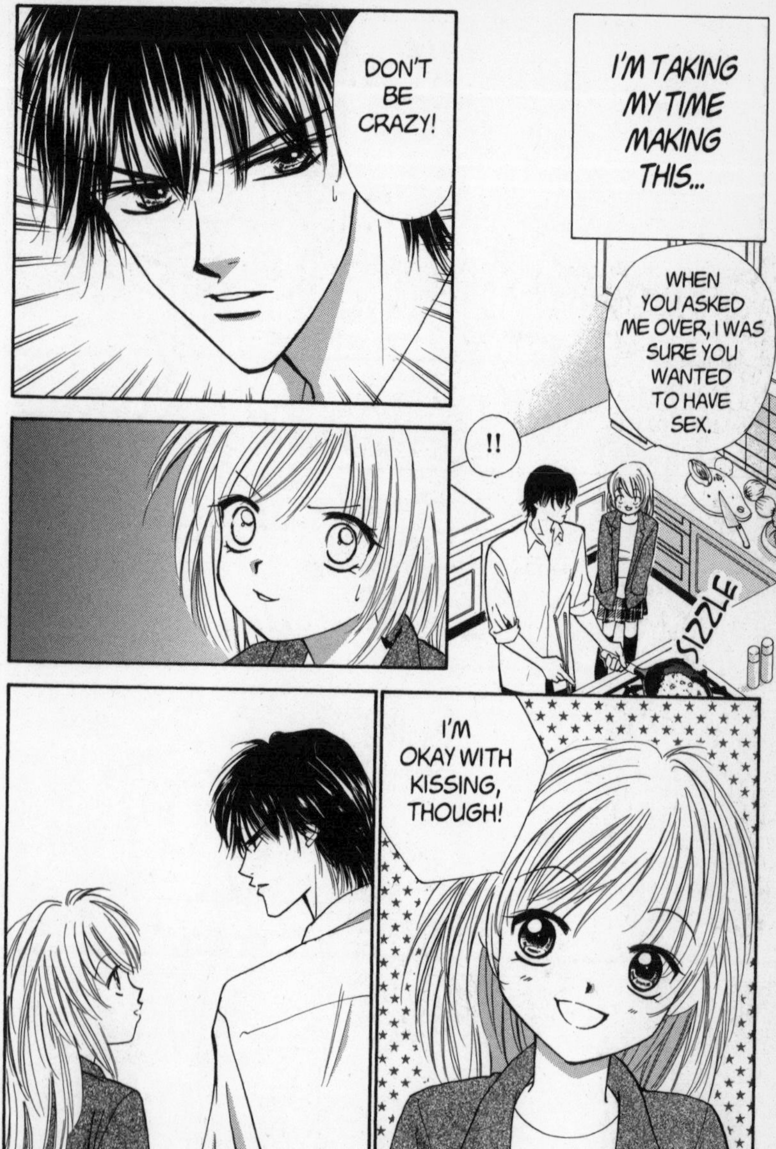
I'M TAKING MY TIME MAKING THIS...
WHEN YOU ASKED ME OVER, I WAS SURE YOU WANTED TO HAVE SEX.
!!
SIZZLE
DON'T BE CRAZY!
I'M OKAY WITH KISSING, THOUGH!

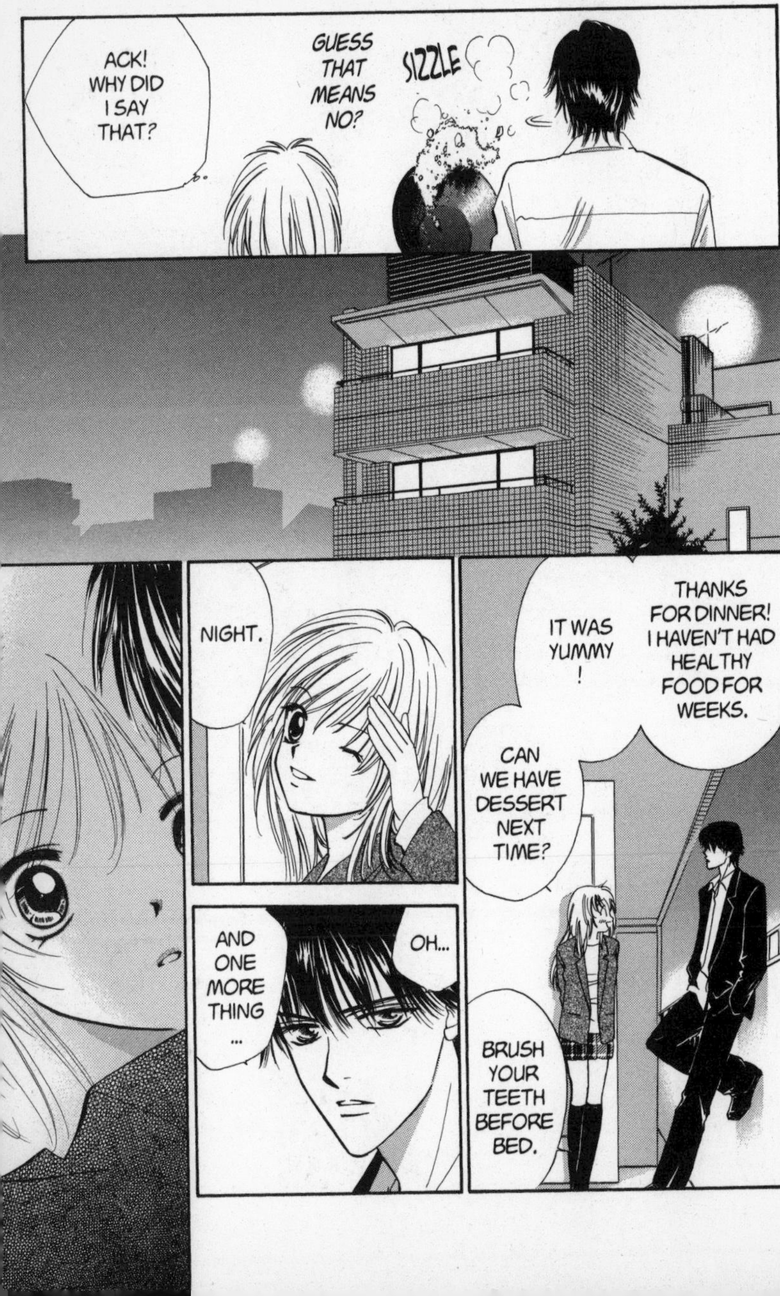
SIZZLE
GUESS THAT MEANS NO?
ACK! WHY DID I SAY THAT?
THANKS FOR DINNER! I HAVEN'T HAD HEALTHY FOOD FOR WEEKS.
IT WAS YUMMY!
CAN WE HAVE DESSERT NEXT TIME?
BRUSH YOUR TEETH BEFORE BED.
NIGHT.
OH...
AND ONE MORE THING...

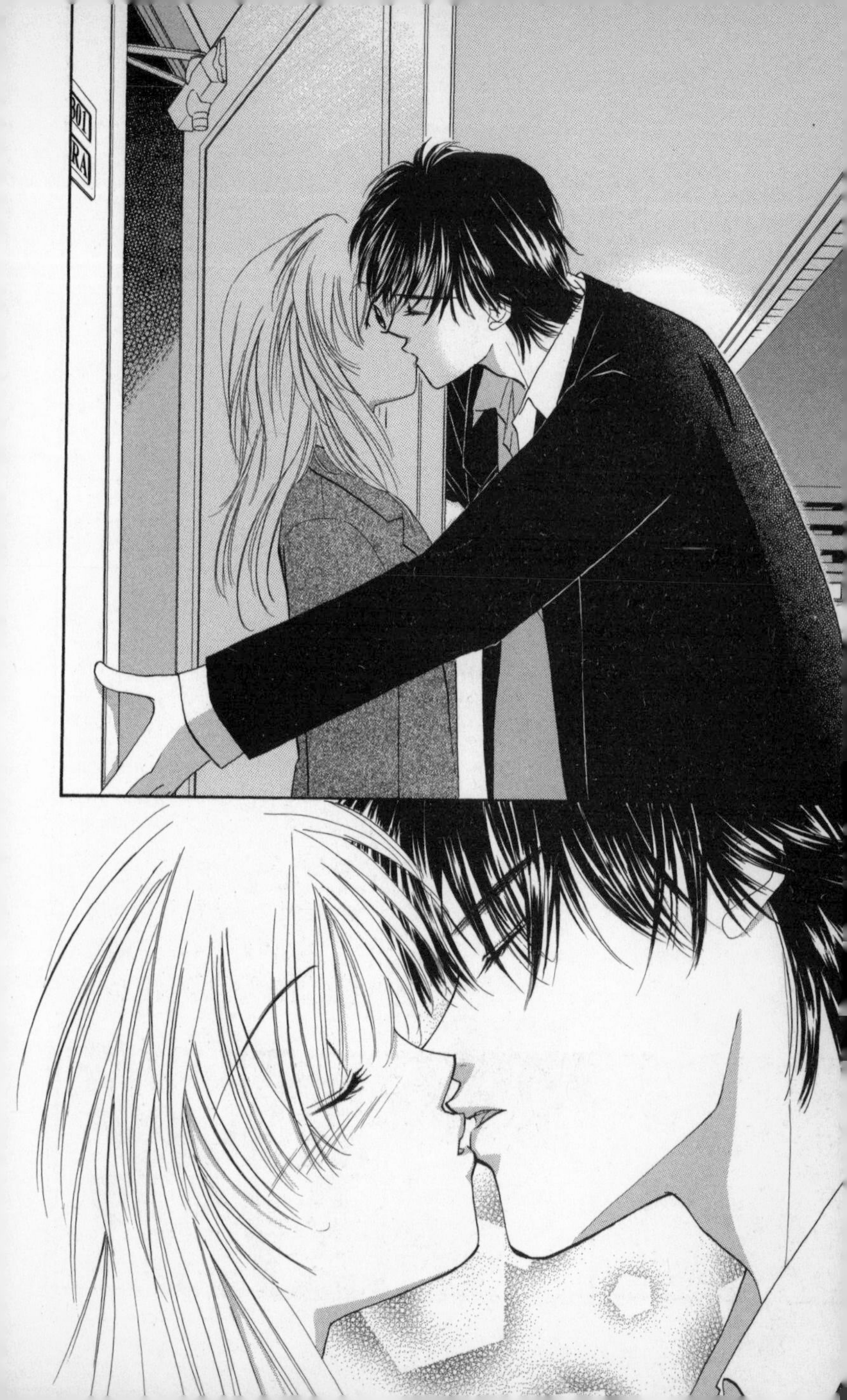

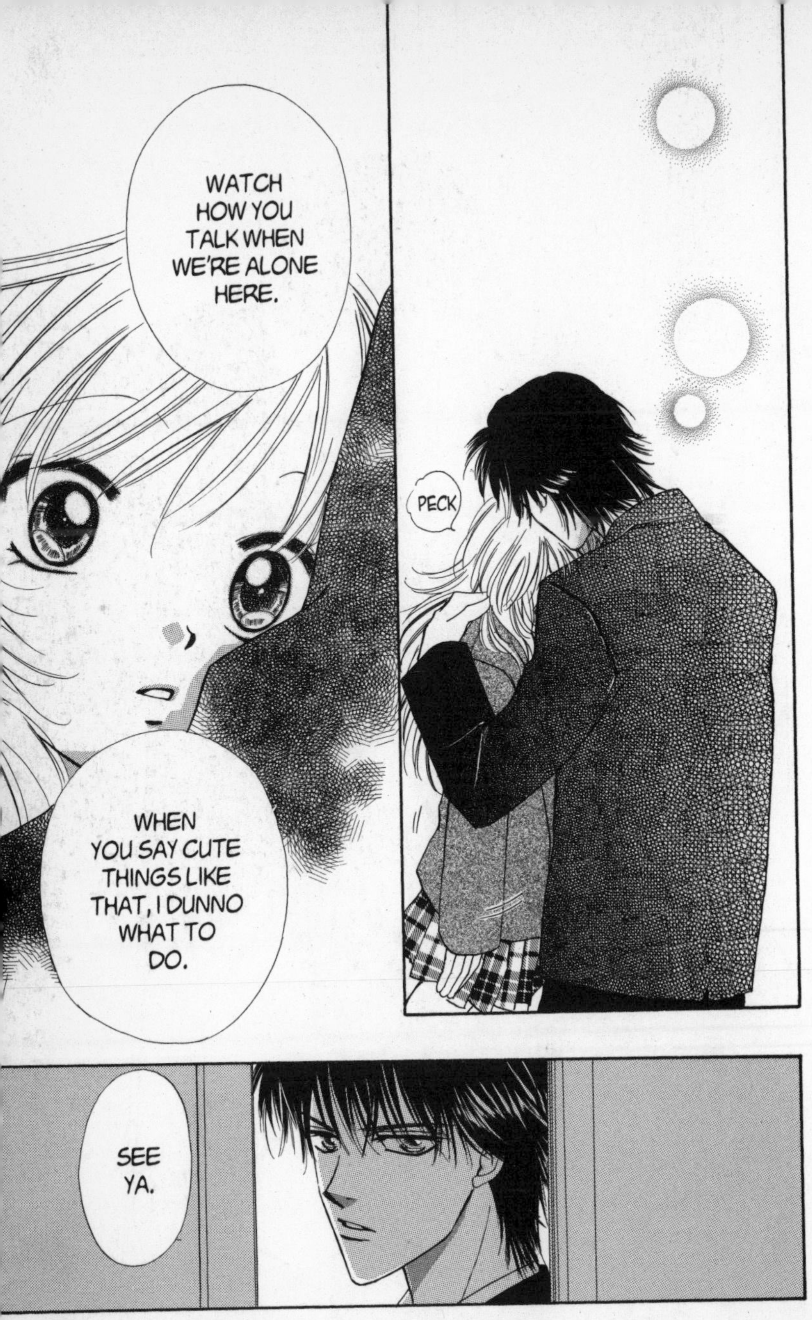
PECK
WATCH HOW YOU TALK WHEN WE'RE ALONE HERE.
WHEN YOU SAY CUTE THINGS LIKE THAT, I DUNNO WHAT TO DO.
SEE YA.

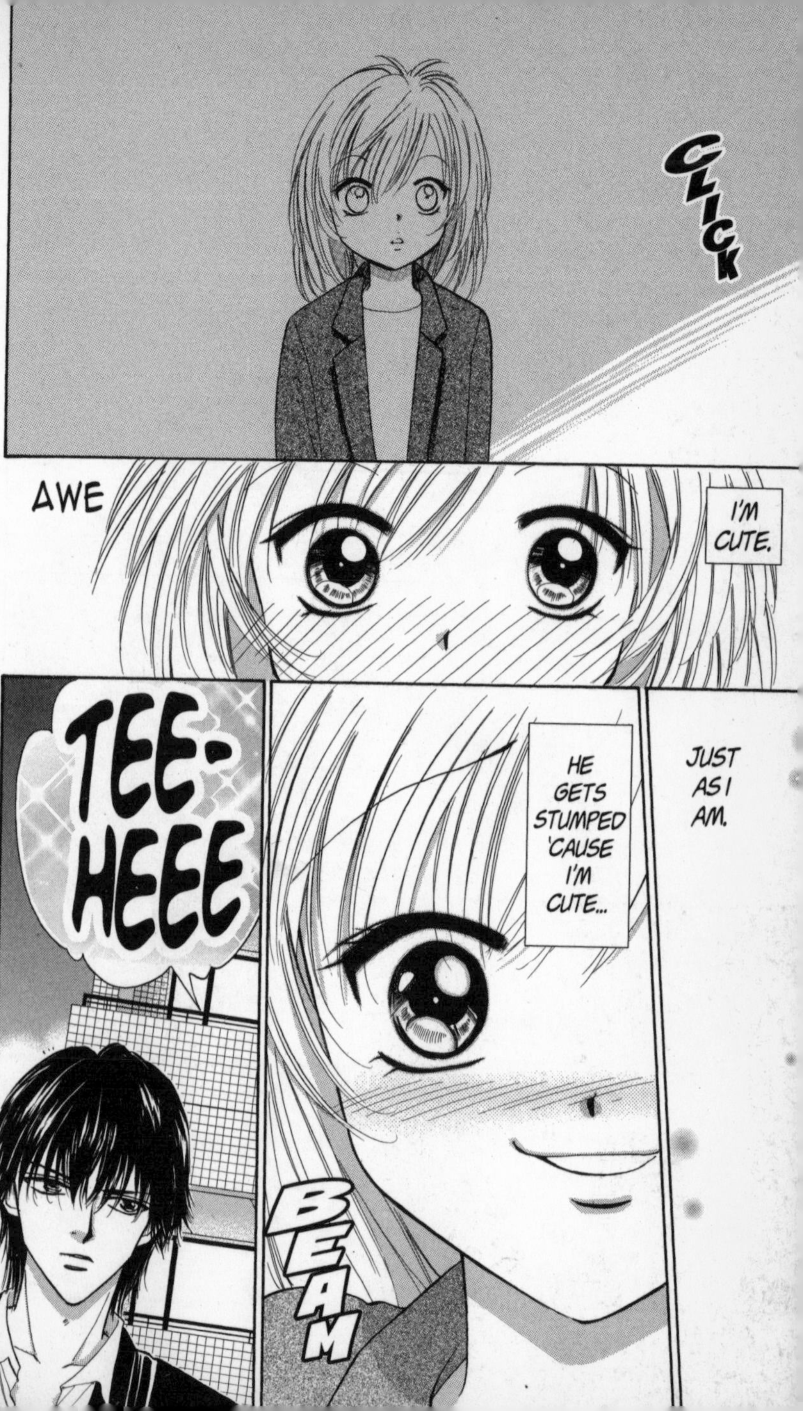
CLICK
I'M CUTE.
AWE
JUST AS I AM.
HE GETS STUMPED 'CAUSE I'M CUTE...
BEAM
TEE-HEEE

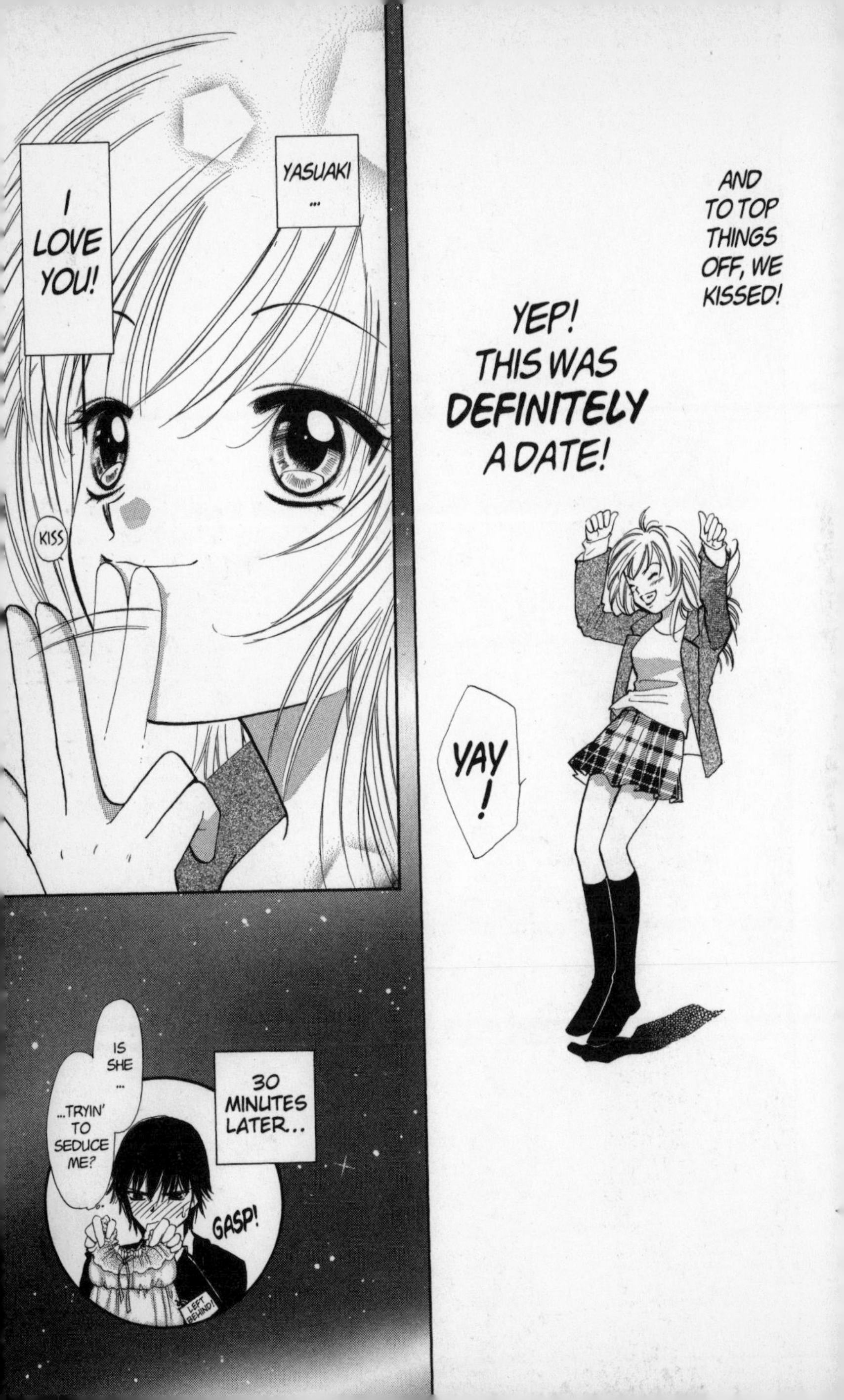
AND TO TOP THINGS OFF, WE KISSED!
YEP! THIS WAS DEFINITELY A DATE!
YAY!
YASUAKI...
I LOVE YOU!
KISS
30 MINUTES LATER...
GASP!
IS SHE...
...TRYIN' TO SEDUCE ME?
LEFT BEHIND!

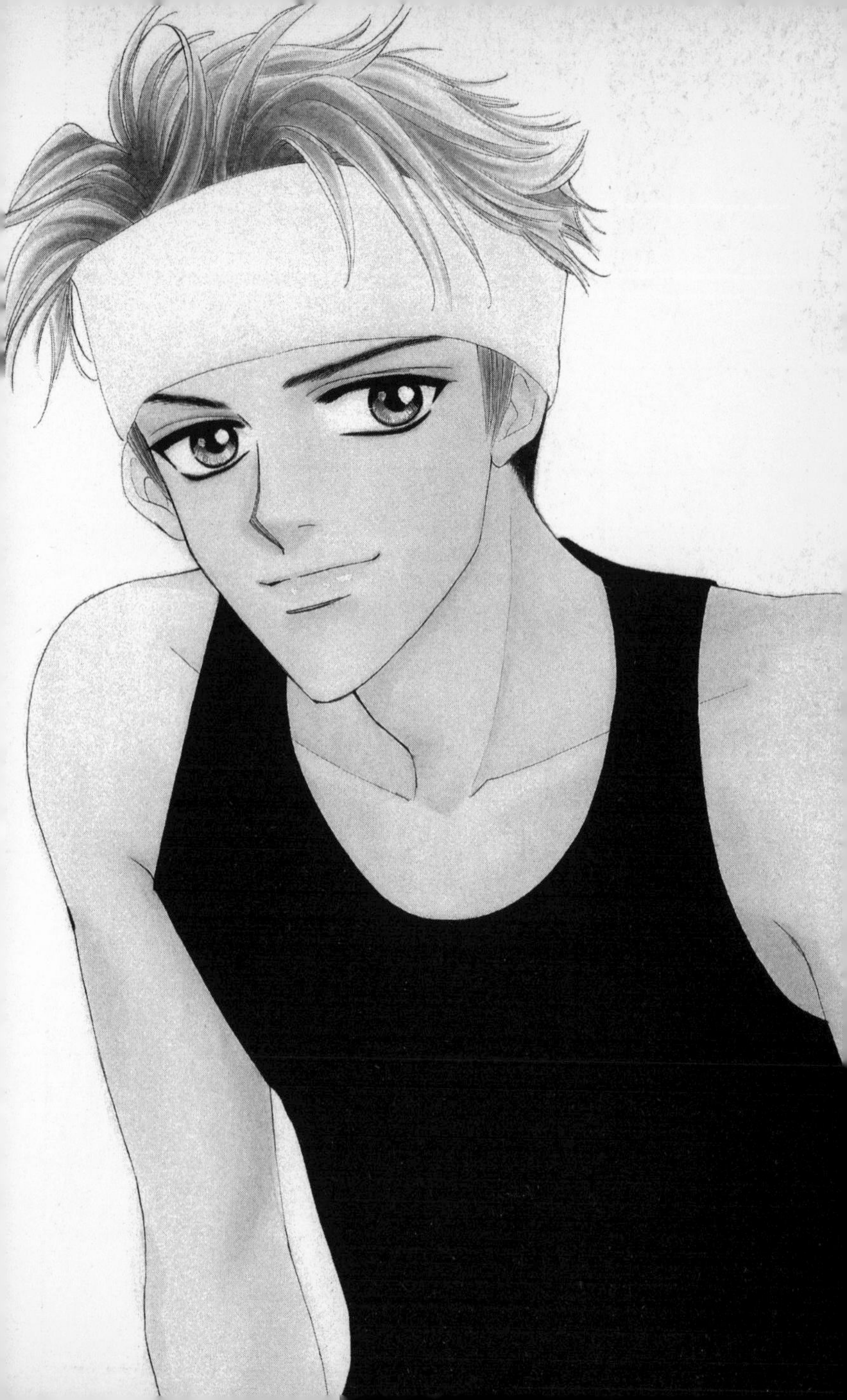

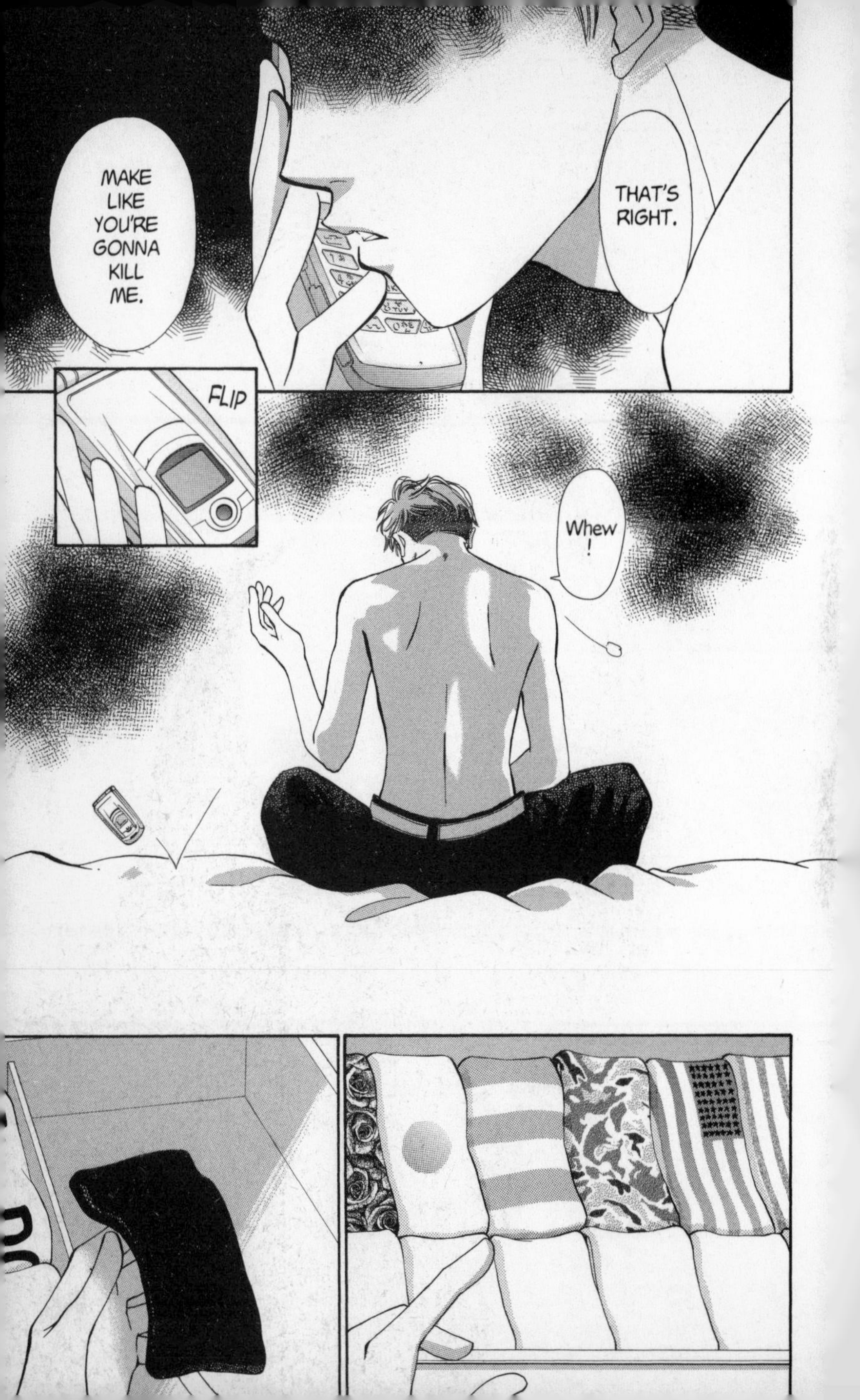
THAT'S RIGHT.
MAKE LIKE YOU'RE GONNA KILL ME.
FLIP
Whew !

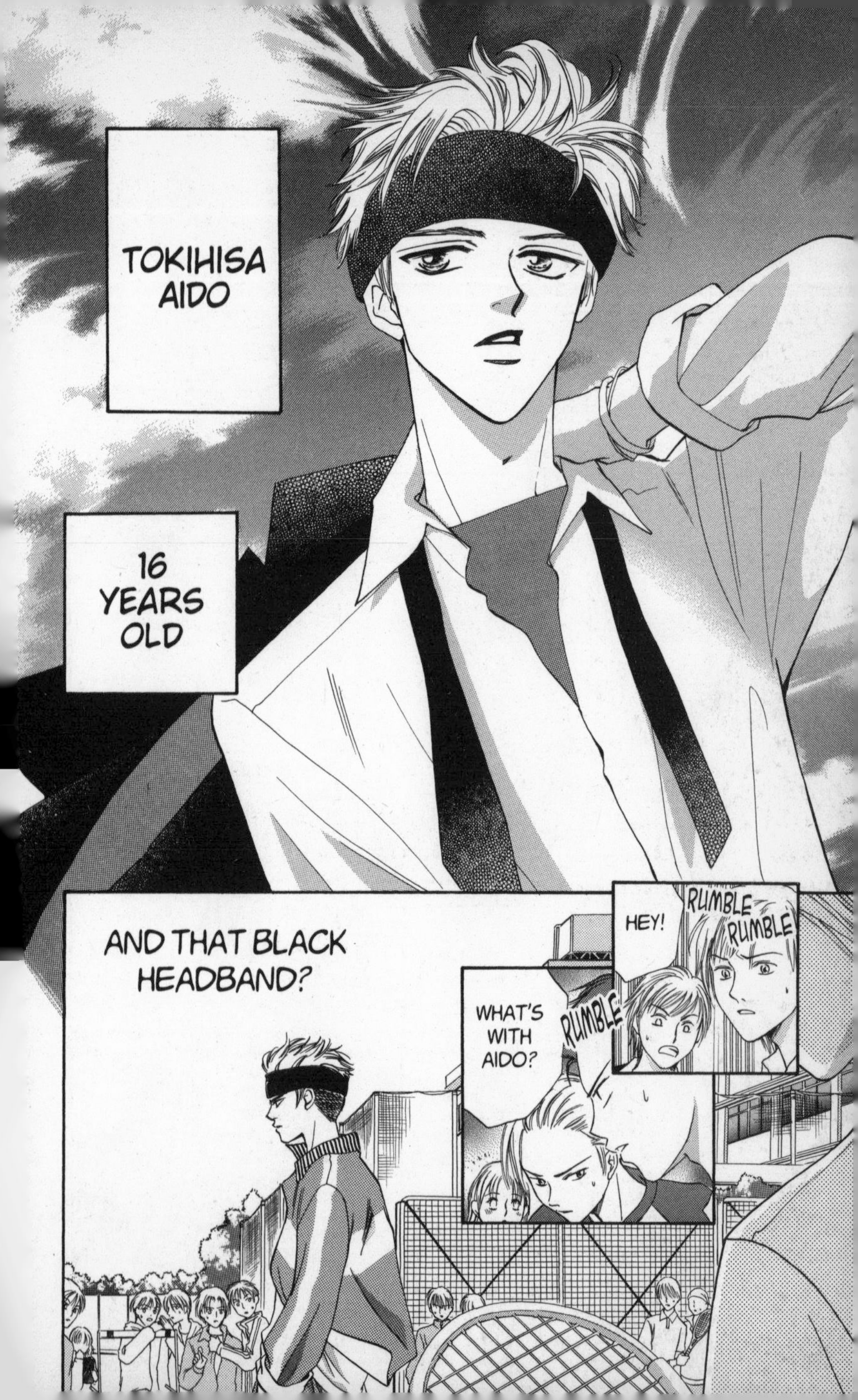
TOKIHISA AIDO
16 YEARS OLD
RUMBLE RUMBLE
HEY!
WHAT'S WITH AIDO?
RUMBLE
AND THAT BLACK HEADBAND?

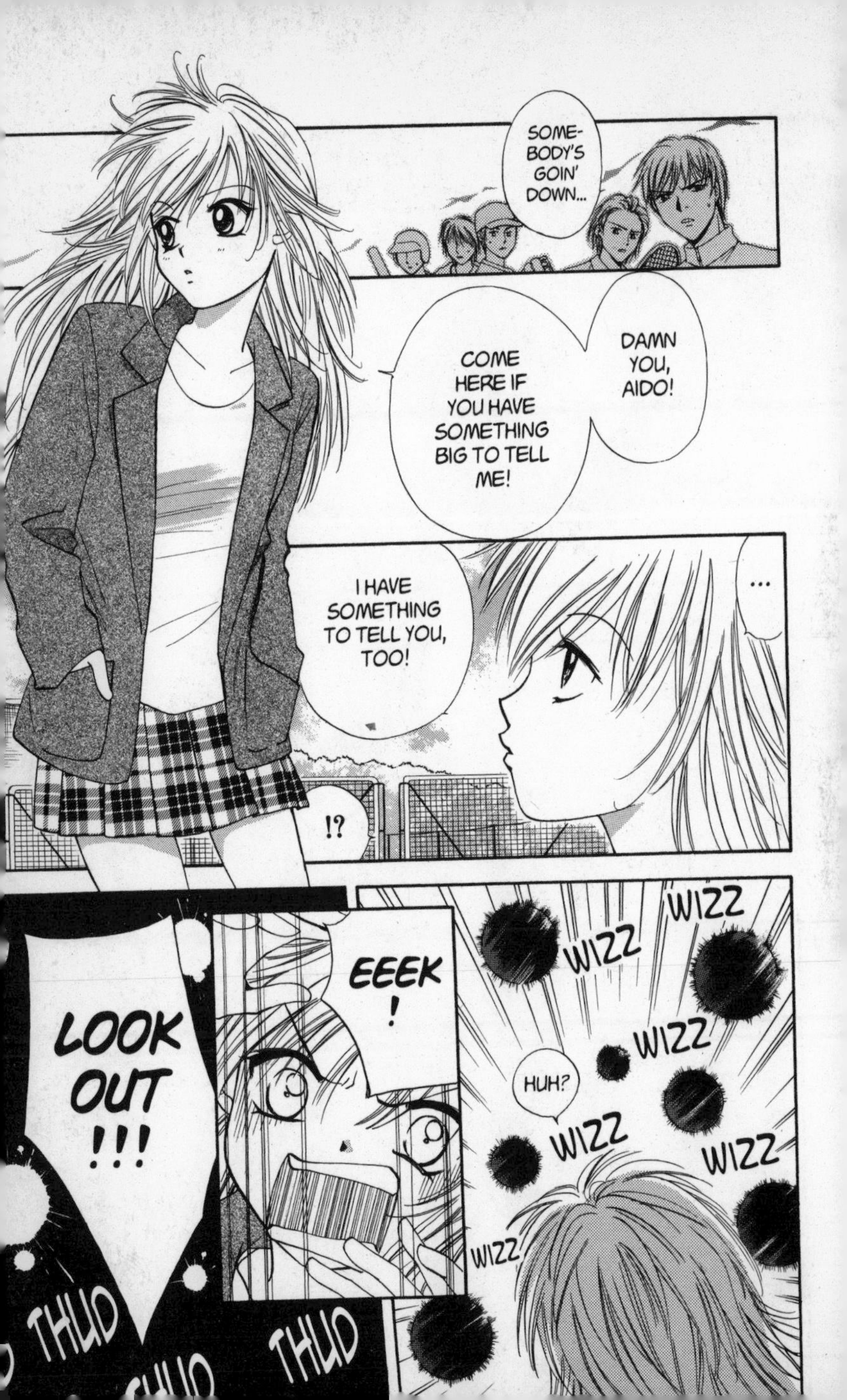
SOME-BODY'S GOIN' DOWN...
DAMN YOU, AIDO!
COME HERE IF YOU HAVE SOMETHING BIG TO TELL ME!
...
I HAVE SOMETHING TO TELL YOU, TOO!
!?
WIZZ
WIZZ
WIZZ
HUH?
WIZZ
WIZZ
WIZZ
EEEK!
LOOK OUT!!!
THUD
THUD

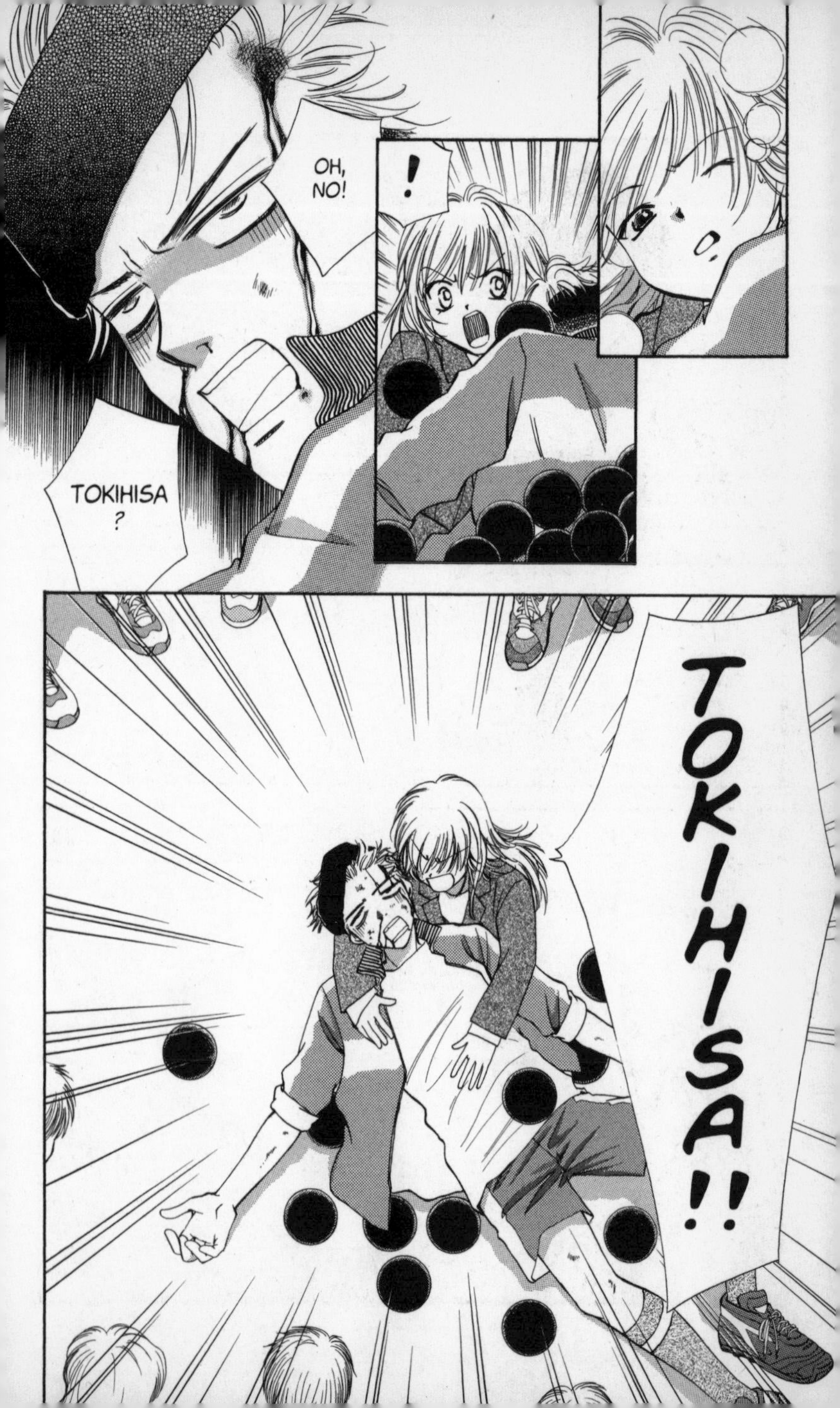
!
OH, NO!
TOKIHISA ?
TOKIHISA!!

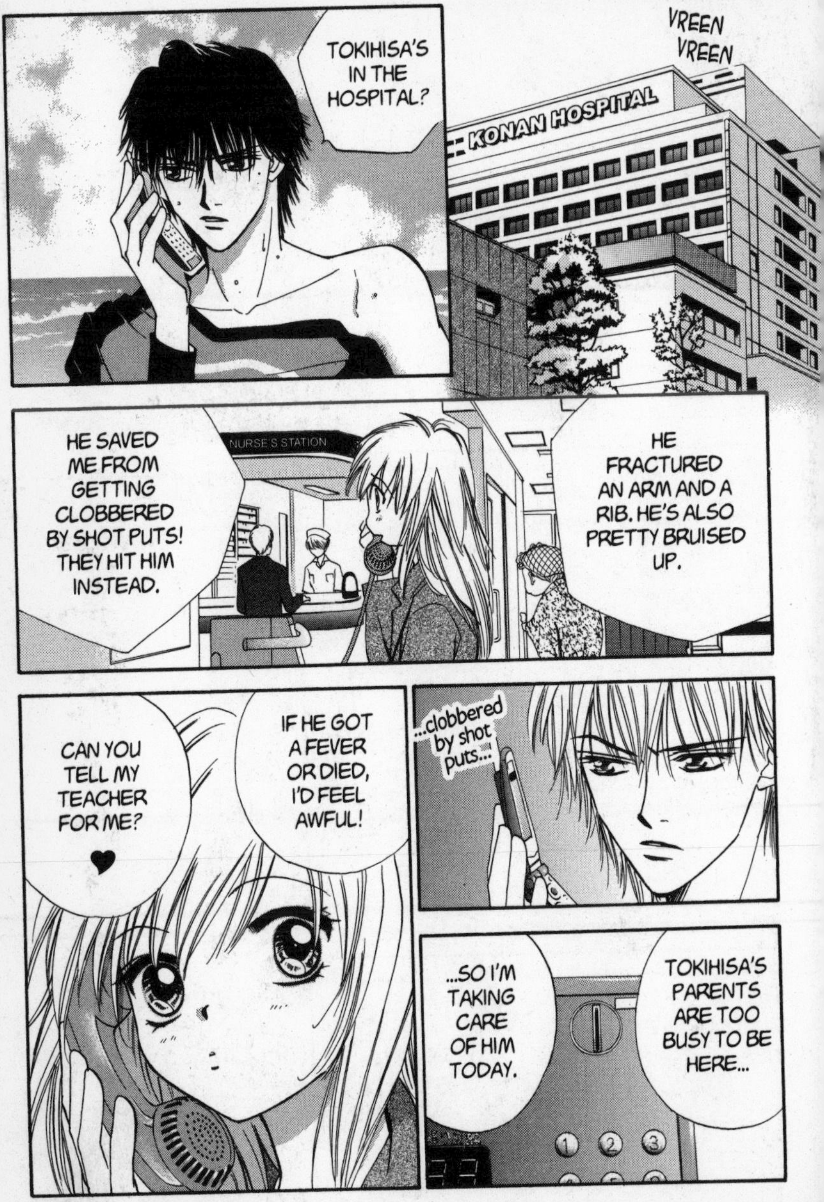
VREEN
VREEN
KONAN HOSPITAL
TOKIHISA'S IN THE HOSPITAL?
HE FRACTURED AN ARM AND A RIB. HE'S ALSO PRETTY BRUISED UP.
NURSE'S STATION
HE SAVED ME FROM GETTING CLOBBERED BY SHOT PUTS! THEY HIT HIM INSTEAD.
...clobbered by shot puts...
TOKIHISA'S PARENTS ARE TOO BUSY TO BE HERE...
...SO I'M TAKING CARE OF HIM TODAY.
IF HE GOT A FEVER OR DIED, I'D FEEL AWFUL!
CAN YOU TELL MY TEACHER FOR ME? ♥

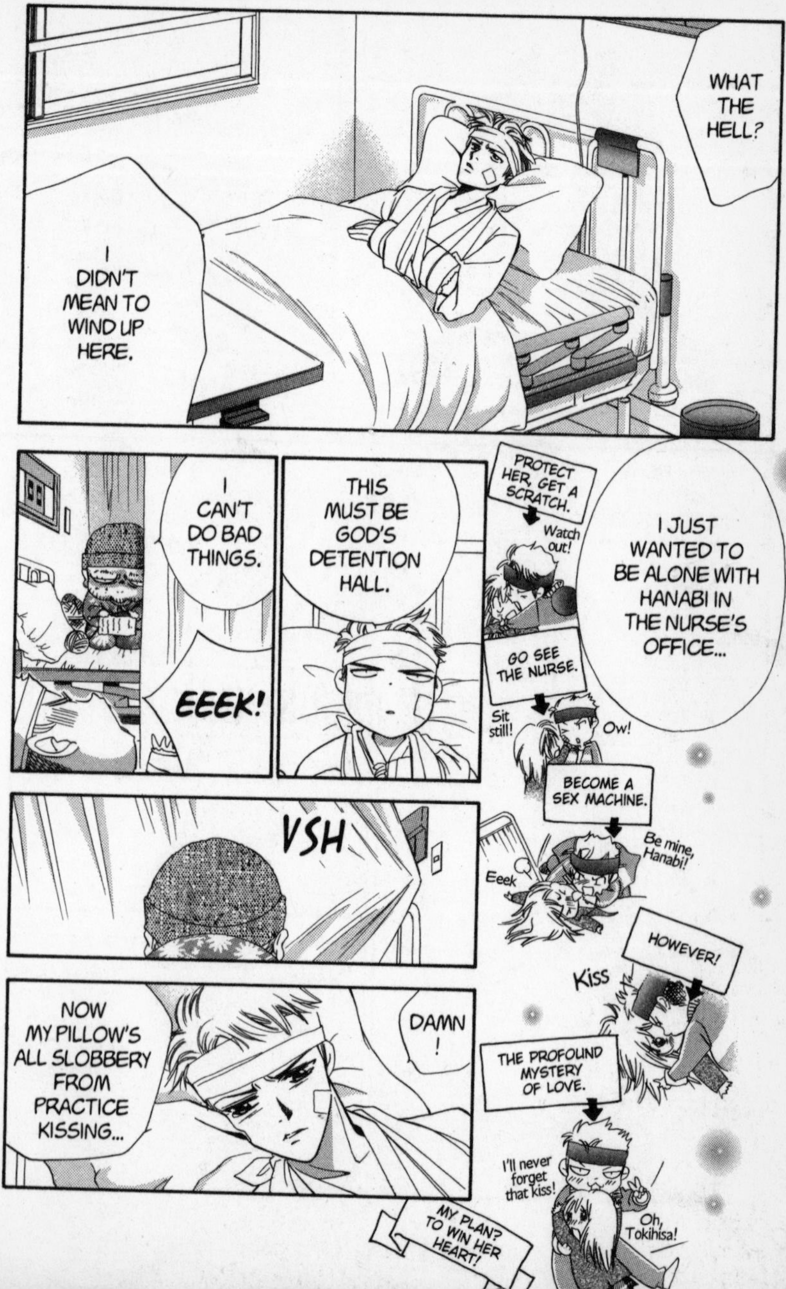
WHAT THE HELL?
I DIDN'T MEAN TO WIND UP HERE.
I JUST WANTED TO BE ALONE WITH HANABI IN THE NURSE'S OFFICE...
PROTECT HER, GET A SCRATCH.
Watch out!
GO SEE THE NURSE.
Sit still!
Ow!
BECOME A SEX MACHINE.
Be mine, Hanabi!
Eeek
HOWEVER!
Kiss
THE PROFOUND MYSTERY OF LOVE.
I'll never forget that kiss!
Oh, Tokihisa!
MY PLAN? TO WIN HER HEART!
THIS MUST BE GOD'S DETENTION HALL.
I CAN'T DO BAD THINGS.
EEEK!
VSH
DAMN!
NOW MY PILLOW'S ALL SLOBBERY FROM PRACTICE KISSING...

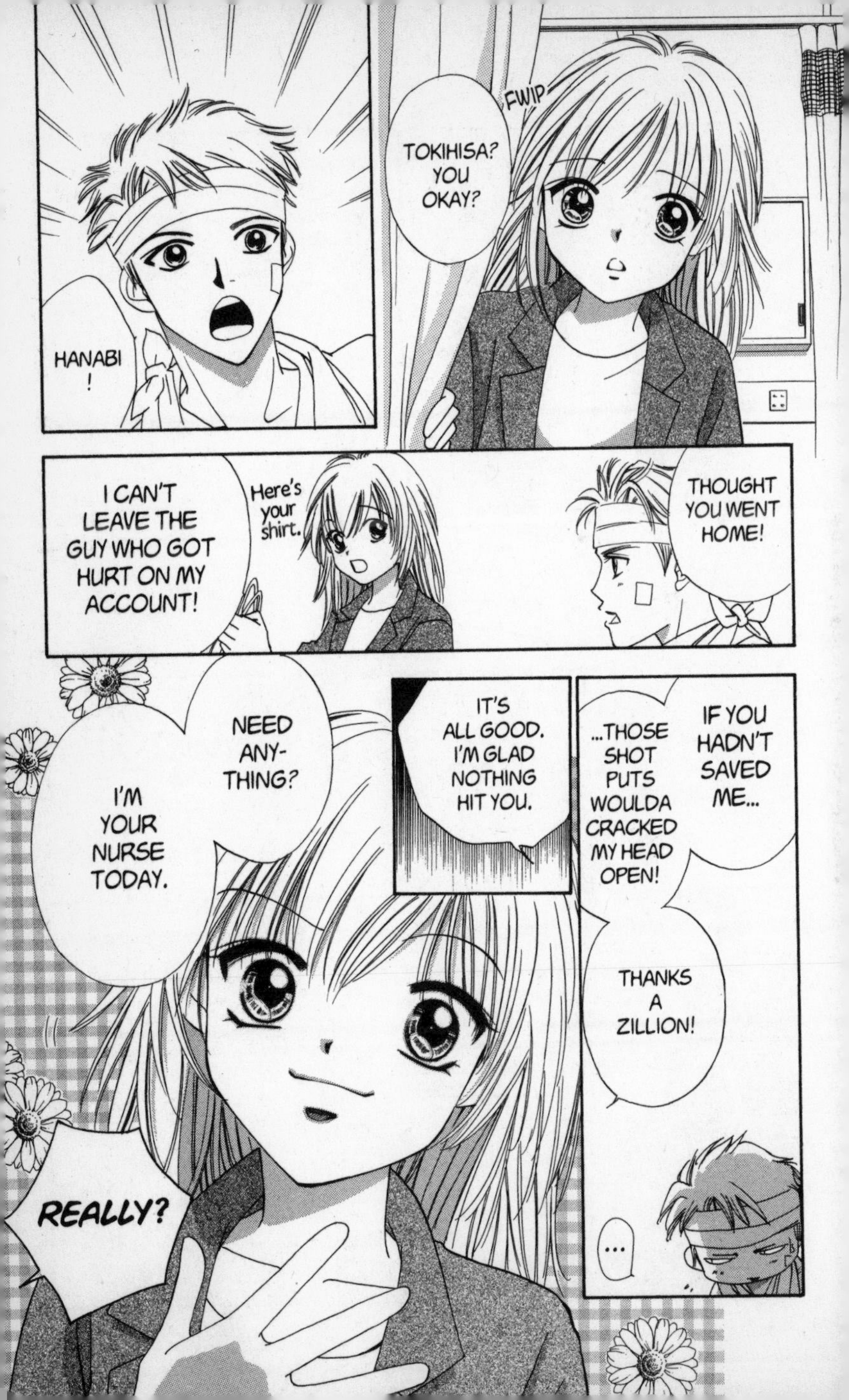
FWIP
TOKIHISA? YOU OKAY?
HANABI!
THOUGHT YOU WENT HOME!
Here's your shirt.
I CAN'T LEAVE THE GUY WHO GOT HURT ON MY ACCOUNT!
IF YOU HADN'T SAVED ME...
...THOSE SHOT PUTS WOULDA CRACKED MY HEAD OPEN!
THANKS A ZILLION!
...
IT'S ALL GOOD. I'M GLAD NOTHING HIT YOU.
NEED ANY-THING?
I'M YOUR NURSE TODAY.
REALLY?

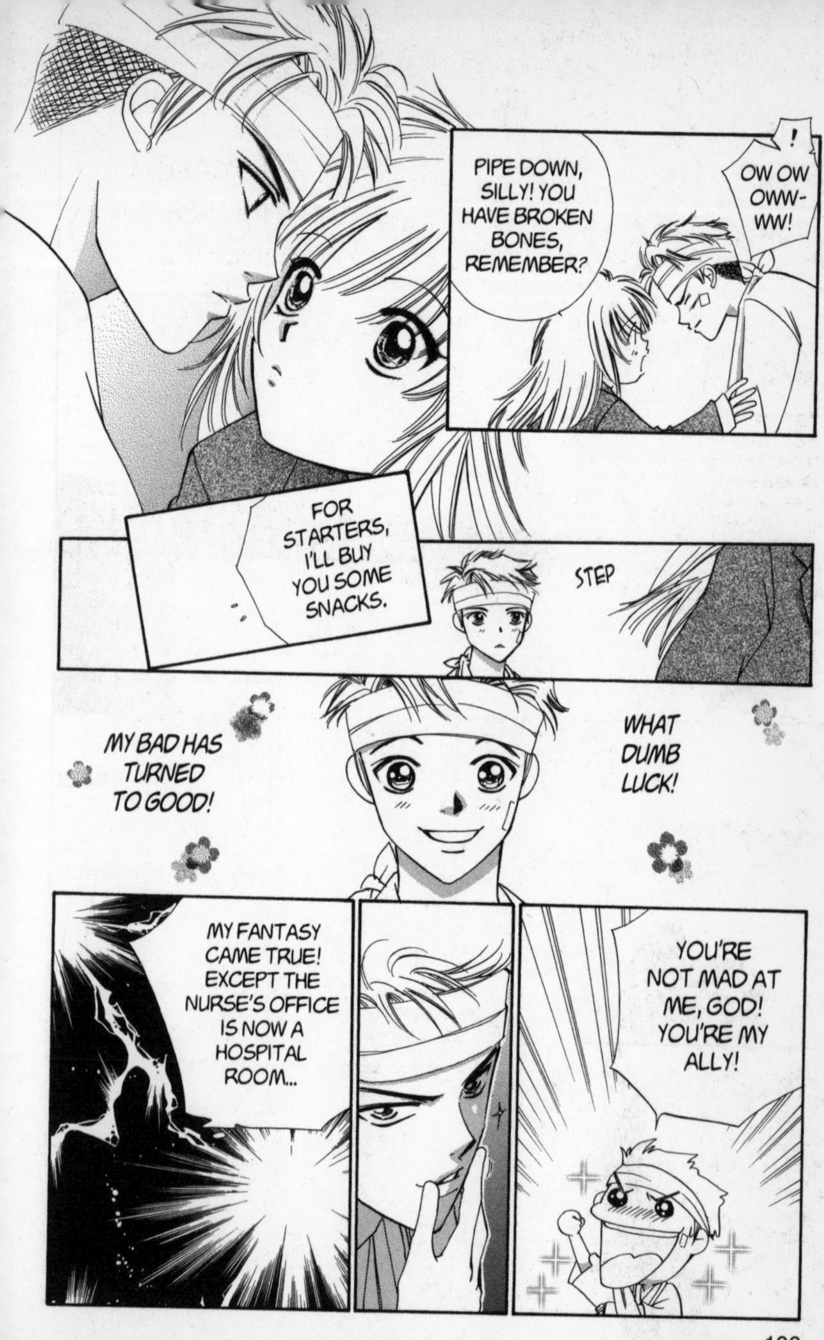
!
OW OW OWW-WW!
PIPE DOWN, SILLY! YOU HAVE BROKEN BONES, REMEMBER?
STEP
FOR STARTERS, I'LL BUY YOU SOME SNACKS.
WHAT DUMB LUCK!
MY BAD HAS TURNED TO GOOD!
YOU'RE NOT MAD AT ME, GOD! YOU'RE MY ALLY!
MY FANTASY CAME TRUE! EXCEPT THE NURSE'S OFFICE IS NOW A HOSPITAL ROOM...

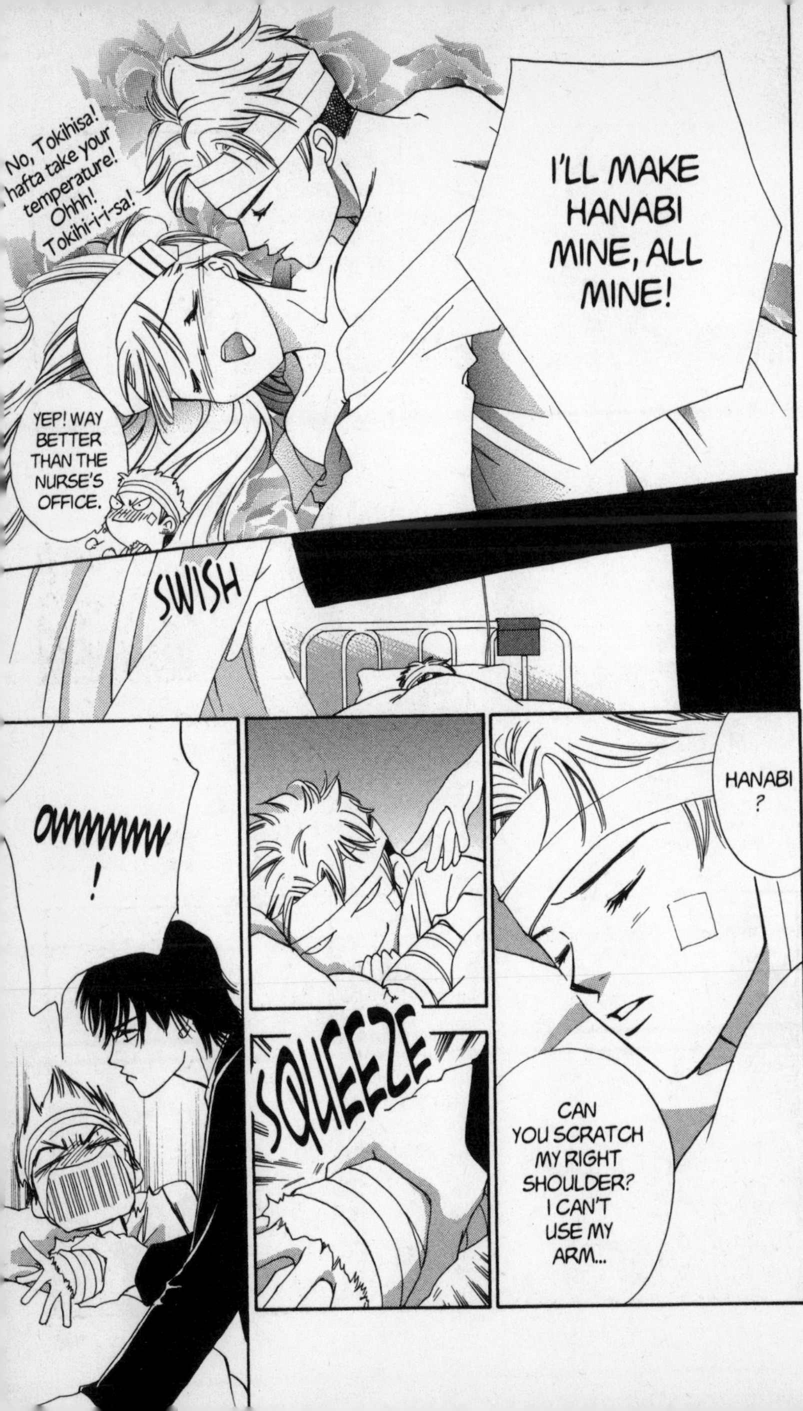
I'LL MAKE HANABI MINE, ALL MINE!
No, Tokihisa! hafta take your temperature! Ohhh! Tokihi-i-i-sa!
YEP! WAY BETTER THAN THE NURSE'S OFFICE.
SWISH
HANABI?
CAN YOU SCRATCH MY RIGHT SHOULDER? I CAN'T USE MY ARM...
SQUEEZE
OWWWWW!

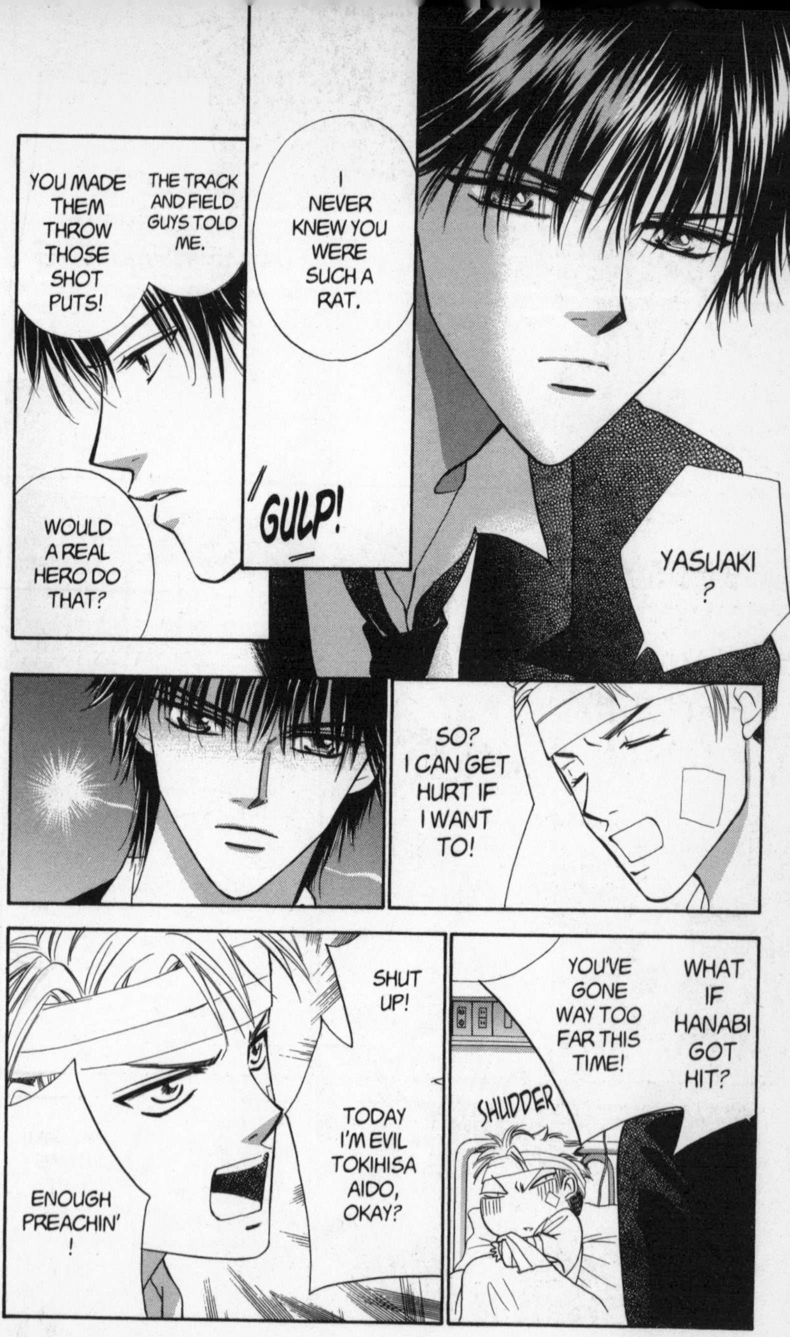
YASUAKI?
I NEVER KNEW YOU WERE SUCH A RAT.
GULP!
THE TRACK AND FIELD GUYS TOLD ME.
YOU MADE THEM THROW THOSE SHOT PUTS!
WOULD A REAL HERO DO THAT?
SO? I CAN GET HURT IF I WANT TO!
WHAT IF HANABI GOT HIT?
YOU'VE GONE WAY TOO FAR THIS TIME!
SHUDDER
SHUT UP!
TODAY I'M EVIL TOKIHISA AIDO, OKAY?
ENOUGH PREACHIN'!

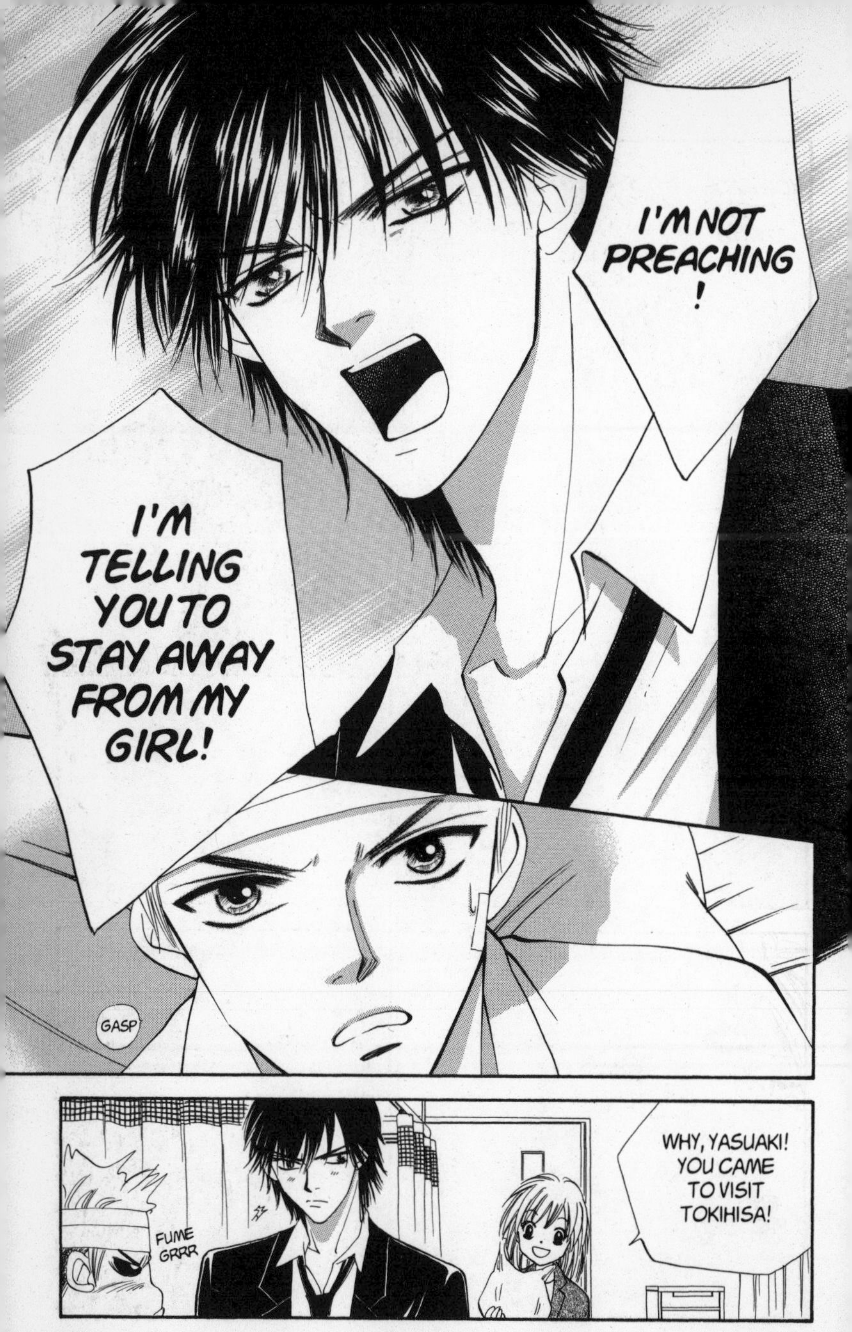
I'M NOT PREACHING !
I'M TELLING YOU TO STAY AWAY FROM MY GIRL!
GASP
WHY, YASUAKI! YOU CAME TO VISIT TOKIHISA!
FUME GRRR

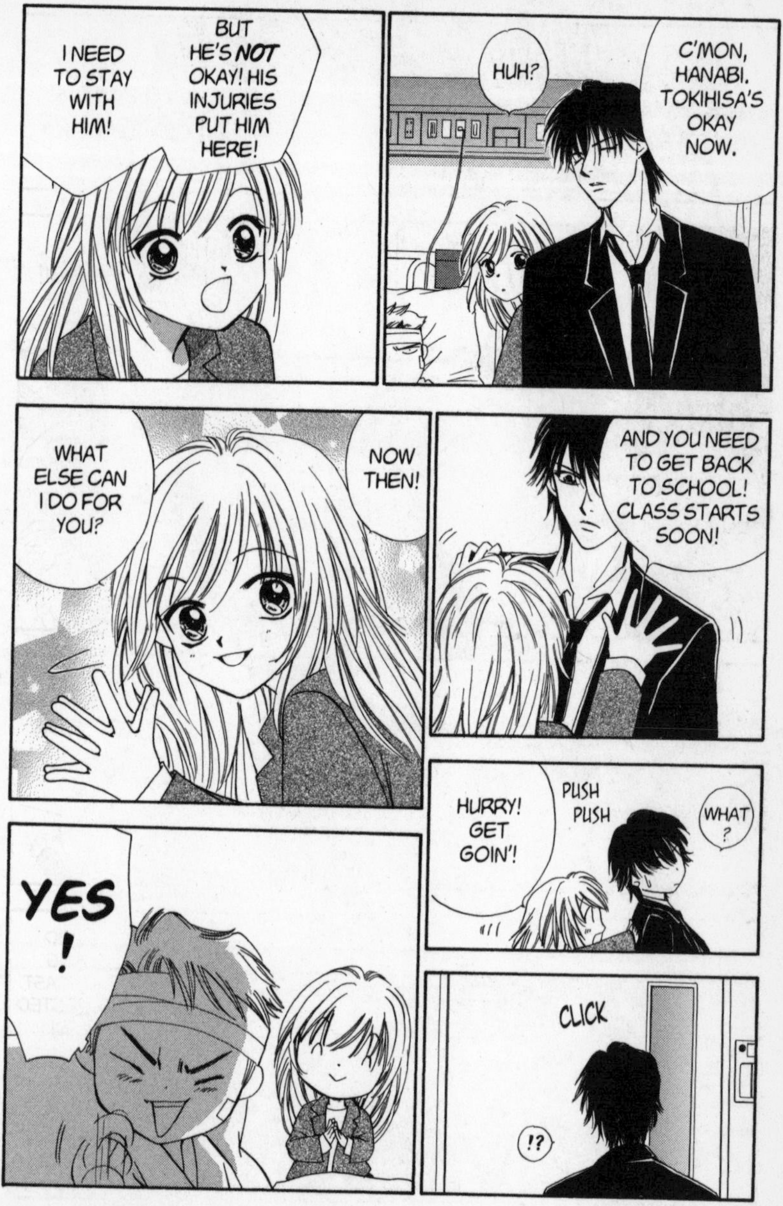
C'MON, HANABI. TOKIHISA'S OKAY NOW.
HUH?
BUT HE'S **NOT** OKAY! HIS INJURIES PUT HIM HERE!
I NEED TO STAY WITH HIM!
AND YOU NEED TO GET BACK TO SCHOOL! CLASS STARTS SOON!
WHAT?
PUSH PUSH
HURRY! GET GOIN'!
CLICK
!?
NOW THEN!
WHAT ELSE CAN I DO FOR YOU?
YES!

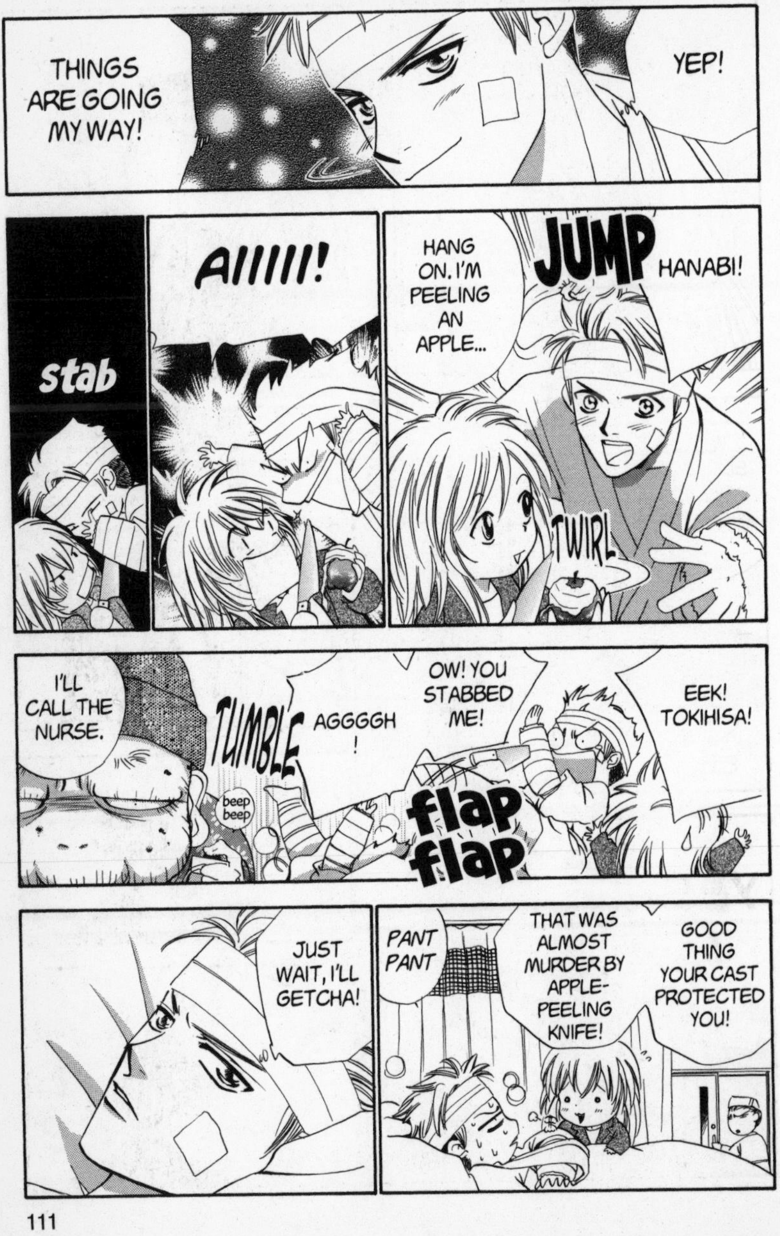
YEP!
THINGS ARE GOING MY WAY!
HANABI!
JUMP
HANG ON. I'M PEELING AN APPLE...
TWIRL
AIIIII!
stab
EEK! TOKIHISA!
OW! YOU STABBED ME!
flap flap
AGGGGH!
TUMBLE
beep beep
I'LL CALL THE NURSE.
GOOD THING YOUR CAST PROTECTED YOU!
THAT WAS ALMOST MURDER BY APPLE-PEELING KNIFE!
PANT PANT
JUST WAIT, I'LL GETCHA!

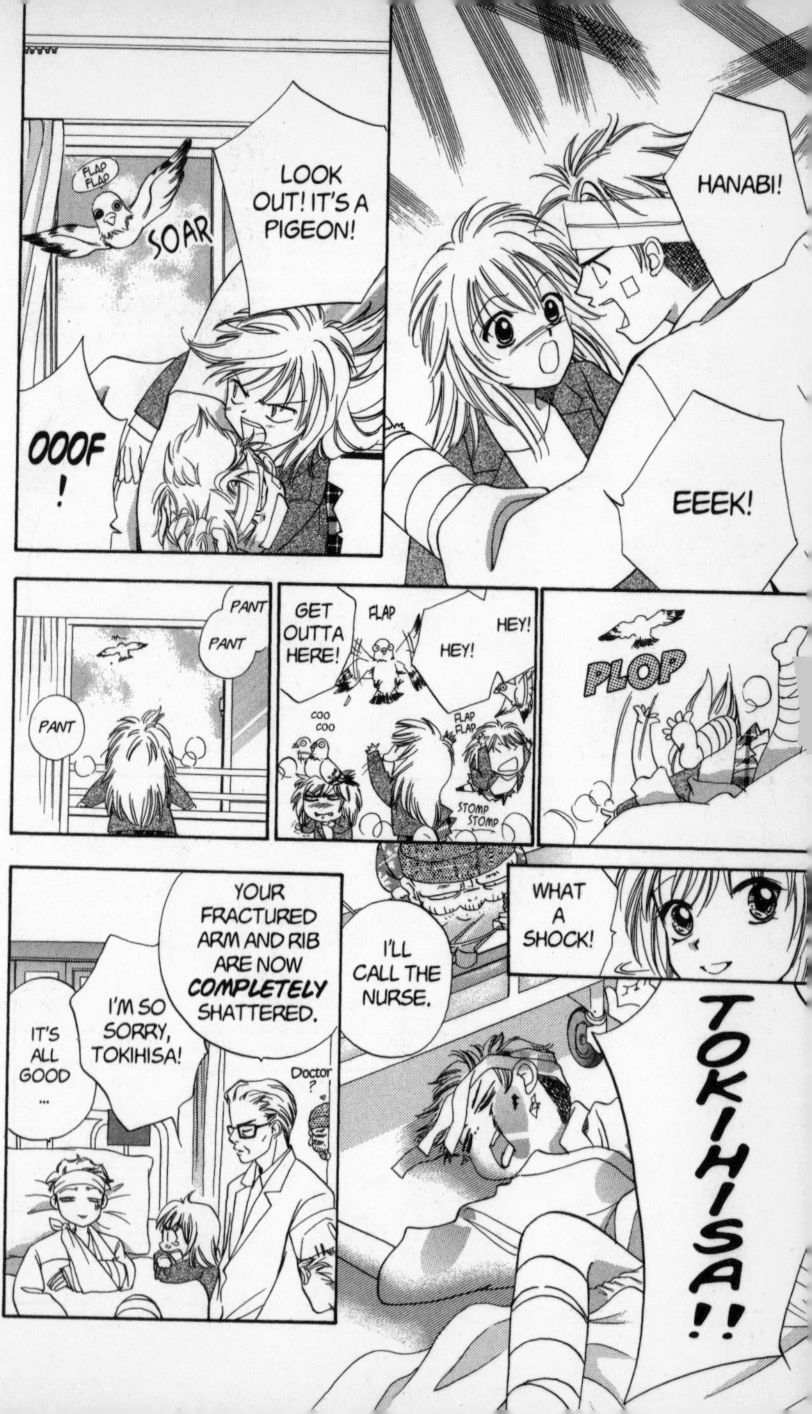
HANABI!
EEEK!
LOOK OUT! IT'S A PIGEON!
FLAP FLAP
SOAR
OOOF!
PLOP
HEY!
HEY!
FLAP
GET OUTTA HERE!
FLAP FLAP
COO COO
STOMP STOMP
PANT
PANT
PANT
WHAT A SHOCK!
I'LL CALL THE NURSE.
TOKIHISA!!
YOUR FRACTURED ARM AND RIB ARE NOW COMPLETELY SHATTERED.
I'M SO SORRY, TOKIHISA!
IT'S ALL GOOD ...
Doctor ?

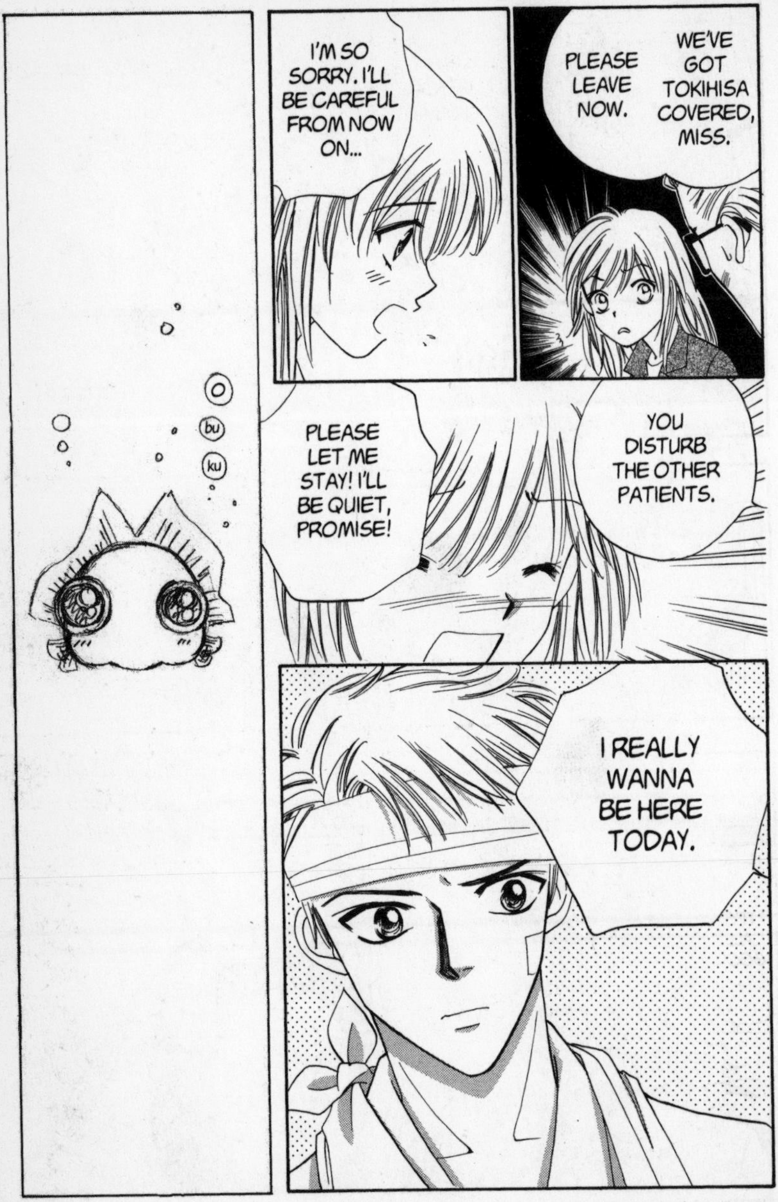
WE'VE GOT TOKIHISA COVERED, MISS.
PLEASE LEAVE NOW.
I'M SO SORRY. I'LL BE CAREFUL FROM NOW ON...
YOU DISTURB THE OTHER PATIENTS.
PLEASE LET ME STAY! I'LL BE QUIET, PROMISE!
I REALLY WANNA BE HERE TODAY.
bu
ku

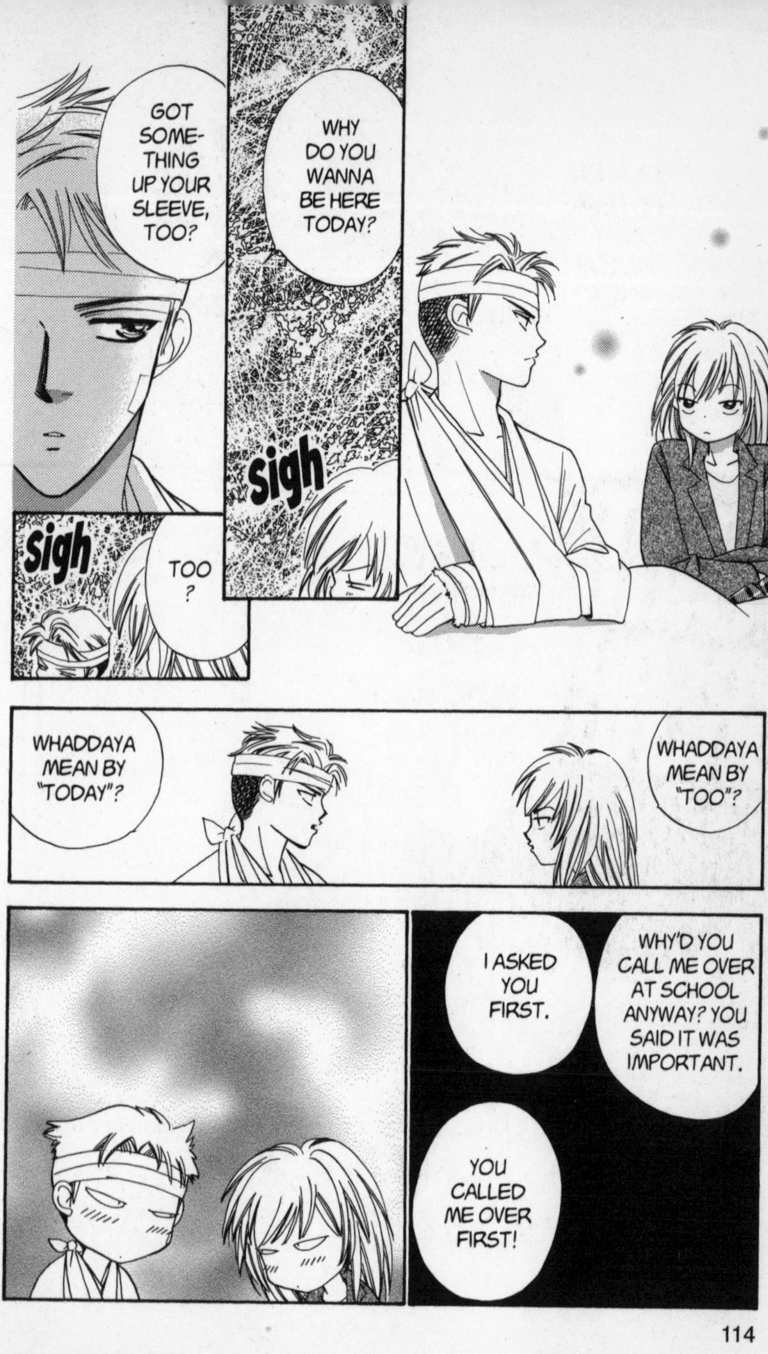
WHY DO YOU WANNA BE HERE TODAY?
sigh
GOT SOME-THING UP YOUR SLEEVE, TOO?
sigh
TOO?
WHADDAYA MEAN BY "TOO"?
WHADDAYA MEAN BY "TODAY"?
WHY'D YOU CALL ME OVER AT SCHOOL ANYWAY? YOU SAID IT WAS IMPORTANT.
I ASKED YOU FIRST.
YOU CALLED ME OVER FIRST!

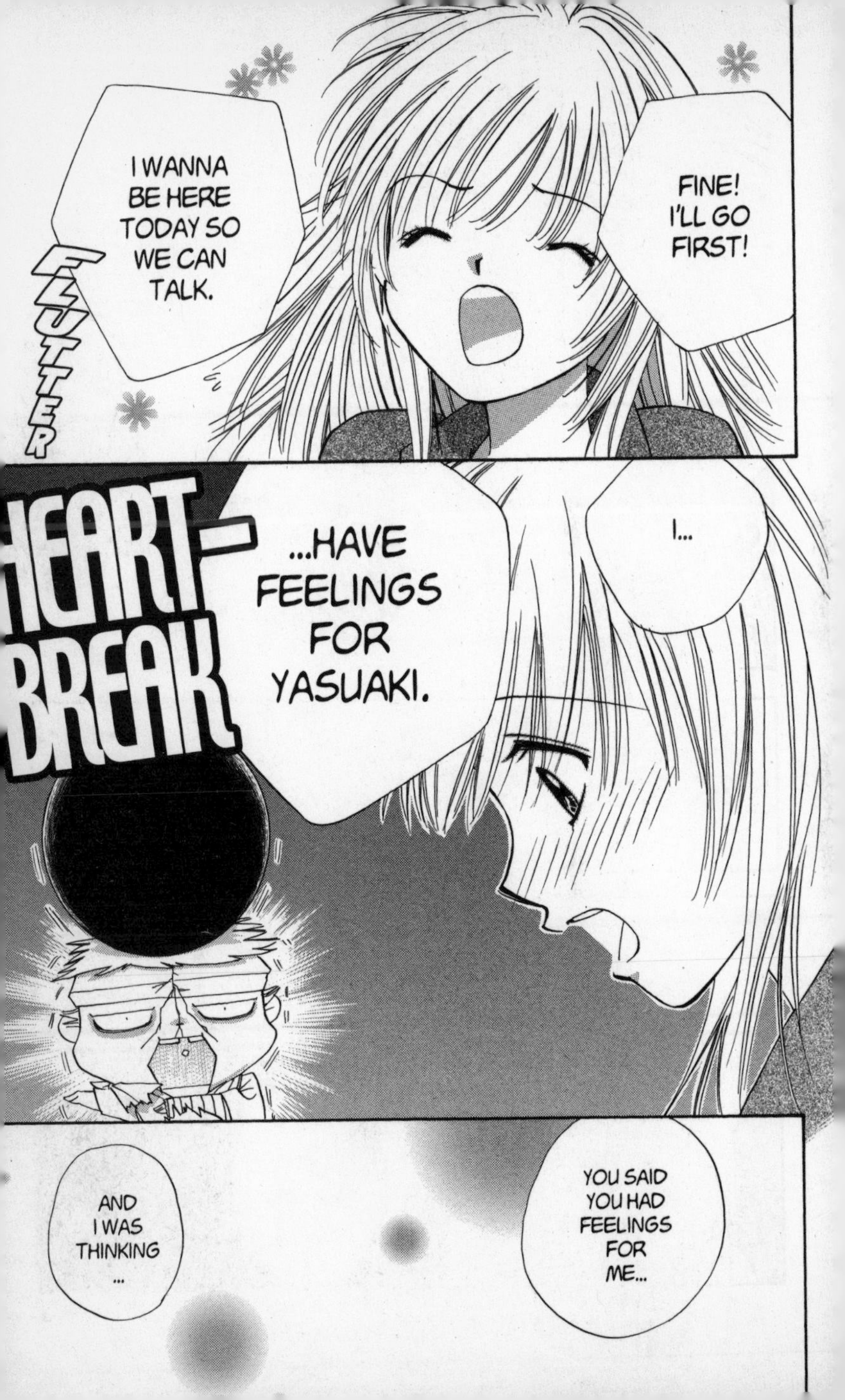

FINE! I'LL GO FIRST!
I WANNA BE HERE TODAY SO WE CAN TALK.
FLUTTER
I...
...HAVE FEELINGS FOR YASUAKI.
HEART-BREAK
YOU SAID YOU HAD FEELINGS FOR ME...
AND I WAS THINKING ...

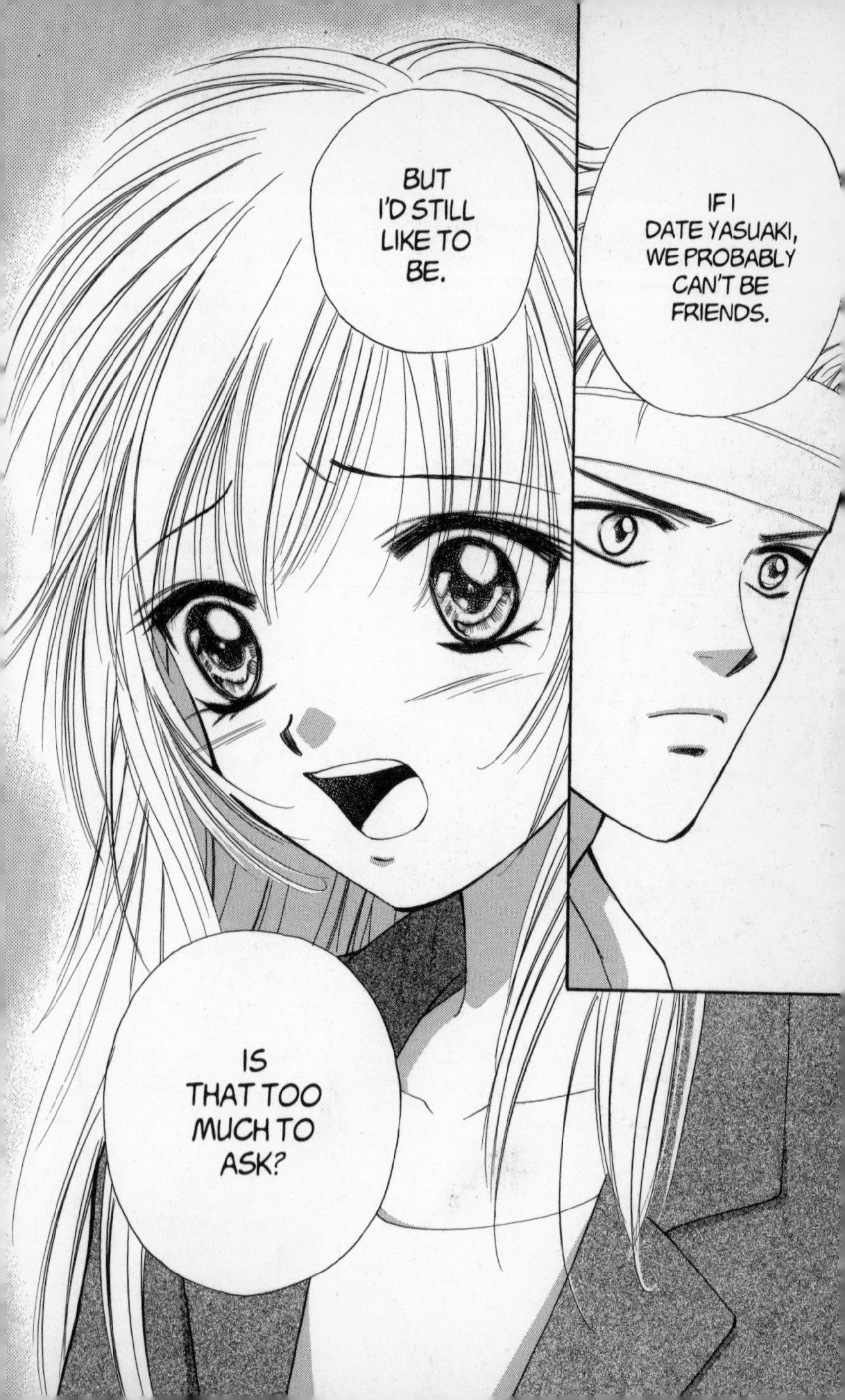
IF I DATE YASUAKI, WE PROBABLY CAN'T BE FRIENDS.
BUT I'D STILL LIKE TO BE.
IS THAT TOO MUCH TO ASK?

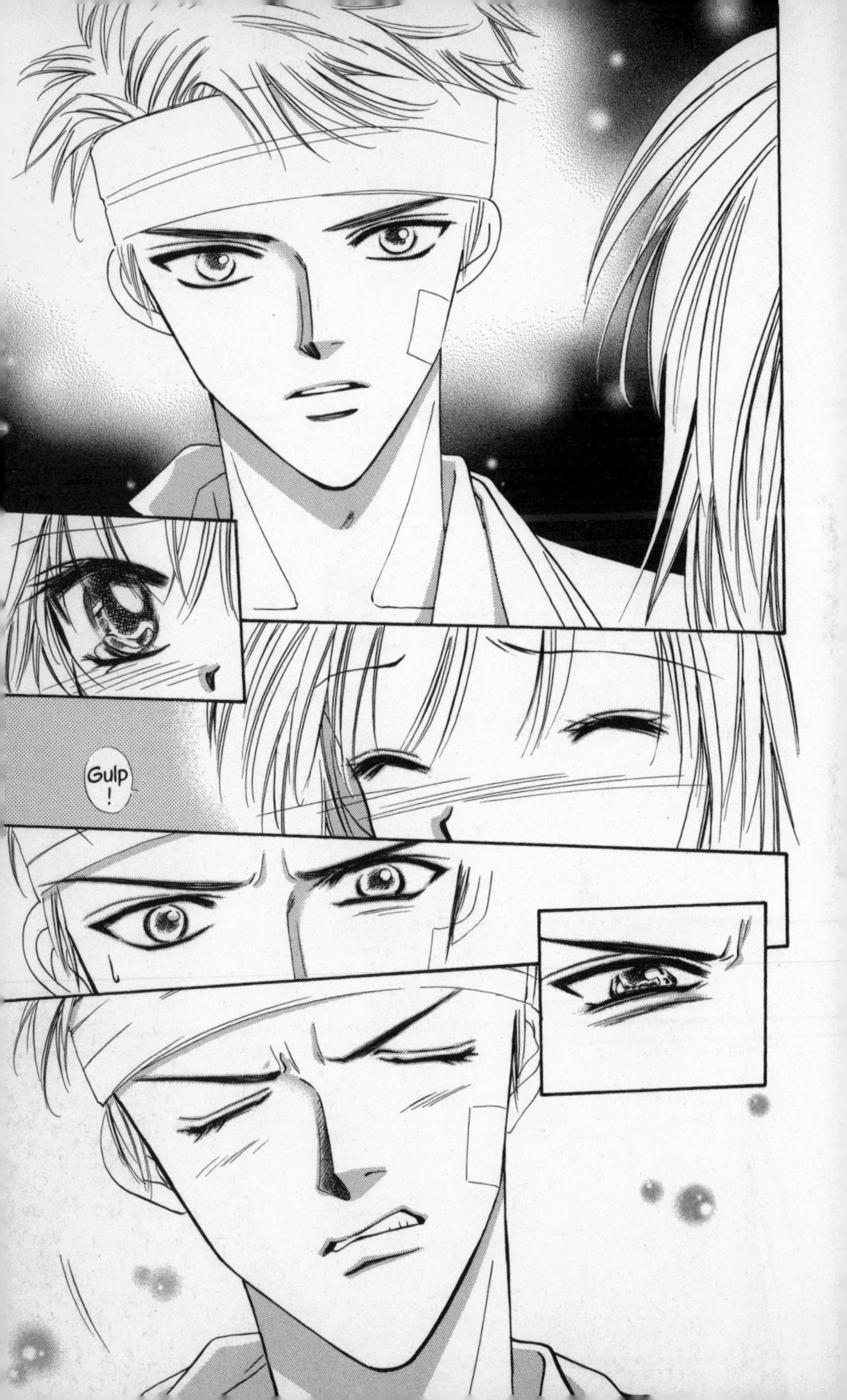
Gulp!

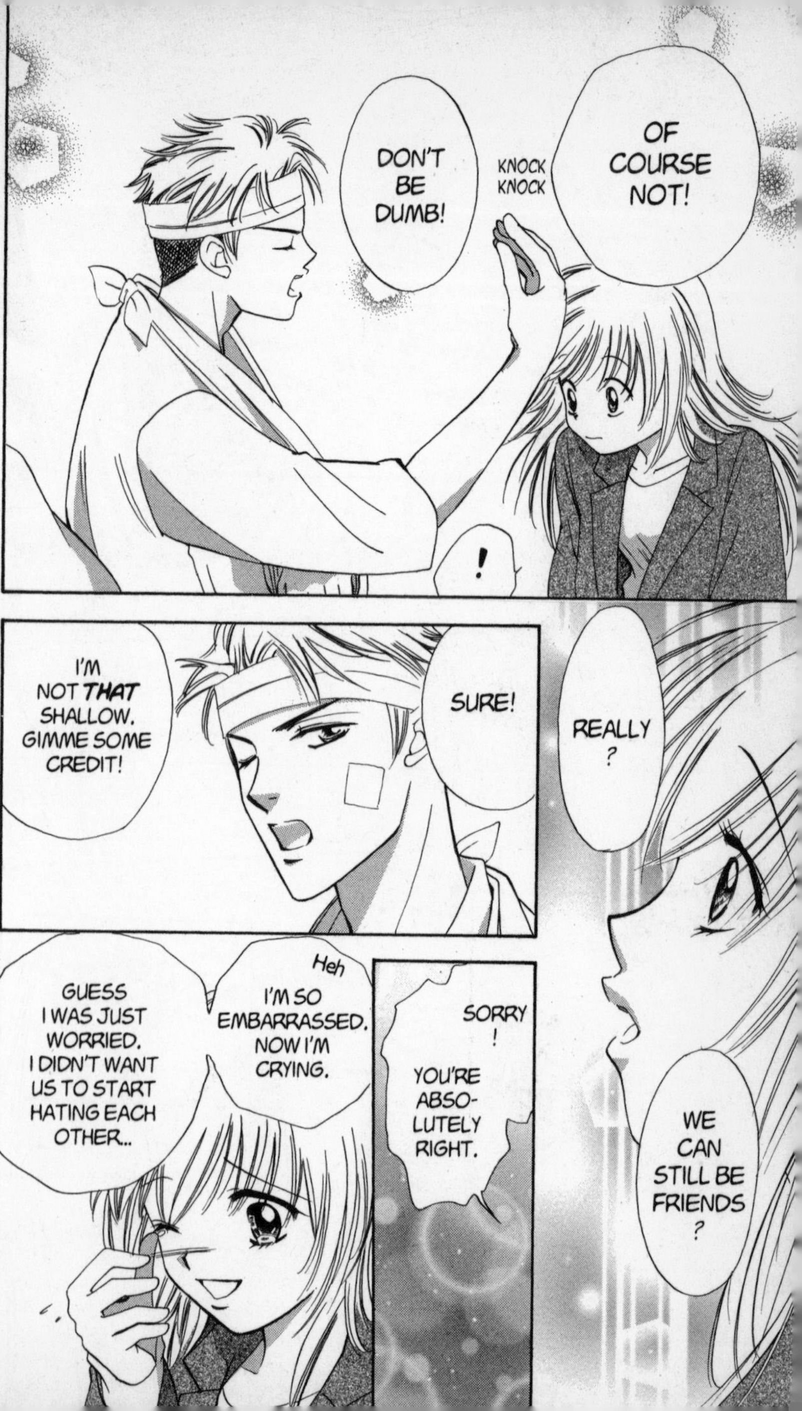
OF COURSE NOT!
KNOCK KNOCK
DON'T BE DUMB!
!
REALLY?
WE CAN STILL BE FRIENDS?
SURE!
I'M NOT THAT SHALLOW. GIMME SOME CREDIT!
SORRY!
YOU'RE ABSOLUTELY RIGHT.
Heh
I'M SO EMBARRASSED. NOW I'M CRYING.
GUESS I WAS JUST WORRIED. I DIDN'T WANT US TO START HATING EACH OTHER...

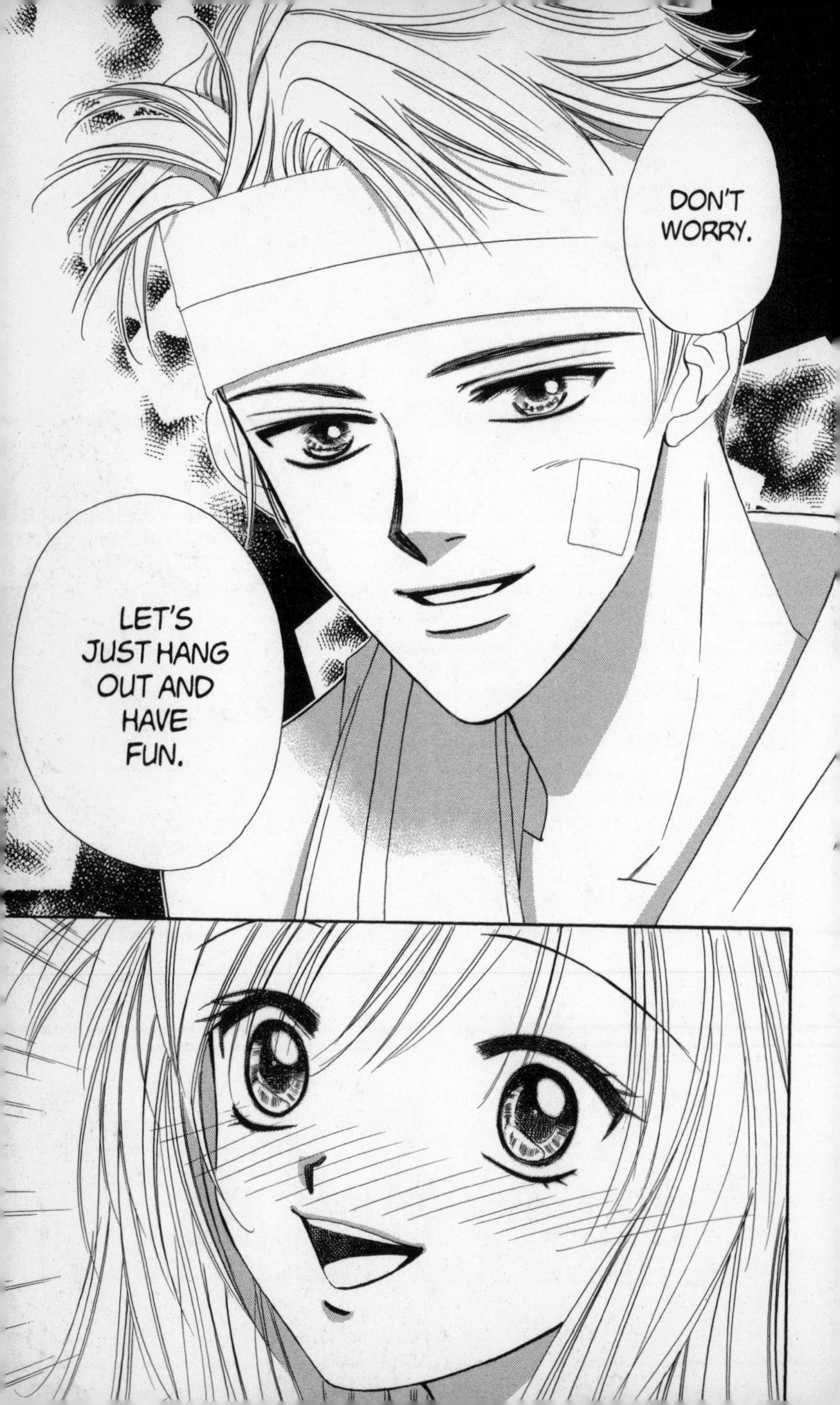
DON'T WORRY.
LET'S JUST HANG OUT AND HAVE FUN.

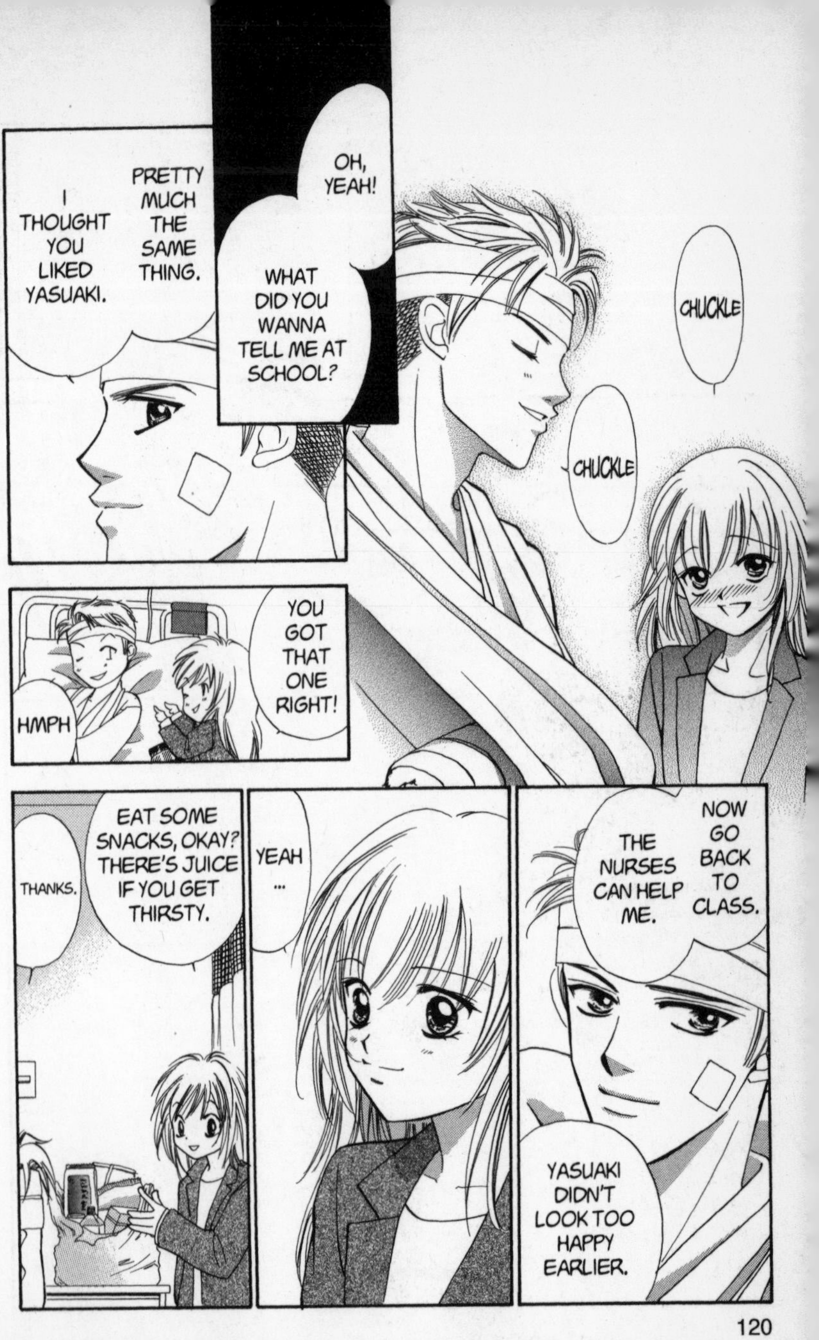
OH, YEAH!
WHAT DID YOU WANNA TELL ME AT SCHOOL?
PRETTY MUCH THE SAME THING.
I THOUGHT YOU LIKED YASUAKI.
CHUCKLE
CHUCKLE
YOU GOT THAT ONE RIGHT!
HMPH
NOW GO BACK TO CLASS.
THE NURSES CAN HELP ME.
YASUAKI DIDN'T LOOK TOO HAPPY EARLIER.
YEAH ...
EAT SOME SNACKS, OKAY? THERE'S JUICE IF YOU GET THIRSTY.
THANKS.

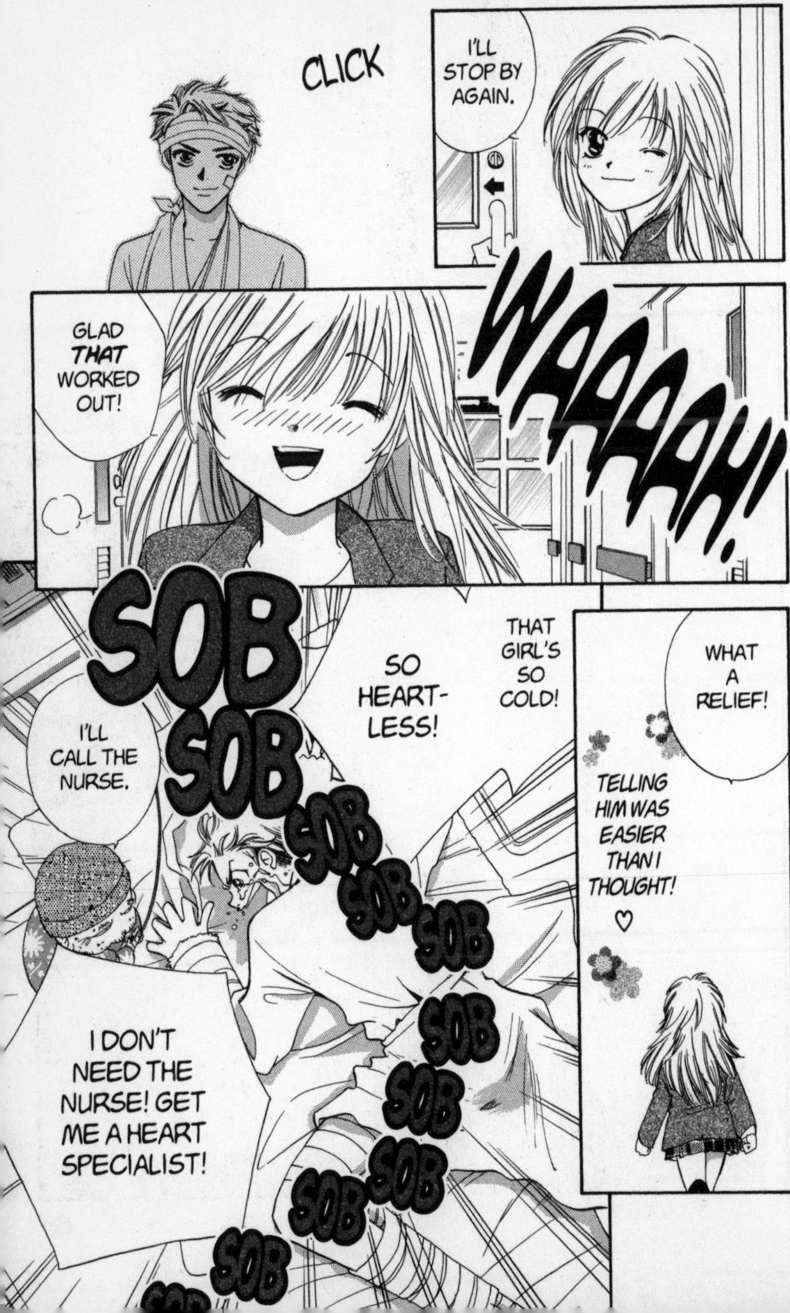
I'LL STOP BY AGAIN.
CLICK
WAAAAAH!
GLAD THAT WORKED OUT!
WHAT A RELIEF!
TELLING HIM WAS EASIER THAN I THOUGHT! ♡
THAT GIRL'S SO COLD!
SO HEART-LESS!
SOB SOB SOB SOB SOB SOB SOB SOB SOB SOB
I'LL CALL THE NURSE.
I DON'T NEED THE NURSE! GET ME A HEART SPECIALIST!

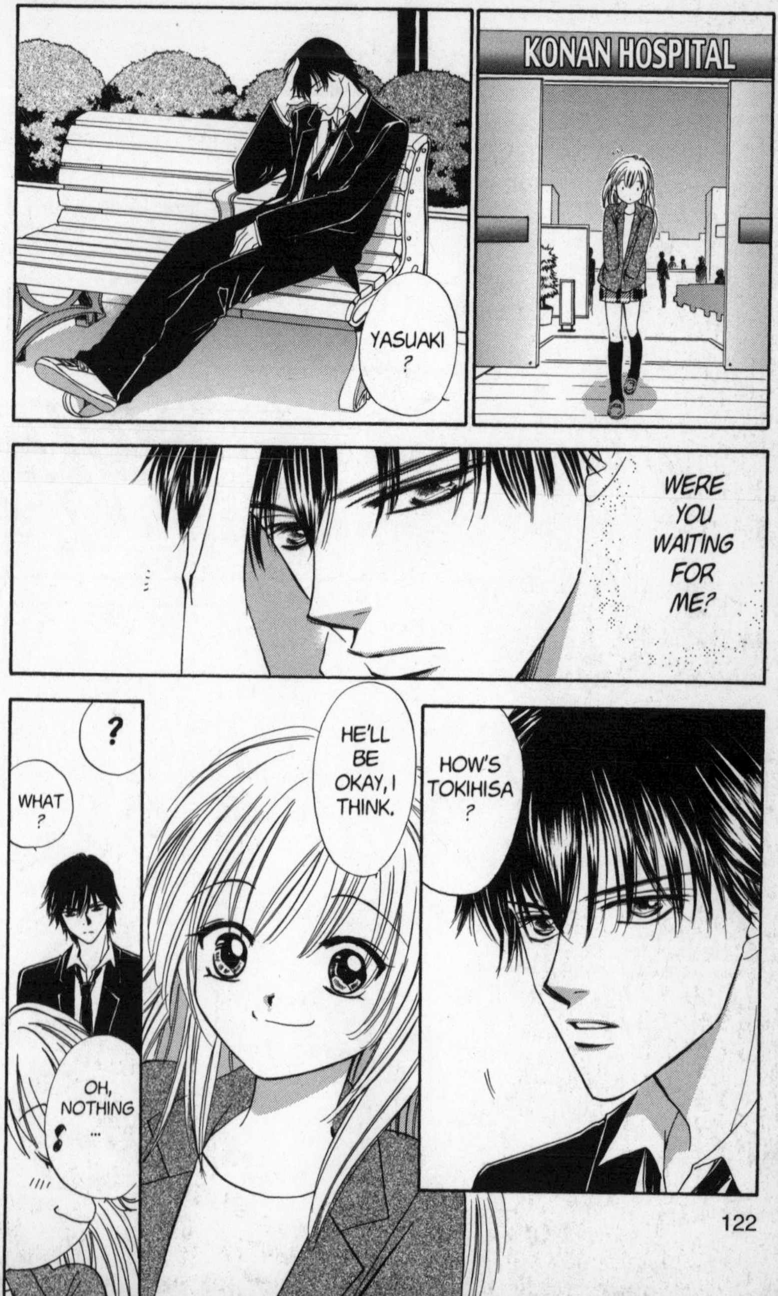
KONAN HOSPITAL
YASUAKI ?
WERE YOU WAITING FOR ME?
HOW'S TOKIHISA ?
HE'LL BE OKAY, I THINK.
?
WHAT ?
OH, NOTHING ...

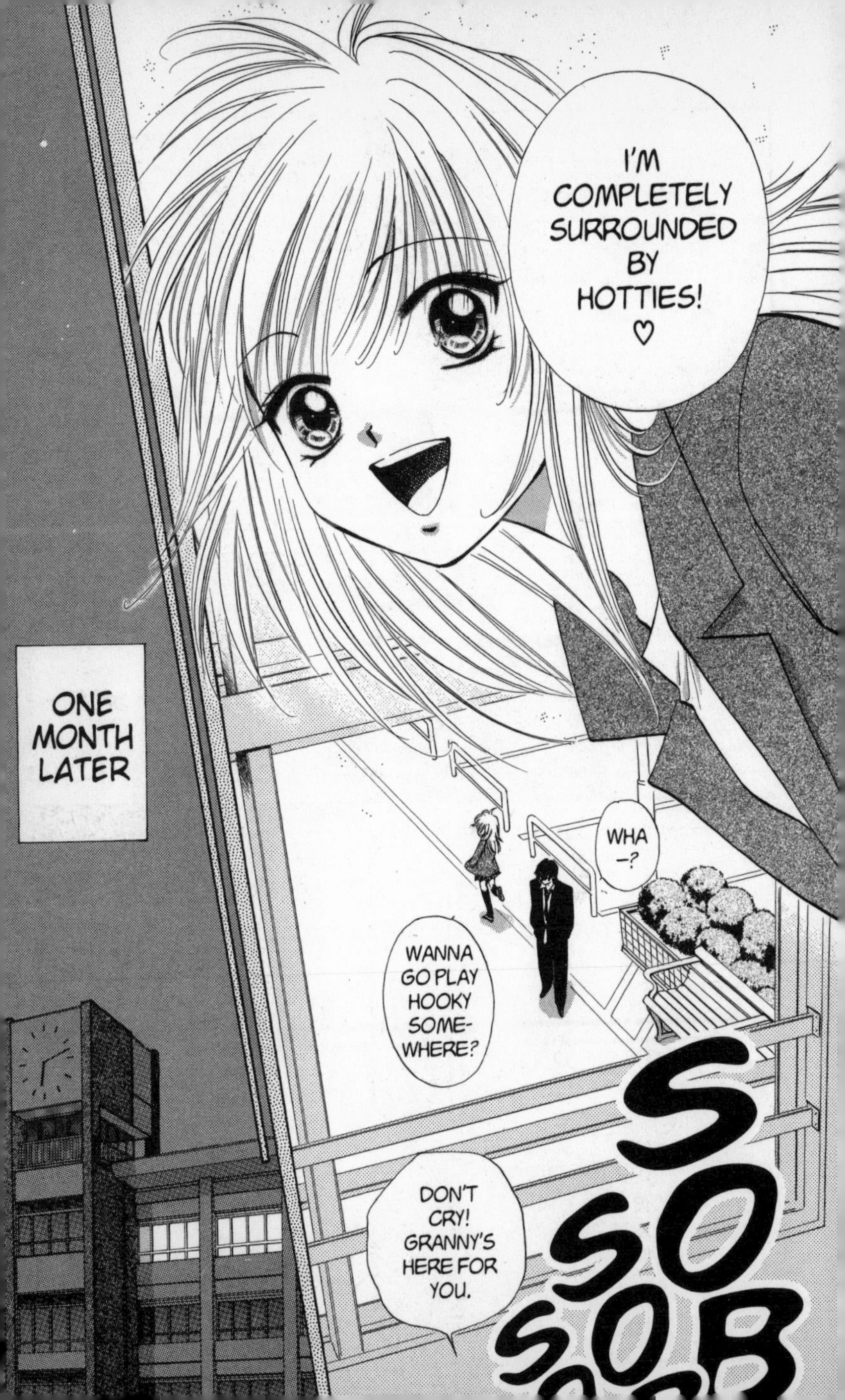

I'M COMPLETELY SURROUNDED BY HOTTIES! ♡
ONE MONTH LATER
WHA-?
WANNA GO PLAY HOOKY SOME-WHERE?
SOB SOB
DON'T CRY! GRANNY'S HERE FOR YOU.

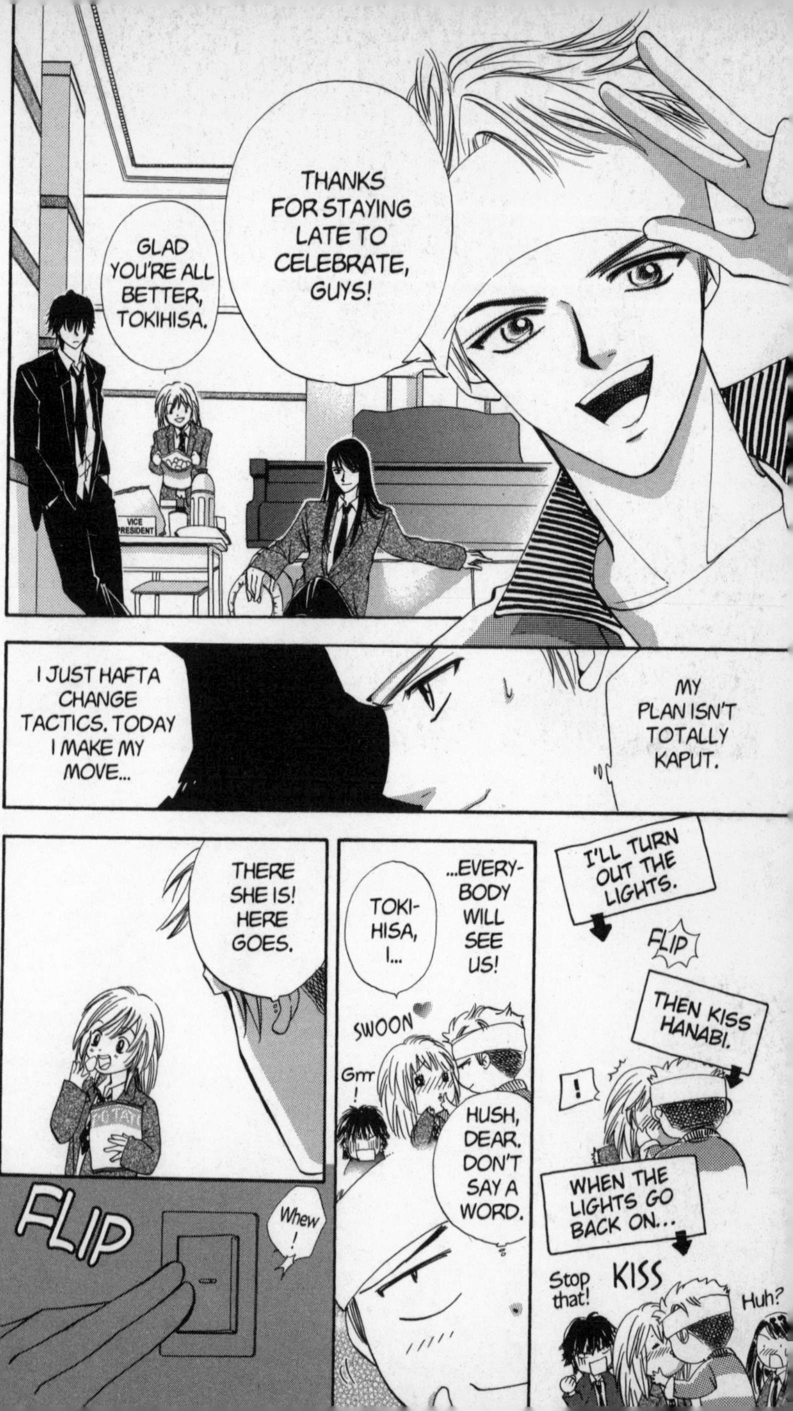
THANKS FOR STAYING LATE TO CELEBRATE, GUYS!
GLAD YOU'RE ALL BETTER, TOKIHISA.
VICE PRESIDENT
MY PLAN ISN'T TOTALLY KAPUT.
I JUST HAFTA CHANGE TACTICS. TODAY I MAKE MY MOVE...
I'LL TURN OUT THE LIGHTS.
FLIP
THEN KISS HANABI.
!
WHEN THE LIGHTS GO BACK ON...
KISS
Huh?
Stop that!
...EVERYBODY WILL SEE US!
TOKIHISA, I...
SWOON
Grrr!
HUSH, DEAR. DON'T SAY A WORD.
Whew!
THERE SHE IS! HERE GOES.
FLIP

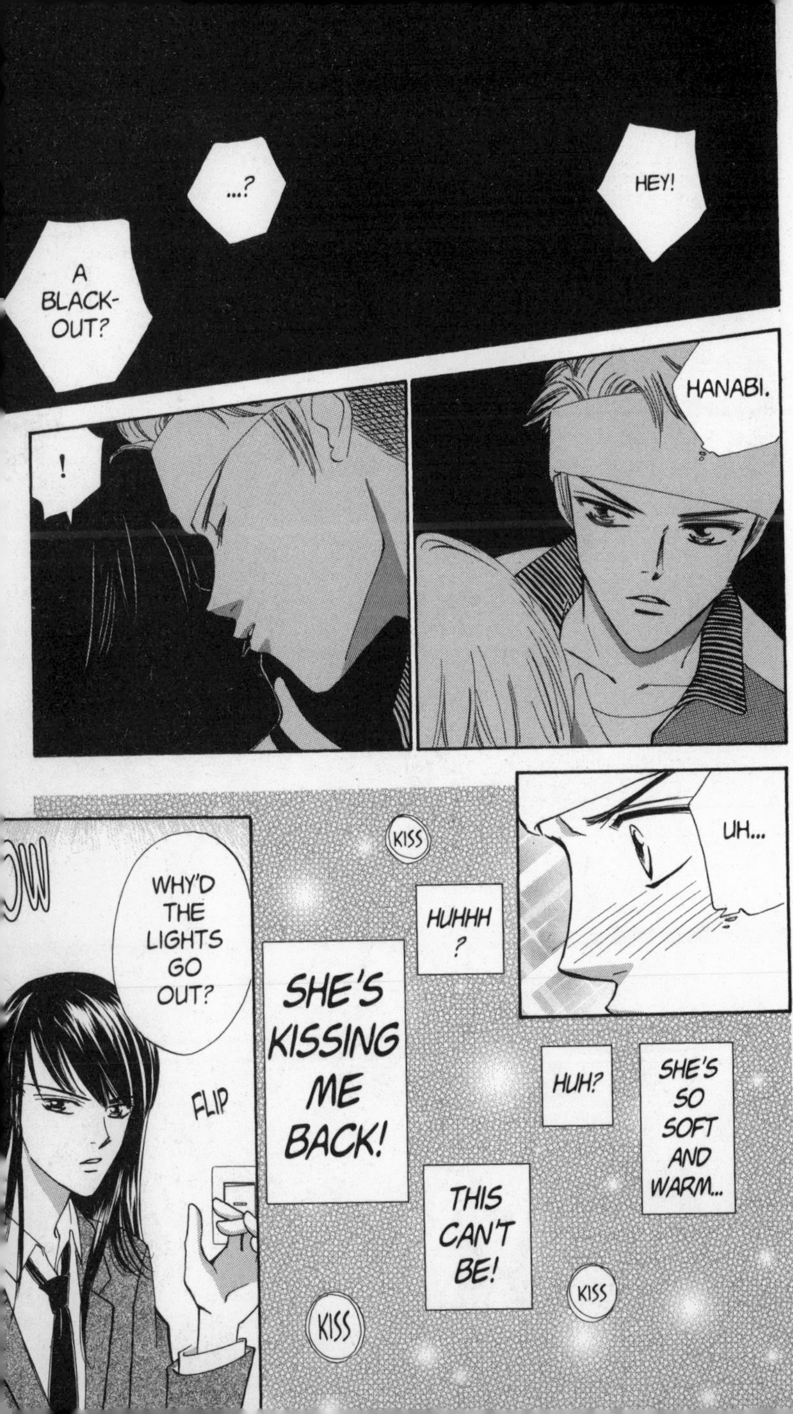
HEY!
...?
A BLACK-OUT?
HANABI.
!
UH...
HUHHH ?
SHE'S SO SOFT AND WARM...
HUH?
SHE'S KISSING ME BACK!
THIS CAN'T BE!
KISS
KISS
KISS
WHY'D THE LIGHTS GO OUT?
FLIP

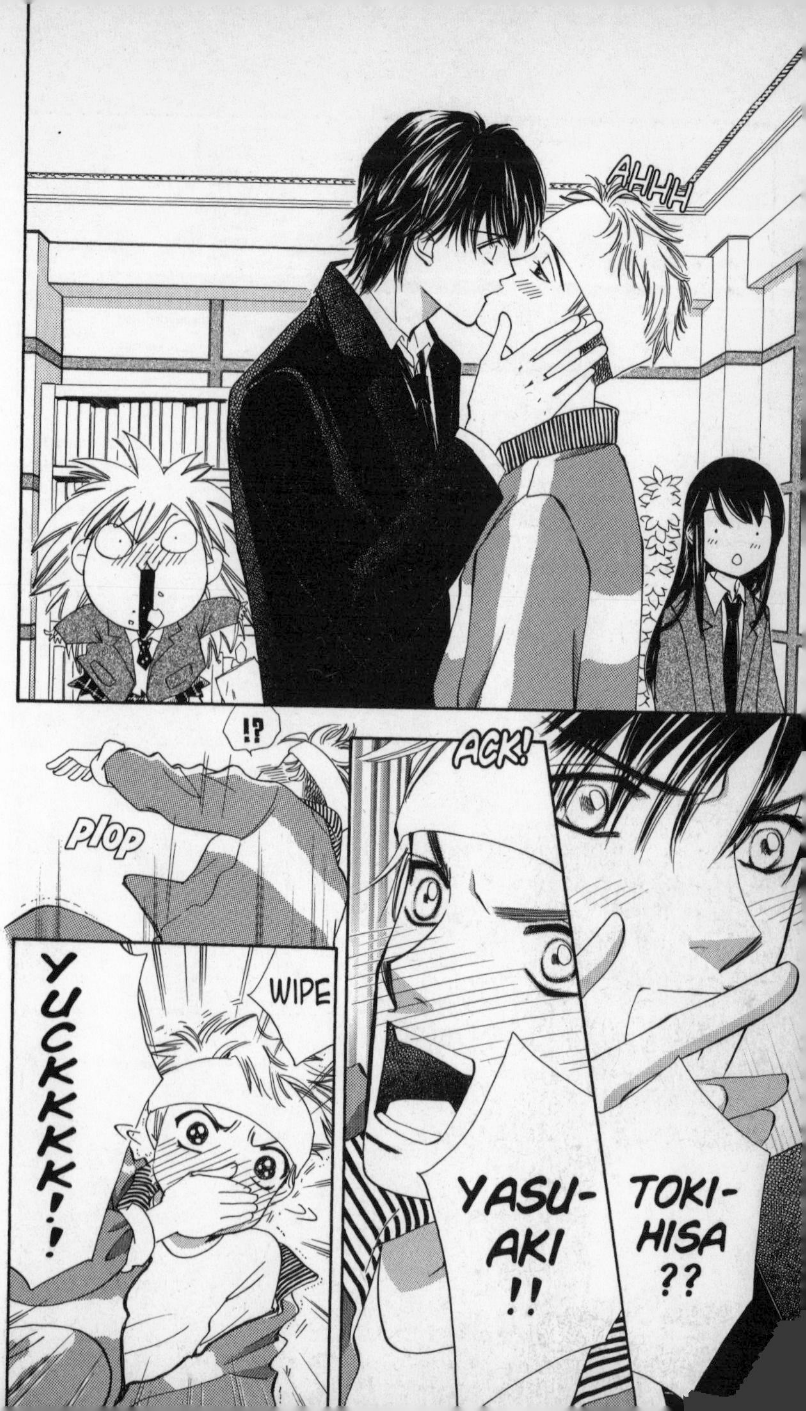
AHHH
ACK!
TOKI-HISA??
YASU-AKI!!
!?
PLOP
WIPE
YUCKKKK!!

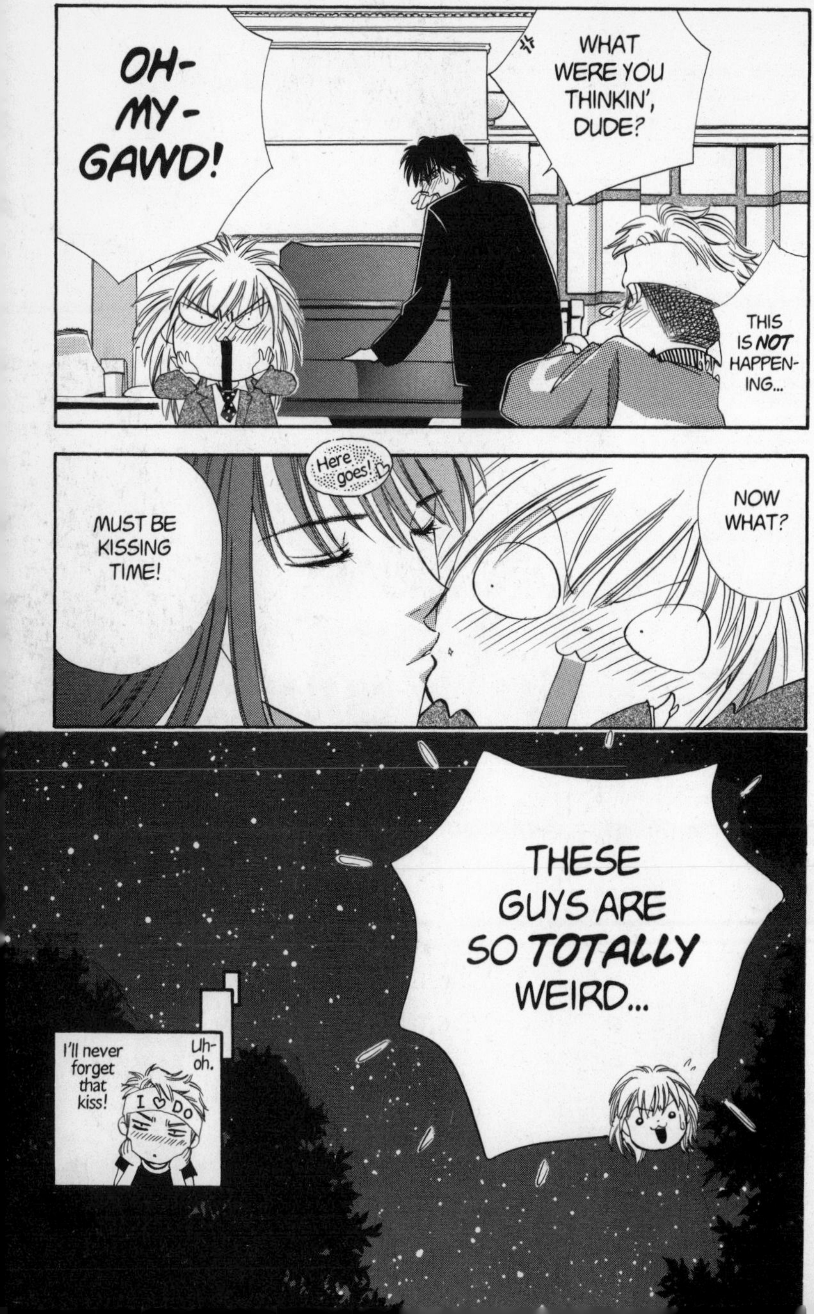
WHAT WERE YOU THINKIN', DUDE?
THIS IS NOT HAPPENING...
OH-MY-GAWD!
NOW WHAT?
Here goes!
MUST BE KISSING TIME!
THESE GUYS ARE SO TOTALLY WEIRD...
Uh-oh.
I'll never forget that kiss!
I ♡ DO

HAPPY
HUSTLE
HIGH

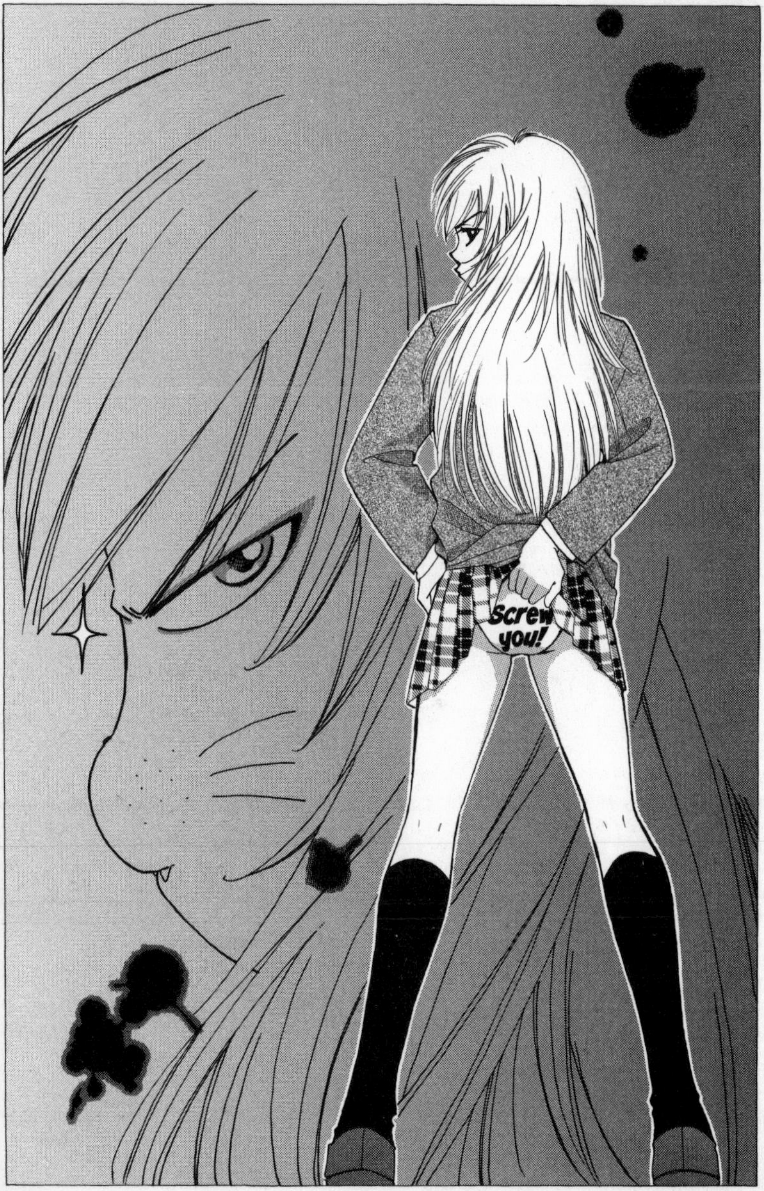
Screw you!

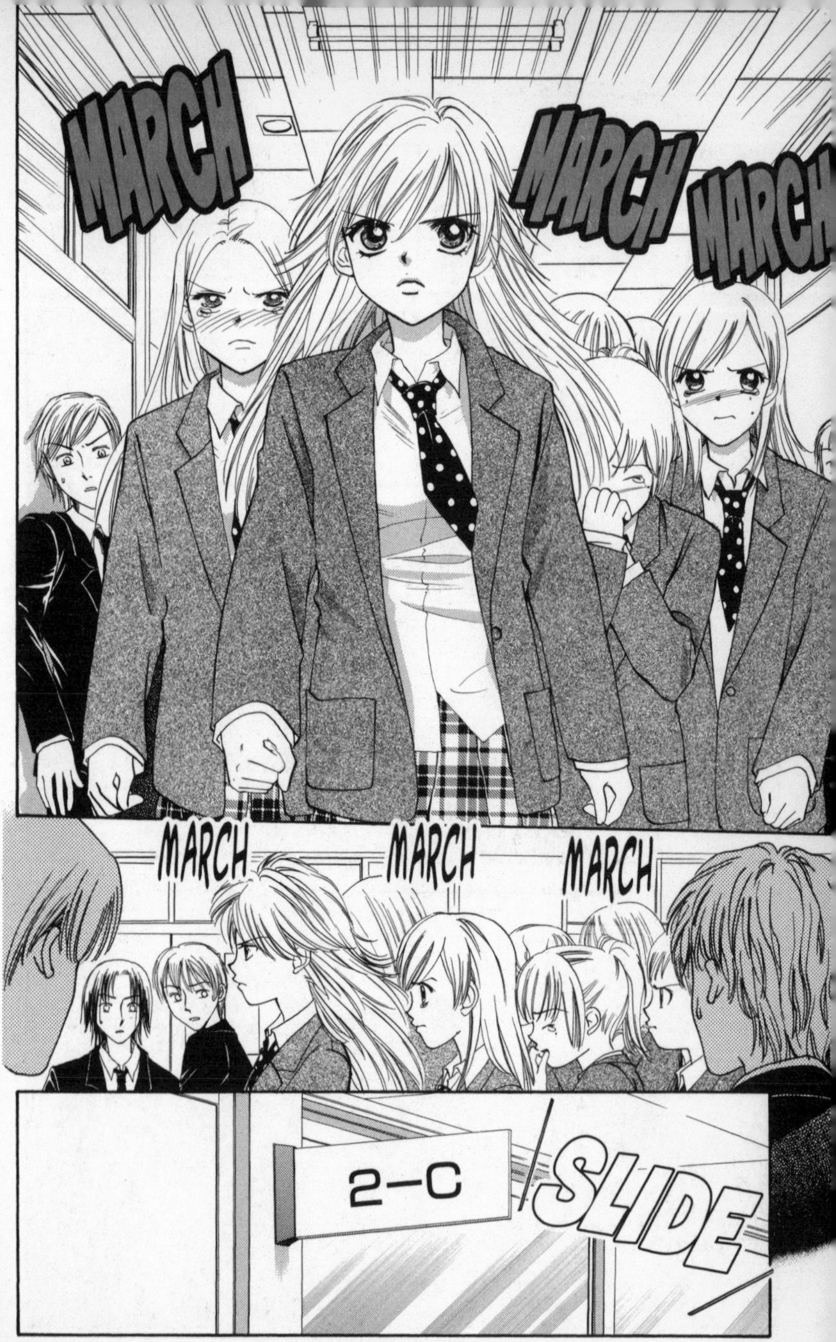

MARCH
MARCH
MARCH
MARCH
MARCH
MARCH
SLIDE
2-C

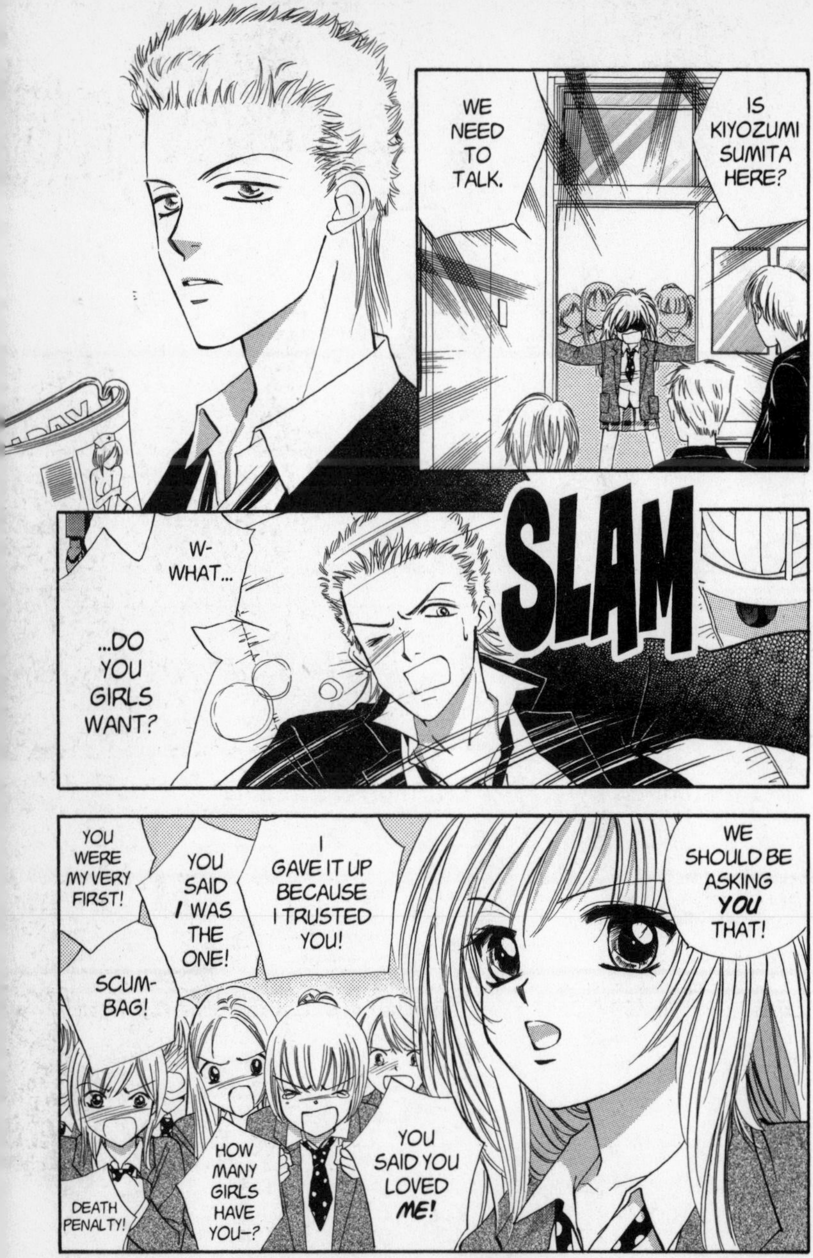
IS KIYOZUMI SUMITA HERE?
WE NEED TO TALK.
SLAM
W-WHAT...
...DO YOU GIRLS WANT?
WE SHOULD BE ASKING **YOU** THAT!
I GAVE IT UP BECAUSE I TRUSTED YOU!
YOU SAID **I** WAS THE ONE!
YOU WERE MY VERY FIRST!
SCUM-BAG!
YOU SAID YOU LOVED **ME!**
HOW MANY GIRLS HAVE YOU–?
DEATH PENALTY!

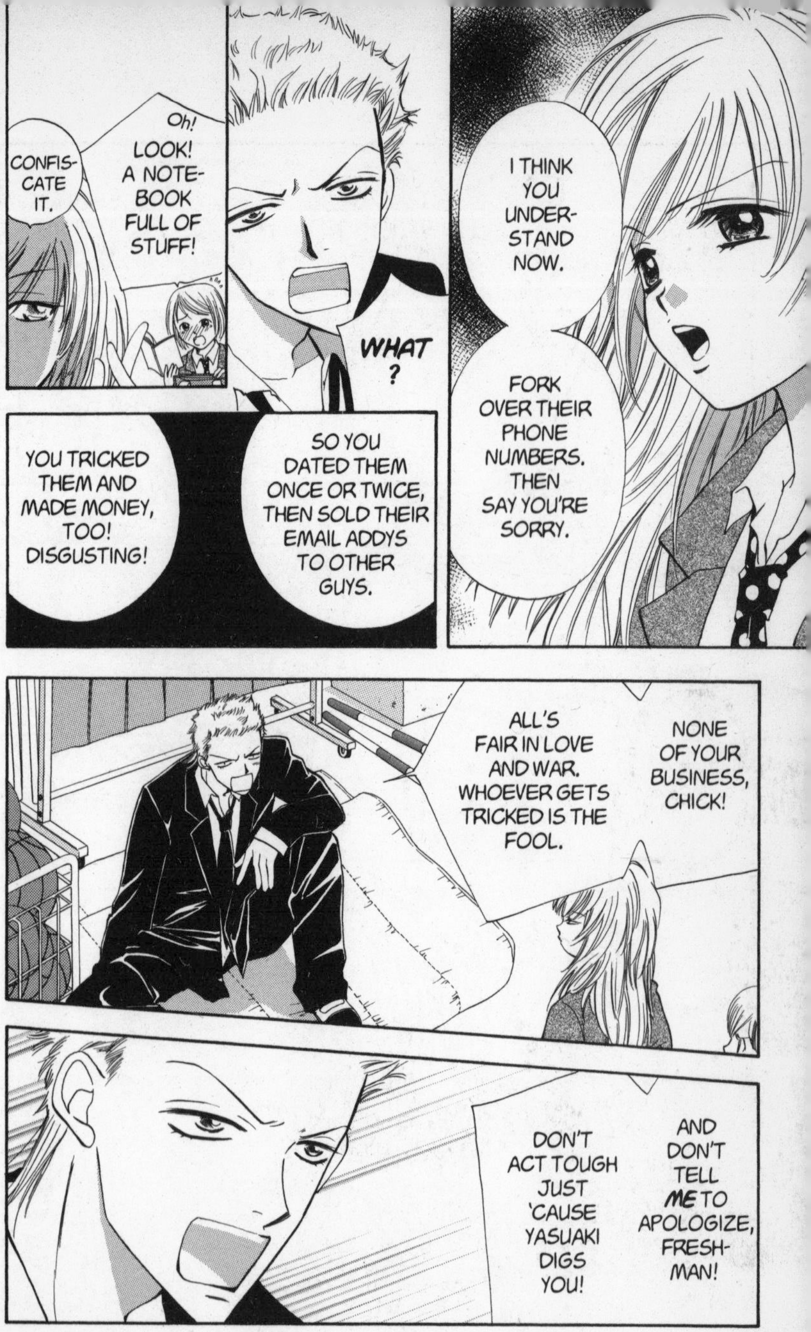
I THINK YOU UNDERSTAND NOW.
FORK OVER THEIR PHONE NUMBERS. THEN SAY YOU'RE SORRY.
WHAT?
Oh! LOOK! A NOTEBOOK FULL OF STUFF!
CONFISCATE IT.
SO YOU DATED THEM ONCE OR TWICE, THEN SOLD THEIR EMAIL ADDYS TO OTHER GUYS.
YOU TRICKED THEM AND MADE MONEY, TOO! DISGUSTING!
NONE OF YOUR BUSINESS, CHICK!
ALL'S FAIR IN LOVE AND WAR. WHOEVER GETS TRICKED IS THE FOOL.
AND DON'T TELL ME TO APOLOGIZE, FRESHMAN!
DON'T ACT TOUGH JUST 'CAUSE YASUAKI DIGS YOU!

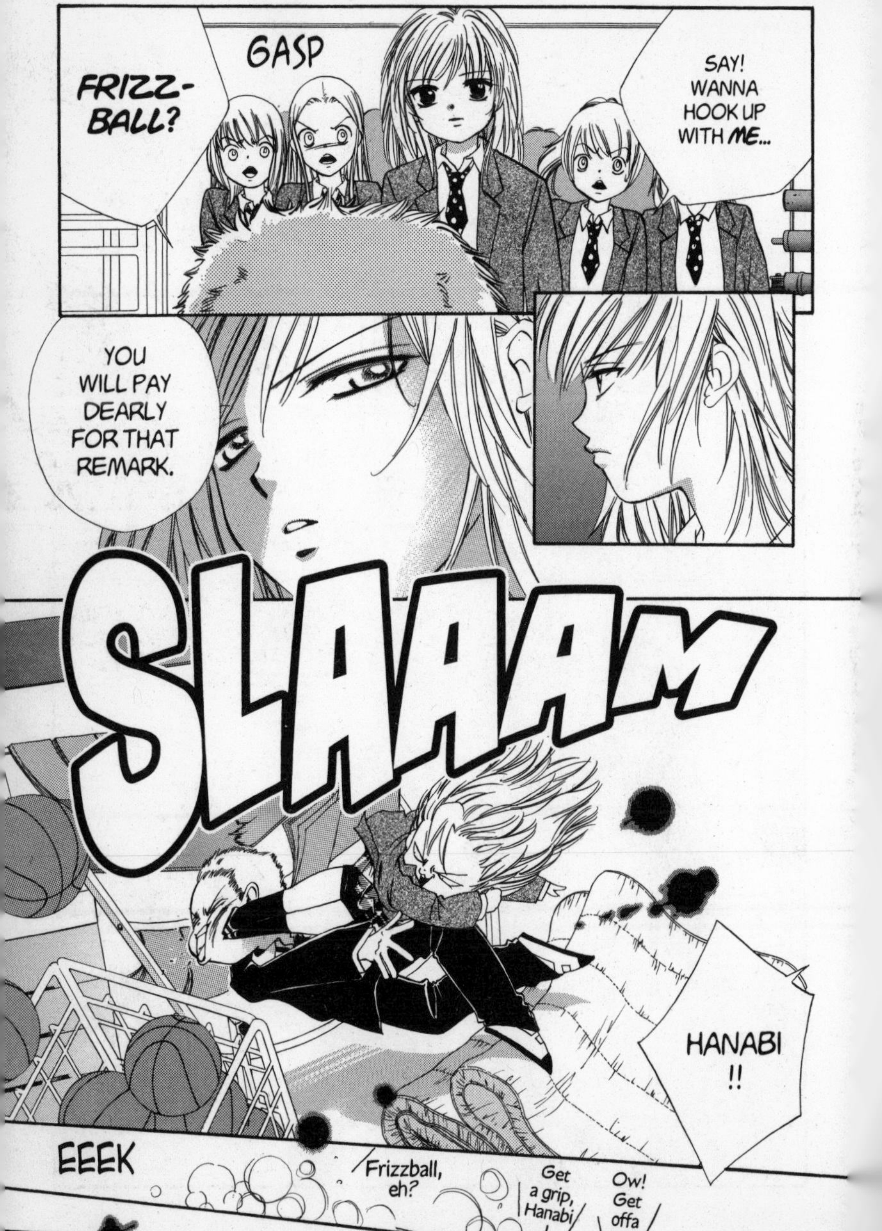
SAY! WANNA HOOK UP WITH **ME**...
FRIZZ-BALL?
GASP
YOU WILL PAY DEARLY FOR THAT REMARK.
SLAAAM
HANABI !!
Ow! Get offa me!
Get a grip, Hanabi!
Frizzball, eh?
EEEK

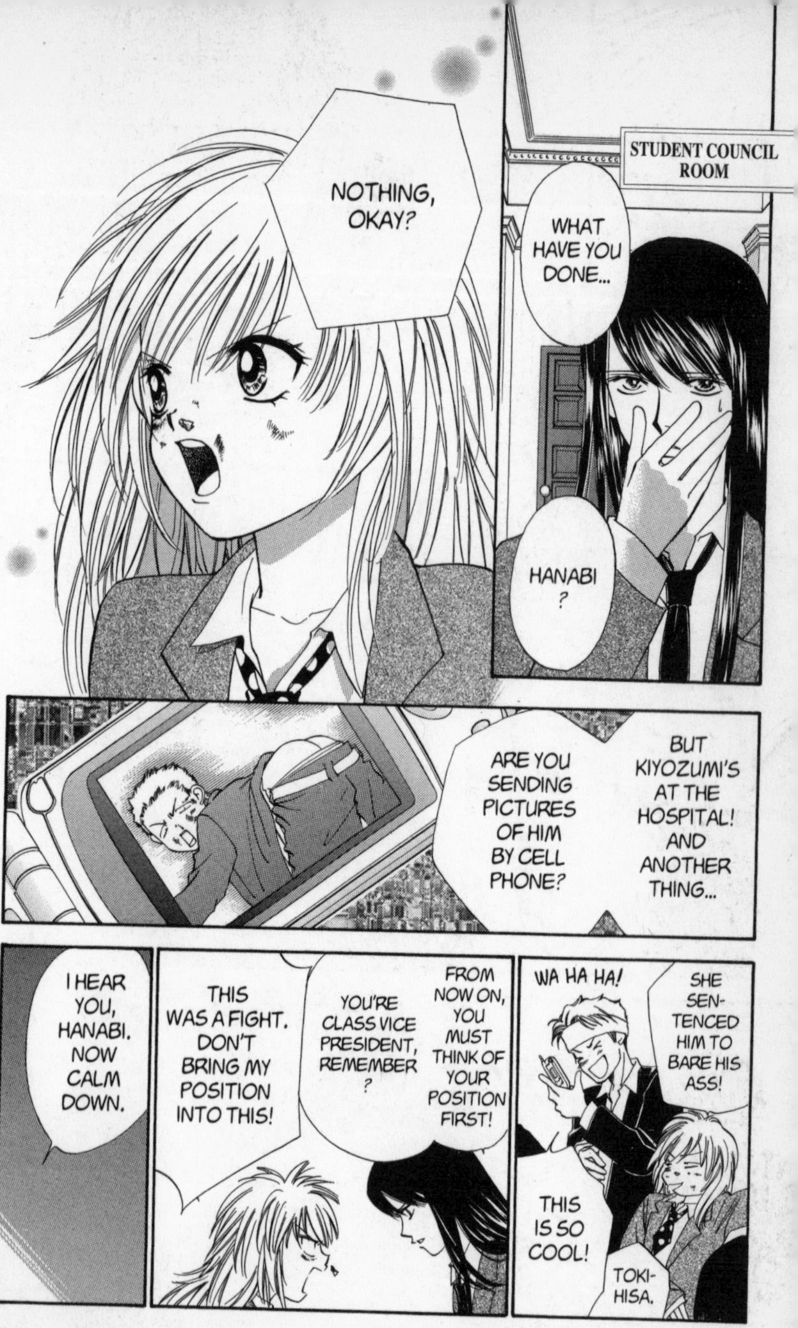
STUDENT COUNCIL ROOM
WHAT HAVE YOU DONE...
HANABI ?
NOTHING, OKAY?
BUT KIYOZUMI'S AT THE HOSPITAL! AND ANOTHER THING...
ARE YOU SENDING PICTURES OF HIM BY CELL PHONE?
SHE SEN-TENCED HIM TO BARE HIS ASS!
WA HA HA!
THIS IS SO COOL!
TOKI-HISA.
FROM NOW ON, YOU MUST THINK OF YOUR POSITION FIRST!
YOU'RE CLASS VICE PRESIDENT, REMEMBER ?
THIS WAS A FIGHT. DON'T BRING MY POSITION INTO THIS!
I HEAR YOU, HANABI. NOW CALM DOWN.

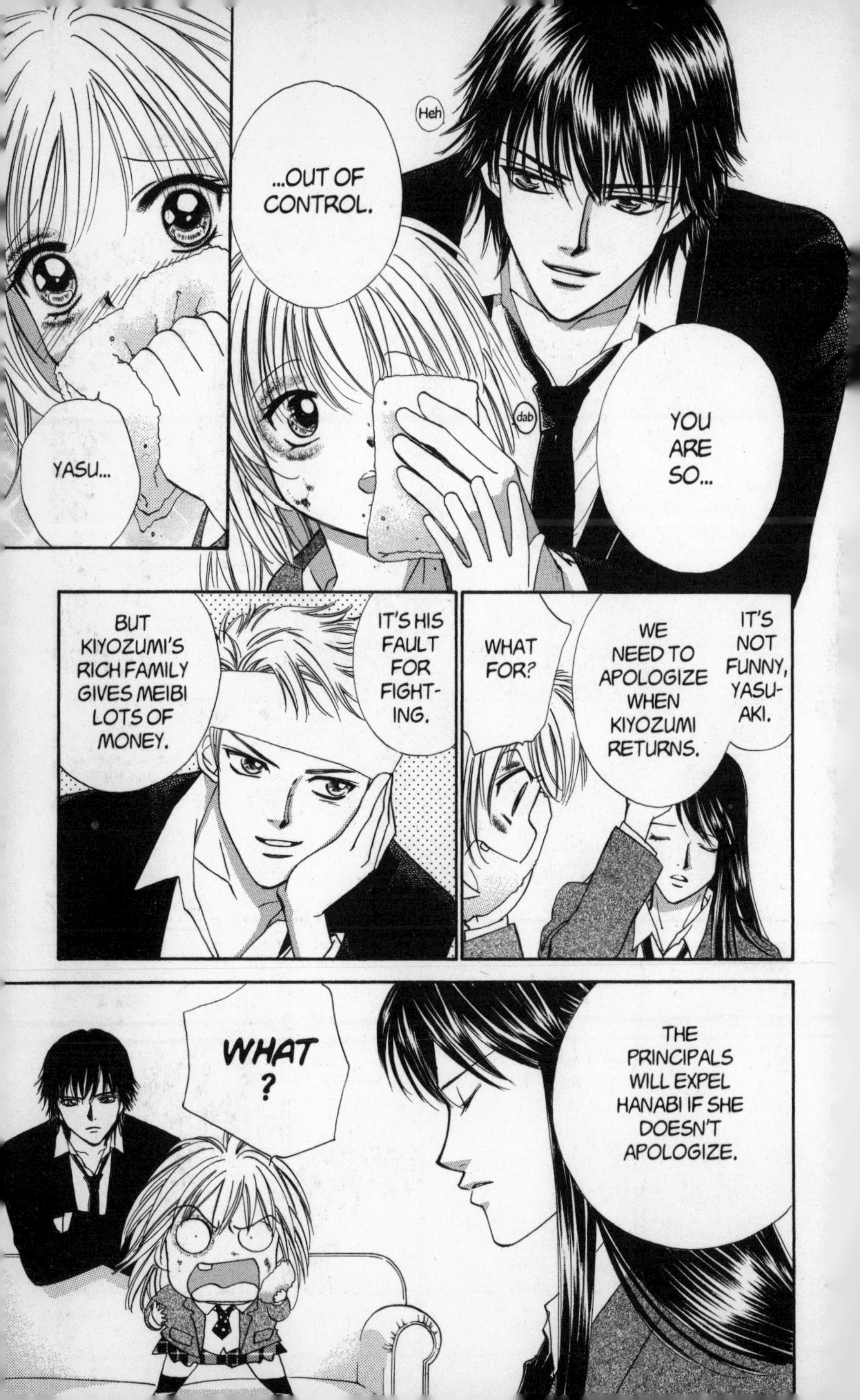

YOU ARE SO...
dab
...OUT OF CONTROL.
Heh
YASU...
IT'S NOT FUNNY, YASU-AKI.
WE NEED TO APOLOGIZE WHEN KIYOZUMI RETURNS.
WHAT FOR?
IT'S HIS FAULT FOR FIGHT-ING.
BUT KIYOZUMI'S RICH FAMILY GIVES MEIBI LOTS OF MONEY.
THE PRINCIPALS WILL EXPEL HANABI IF SHE DOESN'T APOLOGIZE.
WHAT?

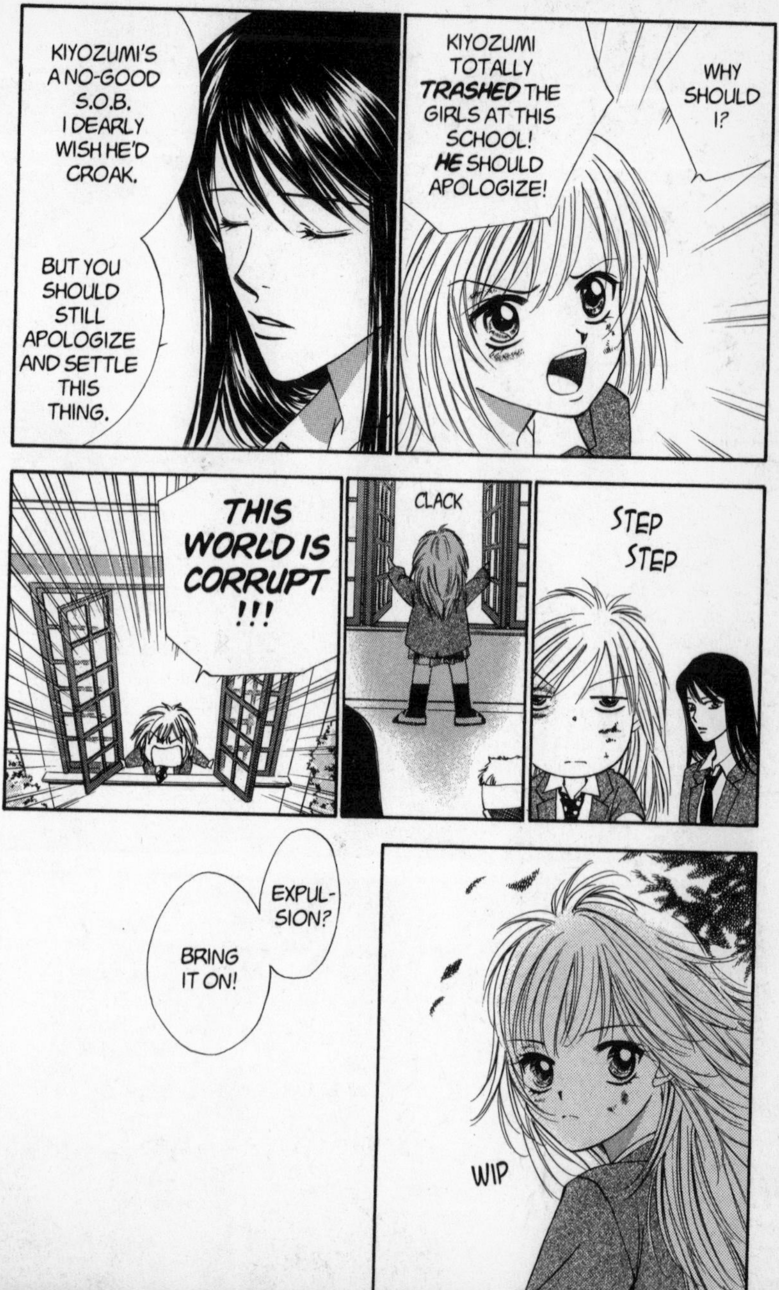
WHY SHOULD I?
KIYOZUMI TOTALLY **TRASHED** THE GIRLS AT THIS SCHOOL! **HE** SHOULD APOLOGIZE!
KIYOZUMI'S A NO-GOOD S.O.B. I DEARLY WISH HE'D CROAK.
BUT YOU SHOULD STILL APOLOGIZE AND SETTLE THIS THING.
STEP STEP
CLACK
THIS WORLD IS CORRUPT !!!
WIP
EXPUL-SION?
BRING IT ON!

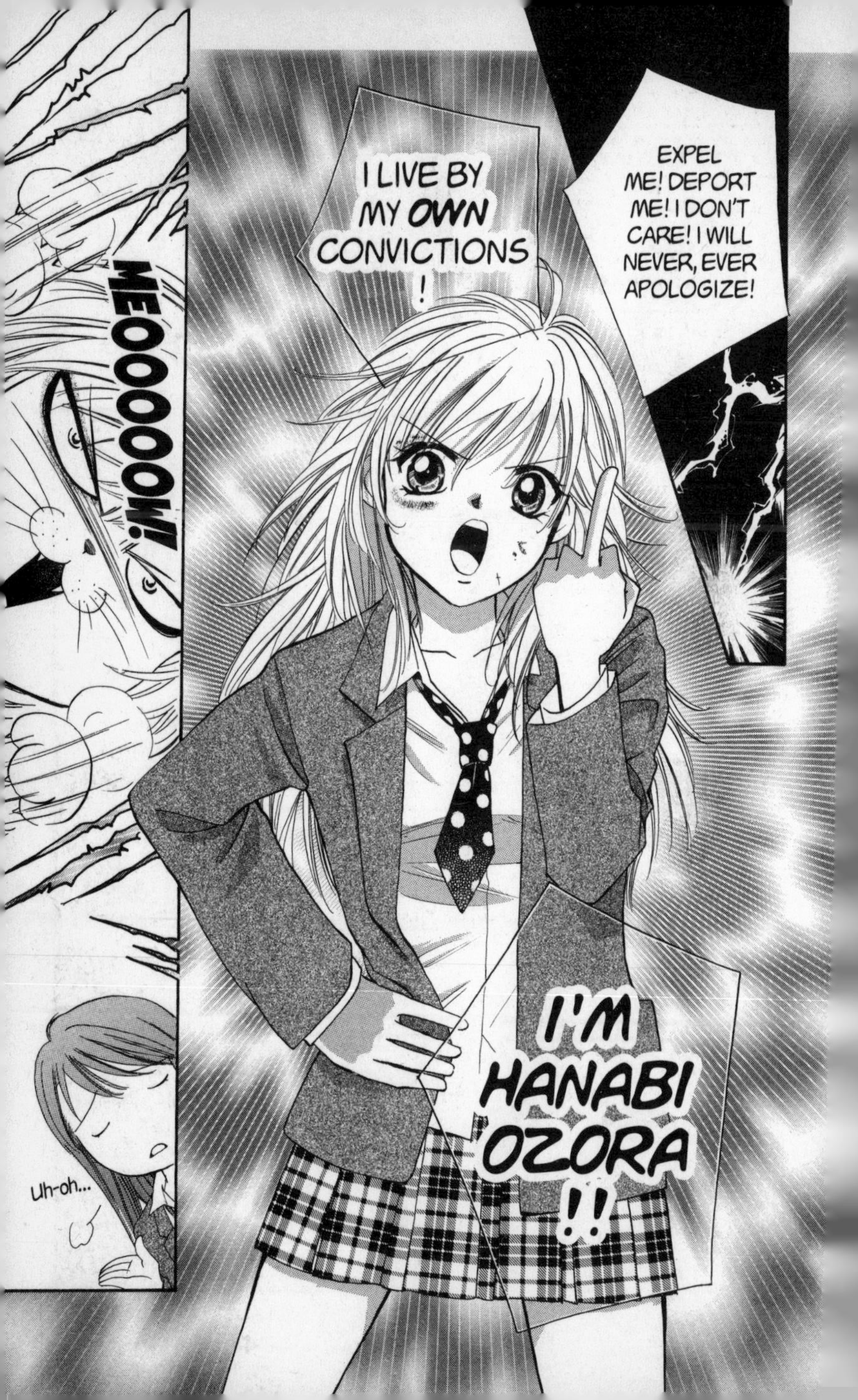
EXPEL ME! DEPORT ME! I DON'T CARE! I WILL NEVER, EVER APOLOGIZE!
I LIVE BY MY OWN CONVICTIONS!
I'M HANABI OZORA!!
MEOOOOOOW!!
Uh-oh...

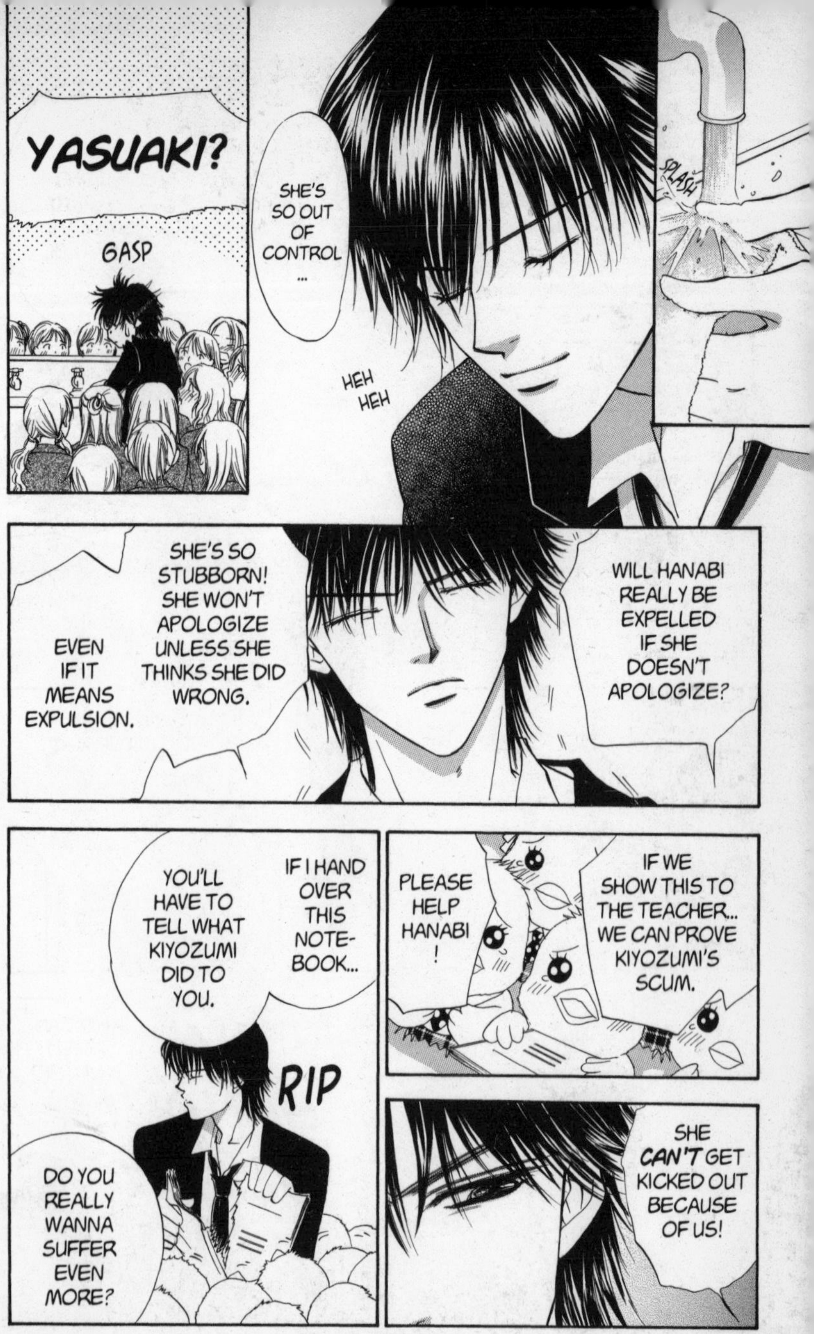
SPLASH
SHE'S SO OUT OF CONTROL ...
HEH HEH
YASUAKI?
GASP
WILL HANABI REALLY BE EXPELLED IF SHE DOESN'T APOLOGIZE?
SHE'S SO STUBBORN! SHE WON'T APOLOGIZE UNLESS SHE THINKS SHE DID WRONG.
EVEN IF IT MEANS EXPULSION.
IF WE SHOW THIS TO THE TEACHER... WE CAN PROVE KIYOZUMI'S SCUM.
PLEASE HELP HANABI!
SHE CAN'T GET KICKED OUT BECAUSE OF US!
IF I HAND OVER THIS NOTE-BOOK...
YOU'LL HAVE TO TELL WHAT KIYOZUMI DID TO YOU.
RIP
DO YOU REALLY WANNA SUFFER EVEN MORE?

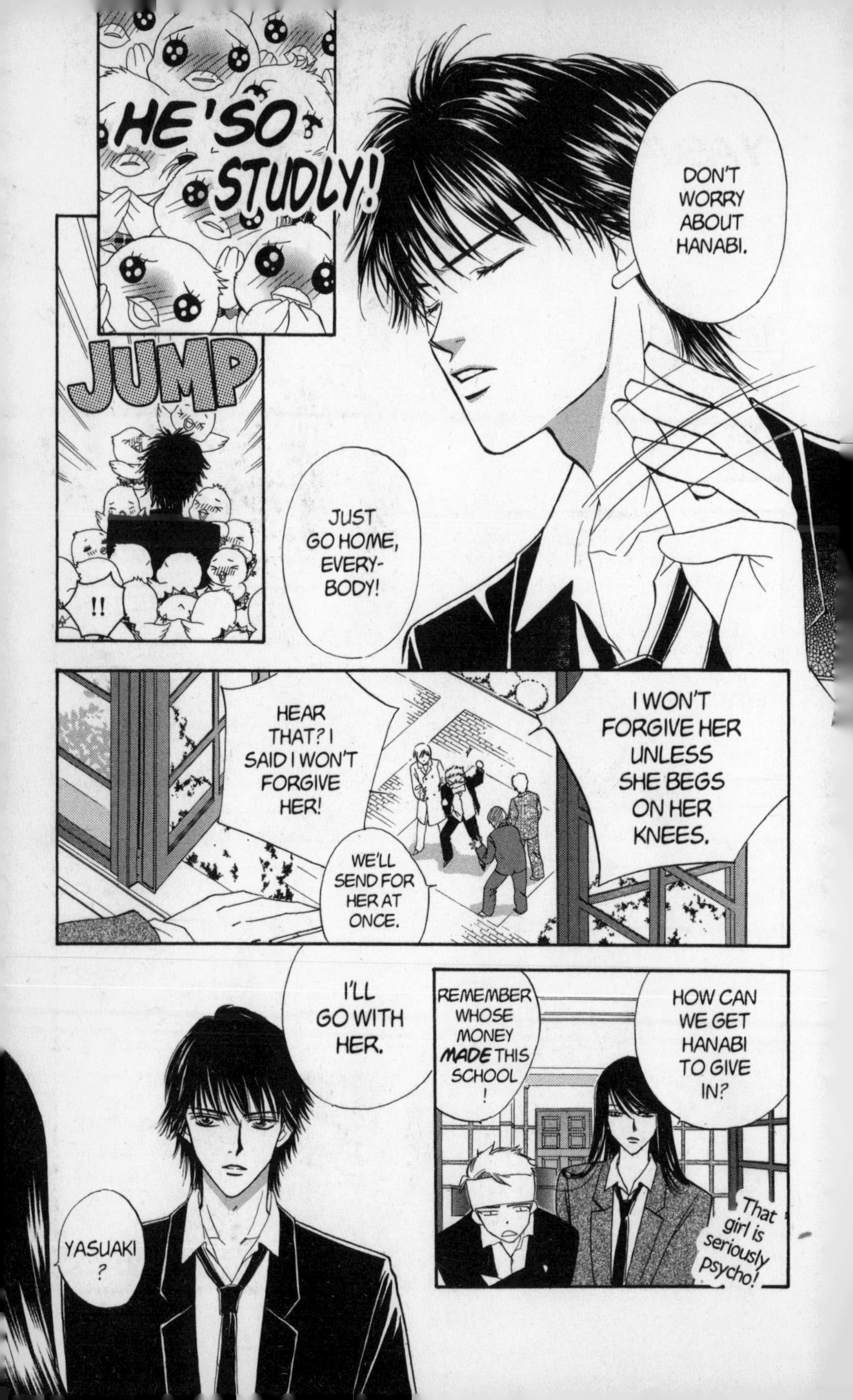
DON'T WORRY ABOUT HANABI.
JUST GO HOME, EVERY-BODY!
HE'SO STUDLY!
JUMP
!!
I WON'T FORGIVE HER UNLESS SHE BEGS ON HER KNEES.
HEAR THAT? I SAID I WON'T FORGIVE HER!
WE'LL SEND FOR HER AT ONCE.
HOW CAN WE GET HANABI TO GIVE IN?
REMEMBER WHOSE MONEY MADE THIS SCHOOL!
That girl is seriously psycho!
I'LL GO WITH HER.
YASUAKI?

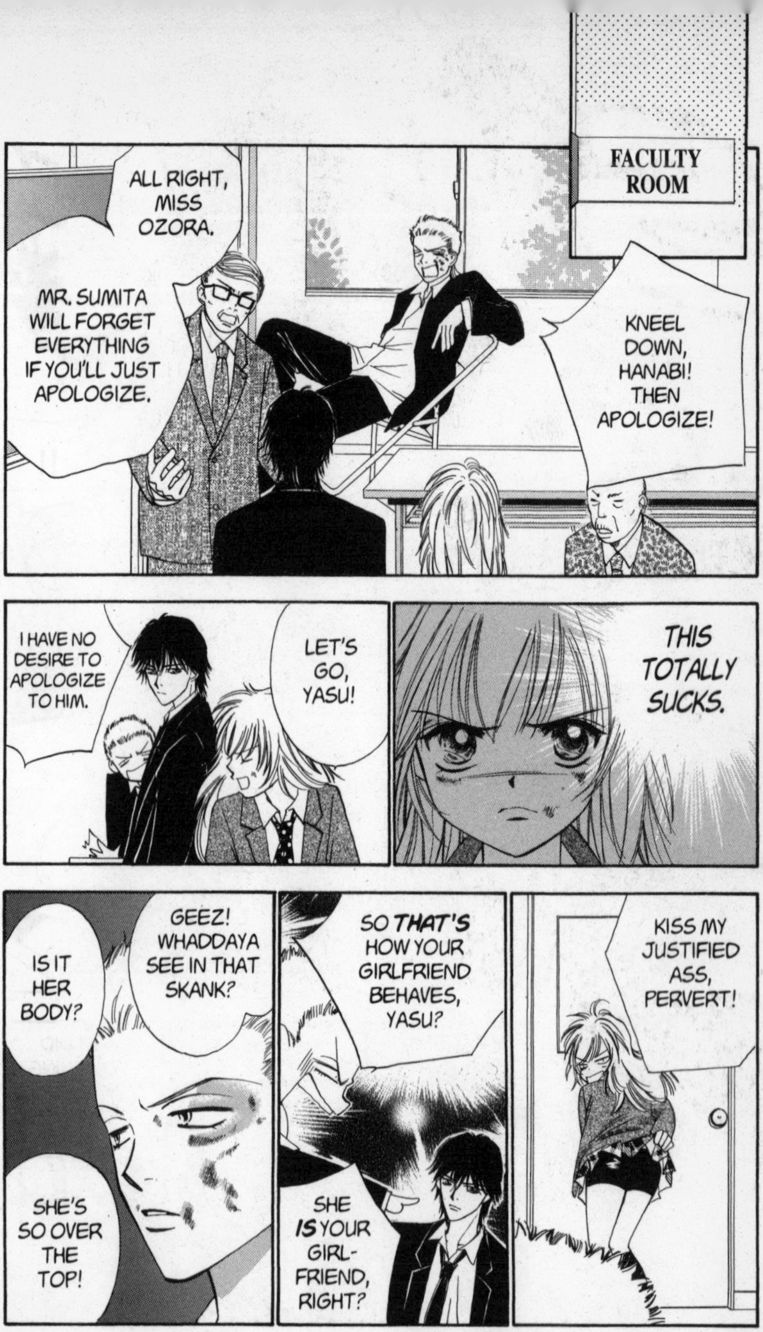

FACULTY ROOM
KNEEL DOWN, HANABI! THEN APOLOGIZE!
ALL RIGHT, MISS OZORA.
MR. SUMITA WILL FORGET EVERYTHING IF YOU'LL JUST APOLOGIZE.
THIS TOTALLY SUCKS.
LET'S GO, YASU!
I HAVE NO DESIRE TO APOLOGIZE TO HIM.
KISS MY JUSTIFIED ASS, PERVERT!
SO THAT'S HOW YOUR GIRLFRIEND BEHAVES, YASU?
SHE IS YOUR GIRL-FRIEND, RIGHT?
GEEZ! WHADDAYA SEE IN THAT SKANK?
IS IT HER BODY?
SHE'S SO OVER THE TOP!

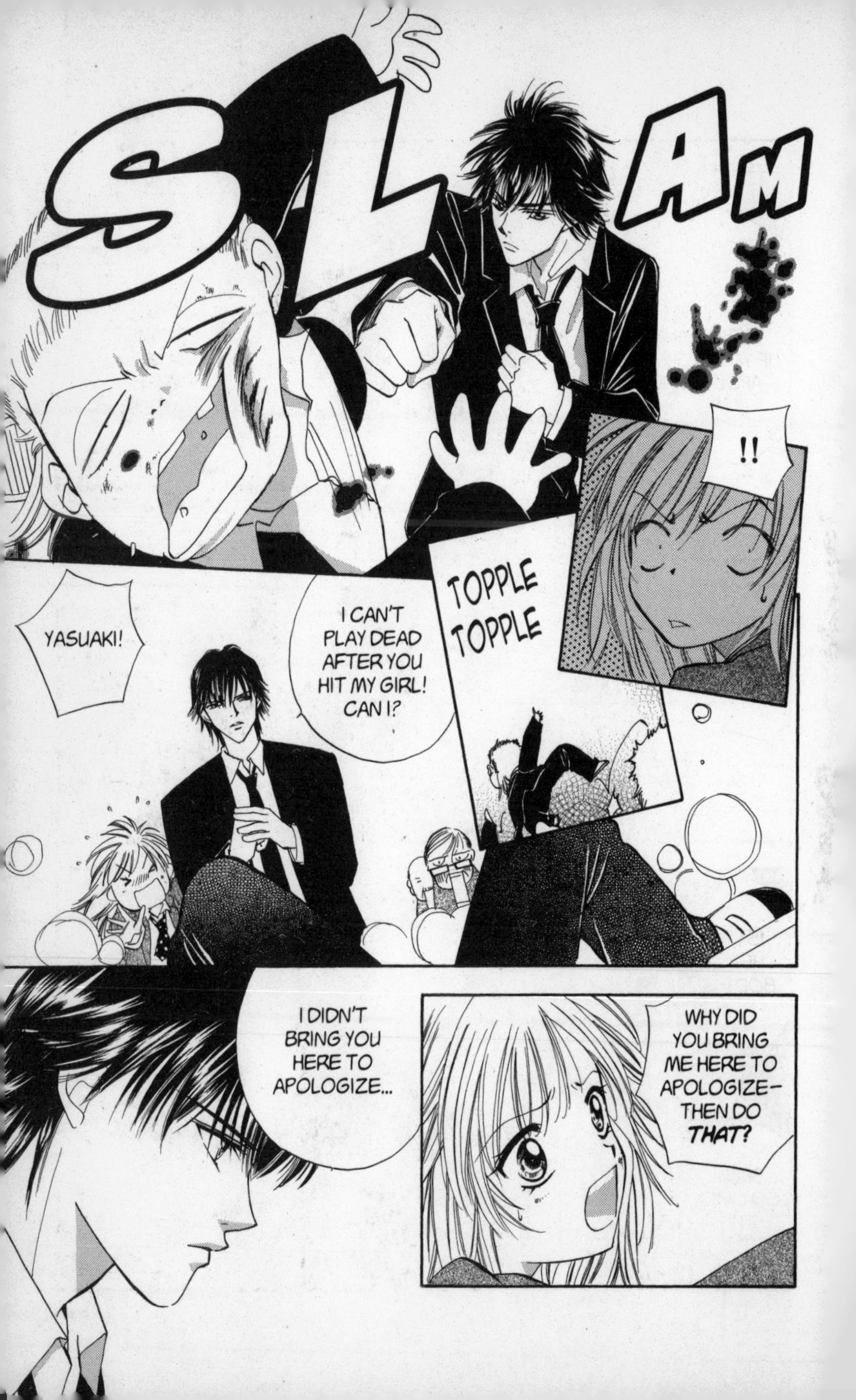
SLAM
!!
TOPPLE TOPPLE
I CAN'T PLAY DEAD AFTER YOU HIT MY GIRL! CAN I?
YASUAKI!
WHY DID YOU BRING ME HERE TO APOLOGIZE- THEN DO *THAT*?
I DIDN'T BRING YOU HERE TO APOLOGIZE...

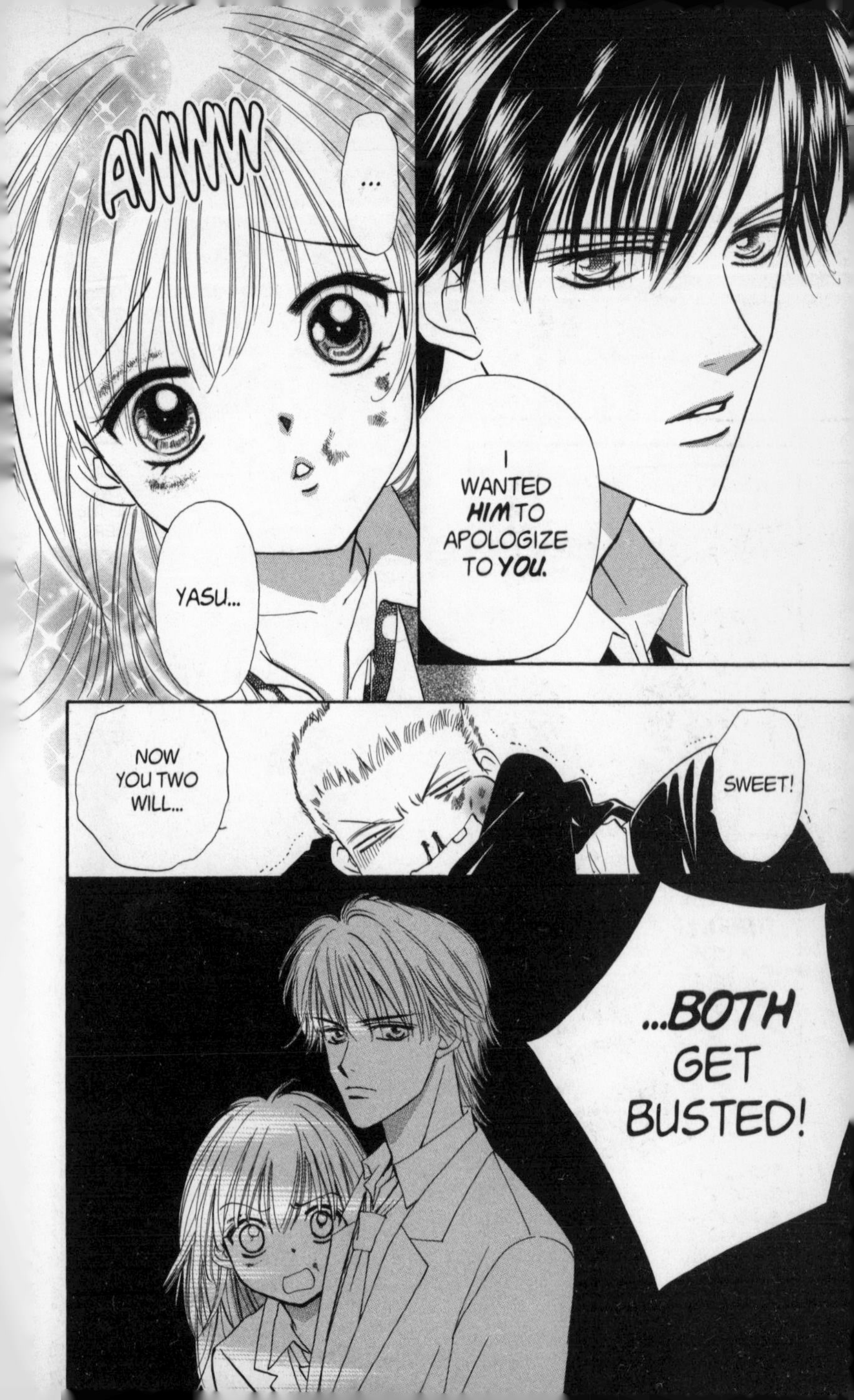
I WANTED HIM TO APOLOGIZE TO YOU.
AWWWN
...
YASU...
SWEET!
NOW YOU TWO WILL...
...BOTH GET BUSTED!

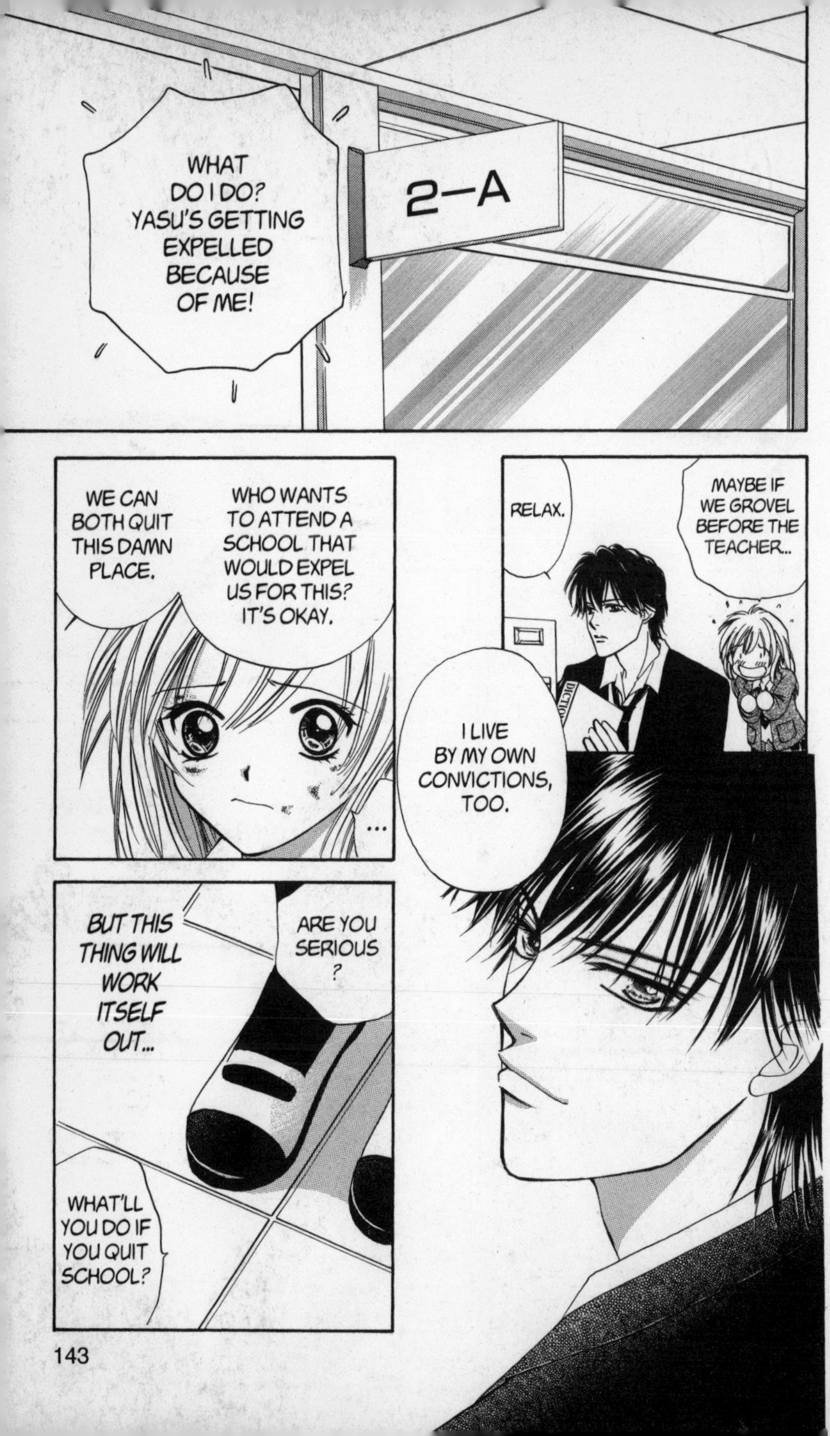
WHAT DO I DO? YASU'S GETTING EXPELLED BECAUSE OF ME!
2-A
MAYBE IF WE GROVEL BEFORE THE TEACHER...
RELAX.
WHO WANTS TO ATTEND A SCHOOL THAT WOULD EXPEL US FOR THIS? IT'S OKAY.
WE CAN BOTH QUIT THIS DAMN PLACE.
...
I LIVE BY MY OWN CONVICTIONS, TOO.
ARE YOU SERIOUS?
BUT THIS THING WILL WORK ITSELF OUT...
WHAT'LL YOU DO IF YOU QUIT SCHOOL?

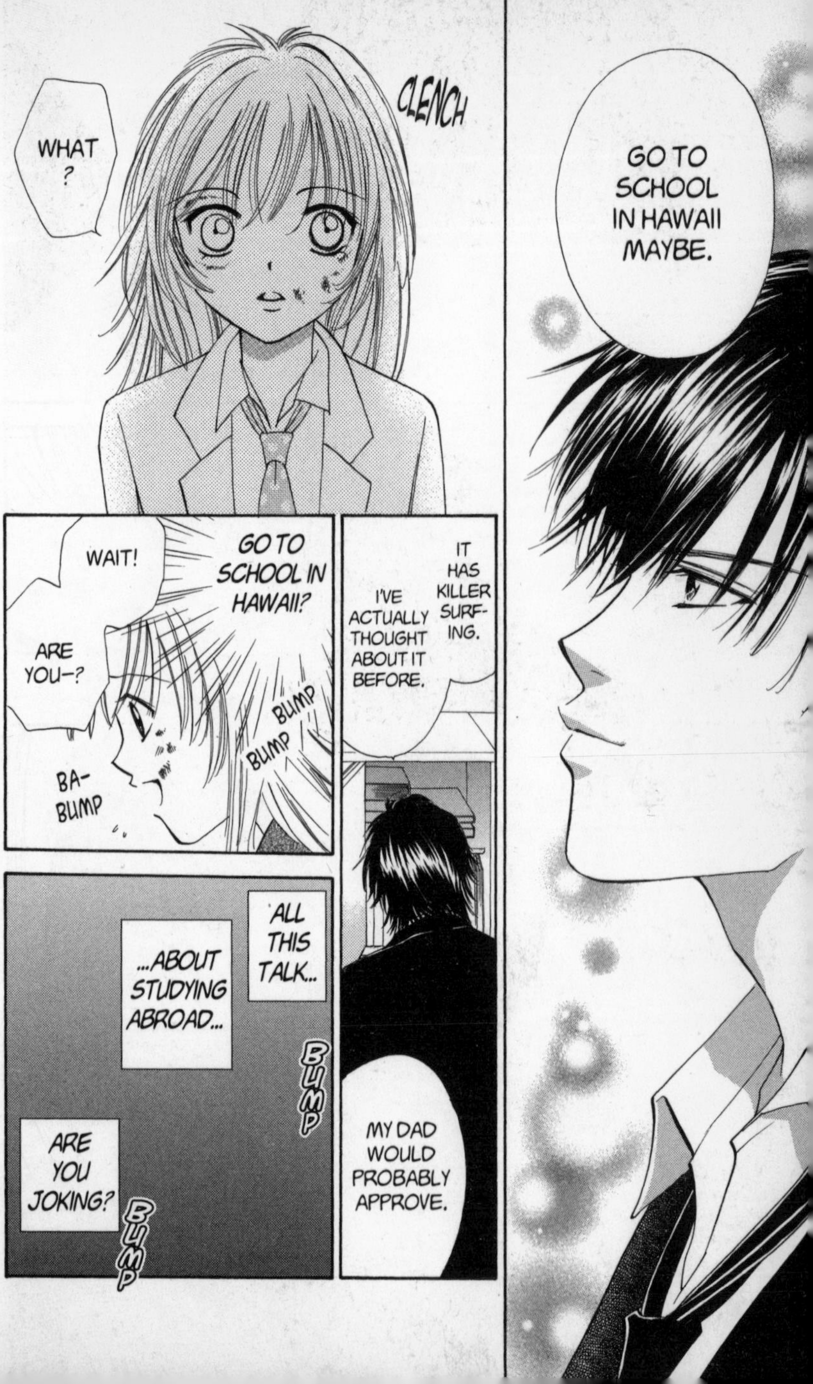
GO TO SCHOOL IN HAWAII MAYBE.
CLENCH
WHAT?
IT HAS KILLER SURF-ING.
I'VE ACTUALLY THOUGHT ABOUT IT BEFORE.
MY DAD WOULD PROBABLY APPROVE.
GO TO SCHOOL IN HAWAII?
WAIT!
ARE YOU-?
BUMP
BUMP
BA-BUMP
ALL THIS TALK...
...ABOUT STUDYING ABROAD...
BUMP
ARE YOU JOKING?
BUMP

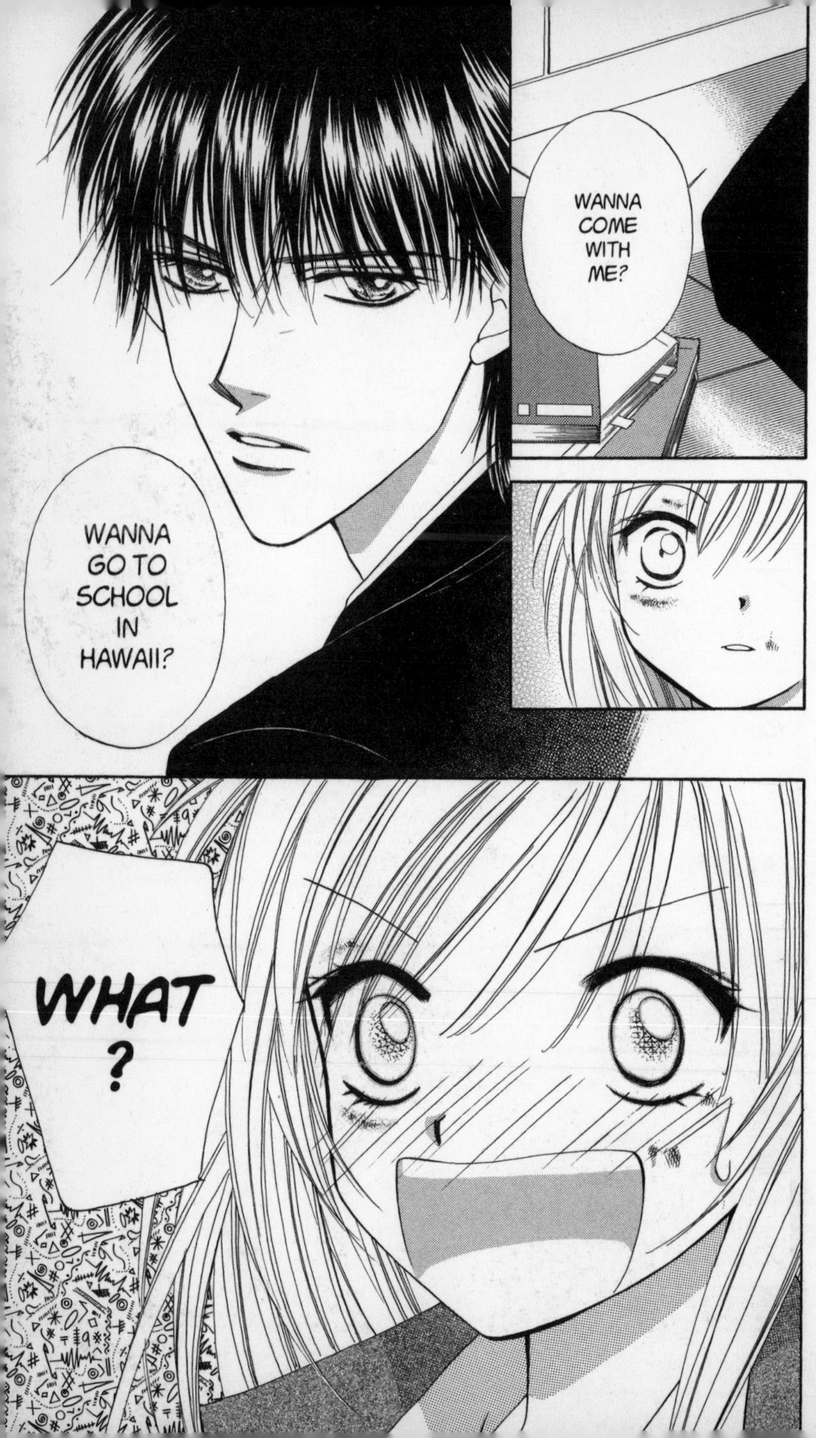
WANNA COME WITH ME?
WANNA GO TO SCHOOL IN HAWAII?
WHAT?

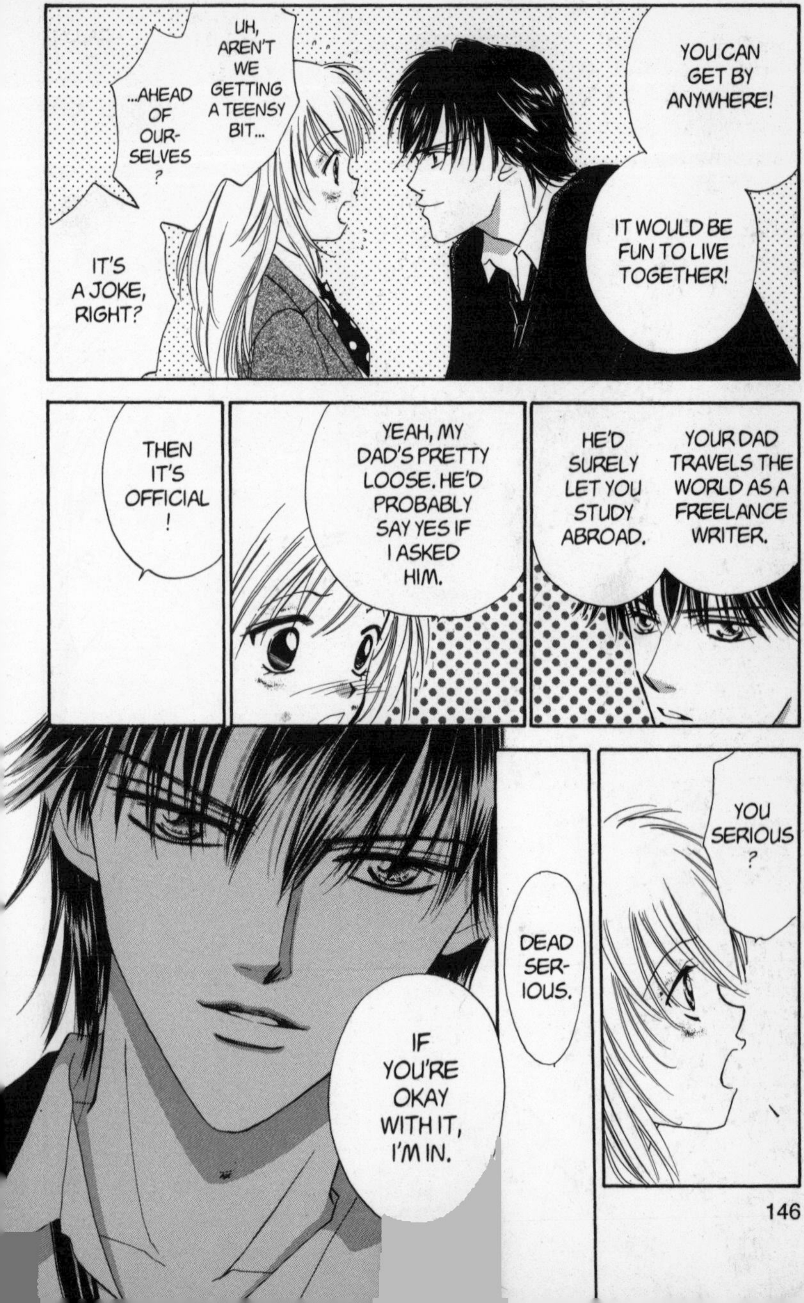
YOU CAN GET BY ANYWHERE!
IT WOULD BE FUN TO LIVE TOGETHER!
UH, AREN'T WE GETTING A TEENSY BIT...
...AHEAD OF OUR-SELVES?
IT'S A JOKE, RIGHT?
YOUR DAD TRAVELS THE WORLD AS A FREELANCE WRITER.
HE'D SURELY LET YOU STUDY ABROAD.
YEAH, MY DAD'S PRETTY LOOSE. HE'D PROBABLY SAY YES IF I ASKED HIM.
THEN IT'S OFFICIAL!
YOU SERIOUS?
DEAD SER-IOUS.
IF YOU'RE OKAY WITH IT, I'M IN.

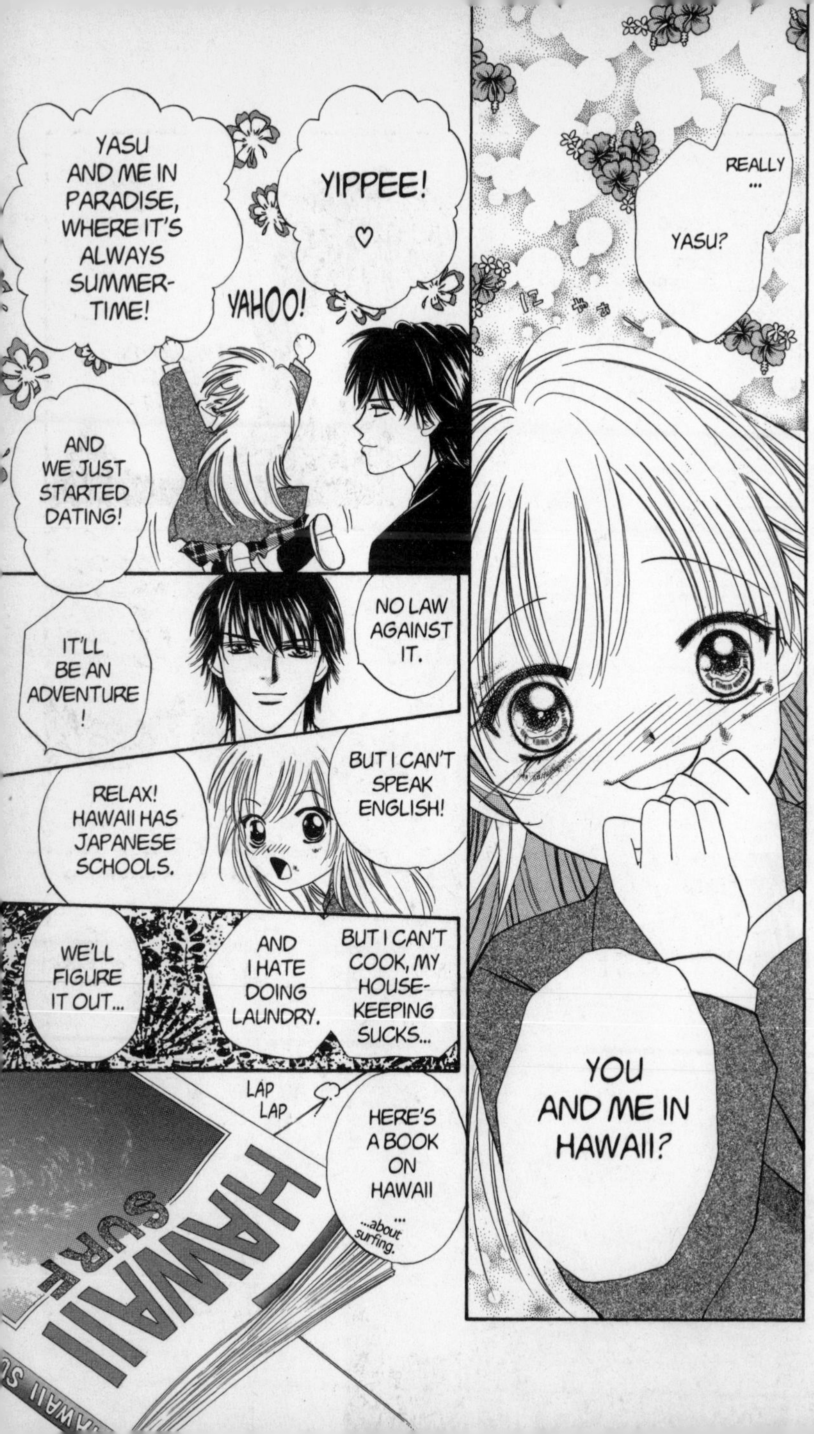
REALLY ... YASU?
YOU AND ME IN HAWAII?
YIPPEE! ♡
YAHOO!
YASU AND ME IN PARADISE, WHERE IT'S ALWAYS SUMMER-TIME!
AND WE JUST STARTED DATING!
NO LAW AGAINST IT.
IT'LL BE AN ADVENTURE!
BUT I CAN'T SPEAK ENGLISH!
RELAX! HAWAII HAS JAPANESE SCHOOLS.
BUT I CAN'T COOK, MY HOUSE-KEEPING SUCKS...
AND I HATE DOING LAUNDRY.
WE'LL FIGURE IT OUT...
HERE'S A BOOK ON HAWAII ...
...about surfing.
LAP LAP
HAWAII SURF

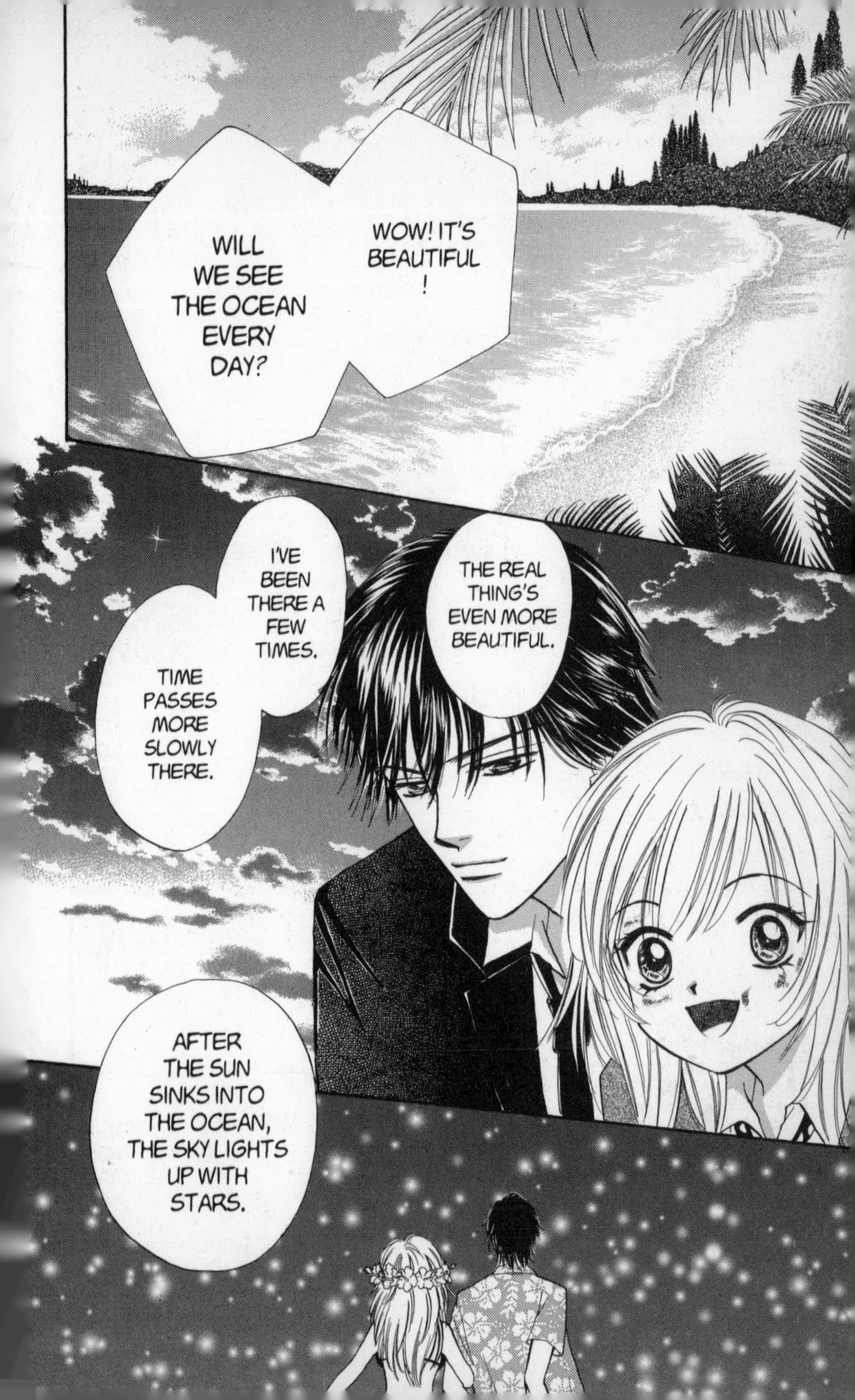
WOW! IT'S BEAUTIFUL!
WILL WE SEE THE OCEAN EVERY DAY?
THE REAL THING'S EVEN MORE BEAUTIFUL.
I'VE BEEN THERE A FEW TIMES.
TIME PASSES MORE SLOWLY THERE.
AFTER THE SUN SINKS INTO THE OCEAN, THE SKY LIGHTS UP WITH STARS.

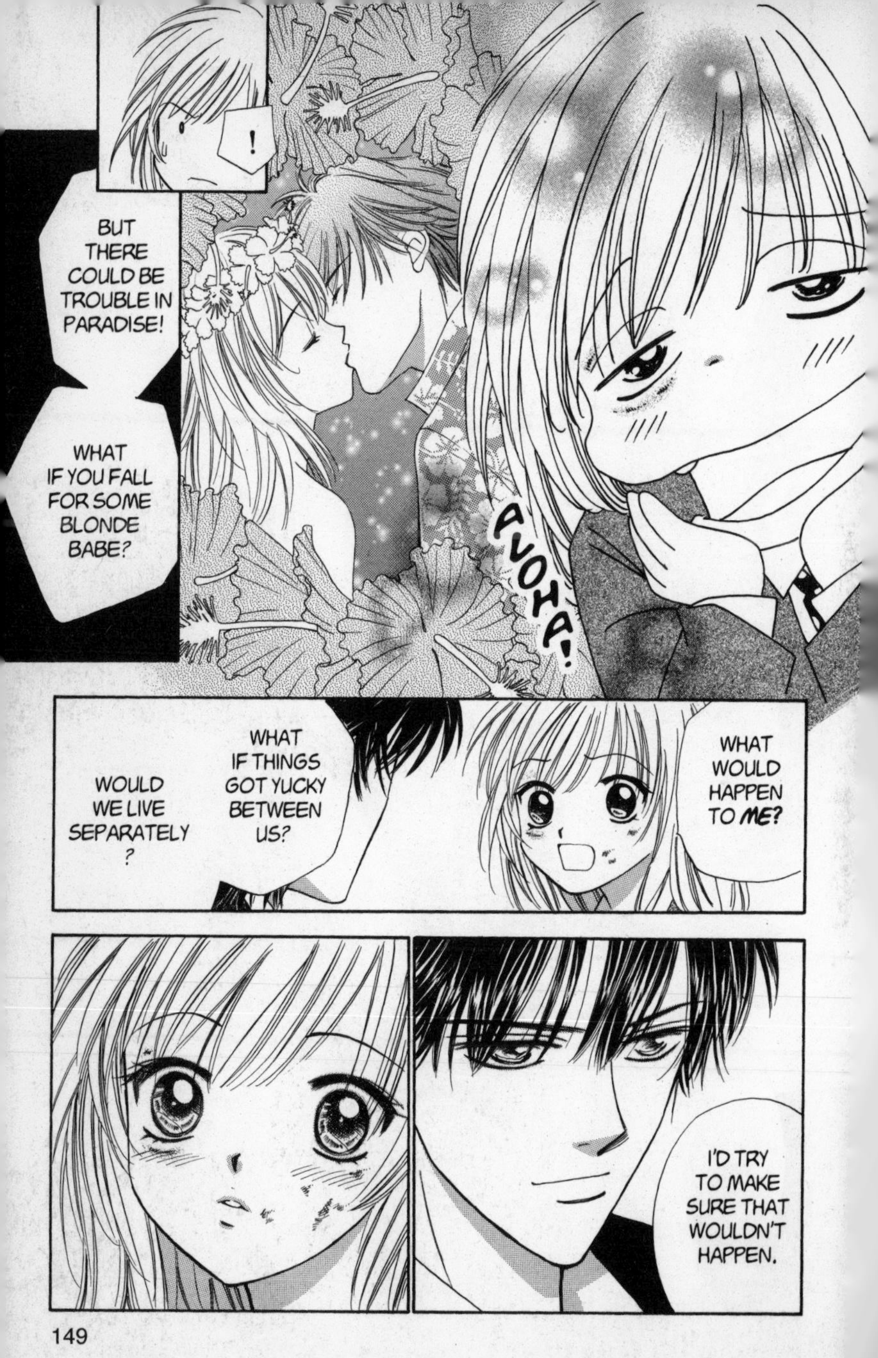
ALOHA!
!
BUT THERE COULD BE TROUBLE IN PARADISE!
WHAT IF YOU FALL FOR SOME BLONDE BABE?
WHAT WOULD HAPPEN TO *ME*?
WHAT IF THINGS GOT YUCKY BETWEEN US?
WOULD WE LIVE SEPARATELY?
I'D TRY TO MAKE SURE THAT WOULDN'T HAPPEN.

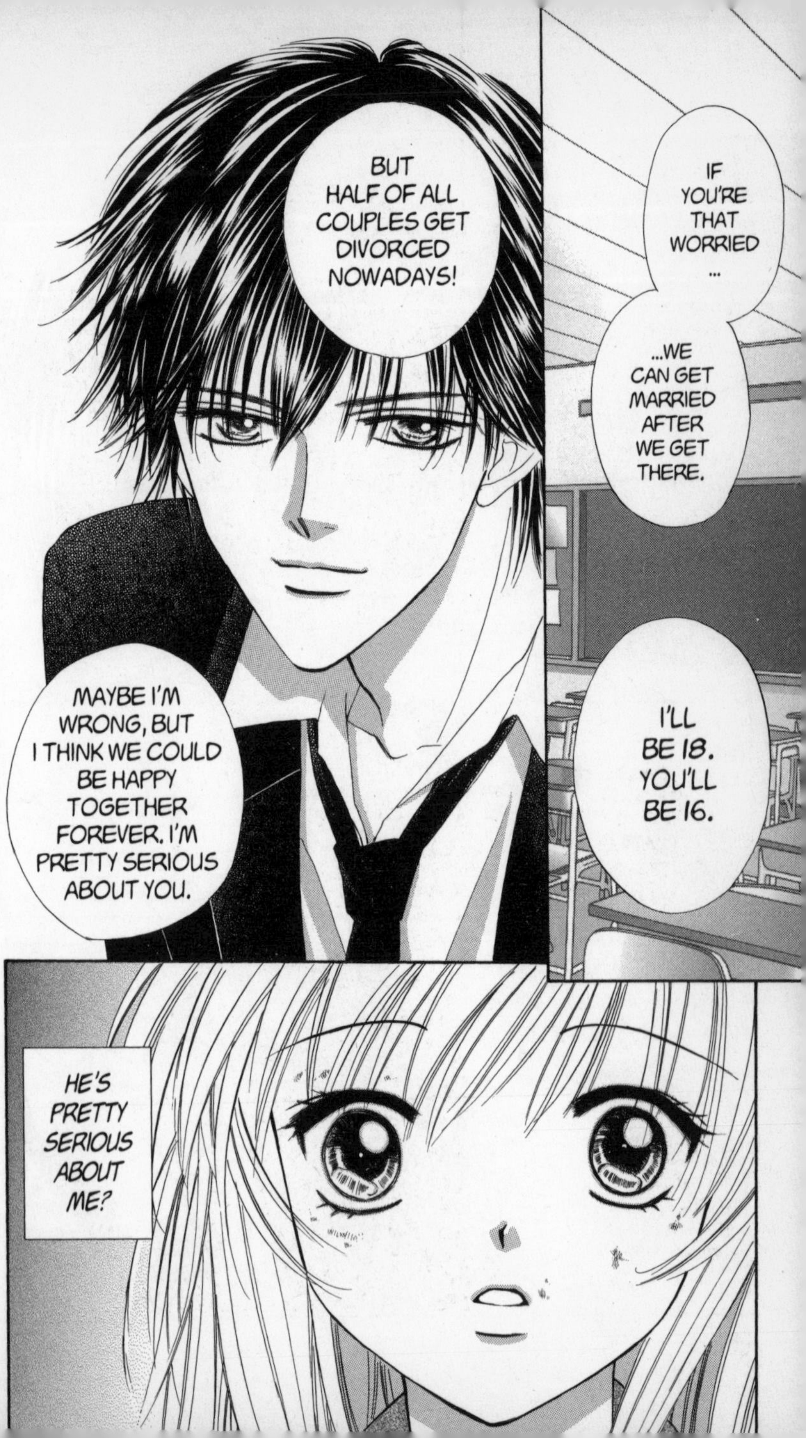
IF YOU'RE THAT WORRIED ...
...WE CAN GET MARRIED AFTER WE GET THERE.
I'LL BE 18. YOU'LL BE 16.
BUT HALF OF ALL COUPLES GET DIVORCED NOWADAYS!
MAYBE I'M WRONG, BUT I THINK WE COULD BE HAPPY TOGETHER FOREVER. I'M PRETTY SERIOUS ABOUT YOU.
HE'S PRETTY SERIOUS ABOUT ME?

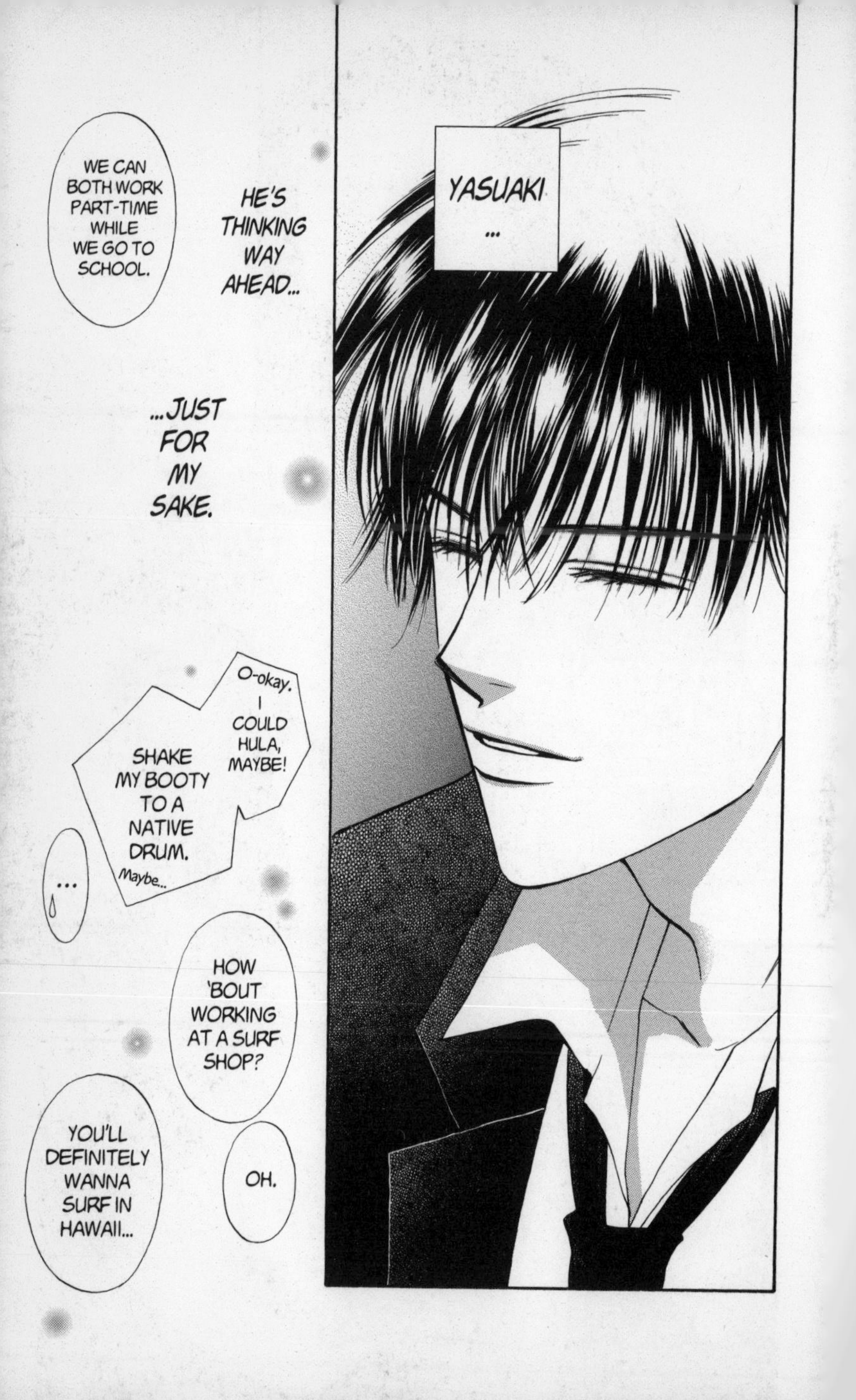
YASUAKI ...
WE CAN BOTH WORK PART-TIME WHILE WE GO TO SCHOOL.
HE'S THINKING WAY AHEAD...
...JUST FOR MY SAKE.
O-okay. I COULD HULA, MAYBE!
SHAKE MY BOOTY TO A NATIVE DRUM.
Maybe...
...
HOW 'BOUT WORKING AT A SURF SHOP?
OH.
YOU'LL DEFINITELY WANNA SURF IN HAWAII...

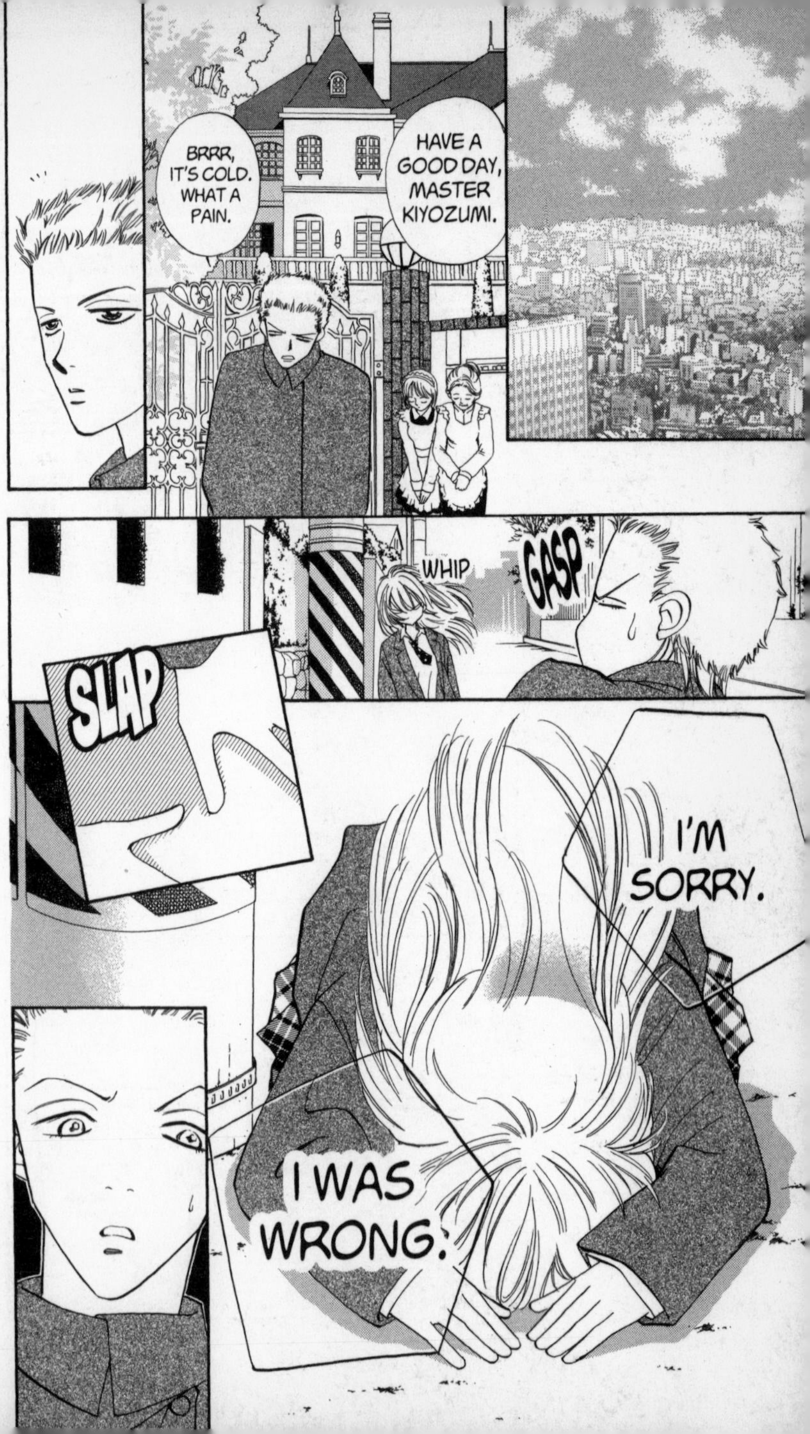

HAVE A GOOD DAY, MASTER KIYOZUMI.
BRRR, IT'S COLD. WHAT A PAIN.
GASP
WHIP
I'M SORRY.
SLAP
I WAS WRONG.

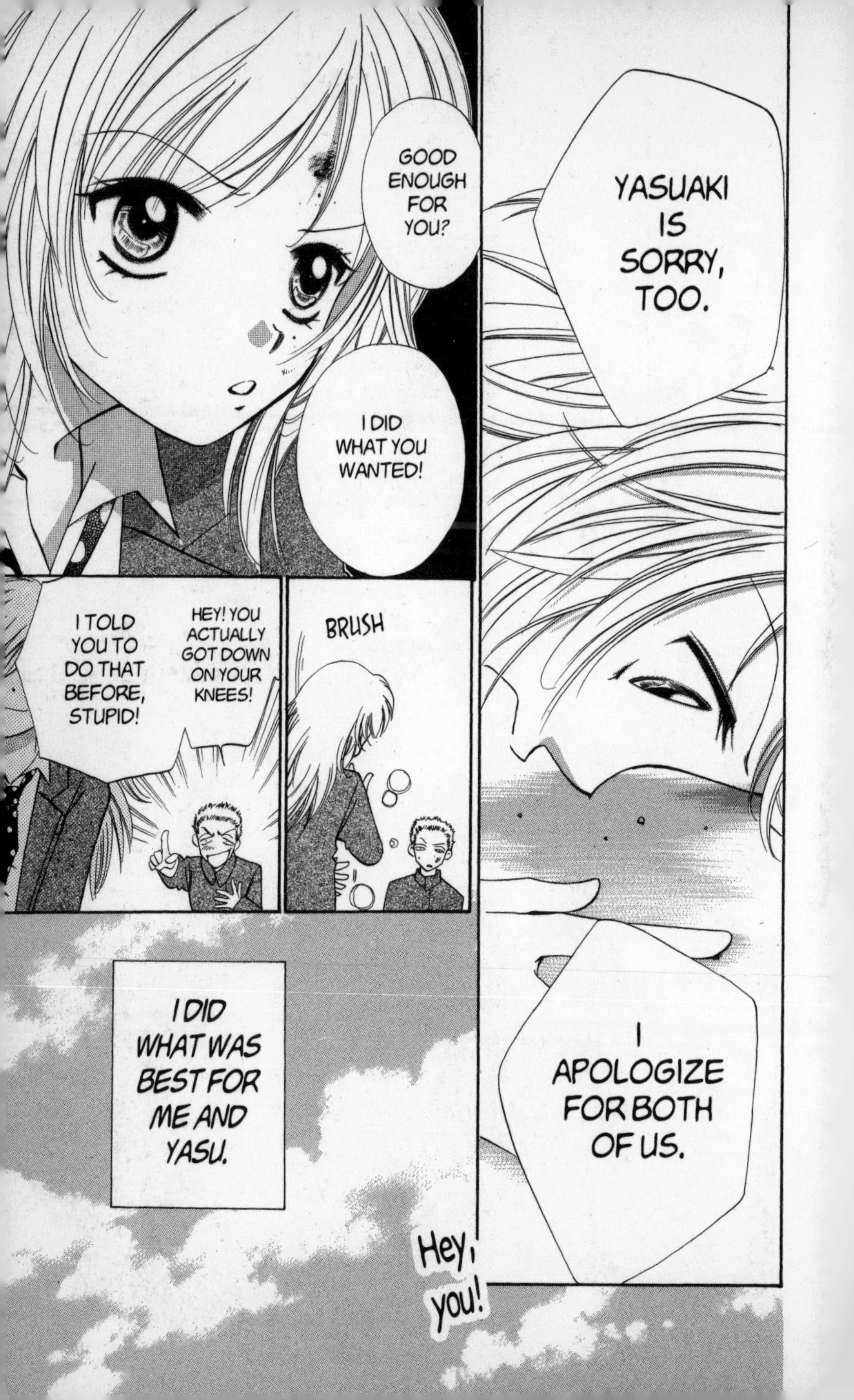
YASUAKI IS SORRY, TOO.
I APOLOGIZE FOR BOTH OF US.
GOOD ENOUGH FOR YOU?
I DID WHAT YOU WANTED!
BRUSH
HEY! YOU ACTUALLY GOT DOWN ON YOUR KNEES!
I TOLD YOU TO DO THAT BEFORE, STUPID!
I DID WHAT WAS BEST FOR ME AND YASU.
Hey, you!

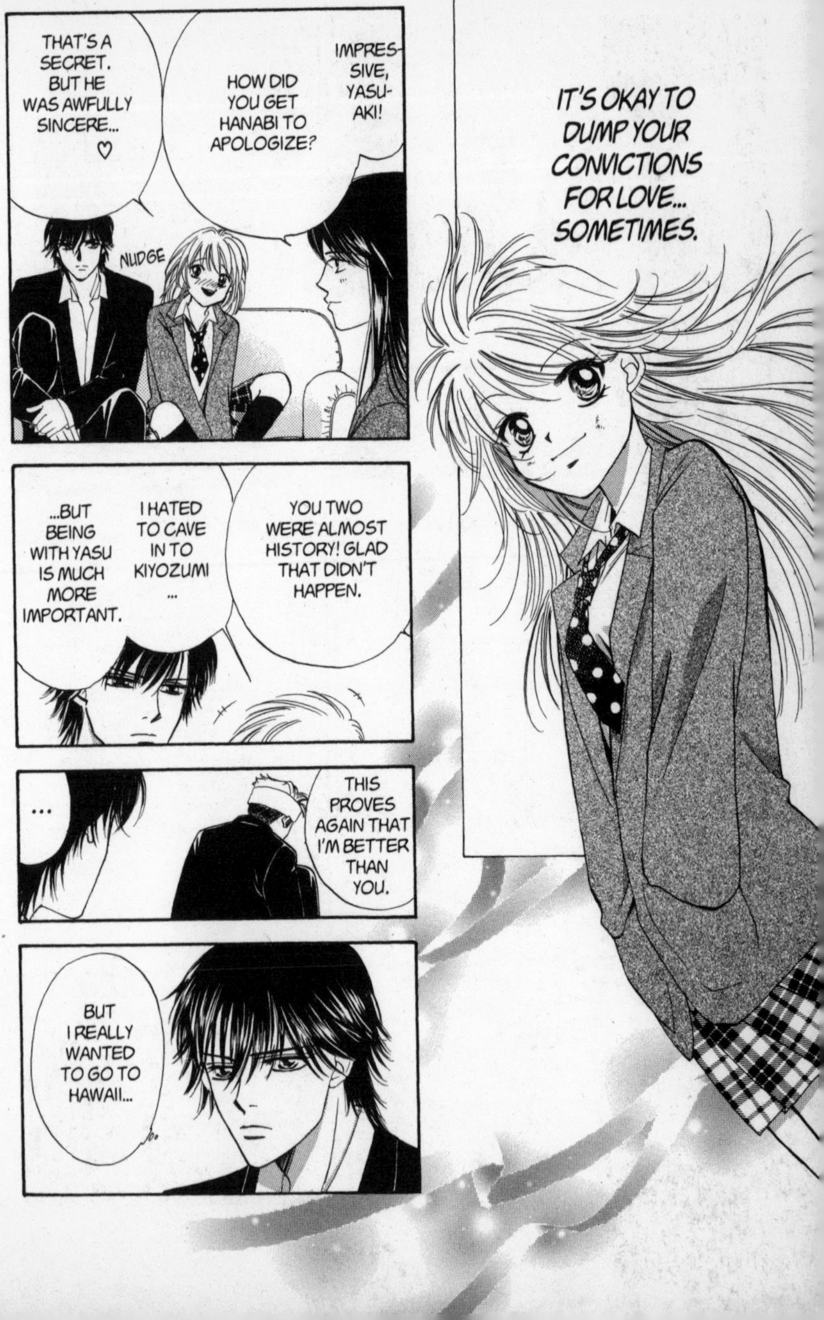
IT'S OKAY TO DUMP YOUR CONVICTIONS FOR LOVE... SOMETIMES.
IMPRESSIVE, YASUAKI!
HOW DID YOU GET HANABI TO APOLOGIZE?
THAT'S A SECRET. BUT HE WAS AWFULLY SINCERE... ♡
NUDGE
YOU TWO WERE ALMOST HISTORY! GLAD THAT DIDN'T HAPPEN.
I HATED TO CAVE IN TO KIYOZUMI ...
...BUT BEING WITH YASU IS MUCH MORE IMPORTANT.
THIS PROVES AGAIN THAT I'M BETTER THAN YOU.
...
BUT I REALLY WANTED TO GO TO HAWAII...

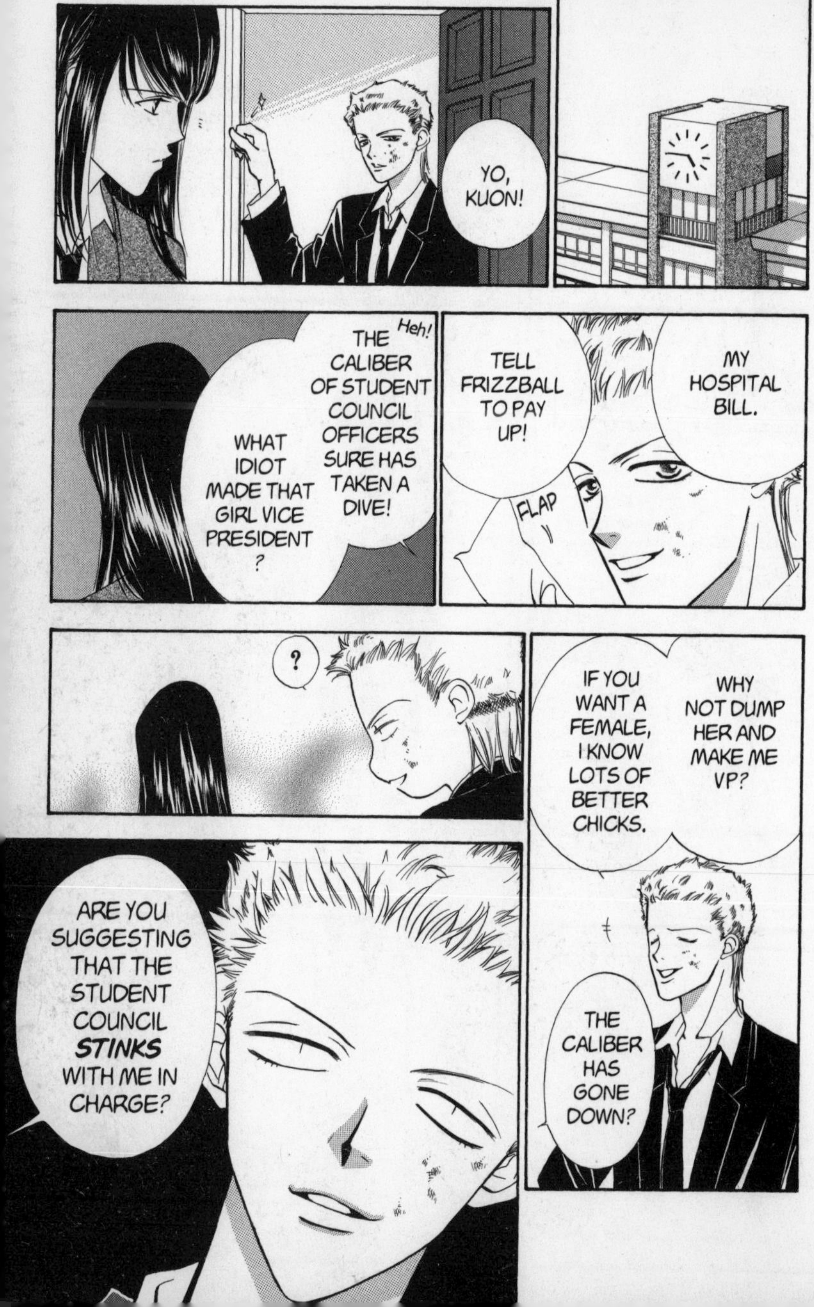
YO, KUON!
MY HOSPITAL BILL.
TELL FRIZZBALL TO PAY UP!
FLAP
Heh!
THE CALIBER OF STUDENT COUNCIL OFFICERS SURE HAS TAKEN A DIVE!
WHAT IDIOT MADE THAT GIRL VICE PRESIDENT?
WHY NOT DUMP HER AND MAKE ME VP?
IF YOU WANT A FEMALE, I KNOW LOTS OF BETTER CHICKS.
THE CALIBER HAS GONE DOWN?
?
ARE YOU SUGGESTING THAT THE STUDENT COUNCIL **STINKS** WITH ME IN CHARGE?

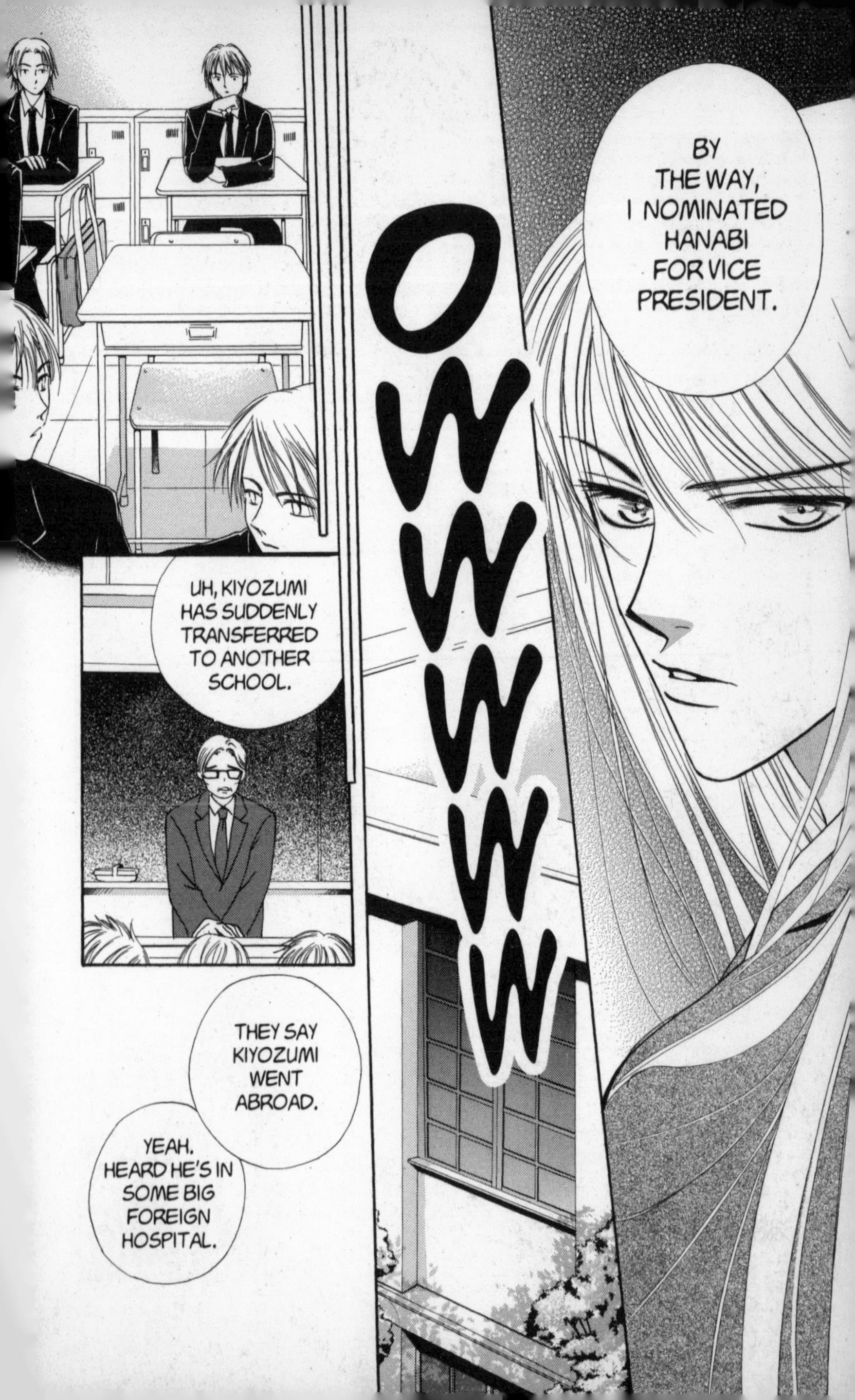
BY THE WAY, I NOMINATED HANABI FOR VICE PRESIDENT.
OWWWWW
UH, KIYOZUMI HAS SUDDENLY TRANSFERRED TO ANOTHER SCHOOL.
THEY SAY KIYOZUMI WENT ABROAD.
YEAH. HEARD HE'S IN SOME BIG FOREIGN HOSPITAL.

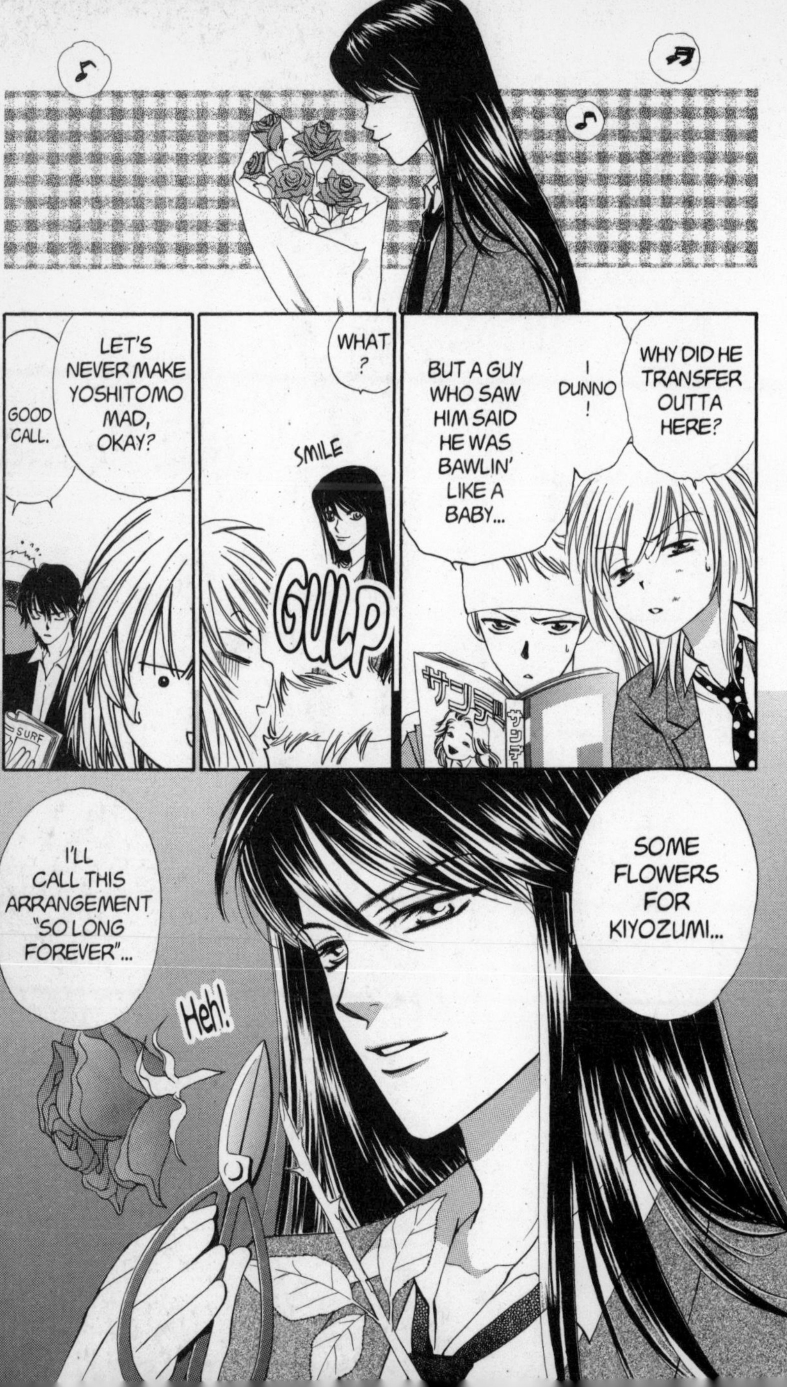
WHY DID HE TRANSFER OUTTA HERE?
I DUNNO!
BUT A GUY WHO SAW HIM SAID HE WAS BAWLIN' LIKE A BABY...
WHAT?
SMILE
GULP
LET'S NEVER MAKE YOSHITOMO MAD, OKAY?
GOOD CALL.
SURF
SOME FLOWERS FOR KIYOZUMI...
I'LL CALL THIS ARRANGEMENT "SO LONG FOREVER"...
Heh!

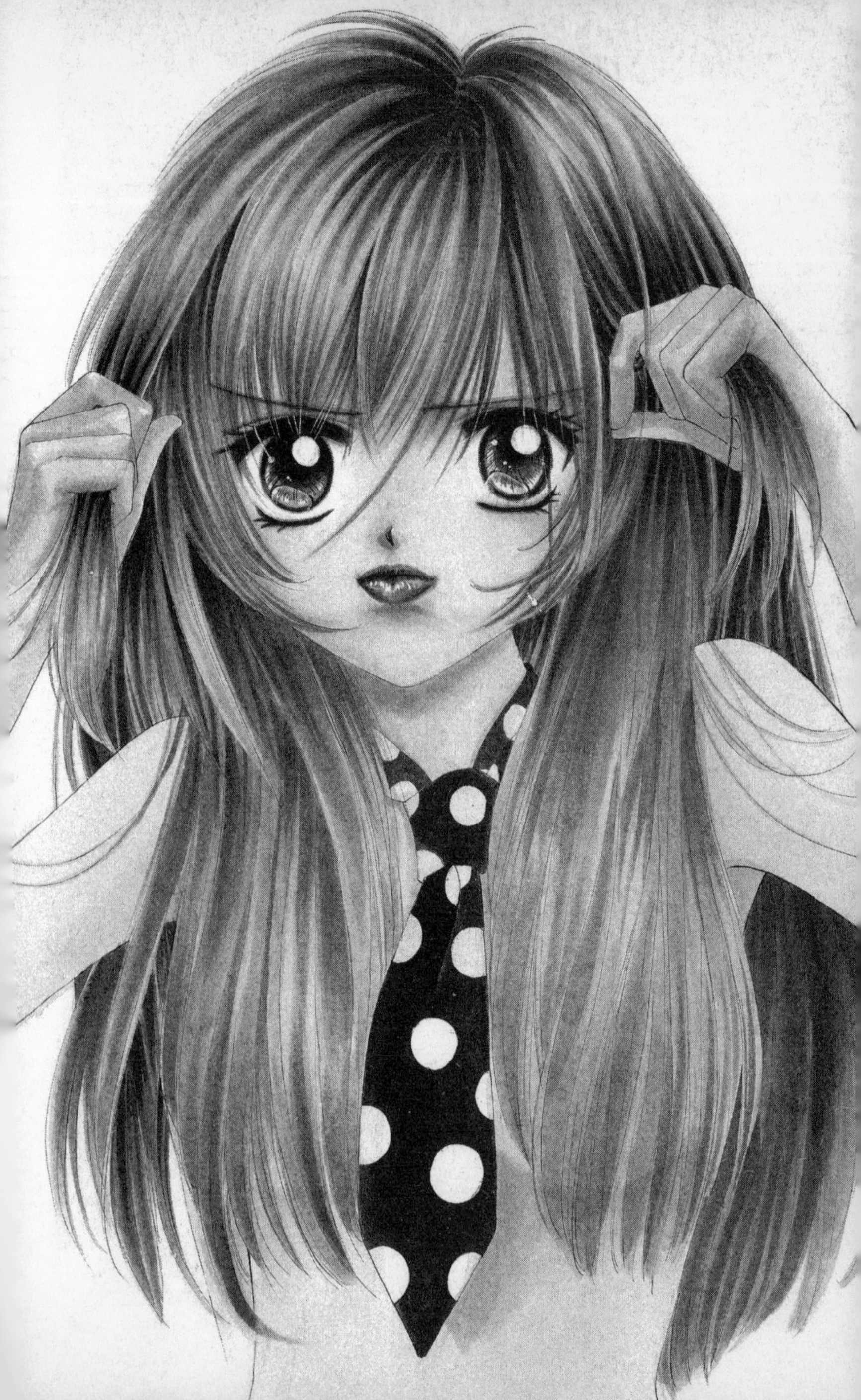

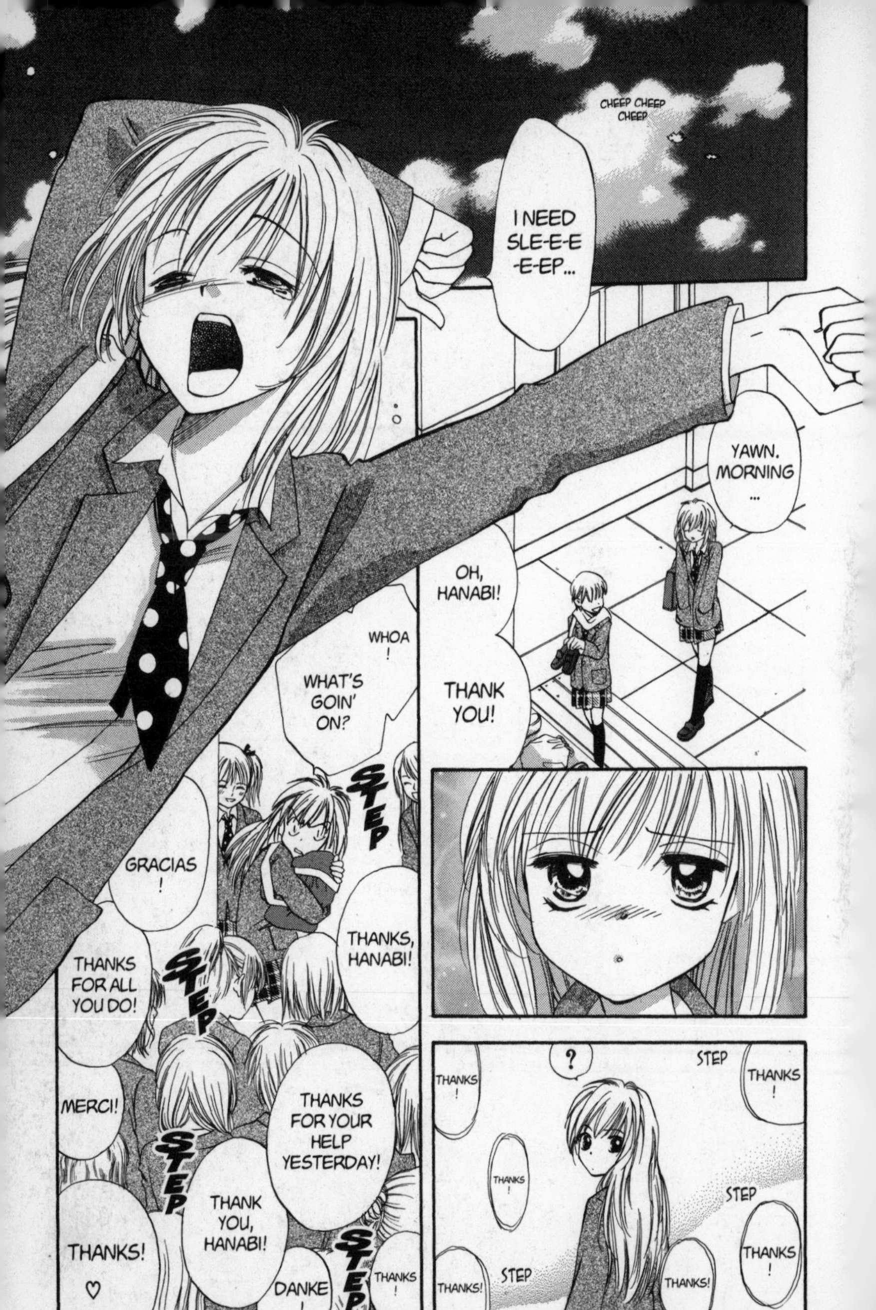
CHEEP CHEEP CHEEP
I NEED SLE-E-E-E-EP...
YAWN. MORNING ...
OH, HANABI!
THANK YOU!
?
STEP
THANKS!
THANKS!
THANKS!
STEP
THANKS!
THANKS!
STEP
THANKS!
WHOA!
WHAT'S GOIN' ON?
STEP
GRACIAS!
THANKS, HANABI!
THANKS FOR ALL YOU DO!
STEP
MERCI!
THANKS FOR YOUR HELP YESTERDAY!
STEP
THANK YOU, HANABI!
THANKS! ♡
STEP
THANKS!
DANKE!

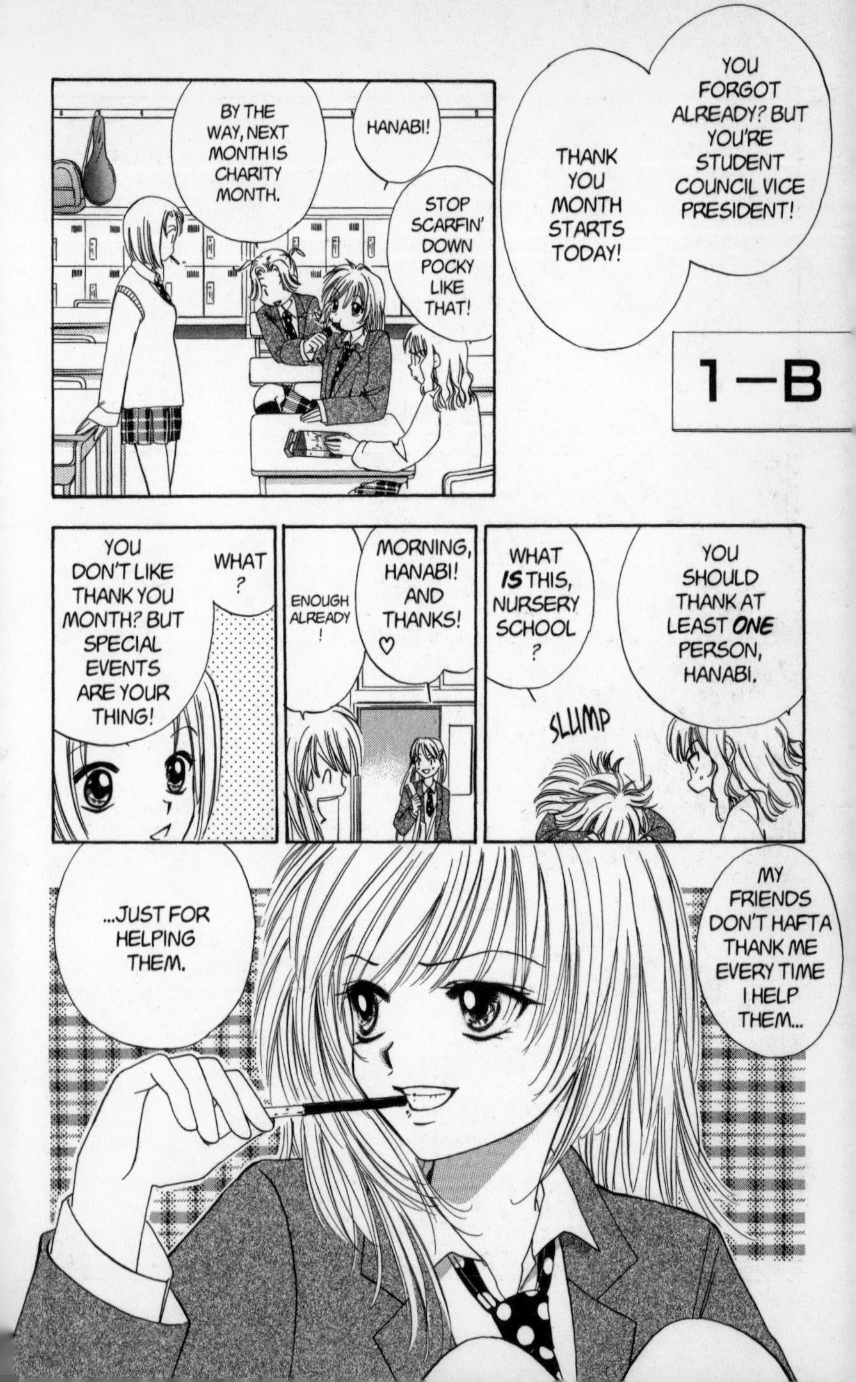
YOU FORGOT ALREADY? BUT YOU'RE STUDENT COUNCIL VICE PRESIDENT!
THANK YOU MONTH STARTS TODAY!
1—B
HANABI!
STOP SCARFIN' DOWN POCKY LIKE THAT!
BY THE WAY, NEXT MONTH IS CHARITY MONTH.
YOU SHOULD THANK AT LEAST ONE PERSON, HANABI.
WHAT IS THIS, NURSERY SCHOOL?
SLUMP
MORNING, HANABI! AND THANKS! ♡
ENOUGH ALREADY!
WHAT?
YOU DON'T LIKE THANK YOU MONTH? BUT SPECIAL EVENTS ARE YOUR THING!
MY FRIENDS DON'T HAFTA THANK ME EVERY TIME I HELP THEM...
...JUST FOR HELPING THEM.

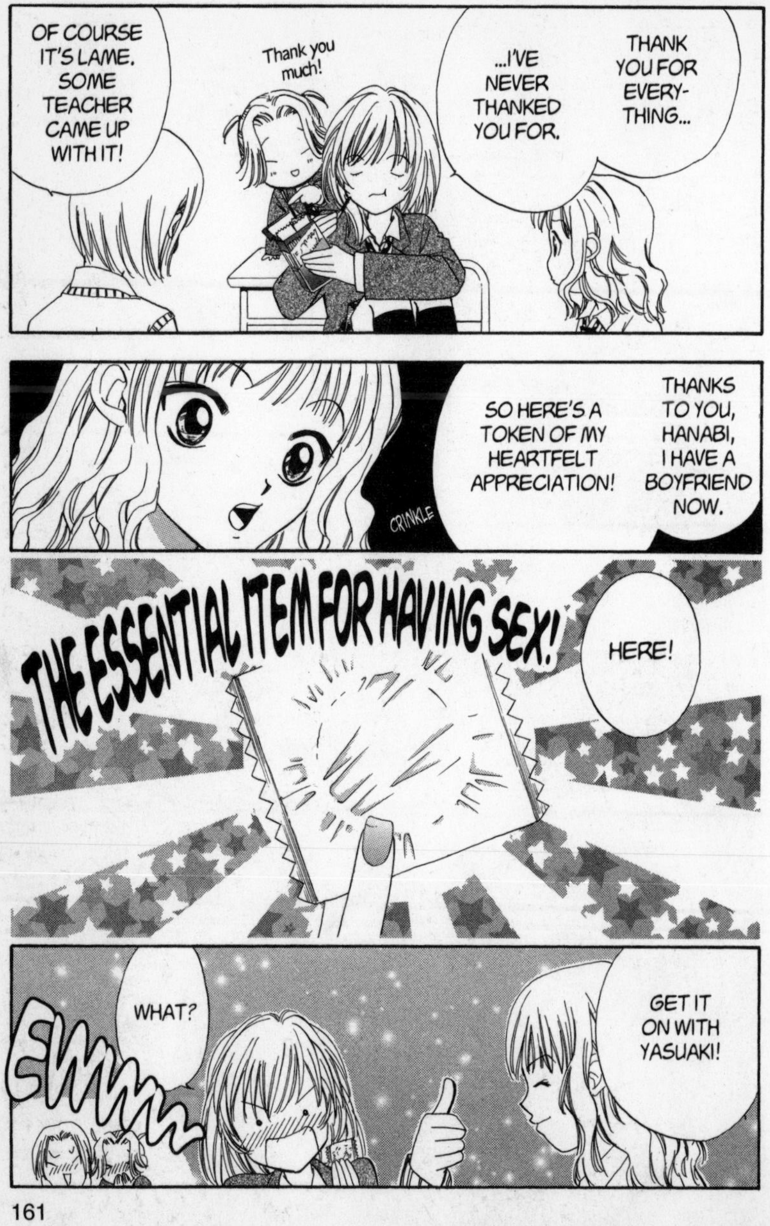
THANK YOU FOR EVERY-THING...
...I'VE NEVER THANKED YOU FOR.
Thank you much!
OF COURSE IT'S LAME. SOME TEACHER CAME UP WITH IT!
THANKS TO YOU, HANABI, I HAVE A BOYFRIEND NOW.
SO HERE'S A TOKEN OF MY HEARTFELT APPRECIATION!
CRINKLE
HERE!
THE ESSENTIAL ITEM FOR HAVING SEX!
GET IT ON WITH YASUAKI!
WHAT?
EWWWW

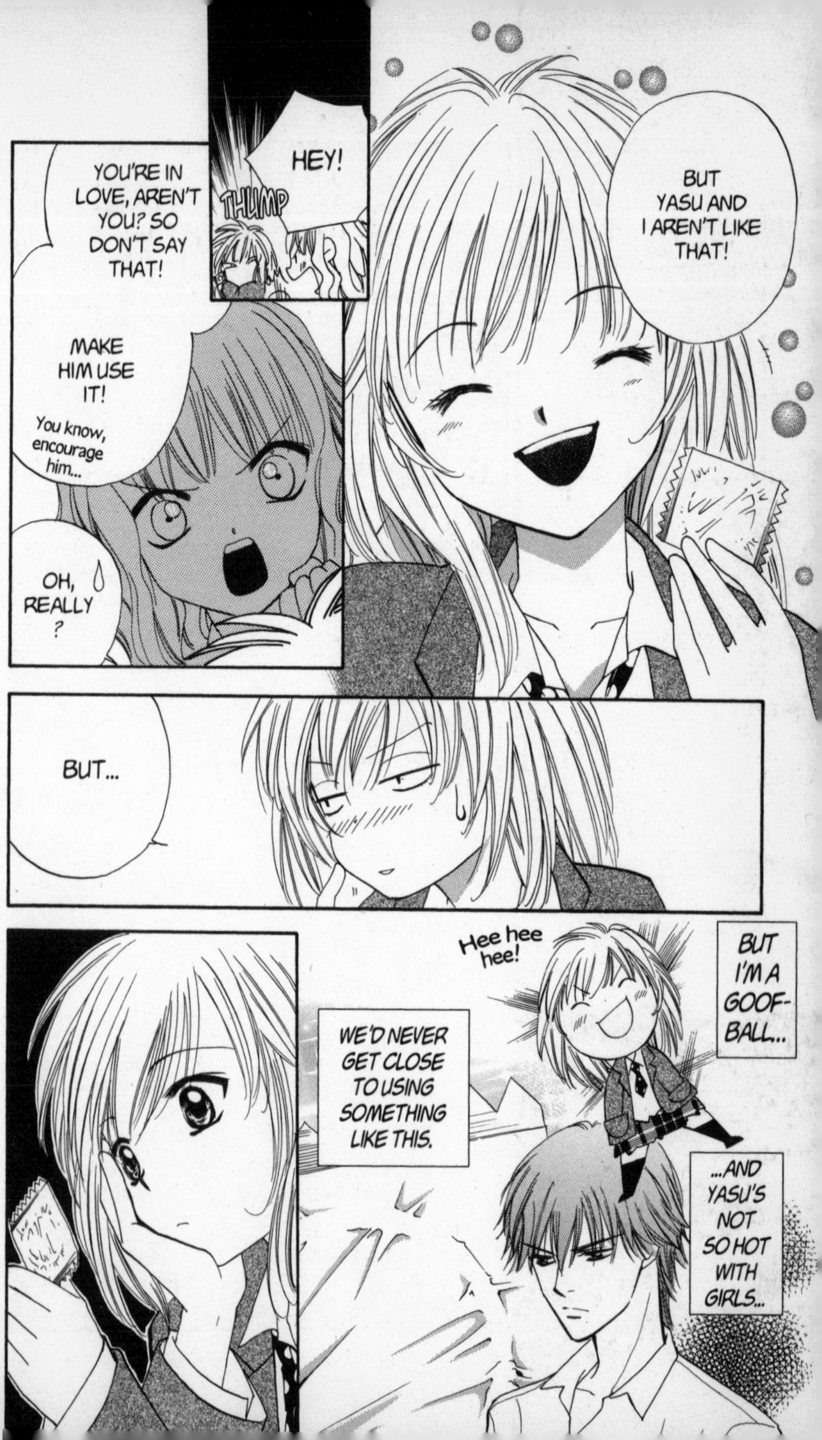
BUT YASU AND I AREN'T LIKE THAT!
HEY!
THUMP
YOU'RE IN LOVE, AREN'T YOU? SO DON'T SAY THAT!
MAKE HIM USE IT!
You know, encourage him...
OH, REALLY?
BUT...
BUT I'M A GOOF-BALL...
Hee hee hee!
...AND YASU'S NOT SO HOT WITH GIRLS...
WE'D NEVER GET CLOSE TO USING SOMETHING LIKE THIS.

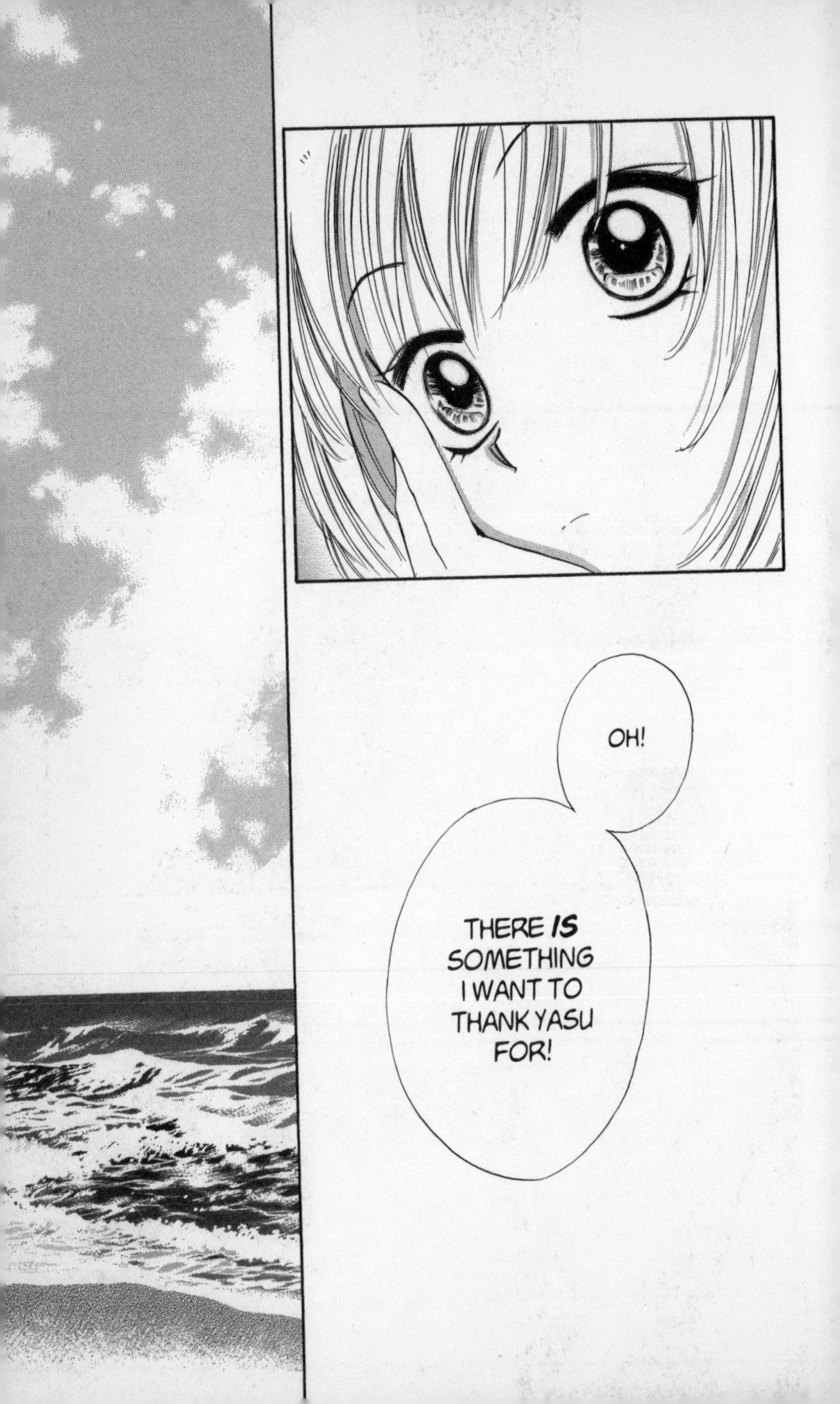
OH!
THERE **IS** SOMETHING I WANT TO THANK YASU FOR!

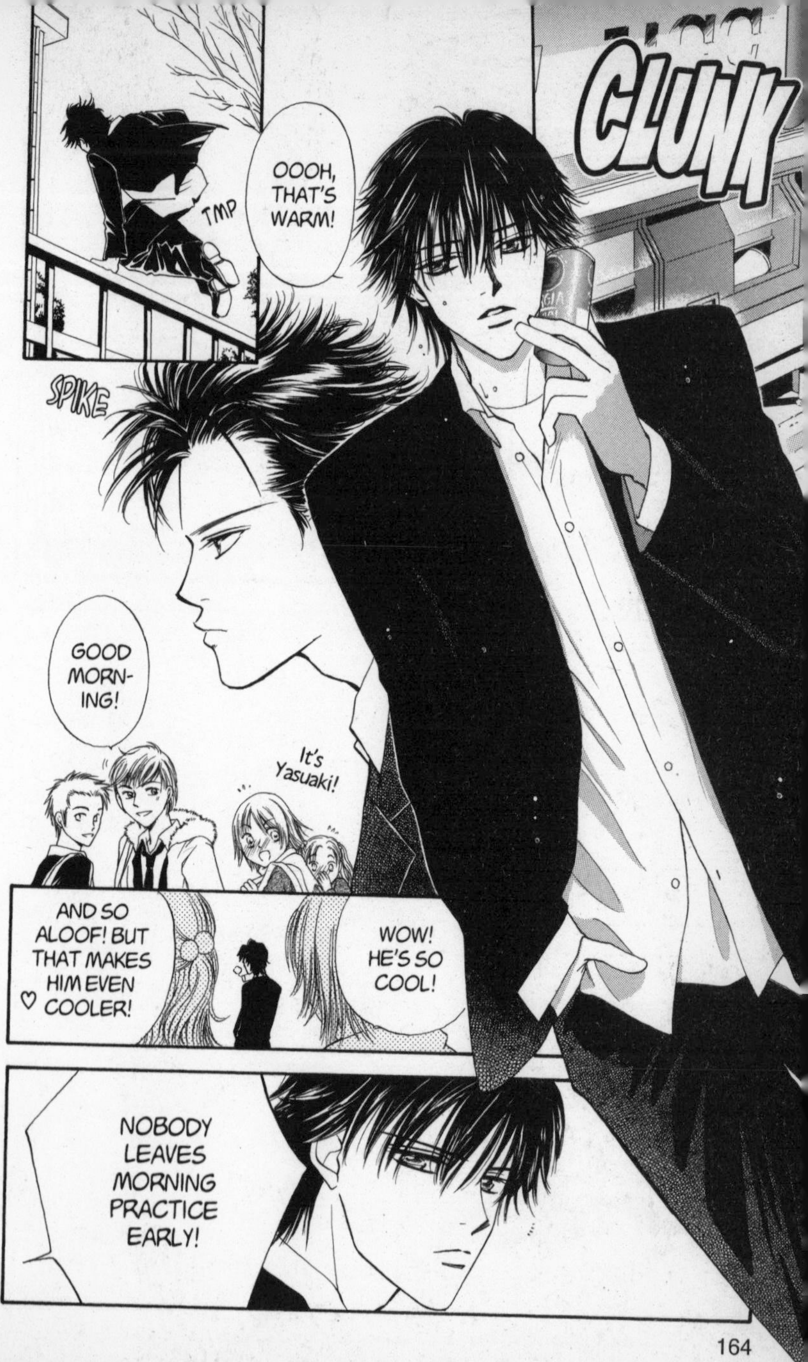

CLUNK
OOOH, THAT'S WARM!
TMP
SPIKE
GOOD MORNING!
It's Yasuaki!
WOW! HE'S SO COOL!
AND SO ALOOF! BUT THAT MAKES HIM EVEN ♡ COOLER!
NOBODY LEAVES MORNING PRACTICE EARLY!

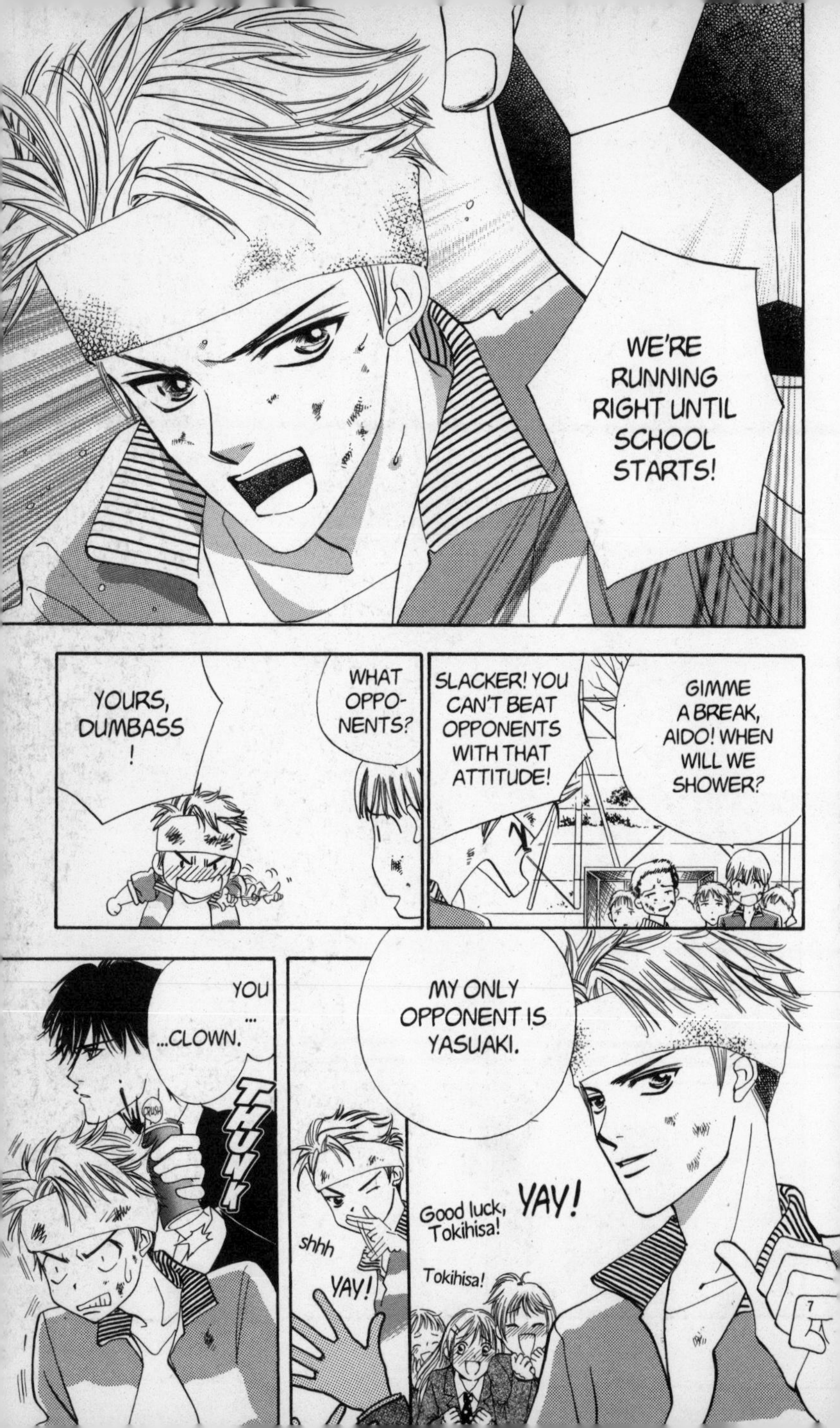
WE'RE RUNNING RIGHT UNTIL SCHOOL STARTS!
GIMME A BREAK, AIDO! WHEN WILL WE SHOWER?
SLACKER! YOU CAN'T BEAT OPPONENTS WITH THAT ATTITUDE!
WHAT OPPO-NENTS?
YOURS, DUMBASS!
MY ONLY OPPONENT IS YASUAKI.
YAY!
Good luck, Tokihisa!
Tokihisa!
shhh
YAY!
YOU ...
...CLOWN.
CRUSH
THUNK

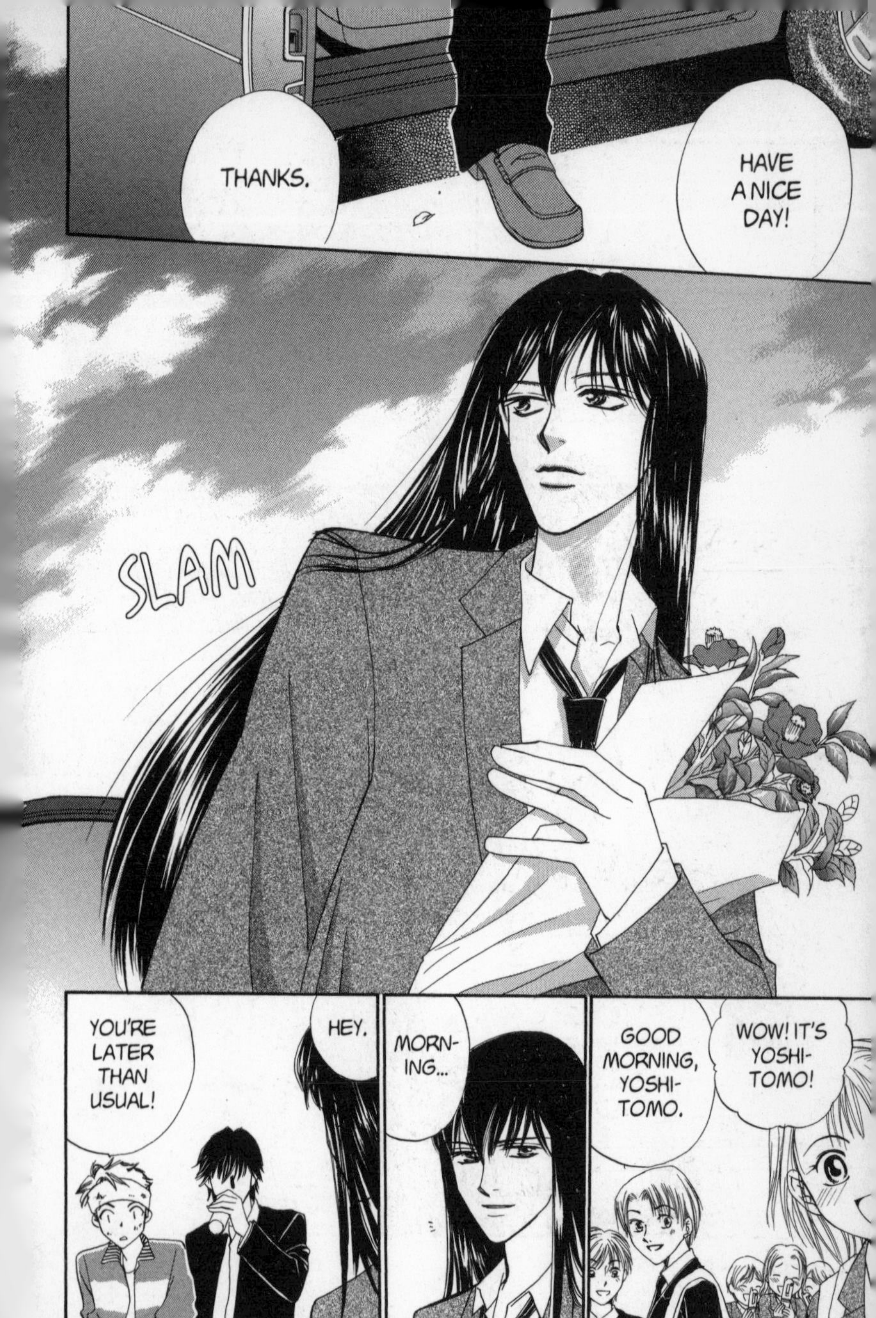
HAVE A NICE DAY!
THANKS.
SLAM
WOW! IT'S YOSHI-TOMO!
GOOD MORNING, YOSHI-TOMO.
MORN-ING...
HEY.
YOU'RE LATER THAN USUAL!

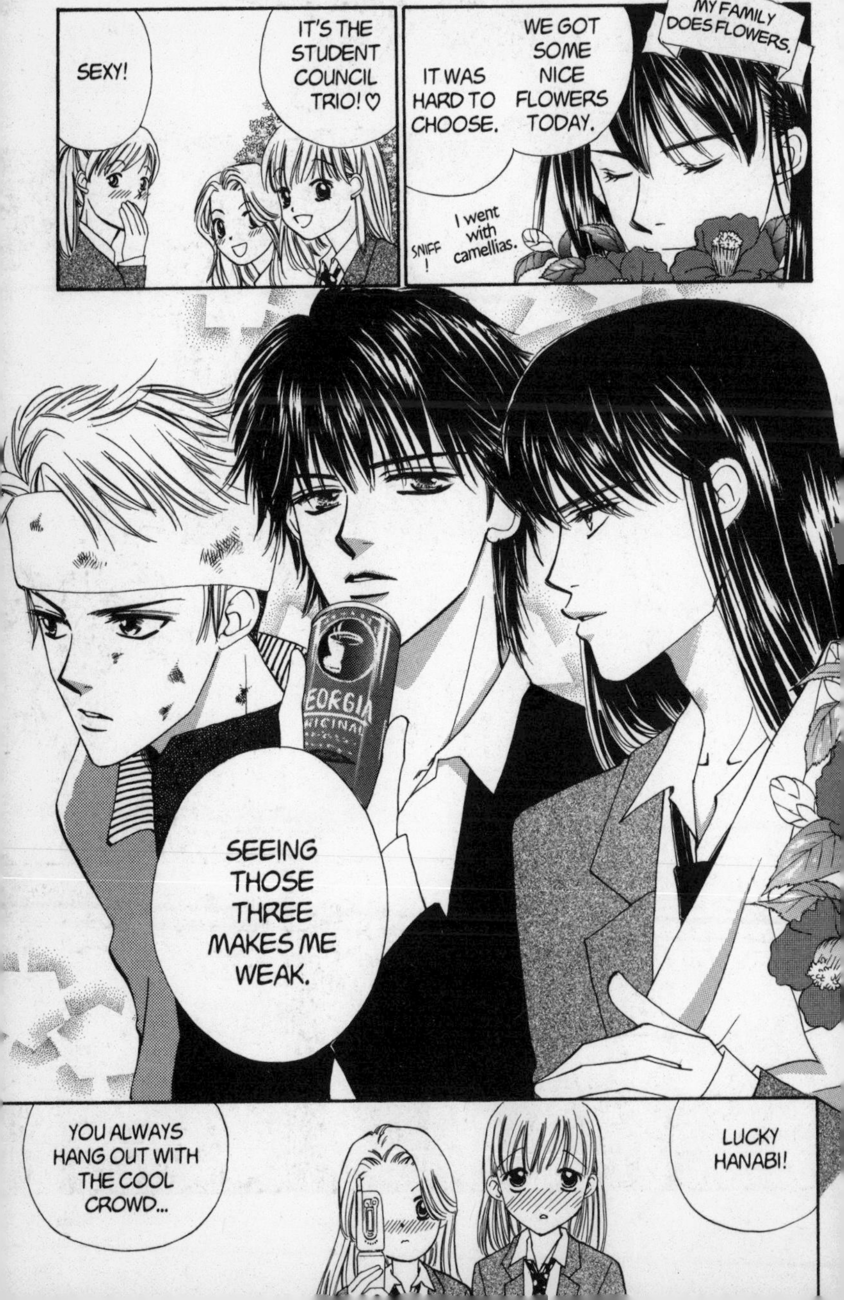
MY FAMILY DOES FLOWERS.
WE GOT SOME NICE FLOWERS TODAY.
IT WAS HARD TO CHOOSE.
SNIFF!
I went with camellias.
IT'S THE STUDENT COUNCIL TRIO! ♡
SEXY!
SEEING THOSE THREE MAKES ME WEAK.
LUCKY HANABI!
YOU ALWAYS HANG OUT WITH THE COOL CROWD...

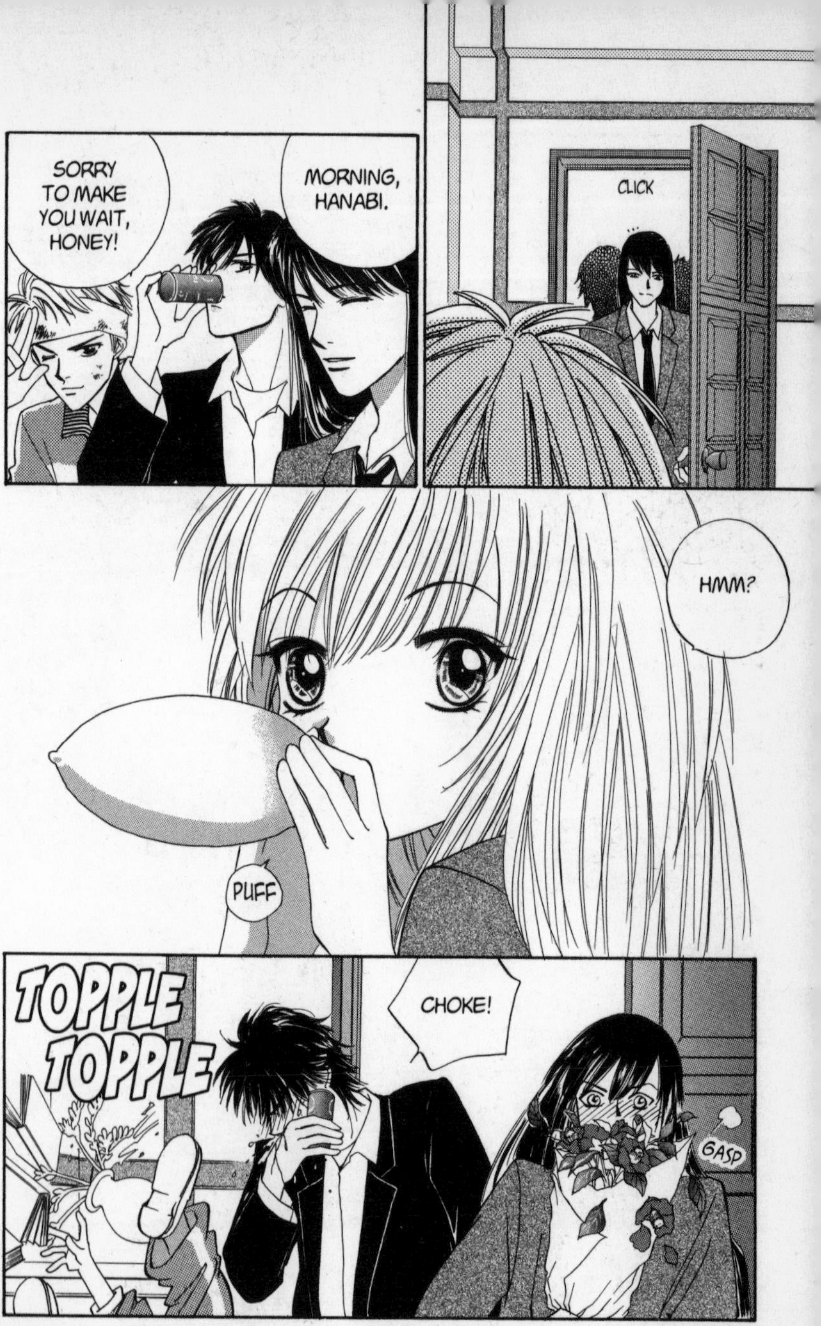
CLICK
MORNING, HANABI.
SORRY TO MAKE YOU WAIT, HONEY!
HMM?
PUFF
CHOKE!
GASP
TOPPLE TOPPLE

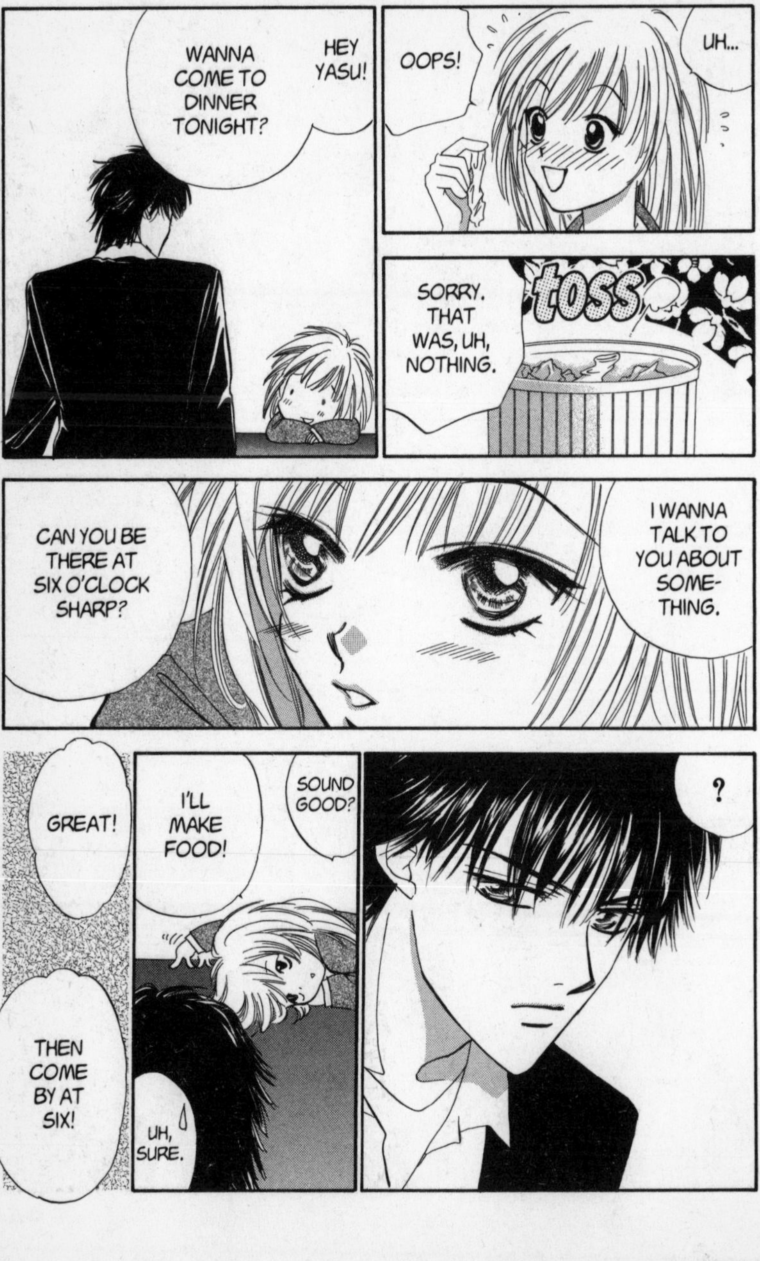
UH...
OOPS!
toss
SORRY. THAT WAS, UH, NOTHING.
HEY YASU!
WANNA COME TO DINNER TONIGHT?
I WANNA TALK TO YOU ABOUT SOME-THING.
CAN YOU BE THERE AT SIX O'CLOCK SHARP?
?
SOUND GOOD?
I'LL MAKE FOOD!
UH, SURE.
GREAT!
THEN COME BY AT SIX!

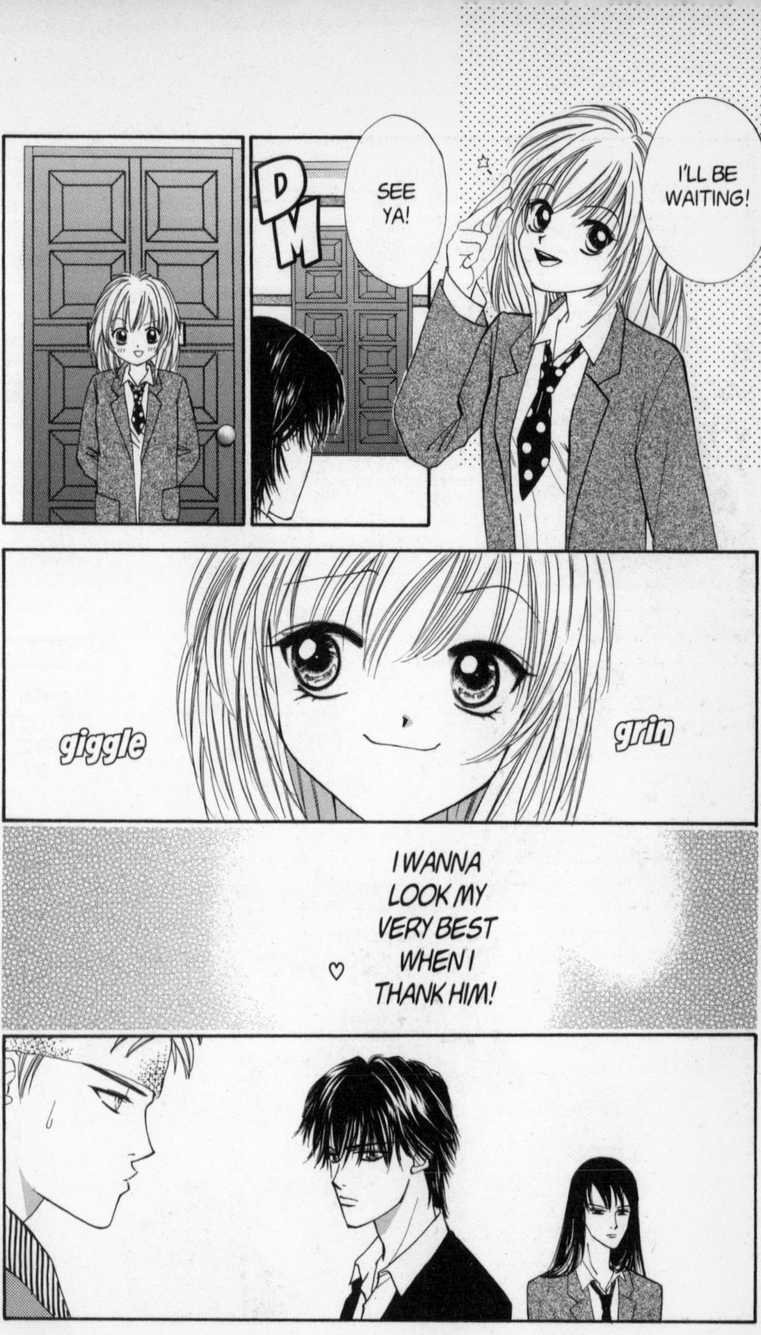
I'LL BE WAITING!
SEE YA!
DM
grin
giggle
I WANNA LOOK MY VERY BEST WHEN I THANK HIM! ♡

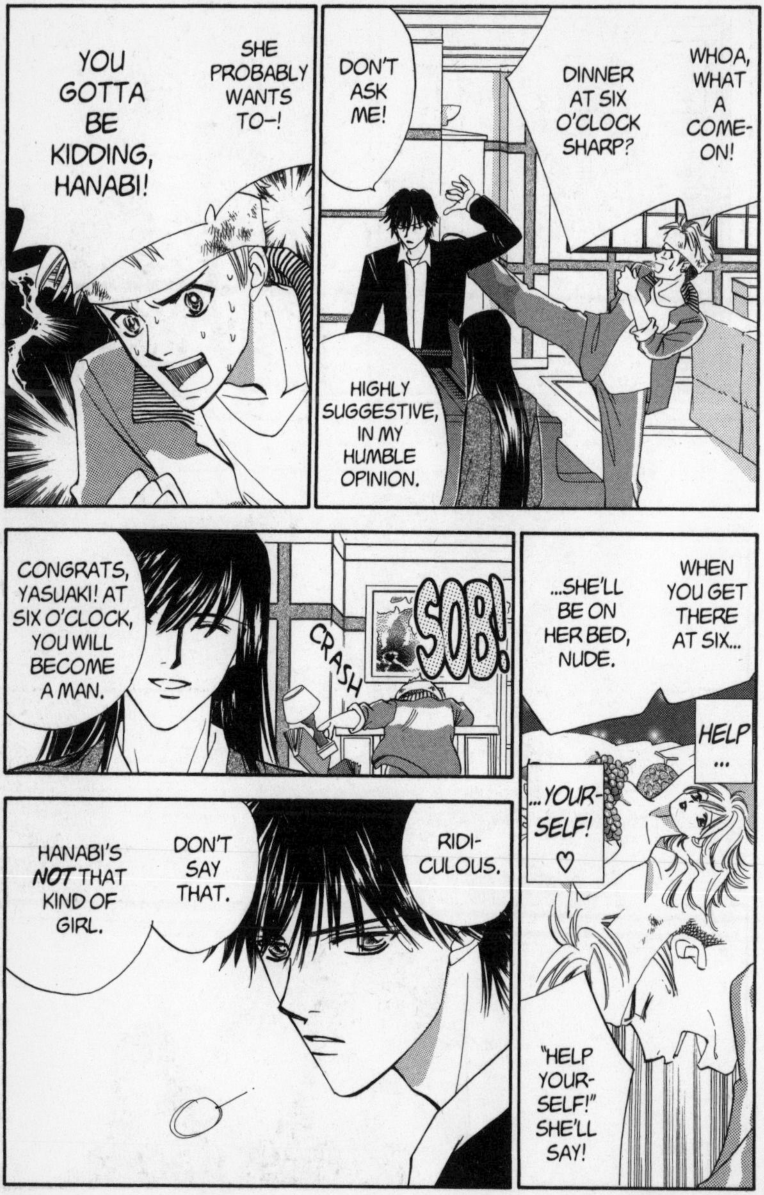
WHOA, WHAT A COME-ON!
DINNER AT SIX O'CLOCK SHARP?
DON'T ASK ME!
HIGHLY SUGGESTIVE, IN MY HUMBLE OPINION.
SHE PROBABLY WANTS TO–!
YOU GOTTA BE KIDDING, HANABI!
WHEN YOU GET THERE AT SIX...
...SHE'LL BE ON HER BED, NUDE.
HELP ...
...YOUR-SELF! ♡
"HELP YOUR-SELF!" SHE'LL SAY!
SOB!
CRASH
CONGRATS, YASUAKI! AT SIX O'CLOCK, YOU WILL BECOME A MAN.
RIDI-CULOUS.
DON'T SAY THAT.
HANABI'S *NOT* THAT KIND OF GIRL.

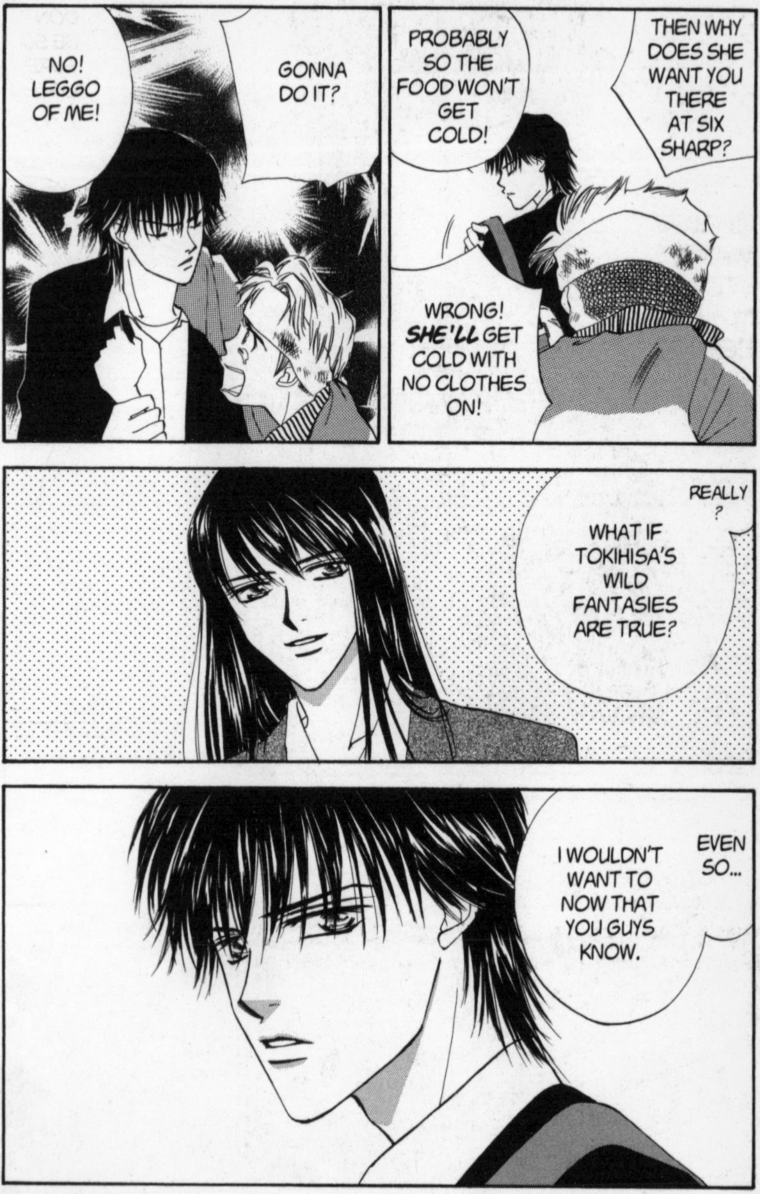
THEN WHY DOES SHE WANT YOU THERE AT SIX SHARP?
PROBABLY SO THE FOOD WON'T GET COLD!
WRONG! SHE'LL GET COLD WITH NO CLOTHES ON!
GONNA DO IT?
NO! LEGGO OF ME!
REALLY?
WHAT IF TOKIHISA'S WILD FANTASIES ARE TRUE?
EVEN SO...
I WOULDN'T WANT TO NOW THAT YOU GUYS KNOW.

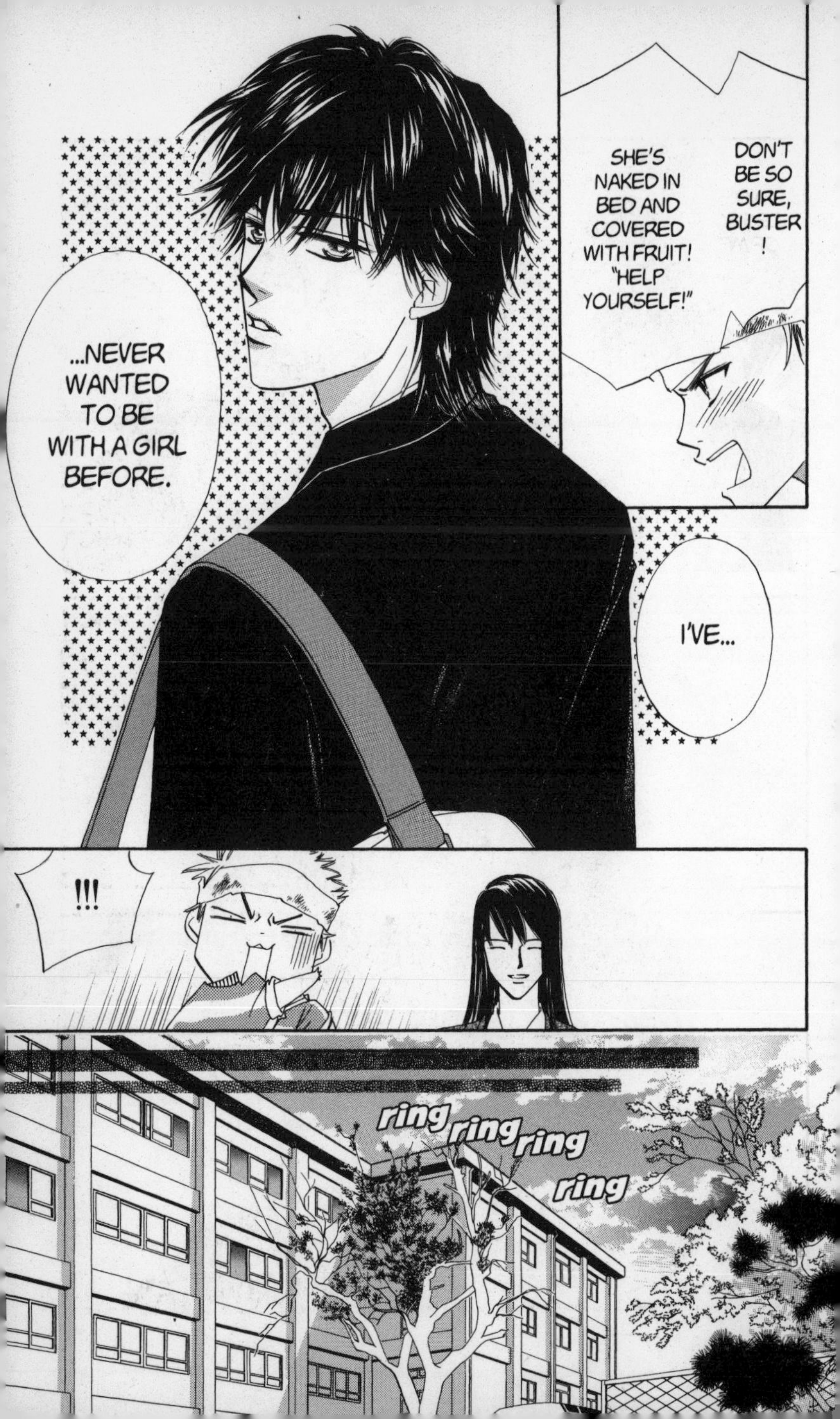
DON'T BE SO SURE, BUSTER!
SHE'S NAKED IN BED AND COVERED WITH FRUIT! "HELP YOURSELF!"
I'VE...
...NEVER WANTED TO BE WITH A GIRL BEFORE.
!!!
ring ring ring ring

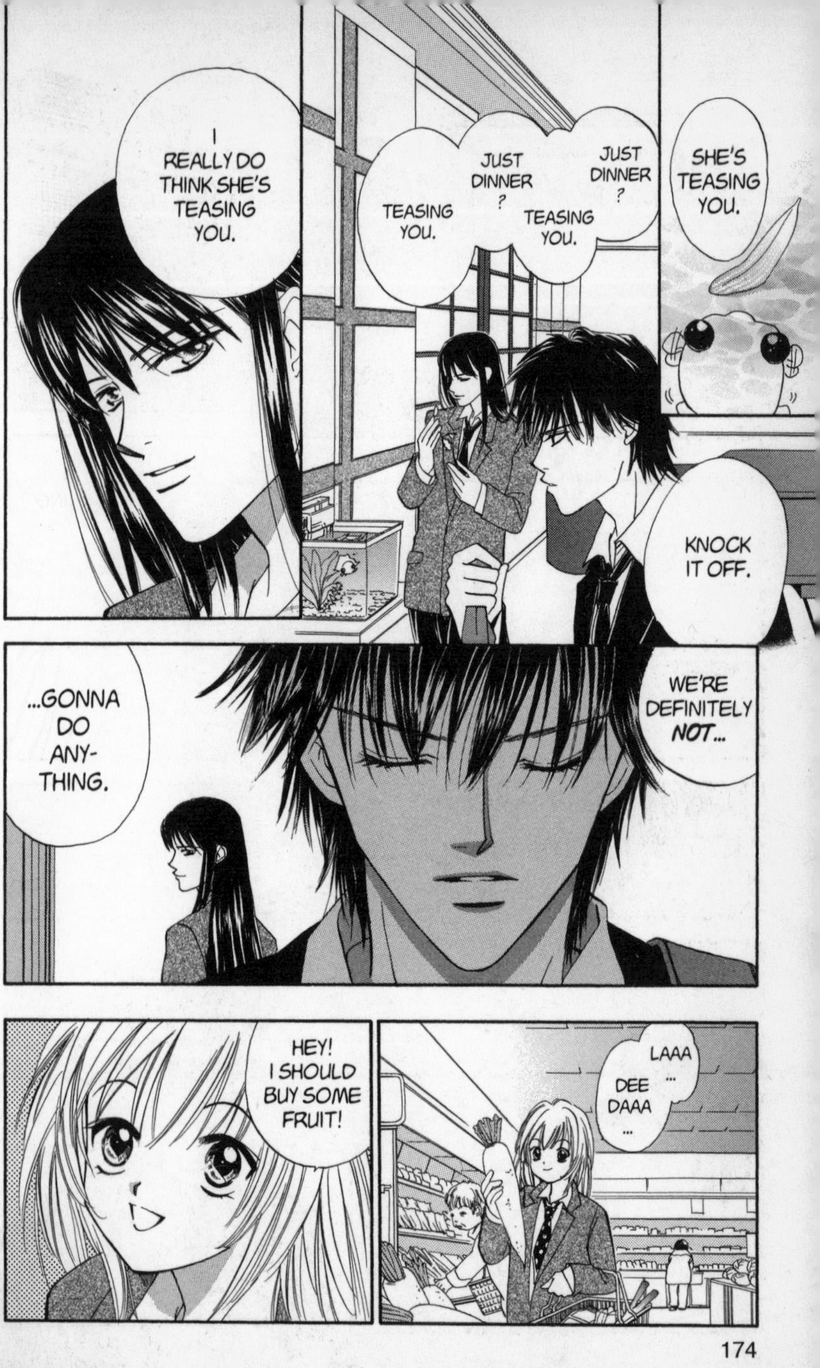
SHE'S TEASING YOU.
JUST DINNER?
JUST DINNER?
TEASING YOU.
TEASING YOU.
KNOCK IT OFF.
I REALLY DO THINK SHE'S TEASING YOU.
WE'RE DEFINITELY NOT...
...GONNA DO ANYTHING.
LAAA... DEE DAAA...
HEY! I SHOULD BUY SOME FRUIT!

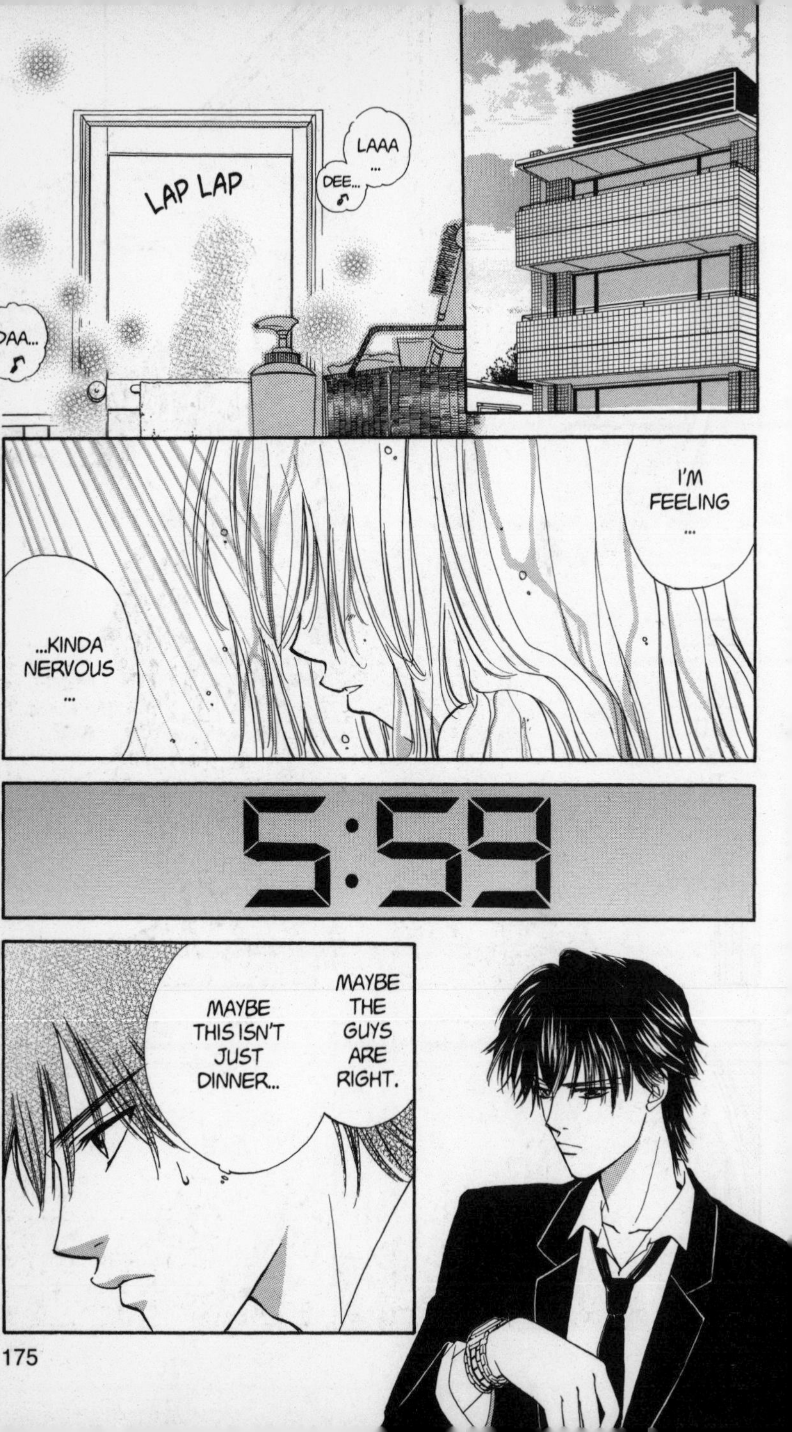
LAAA...
DEE... ♪
LAP LAP
DAA... ♪
I'M FEELING...
...KINDA NERVOUS...
5:59
MAYBE THE GUYS ARE RIGHT.
MAYBE THIS ISN'T JUST DINNER...

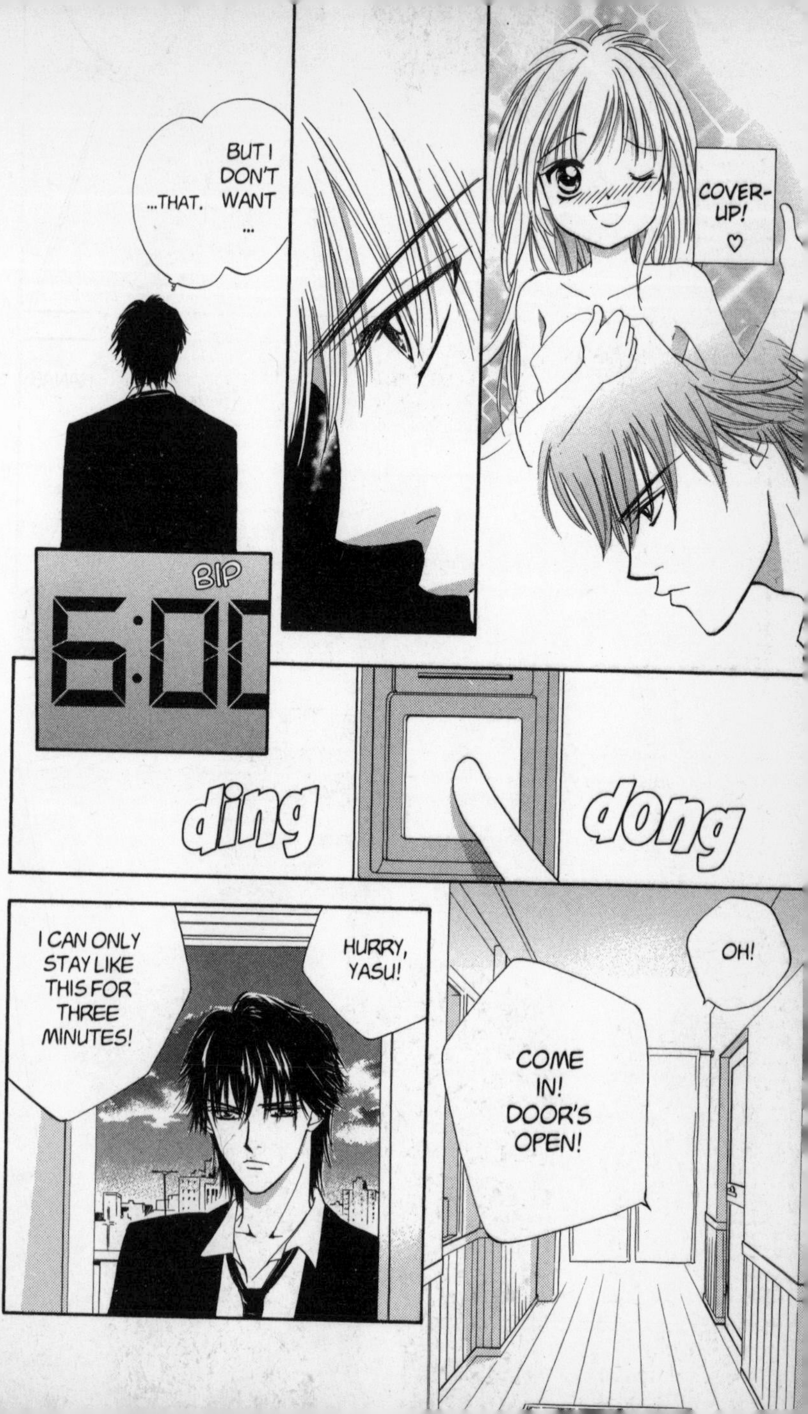

COVER-UP! ♡
BUT I DON'T WANT ... ...THAT.
BIP
6:00
ding
dong
OH!
COME IN! DOOR'S OPEN!
HURRY, YASU!
I CAN ONLY STAY LIKE THIS FOR THREE MINUTES!

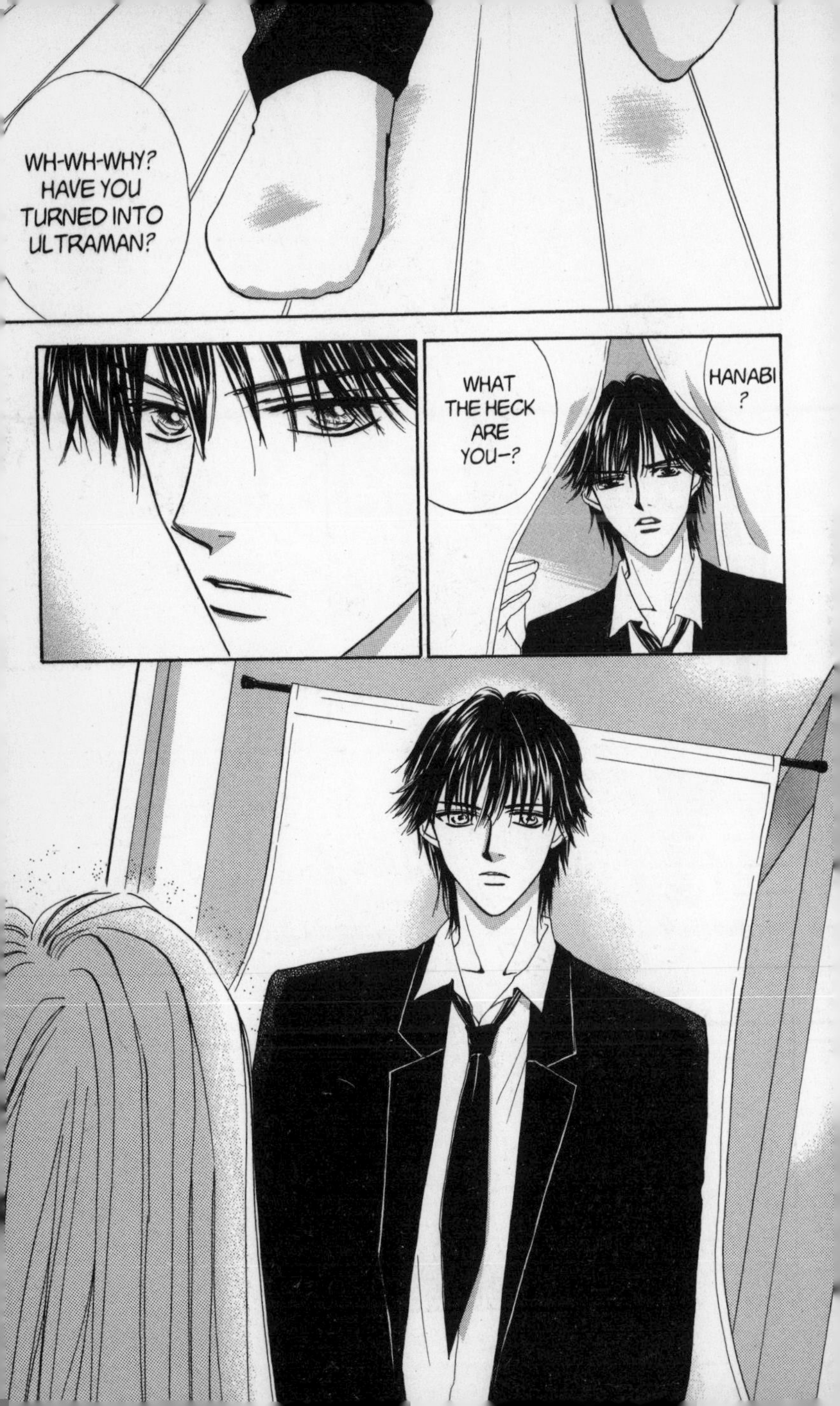
WH-WH-WHY? HAVE YOU TURNED INTO ULTRAMAN?
HANABI ?
WHAT THE HECK ARE YOU-?

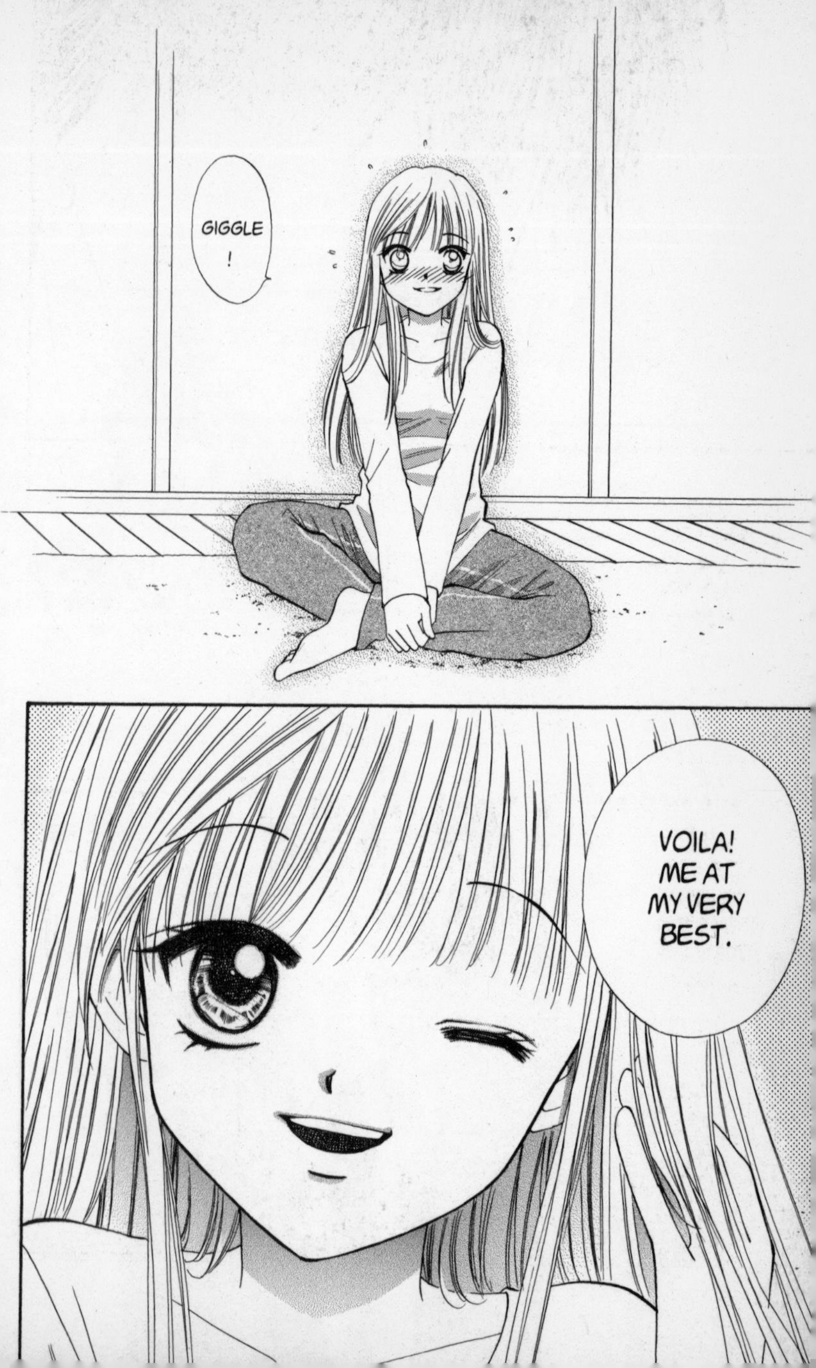
GIGGLE !
VOILA! ME AT MY VERY BEST.

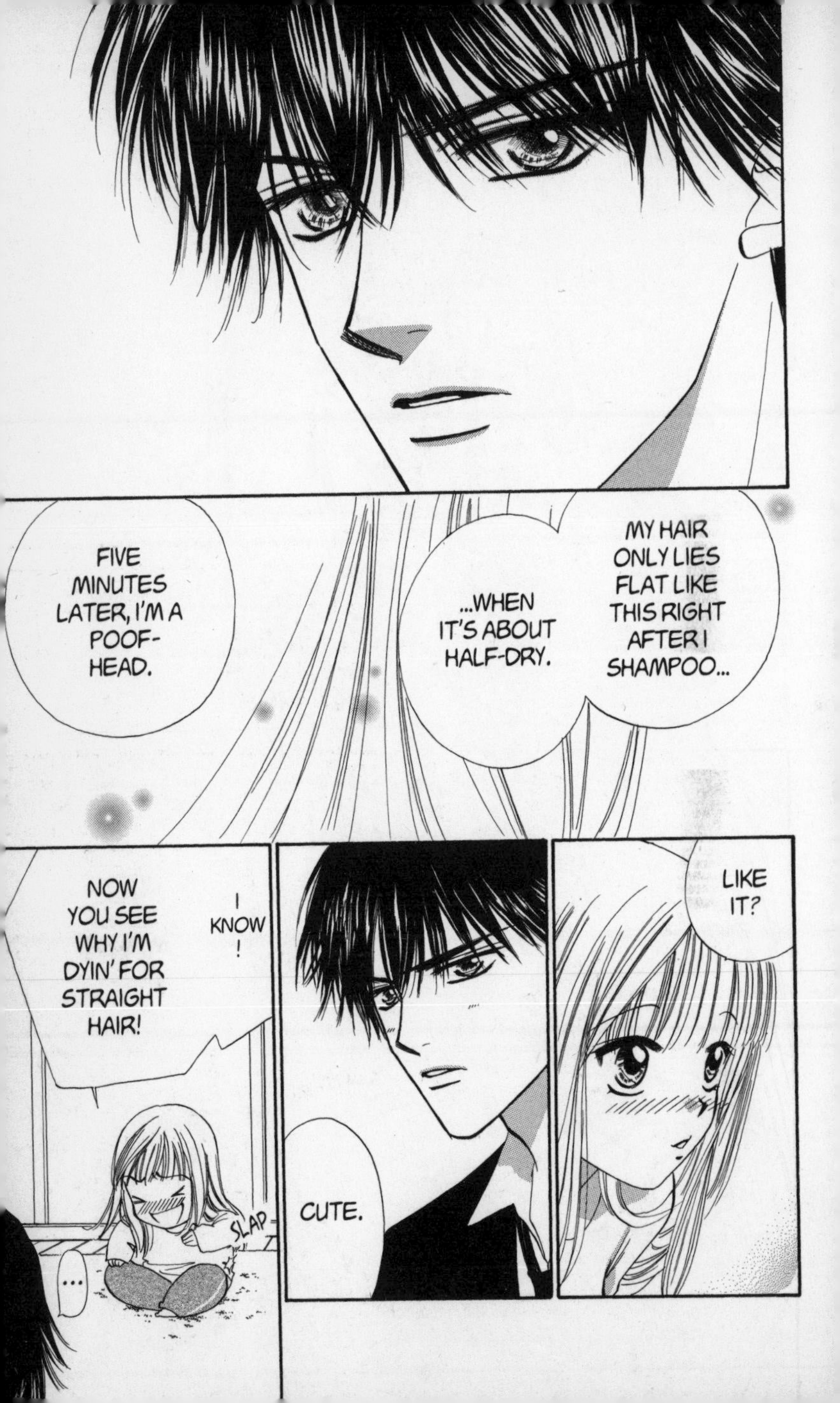
MY HAIR ONLY LIES FLAT LIKE THIS RIGHT AFTER I SHAMPOO...
...WHEN IT'S ABOUT HALF-DRY.
FIVE MINUTES LATER, I'M A POOF-HEAD.
LIKE IT?
CUTE.
I KNOW!
NOW YOU SEE WHY I'M DYIN' FOR STRAIGHT HAIR!
SLAP
...

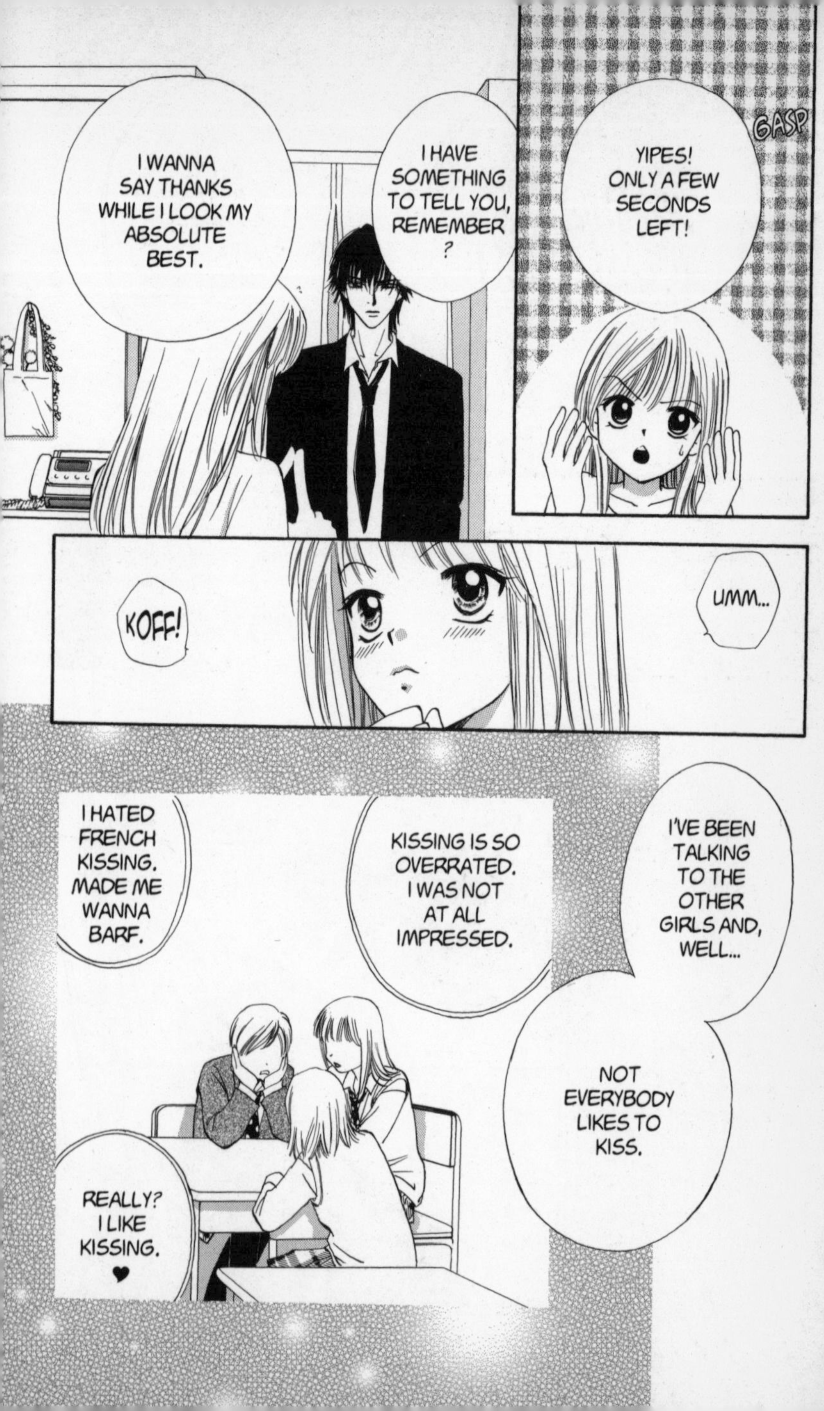
GASP
YIPES! ONLY A FEW SECONDS LEFT!
I HAVE SOMETHING TO TELL YOU, REMEMBER ?
I WANNA SAY THANKS WHILE I LOOK MY ABSOLUTE BEST.
UMM...
KOFF!
I'VE BEEN TALKING TO THE OTHER GIRLS AND, WELL...
NOT EVERYBODY LIKES TO KISS.
KISSING IS SO OVERRATED. I WAS NOT AT ALL IMPRESSED.
I HATED FRENCH KISSING. MADE ME WANNA BARF.
REALLY? I LIKE KISSING. ♥

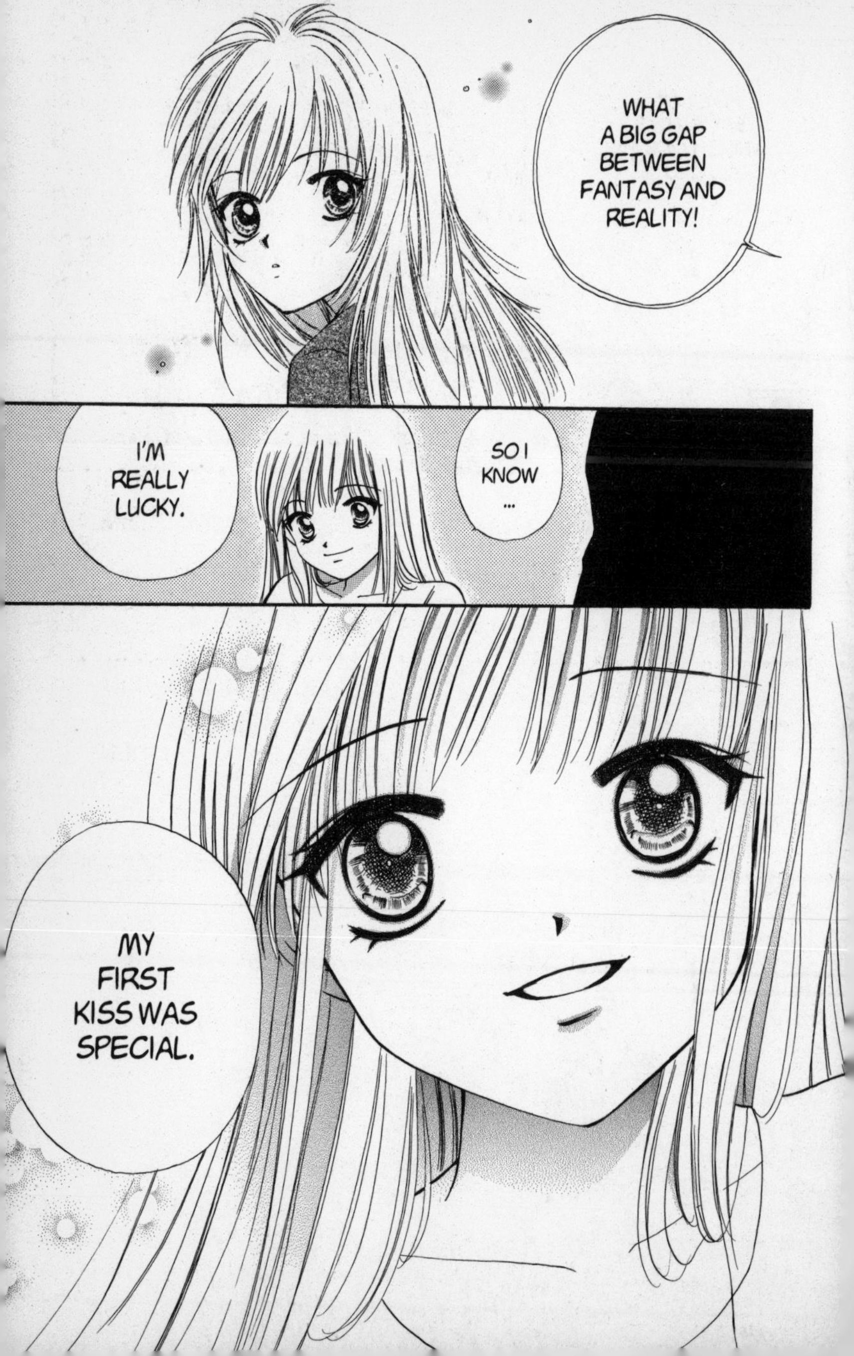
WHAT A BIG GAP BETWEEN FANTASY AND REALITY!
SO I KNOW ...
I'M REALLY LUCKY.
MY FIRST KISS WAS SPECIAL.

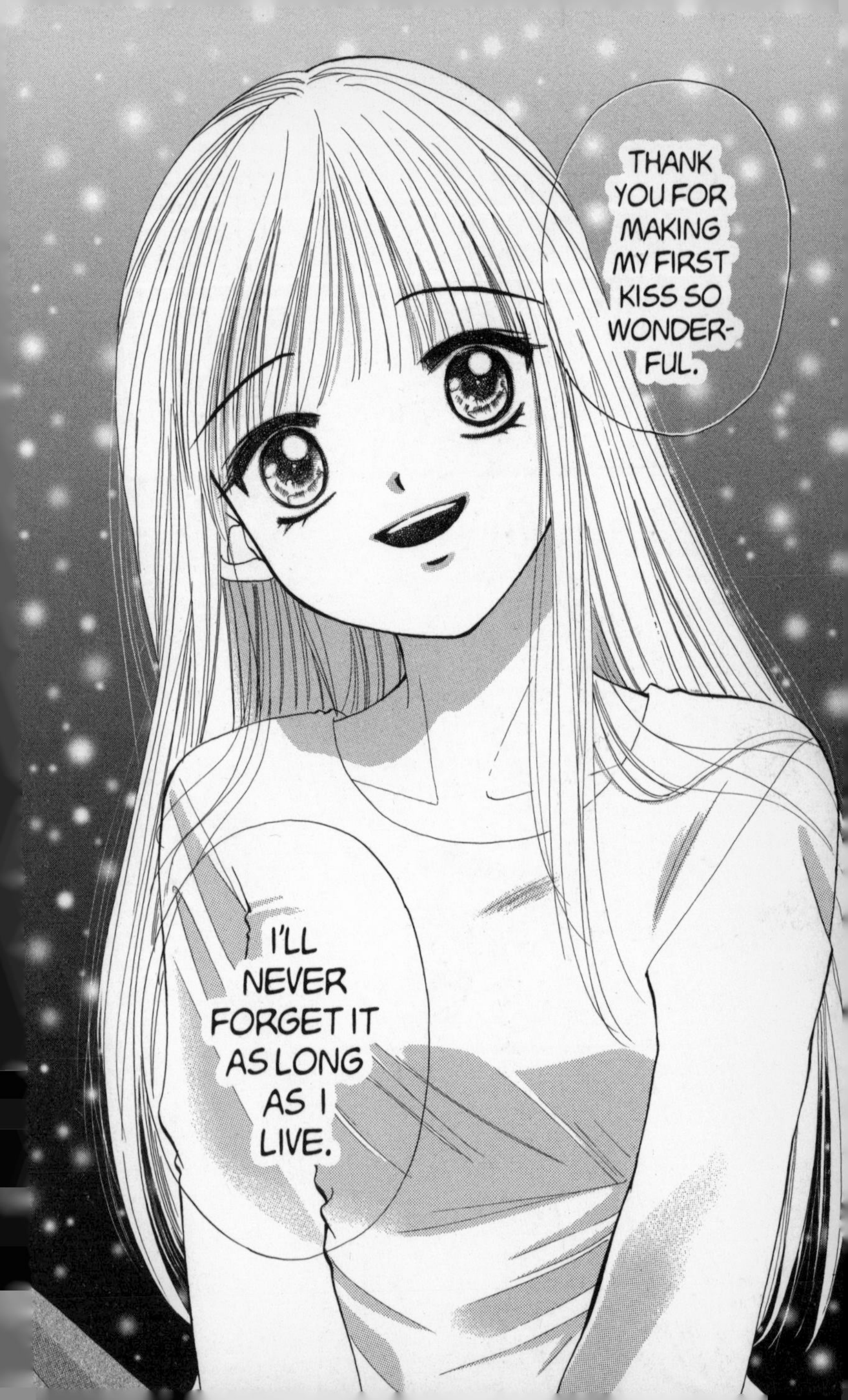
THANK YOU FOR MAKING MY FIRST KISS SO WONDER-FUL.
I'LL NEVER FORGET IT AS LONG AS I LIVE.

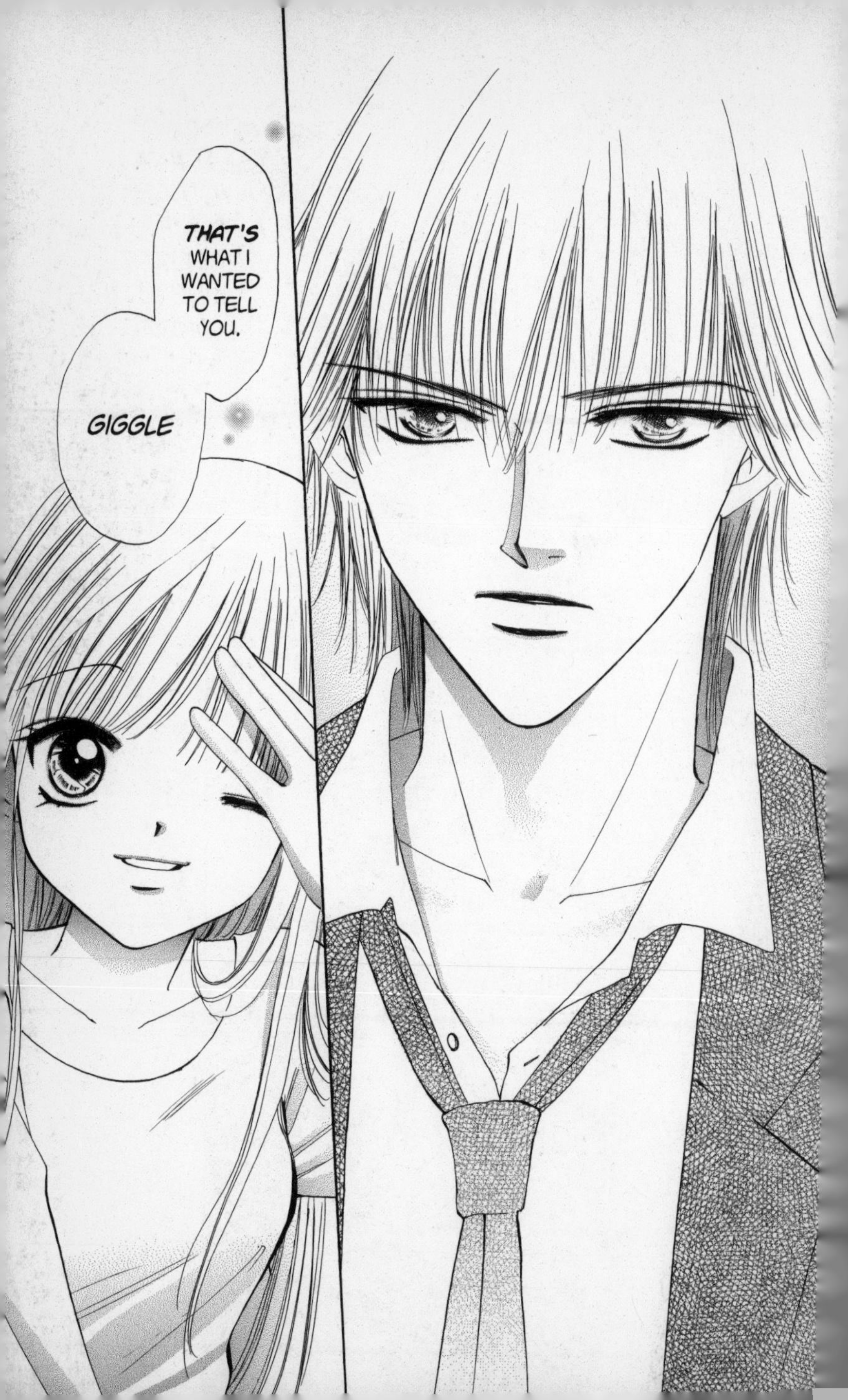
THAT'S WHAT I WANTED TO TELL YOU.
GIGGLE

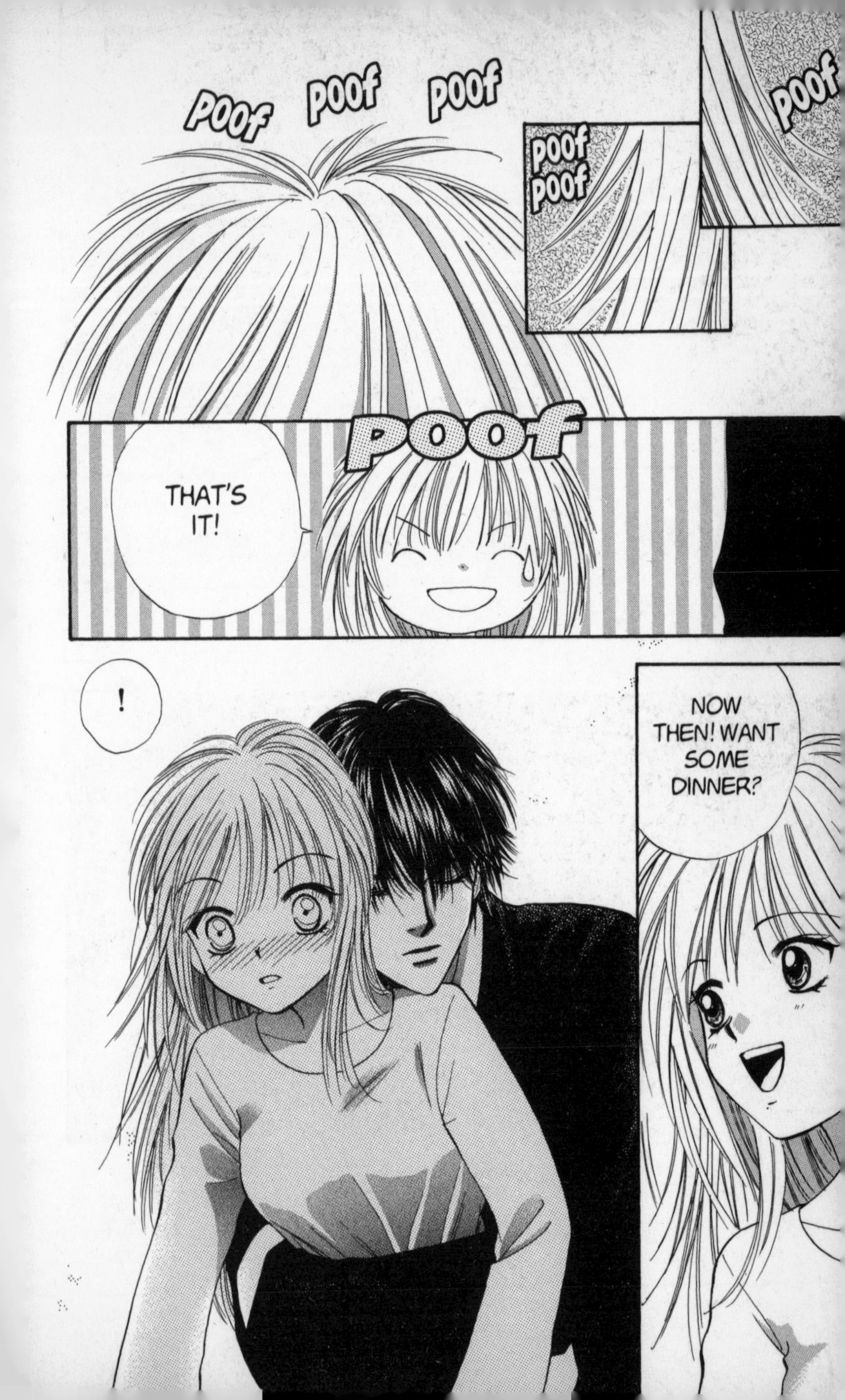
POOF
poof poof
POOF poof poof
POOF
THAT'S IT!
NOW THEN! WANT SOME DINNER?
!

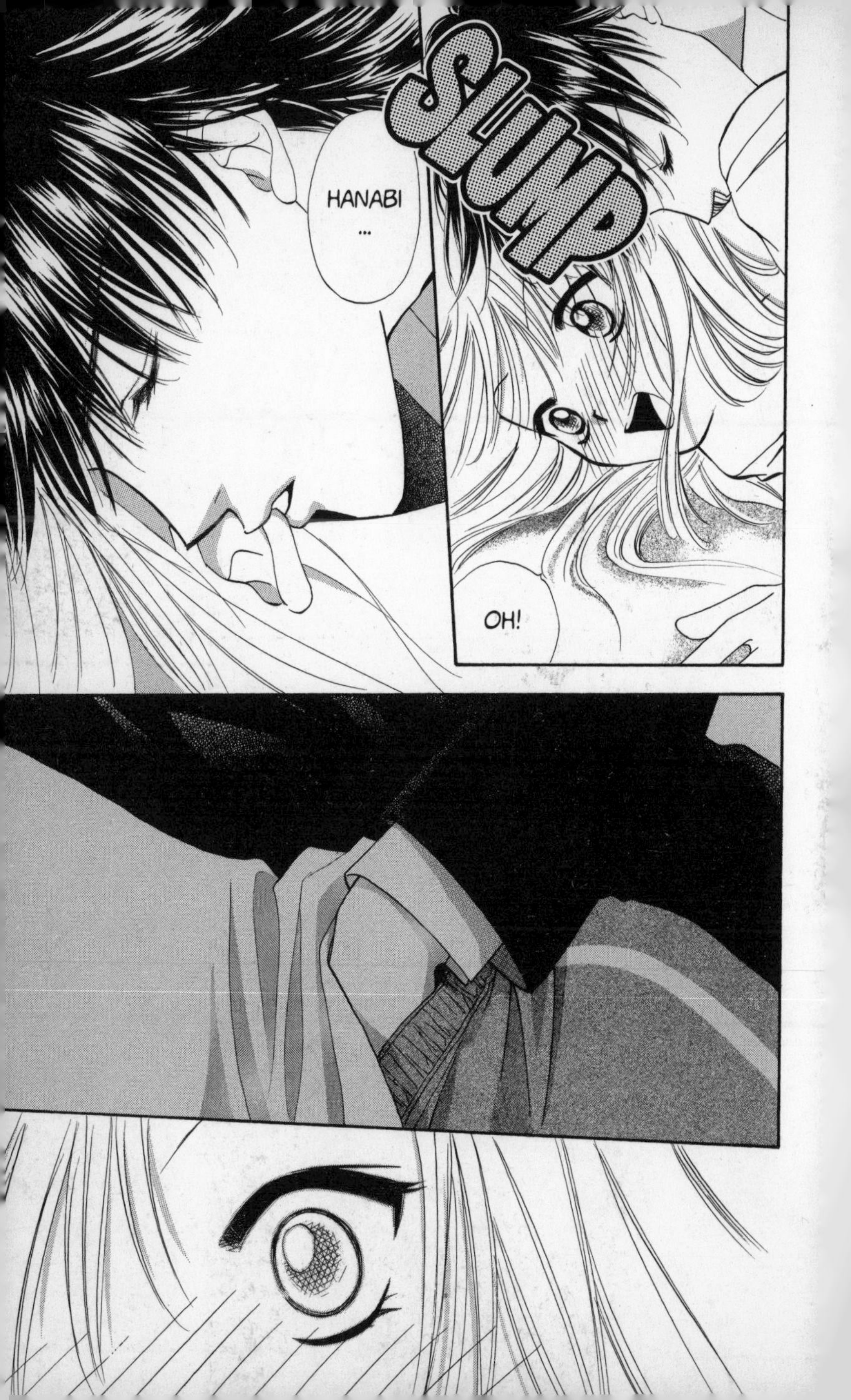
SLUMP
OH!
HANABI ...

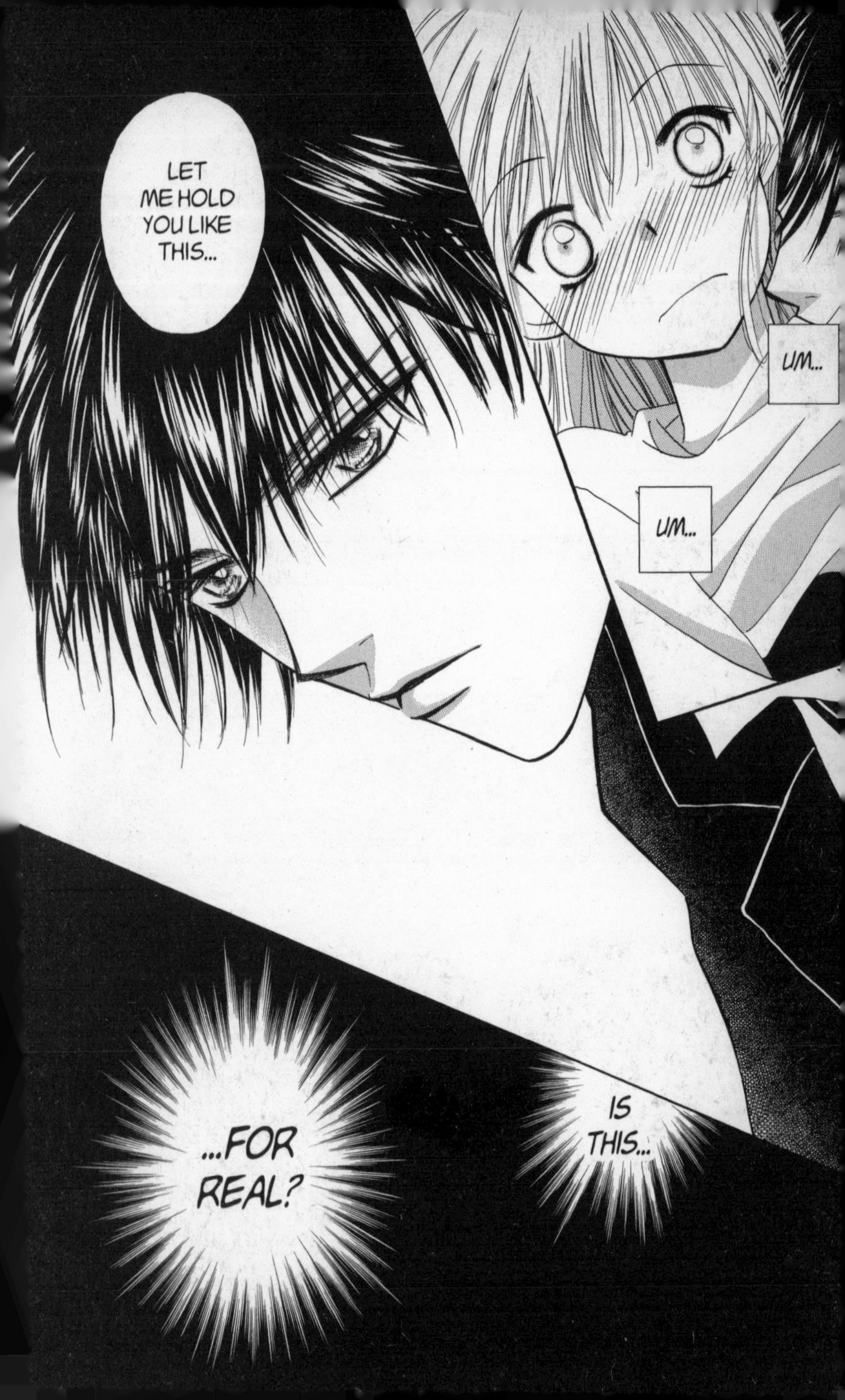
UM...
UM...
LET ME HOLD YOU LIKE THIS...
IS THIS...
...FOR REAL?

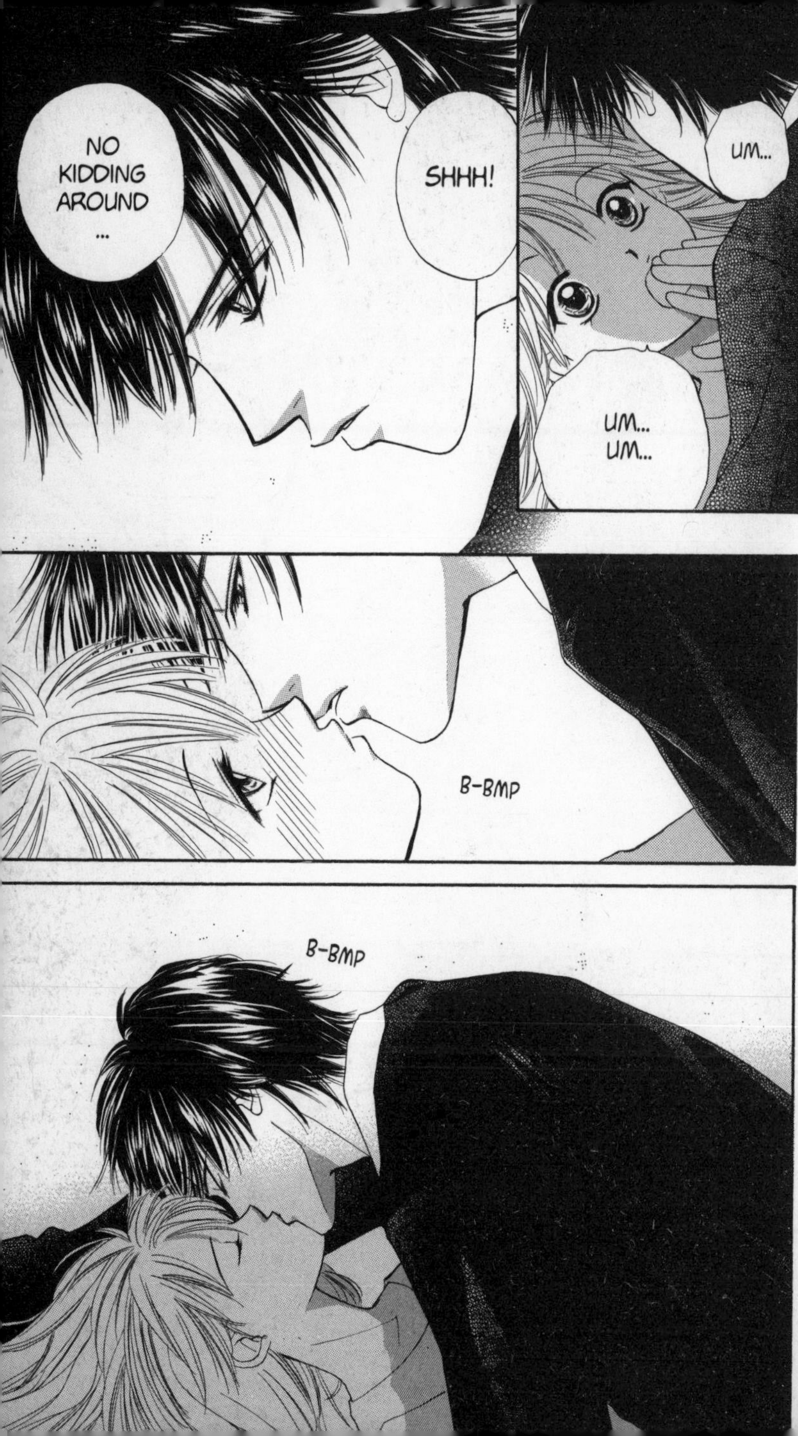
UM...
UM... UM...
SHHH!
NO KIDDING AROUND ...
B-BMP
B-BMP

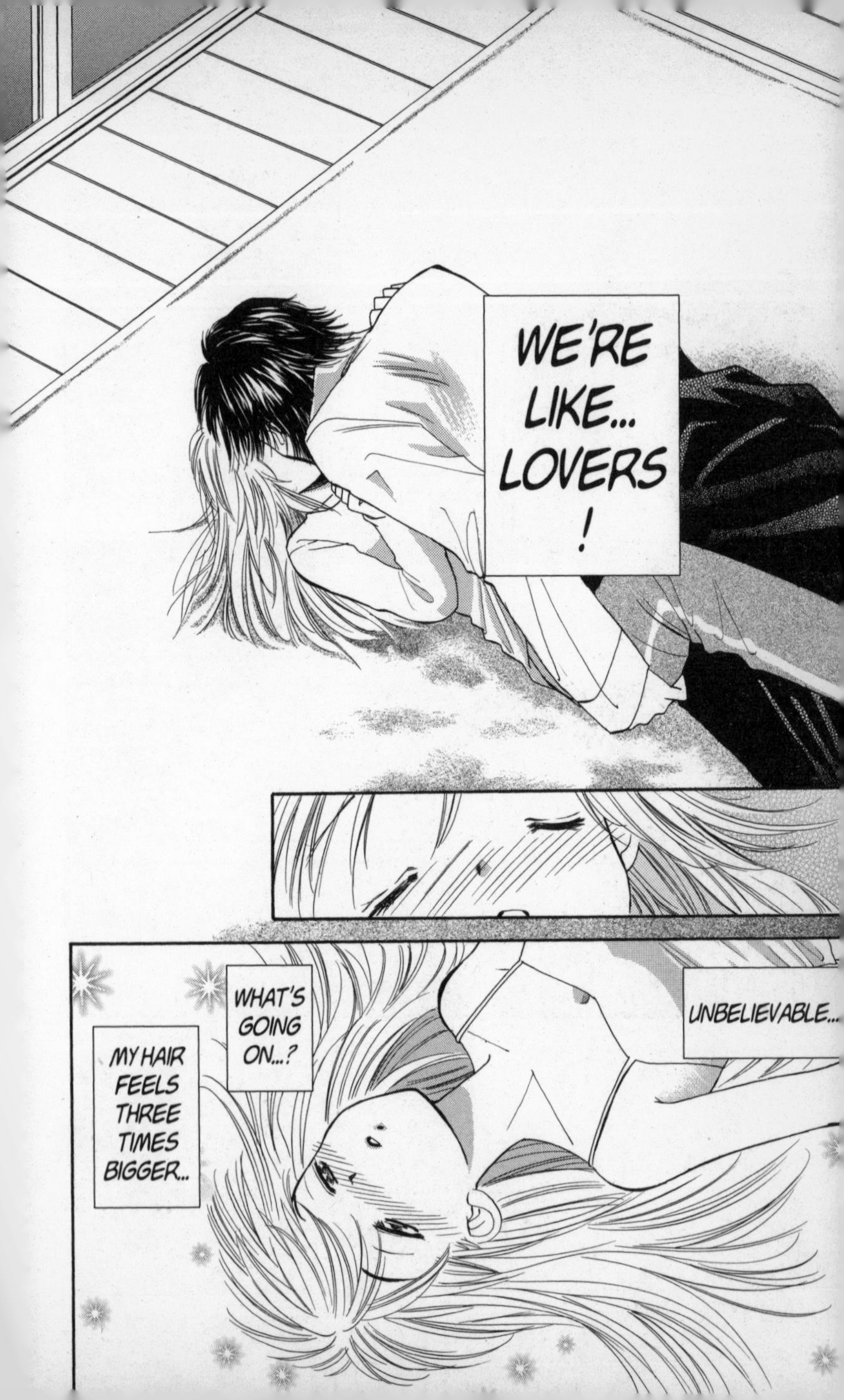
WE'RE LIKE... LOVERS!
UNBELIEVABLE...
WHAT'S GOING ON...?
MY HAIR FEELS THREE TIMES BIGGER...

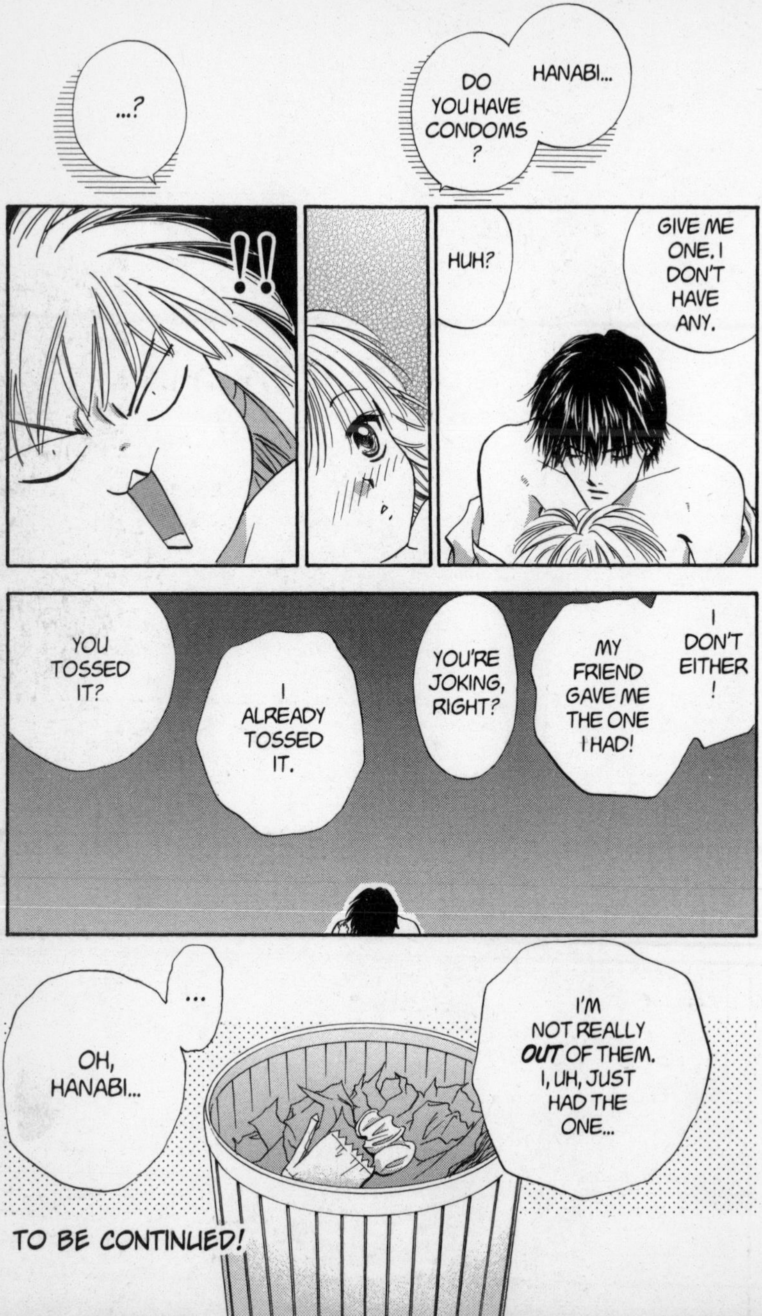
HANABI... DO YOU HAVE CONDOMS?
...?
GIVE ME ONE. I DON'T HAVE ANY.
HUH?
!!
I DON'T EITHER!
MY FRIEND GAVE ME THE ONE I HAD!
YOU'RE JOKING, RIGHT?
I ALREADY TOSSED IT.
YOU TOSSED IT?
I'M NOT REALLY *OUT* OF THEM. I, UH, JUST HAD THE ONE...
...
OH, HANABI...
TO BE CONTINUED!

HAPPY HUSTLE HIGH
Vol. 2

Story and Art by Rie Takada

English Adaptation/Janet Gilbert
Translation/June Honma
Touch-up Art & Lettering/Rina Mapa
Design/Izumi Evers
Editor/Kit Fox

Editor in Chief, Books/Alvin Lu
Editor in Chief, Magazines/Marc Weidenbaum
VP of Publishing Licensing/Rika Inouye
VP of Sales/Gonzalo Ferreyra
Sr. VP of Marketing/Liza Coppola
Publisher/Hyoe Narita

Printed in the U.S.A.

Published by VIZ Media, LLC
P.O. Box 77010
San Francisco, CA 94107

10 9 8 7 6 5 4 3 2
First printing, May 2005
Second printing, October 2007

www.viz.com
store.viz.com

RATED T+ FOR OLDER TEEN

PARENTAL ADVISORY
HAPPY HUSTLE HIGH is rated T+ for Older Teens. Contains strong language and sexual themes. Recommended for older teens (16 and up).

ratings.viz.com

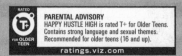

EDITOR'S RECOMMENDATIONS

If you enjoyed this volume of
HAPPY HUSTLE HIGH

then here's some more manga you might be
interested in.

© 2000 Kaneyoshi
Izumi/Shogakukan, Inc.

Doubt!! by Kaneyoshi Izumi: A wise man once said,
"There are only two kinds of people: those that make
wide, sweeping generalizations, and those that
don't." Unfortunately, body-image-challenged Ai definitely falls into the former category for, as she sees
it, there are really only two kinds of girls: those who
get noticed by boys, and those—like herself—who
don't. Will an ultimate makeover change her luck
with the fellas, or will she inevitably become just
another vacuous slave-to-fashion?

© 2002 Kaho Miyasaka/
Shogakukan, Inc.

Kare First Love by Kaho Miyasaka: Shy and oh-so-
insecure Karin Karino is getting ready for her first
shot at teenage love, but at what cost? It sure is
great that the attractive and artistically inclined
Kiriya has taken a fancy to her bespectacled charms,
but things are bound to get messy when her
classmate Yuka, in a fit of jealousy, pushes Karin
down a staircase! They say love hurts, but this might
be taking things a bit too far.

© 2001 Miki
Aihara/Shogakukan, Inc.

Hot Gimmick by Miki Aihara: If some people have
the misfortune of being born under an unlucky star,
then Hatsumi Narita must've been born under an
unlucky galaxy. Scheming neighbors and demented
classmates are but a few of the many woes that
befall this hapless heroine. But at least hope springs
eternal...right? Not only is Miki Aihara's *Hot Gimmick*
one of the most talked-about shôjo titles from Japan,
it's rapidly becoming one of the most popular ones in
the U.S. too!

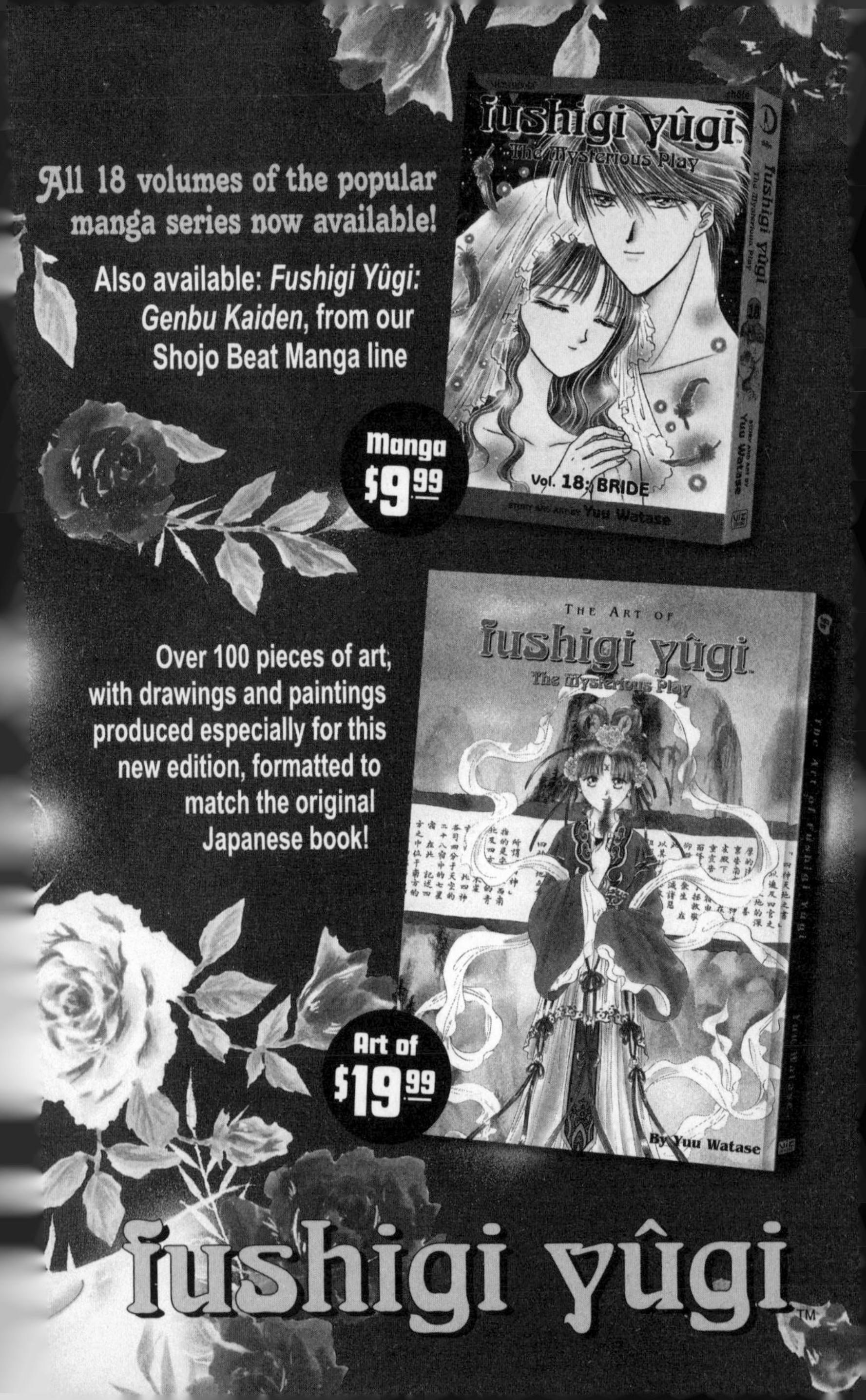
All 18 volumes of the popular manga series now available!
Also available: Fushigi Yûgi: Genbu Kaiden, from our Shojo Beat Manga line
fushigi yûgi
The Mysterious Play
Vol. 18: BRIDE
Yuu Watase
Manga $9.99
Over 100 pieces of art, with drawings and paintings produced especially for this new edition, formatted to match the original Japanese book!
THE ART OF
fushigi yûgi
The Mysterious Play
By Yuu Watase
Art of $19.99
fushigi yûgi™

GET THE COMPLETE FUSHIGI YÛGI COLLECTION

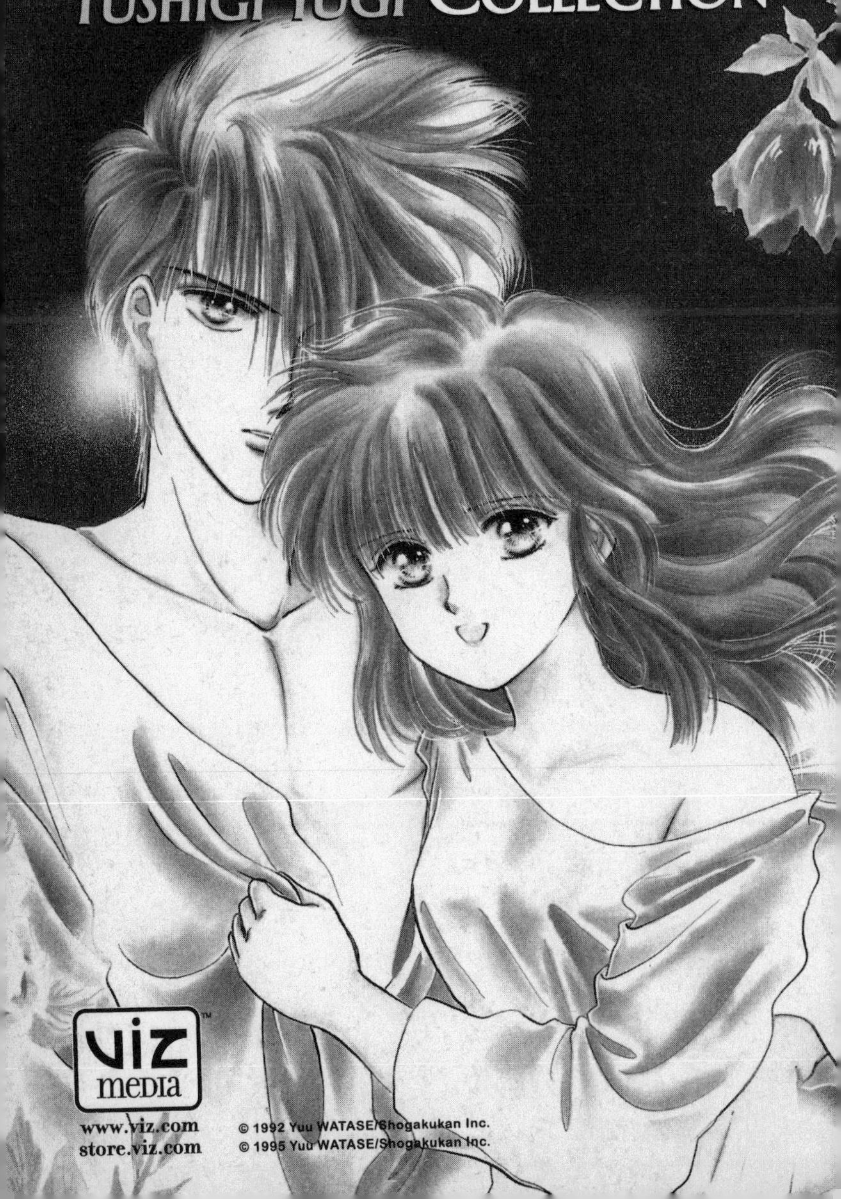

viz media

www.viz.com
store.viz.com

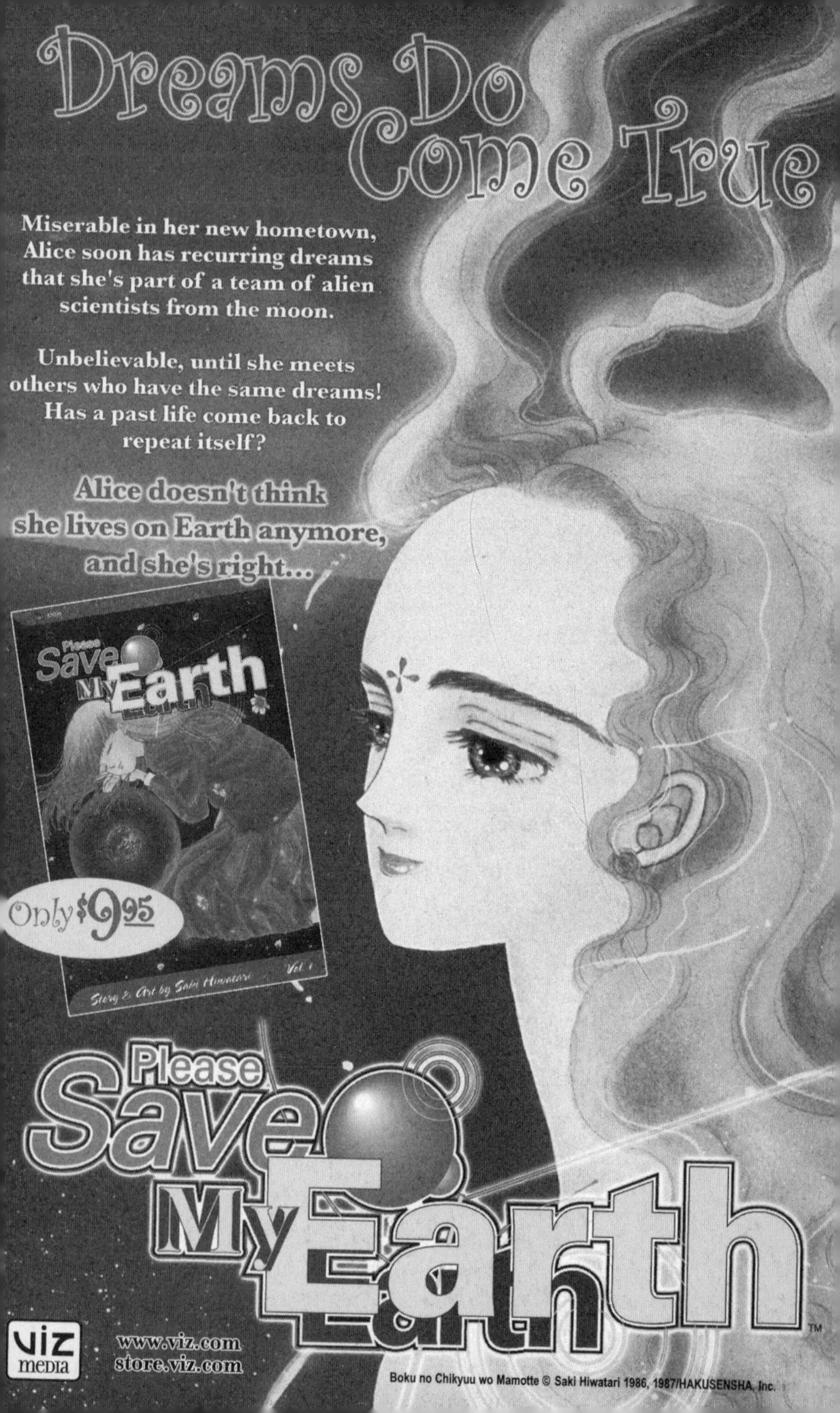
Dreams Do Come True
Miserable in her new hometown, Alice soon has recurring dreams that she's part of a team of alien scientists from the moon.
Unbelievable, until she meets others who have the same dreams! Has a past life come back to repeat itself?
Alice doesn't think she lives on Earth anymore, and she's right...
Please Save My Earth
Story & Art by Saki Hiwatari
Vol. 1
Only $9.95
Please Save My Earth™
viz media
www.viz.com
store.viz.com
Boku no Chikyuu wo Mamotte © Saki Hiwatari 1986, 1987/HAKUSENSHA, Inc.

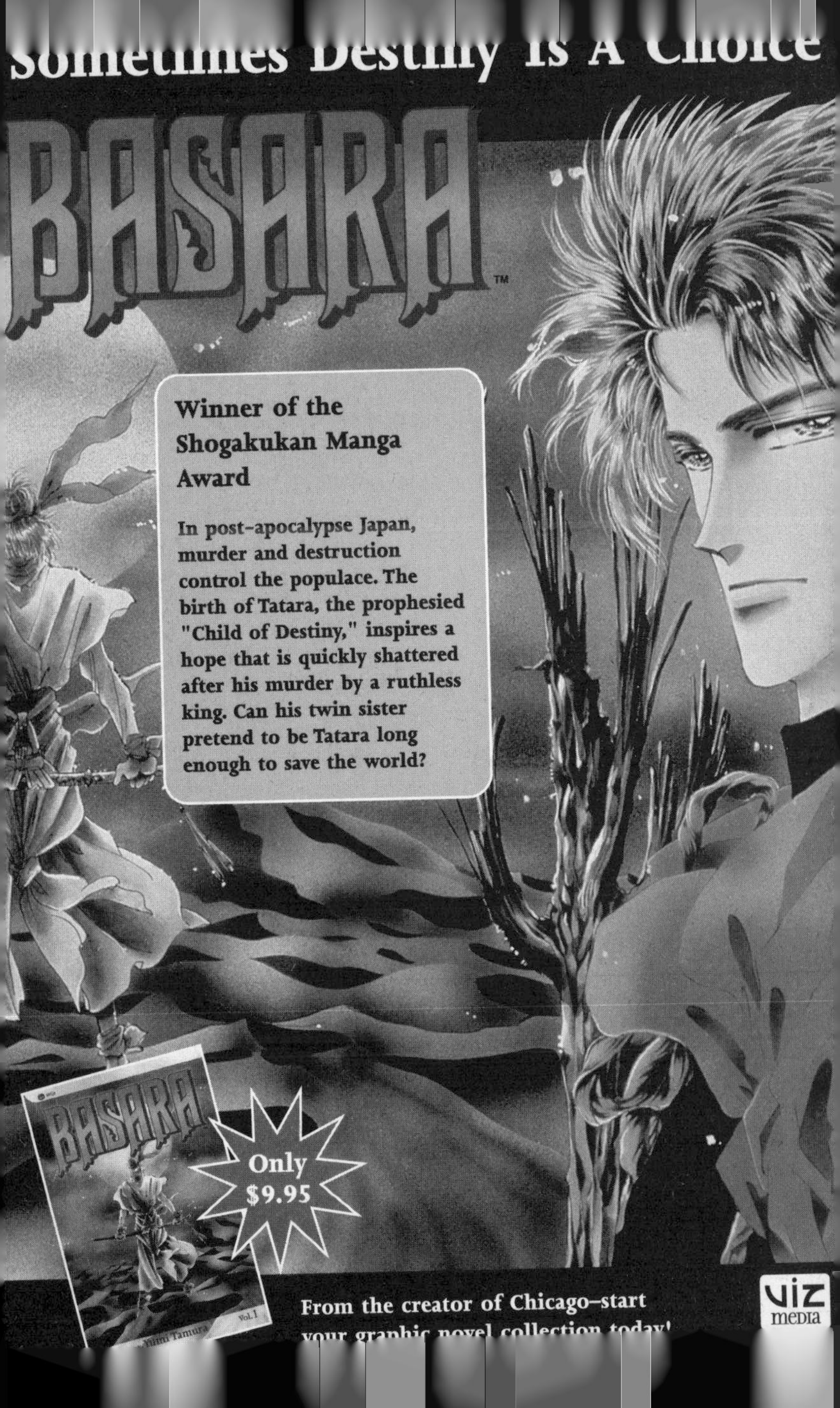
Sometimes Destiny Is A Choice
BASARA™
Winner of the Shogakukan Manga Award
In post-apocalypse Japan, murder and destruction control the populace. The birth of Tatara, the prophesied "Child of Destiny," inspires a hope that is quickly shattered after his murder by a ruthless king. Can his twin sister pretend to be Tatara long enough to save the world?
Only $9.95
From the creator of Chicago–start your graphic novel collection today!
viz media

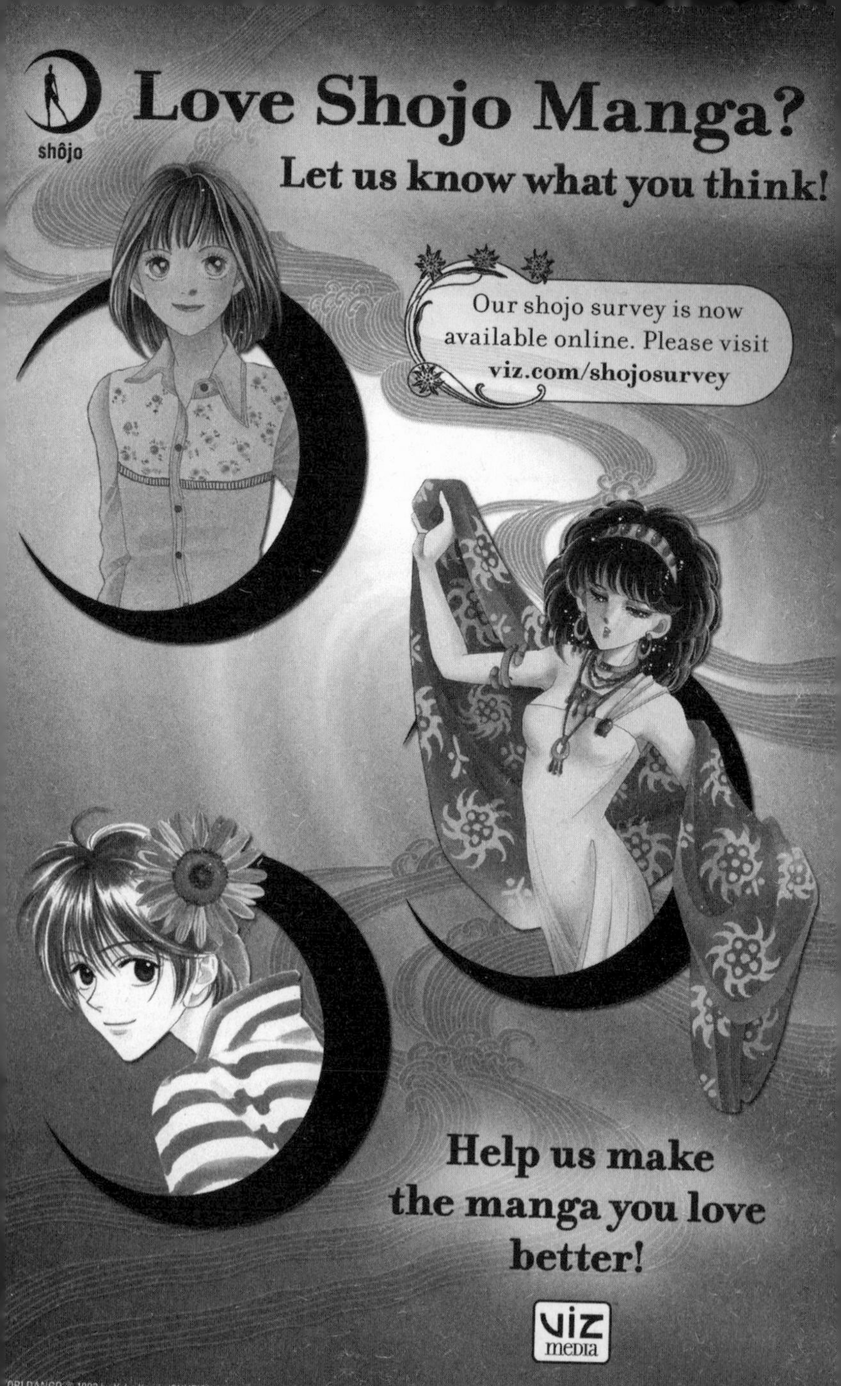